THE RIGHT TO
create

THE RIGHT TO
create

Judith Groch

Boston   LITTLE, BROWN AND COMPANY   *Toronto*

Published simultaneously in Canada
by Little, Brown & Company (Canada) Limited

PRINTED IN THE UNITED STATES OF AMERICA

To my father, Eli Goldstein

Acknowledgments

THE MANUSCRIPT of this book was read by Dr. Joseph Katz, Executive Director of the Institute for the Study of Human Problems, Stanford University, and Dr. Eli Goldstein, Professor of Clinical Medicine, New York Medical College. I am deeply indebted to Dr. Katz for his constructive comments and suggestions, and for the stimulus of his interest and encouragement. Errors of fact or interpretation are, however, my own responsibility. Dr. Goldstein's wise counsel, his literary taste, and his devotion to gracious writing have helped to make this book a more lucid and readable work.

I also wish to thank Miss Nancy Gross for invaluable support at the outset of this venture. To a considerable extent this book owes its existence to her editorial vision.

The manuscript was typed by my loyal friend Mrs. Elaine R. Werblud, who also, cheerfully and generously, assisted in checking the reference material.

To my husband and children I owe a special debt for their good humor and felicitous cooperation.

Contents

THE RIGHT TO
create

1. Man and the Mindless Inventor

Nature with equal mind,
Sees all her sons at play,
Sees man control the wind,
The wind sweep man away.
— MATTHEW ARNOLD

THE STORY of human creativity and the epic of man are companion tales. The entire structure of culture, from the first primitive tools used for cutting roots at the dawn of human history to the soft whirring of the computers in the space laboratory, from the first magic incantations to the finest structures of ethics and religion, originated in the creative acts of human beings. Although higher animals possess in crude form the rudiments of most intellectual processes, man in his ability to learn, reason, speak, and create is unrivaled. He alone dreams of immortality and weeps in the face of tragedy; only man intercepts his destiny and conjures the infinite; only man knows that he creates. Because he is highly intelligent, adaptable, and creative, man has become king of beasts and on occasion, confidant of angels. In the sense that man participates consciously in the creative process, he is godlike; in the sense that man is godlike in his aspirations but is neither omniscient nor omnipotent, he is human. Since man's biological antecedents are animal, he is also part beast. In all of creation man's heritage is without precedent.

If we strip away the artifacts of human history and go back

to that dim, unremembered time before the oldest stone tools were flaked, before the earliest words were spoken, and before the first hope became conscious in the brain of our lost progenitors, we find ourselves in the timeless world of the brute, where mindless nature is the creative force and man has not yet appeared. Here dwell the butterfly and the beaver; discarded trilobites and condemned dinosaurs sleep at nameless crossroads. Here restless atoms and molecules burn out and are replaced and fiery stars consume themselves while others are born. In nature's realm the pageant of creation is marvelous to behold, the creative process extraordinarily intricate and the miracles of nature's invention seemingly without end.

Blind Creation

The creative principle is a fundamental property of our universe. It operates everywhere, but is most dramatically evident in the evolution of life upon that small, green particle spinning through the cosmos to which we have given the name Earth. Primordial creation, the creation of something out of the infinity of nothing, is not only beyond man's powers, it is at present beyond the grasp of the human mind. We know neither how, nor why matter came into being.

In the first eon of geological time the earth was a savage wasteland of gravel, stone, and water. As the millennia passed, the naked continental platforms were gradually carpeted with green, adorned with moss and ferns, and strung with garlands of flowers. As if such raiment were not sufficient glory, sea and air soon rang with the roar and squeak, cry and song of living creatures. The origin of life and the dawn of organic evolution still remain veiled in mystery, although we hope ultimately to comprehend the critical events which transpired in the sunless waters of the young earth. But from the first eccentric molecules which had discovered how to reproduce themselves to the single fertilized egg cell destined to read books about itself, the potential for change, novelty, and creative activity is inherent in life.

Nature's creative force is latent in the genetical system which directs the growth patterns of each new generation of plant or animal. All living organisms, simple one-celled protozoa as well as the newly conceived child, possess instructions for making more of their own kind. This genetic information is coded within the chromosomes and genes of the cell nucleus. The laws of biological organization are still obscure. Present evidence indicates that the directions for producing the complex patterns of a new life are contributed by the long, spiraling DNA molecule in interaction with other cellular constituents. In multicellular animals only specialized reproductive cells utilize all the coded information. In some way the other cells form "cover up" substances — control molecules — which prevent bone cells or lung cells from reading information which does not concern them.

Conservation and innovation are the two great interlocking principles intrinsic to life. Self-reproduction, the propagation of what already exists, is the conservative force. As the agent of tradition it insures the preservation of life. But simply to resist the tide of death and to build inventory is not enough. The potential for change and novelty is also embodied within the genetical system. The creative force, the second great principle of life, is responsible for the profusion of living forms with which our earth abounds. The dark waters of the abyss and the glittering sands of the desert, dank, rocky crevices and leafy treetops are all home to some living creature. "The course of nature," said Isaac Newton, "seems delighted with transmutations." If we look carefully at a bunch of daisies, it is apparent that despite their overall resemblance, no two are identical. If life's duplication processes were to produce exact replicas of the parent generation, life could not have evolved. Nature is neither an assembly line nor a museum; life is neither static, nor repetitious. The canvas of life is an evolving masterpiece whose creator is itself.

Two major factors account for variation and innovation in the master plans of life. In sexual reproduction, the almost universal means by which animals and plants procreate, the instructions for the design and development of a new individual are contributed by two different parents, who themselves bear the complex strands of a long genetic past. Like an enormous deck of cards, chromosomes and genes are constantly shuffled and reshuffled, making possible an astronomical number of new combinations. Genetic variability of this kind manifests itself in offspring which resemble their parents, but vary in small details. The more radical alteration in the genetic code is the mutation, a change in the structure or composition of the chromosomes and, in particular, of the genes. Mutations are mainly random occurrences which have no predetermined relationship to the needs of the organism.

Life's "imagination" inheres, therefore, in the constant rearrangement of potential parts, and in the genetic accident — the "new idea" in the design of life. But without an organizing principle to orient scattered, largely random evolutionary changes, the result would be biological gibberish — not evolution. It is the process of natural selection which is the orienting force in evolution, giving order and form to the unprocessed novelties born of nature's fertile "imagination." According to Darwin's principle of natural selection, those plants and animals survive and reproduce which are best equipped to meet the demands of an environment which is itself changing. Modern theories of evolution maintain that the environment, in providing the challenge to which a species must respond, becomes the directive force in the evolutionary process. Ruthless, slow and erring, but magnificently successful, natural selection acts as the agent of creativity, determining in many complex and subtle ways not only which of nature's innovations shall be cast off, but which shall endure and assert themselves in successive generations. In departing from the status quo, in revealing the road to the future, mutation and selection are to nature what genius is to mankind.

As the originator of abundant and diverse forms of life, nature is a supreme and tireless artist. But as a creator, nature is also mindless and blind. Lacking intelligence and conscious purpose, nature blunders, makes "mistakes" and is usually a cruel judge of innovation. Mutations which are too radical for the environment in which they occur are lethal to their carriers. Natural selection has been described as opportunistic. It perpetuates what is immediately advantageous and, incapable of foresight, ignores what might be of use in the future. Finally, organic evolution operates with neither purpose nor plan, with neither pride nor regret in its achievements. Although man may regard himself as the crowning glory of creation, there is no evidence to indicate that he was planned as evolution's ultimate triumph.

Death and waste, failure and folly are everywhere in nature's realm. But blind trial-and-error procedures are a privilege nature can afford in a venture where time and material are infinite, and the destination is no one's concern. If nature lacks the mind to plan its experiments, we must never forget that it also lacks the heart, even once in a moment of sentiment or grace, to suspend its own inexorable principles. There are creatures favored of nature — and man is one — but nature can have no favorites.

The Conscious Creator

After eons of successive change there evolved an intelligent, introspective, creative animal who dared to challenge nature in its own demesne. In the vast expanse of geologic time, man is a latecomer who, in the words of Loren Eiseley, "slipped . . . out of the green twilight of nature's laboratory" only a few minutes ago. Since his advent, however, nothing on this planet has been the same. Unable to match the grandeur and cosmic scope of nature's creation, man is, in one respect, superior to the forces which sired him: he is a conscious creator who knows what he wants, and sets forth with imagination, intelligence, and foresight in pursuit of goals of his own choice. The source of man's inspiration, like the origin of his values, may lie in the unconscious or preconscious realms of the mind, but the human being recognizes his painting or his philosophy as his own response to a goal he has knowingly selected or accepted. "Art," said Eric Gill, "is deliberate skill — skill with mind behind it." The gossamer webs and suspension bridges of the spider are neither art nor invention as we understand these terms. In place of a unique and individual mind capable of making its own decisions, inborn instructions coded in the genetic material of spider cells provide that every spider, according to its species, shall become a master of geometric design and a wizard of civil engineering. Similarly, the design and construction of the beaver dam and the hive of the honeybee originate in genetically "programmed" behavior, not in rational acts of choice. If man wishes to dwell in the desert, he uses his brain to provide air-conditioned oases and other amenities of civilization where he finds nature has been derelict. If he wishes the desert to bloom, he does not have to wait centuries in the hope that a successful plant species will evolve. Instead, he intervenes in nature's slow, inefficient process by artificially selecting for breeding those plant specimens with desirable characteristics, eliminating those which do not suit him.

With intelligence and daring this precocious evolutionary infant has usurped nature's traditional control over the destiny of her issue and has set about redecorating his planet and rearranging its furnishings with genius and dazzling speed, but also with a touch of madness. In his brief sojourn, the thinking talking creature with his top-heavy brain and dexterous fingers has created a fairy-tale kingdom of tools. Using hardware extensions of his body and mind, man has acquired immense power to exploit nature for his own purposes — without genetic expense to himself.

One hundred and thirty million years ago, the archetypal bird looked down upon the monster dinosaurs and drowned swamps of the Mesozoic era. Today the bird soars over the heads of human beings and the rooftops of sprawling cities, but the skills and accomplishments of the modern bird remain basically unchanged. A mere half century after inventing a machine which for twelve seconds bore him through the air in clumsy imitation of a bird, man has constructed wingless spaceships with which to pursue his dreams across the virgin cosmos. Until a generation ago, the distance a person could travel in a lifetime, either on foot or by vehicle, was an average of thirty thousand miles. Today, several million men have traveled more than three million miles, airline pilots far exceed this mileage, which in turn is but a week's outing for a Gemini astronaut.

In evolving man, nature has produced a creature who if he cannot yet create life, has the power to end it. Whether from our point of view — and the point of view is important — our species of conscious creators is a testament to nature's creative genius or whether we are destined to be evolution's supreme disaster on this earth, prematurely reducing millions of years of creation to primitive rubble, is a momentous decision which we now face. Man has a vested interest in his survival, but nature, being without purpose, could not be expected to grieve over the failure of one of its experiments. In the story of evolution, extinction is the rule; survival, the exception.

The proud *Tyrannosaurus rex* and all his lesser relatives were dispatched to oblivion, perhaps, because it was too late in their evolutionary commitment to adapt to a changing environment. Of the sixteen orders of reptiles which once dominated the earth and its seas, only four (lizards and snakes, crocodiles, turtles, and the little known tuatara) are the scant relics of this mighty empire. Nevertheless, the proud reign of the "unsuccessful" dinosaurs lasted an impressive 130 million years, compared to a mere two million years so far for the genus *Homo*. From our perspective, the offensive cockroach is certainly one of nature's less glorious accomplishments. Yet this lowly pest has survived with little change since it evolved in the great coal ages some 300 million years ago, and is so well adapted to the vicissitudes of its environment, both natural and man-made, that in the event of Armageddon, it will probably crawl out of the walls after the best and the worst of us are gone.

It would be sentimental to regard nature as a wise or perfect creator. The system of natural selection stumbles down blind alleys, and makes genetic errors, often leaving disaster in its wake. For all its wonders and vaunted wisdom, the marvelous human body is a complex playground for mischief, illustrating poor planning, contradiction, and obsolescent design. The entrance to the retina of the optic nerve lies in the path of incoming light, producing a point, insensitive to light, known as the "blind spot." The human body's immunological defenses evolved in egg-laying vertebrate animals before the mammalian orders appeared on earth. The system is remarkable, but fallible. The unborn young of the mammal are nourished not in eggs, but within the mother's body causing a complication which could not have been anticipated in the days of egg hatchers. Occasionally, the mother's body reacts to the fetus as if it were a foreign invader. Designed with the premise that anything foreign is dangerous, the immunological defense system in certain cases cannot distinguish between a much desired baby and a hostile army of bacteria. Only man can sometimes compensate for nature's lack, either of past foresight or present flexibility.

If we look out beyond our familiar earth into the starry skies and consider that our planet is but one among hundreds of millions of planets which may be inhabited, the possibility that man may sweep the earth clean of higher forms of life cannot matter to a harsh, insensitive creative process for which time is eternal and the entire universe its laboratory. Imagine that there may be hundreds of millions of "species" of planets on which life not only might prosper, but might evolve in a form better suited than *Homo sapiens* to survive in an artificial environment. A setback on this planet would mean less than the loss of a species of ant. Cosmic perspective, if not exactly heartwarming, is instructive.

If nature errs in the long-range design of one of its species, that species is doomed; others will take its place. In evolving man, an animal with the intelligence to intervene in the work of nature but who has difficulty in summoning those other qualities of spirit and heart — generosity, foresight, patience — which are necessary accompaniments of intellect, nature may have used the wrong formula. Being narrowly opportunistic, nature makes no genetic investment in the future beyond the immediate preservation of life. Staring at the colossus of dinosaur bones entombed in a museum vault, small, puny man may flatter himself that he has escaped the mindless domination of nature, but at the end of his second million years, this infant among species has already learned how to commit suicide. Sober reflection suggests that we may be a hastily and ill-conceived invention: a false start. When compared to the slow pace of earlier evolutionary changes, the evolution of the bulging human brain from the more modestly endowed organ which filled the skull box of our apelike ancestors, took place — according to present evidence — with an explosive burst of speed. If we were appraising an invention, not a human being; an intelligent creator, not a mindless process, it would be a reasonable conjecture that nature should scrap the present model and try again. With less haste, perhaps, nature might succeed next time in evolving an animal in which intelligence and emotional maturity are better integrated.

To this appalling prospect, there is, fortunately, a more cheerful alternative. Man does not regard himself as a tentative experiment and he need not languish in nature's laboratory waiting for that heartless old inventor to clean house. Whereas nature operates with blind force, man proceeds with knowledge, intelligence, and a measure of control over his fate. As he charts his destiny, man too often suffers from distorted vision, but he is not blind. In endowing the human being with what is probably the finest brain it has yet evolved, in bestowing the gift of language, and in the provision of supplementary blessings such as agile fingers, stereoscopic vision, and erect stature, nature has invested man with the power to direct his own future. Man has the opportunity, granted to no other animal, to make amends through his cultural (nongenetic) evolution for the failure of genetic evolution to anticipate that the brain it had evolved would one day, for example, desire to make organ transplants, give blood transfusions, or would require the delicate pink lung tissue to breathe fumes from automobile exhausts and industrial garbage. Man has the power to understand the "rules" he cannot alter, and the freedom to alter his own behavior in accordance with these rules.

From Human to Humane

Observing that man, particularly at his present disagreeable stage of development, is not the final, unsurpassable achievement of evolution, the distinguished naturalist Konrad Lorenz has made the trenchant observation "that the long-sought missing link between animals and the really humane being is ourselves!" The ancient and melancholy platitude that you can't change human nature is a nasty, but persistent myth which endures because it is useful. That man, belligerent, selfish, and intractable, is born to steal, fight, wage war, and to do as he has always done is a perverse conception which ironically ignores the fact that even to thoughtful students of our species it is not yet clear what is meant by human nature. Until infanticide was made unfashionable, as being "against human nature," it was an almost universal practice, effectively helping to adjust man's number to his means. A social scientist surveying the scene in ancient times might justifiably have concluded that the murder and sacrifice of the weak or unwanted was a "natural" act, entirely compatible with human nature.

Since antiquity men have endeavored to define the nature of human nature, to discover that elusive entity, irreducible and universal, unmodified by the diverse trappings of culture. In the eighteenth century, man was regarded as a "naked reasoner" whose natural and noble core, immutable like the universe itself, existed beneath his cultural wardrobe. Classical anthropology considered man a "talented ape" whose basic nature could be discerned in universal cultural practices presumed to reflect basic human requirements. Throughout history, human nature has been enlisted in the service of such varying political and social causes as liberty, racism, imperialism, capitalism, Marxism, sexual freedom, educational reform, and the status quo.

The congruence between man's innate capacities and his actual behavior still remains a critical issue for behavioral and social scientists, as well as for philosophers and theologians. Anthropological evidence strikingly demonstrates that there are many styles of being human. The idea of human nature as immutable, unmodified by local custom and social practices may be an illusion. It has been suggested that man is to be defined neither by his innate capacities nor by his actual behavior, but "by the way in which the first is transformed into the second."

Human nature may be difficult to observe, but to possess such a nature means to be capable of learning and altering the behavior which derives from this nature. An outstanding characteristic of human behavior is that its patterns are not inevitable, that it is flexible and adaptable; that it can, indeed, must change. Choice and possibility are inherent in the design of the versatile human brain and its nervous system. The essence of the human condition is the individual's freedom to learn. Man profits not only from his own experience but from the wisdom or folly of those who have lived before him, and alters his behavior in accordance with his immediate or future needs. The bee makes wax, never plastic; the silkworm makes silk, not nylon. The computer calculating the route to the moon does not suddenly stop to compose a sonnet to that lovely celestial orb, and it will relentlessly grind out calculations or translate foreign languages even if its "life" is threatened by the outbreak of a fire in its laboratory, or holocaust in the outside world. Biological freedom, however, is the cherished gift of the human species. Man can spin and brew, scan the heavens or his poems, calculate, compose, translate, or stop what he is doing to go fishing or to help a friend. Aggression may be a form of behavior we share with our animal brethren, but being human we can also consider the paradox that some fights are lost in the fighting.

Just as the child learns to alter his self-centered behavior to meet the demands of his society, the bride and groom adjust their individual behavior in the interest of wedded bliss and adapt once again to the novel condition of parenthood; just as Augustine the profligate and heretic became Saint Augustine the theologian and church father, so there is no biological reason why most normal human beings cannot modify their attitudes and remodel their behavior in appropriate circumstances.

For the growing child, for the reformed delinquent, for the American who becomes a Buddhist priest, and the child of the Negro ghetto who rises to government office, the change in behavior is as much a matter of education and motivation as specific ability. This does not mean that goodwill and perseverance are all one needs to behave like Mozart or to think like Einstein, or that the revision of early prejudices and deeply ingrained attitudes is easily or perfectly achieved. Nor does this mean that human nature is entirely malleable and that therefore, if you know how, human behavior can be arbitrarily manipulated and adapted without suffering any ill effects. What human nature is may not yet be understood, but as Paul Goodman has observed, good teachers and psychologists who deal directly with children know that some practices are "against human nature," or at least against the natures of the young people in their charge. A human being who abandons his own identity, who loses that inner sense of coherence which enables him to recognize himself, who adjusts to circumstances by becoming what others wish him to be, does so at his own peril. Man's adaptable, versatile brain is the biological organ of possibility and choice. Because the patterns of human behavior are not inevitable, because we are relatively free from the direct coercion of instinct and reflex, freedom is inherent in the brain's design.

Our generic biological freedom may nevertheless be a heavy burden. As Erich Fromm and John Dewey before him have warned, modern man feeling alone and insignificant is increasingly tempted, in matters ranging from his political affairs to the conduct of his personal life, to surrender his unique human prerogatives in return for external authority or the security of a conformist life. Freedom is power — but it is the power to do wrong as well as right. There are times when it is easier to be told what to do, rather than to make one's own decision and assume the responsibility for the consequences. But whenever man is forced, as in a totalitarian state, or willingly agrees to live like a machine or an obedient animal, he abdicates his human privileges and risks being profoundly miserable.

The faculty common to all whose nature is human, separating man from even the most cunning and educable ape or dolphin, is his superior ability to learn and to transmit his experience to others. Correspondingly, whether in the playground or in the Pentagon, he is supremely dependent upon learning for survival. Biological freedom would be useless, even disastrous, if the brain could not profit from experience and communicate what it has learned to others. The acquisition of knowledge through experience is called learning; the knowledge which is communicated from brain to brain — instead of gene to gene — is called culture. What Jerome Bruner calls " 'educated' learning," man's ability to learn today what he will need tomorrow, is the specialization of our species. In childhood we learn not only what is of immediate and obvious value, but what, despite lack of present significance, we are told will be required in the future. Educated learning, however, is not merely the occupation of children required to study fractions, liquid measures, or great inventions; it is now a lifelong imperative for the adult. Living in the second half of the twentieth century, the adult cannot afford to stop learning. Like the child, he must continue to prepare for the future — a future which is evolving before his very eyes.

Our toys and gadgets have acquired a global bounce and screech. Modern communication and transportation methods have, for better or worse, made strange bedfellows of people once widely separated by distance, oceans, mountain ranges, and even the nearby jungle. Babylon can no longer disappear quietly into the pages of history, leaving other states to tend the affairs of civilization; if a Roman Empire falls today, its death toll will be heard between the antipodes of the planet. The power we wield reaches not only around the earth and outward into space, but forward through time, down to generations of people still unborn. The golden rule, even now more the exception than the rule, applies not only to one's fellowman, but to one's descendants as well. The germ plasm we foul today through radiation or noxious chemicals may cause us no anguish, but will be the sorrow of future generations. The forests we decimate and the creatures we drive to extinction will not revive to serve our children, or their children.

From the time man first settled down to farming, he has violated nature's delicate balance, interfering with natural habitats and with patterns of rebirth. Until recently man did not worry about using up his planet. There seemed to be so much of it. Man has always tapped the earth's water resources to slake his thirst, for power, and for sanitation, but his effect was negligible compared to the violent alteration of these resources by the contaminants of the industrial and nuclear ages, or by the construction of hydroelectric dams which alter the drainage patterns in the natural watershed. Each morning Americans leave their homes freshly bathed and clothed, but our rivers carry detergents instead of fish. As our industrial talents flourish unchecked, the atmosphere, which has always absorbed our waste products — from the carbon dioxide we exhale and the combustion products of early man's campfires to those of the factory — now endures, we suspect somewhat uneasily, its ever-increasing burden of human waste. Once the earth could afford the gifted, selfish predator it had brought forth. Now we have become too expensive. The earth's natural resources no longer supply the needs of a few nibbling mice, but of hordes of hungry, fire-breathing dragons.

Most of our scientific progress has occurred in the last four hundred years, and the period since the turn of the century has no counterpart in man's history. As the growth of scientific and technological knowledge continues to accelerate, our power to alter the environment is estimated to be increasing at a logarithmic rate. A considerable part of what we confidently call progress is actually scientific and technological progress. In this respect, airplane design has progressed and so has medical knowledge.

A single scientific innovation is a step in a self-stimulating chain reaction in which one event stimulates the next, this in turn giving rise to several others. Technology advances and social change follows. Suddenly we find ourselves trapped in a wildly proliferating network of technological and social change whose growth we feel powerless to control and from which there appears to be no deliverance. The invention of the gasoline engine led to the mass production of the automobile. Within a few decades innovations in transportation spawned the high- and thruways, the bumper-to-bumper weekend, the neon landscape, the suburb, the motel, the drive-in theater. Urban blight and flight ensued and finally major changes in America's living and working patterns evolved.

As our power to tinker with the environment increases, as the pace accelerates, the margin for error shrinks and the time for revision, adjustment and social adaptation contracts. The second chance, on which our forebears could count, may no longer be offered, and nature certainly has no intention of rescuing us from our predicament.

Lacking instinctive behavioral mechanisms to offset the unforeseen circumstances of his material culture, man is an ill-adapted animal. In order to survive, animals and plants must adapt physically to their environment through biological (genetic) evolution. Man can adapt the environment to himself by means of his cultural (nongenetic) evolution. The lessons of evolution, however, remain valid. Like all other animals, man must establish cordial relations between himself and his environment, or perish. But man is part of his environment. The most lethal alterations in the environment are not the slow changes of climate or food supply occurring over the millennia, but the swift and radical alterations man makes himself. There can be no successful rapprochement with nature until man learns to live with himself.

Indifference, resignation, or wishful thinking disguised as hope are hardly appropriate attitudes for people who have come to roost on a volcano. Ignorance of our biological history and of the mechanisms of human behavior is equally unhealthy. This is no time to resort to the defeatist myth of immutable human nature, to mutter tired phrases such as hopeless idealism, or to announce irrefragably that the profound social changes required are unrealistic. If the prescription for human society sounds like idealism or utopia, then it is intended to. The time is late, and the times dangerous. Just when men have abandoned utopia, utopia has become a necessity.

Fortunately for the equanimity of the dim-witted dinosaurs, but unfortunately for the future of the monster reptiles, no erudite dinosaurs convened in the late days of the Cretaceous era to warn of impending catastrophe, or to relate what befell other species in similar circumstances. But man is better endowed. He can learn from the lessons of the past and to a considerable extent he creates his own future. If man wants to, it is within his power to use his intelligence and his creative gifts to bypass the road to either physical or spiritual extinction. He sees the handwriting on the wall, but will he read it?

If man is to endure, he must divert his talent and energies to the solution of those urgent problems, including formidable moral and ethical problems inherent in his awesome power to tamper with his environment, or be sacrificed to his immature genius. He must use the brain nature has given him, not only to give insulin to the diabetic and spectacles to the myopic, not merely to design more proficient computer circuits, but to discover the long-range goals which favor his survival. He must use his computers and other machines with intelligence and sound purpose. It is his task to compensate for nature's apparent failure to produce a more agreeable relationship between human ingenuity and human self-control. Nature invented the two-legged learning, dreaming animal. It is man's responsibility to become a generous, compassionate and wise animal, to earn the prematurely bestowed epithet: *sapiens.*

2. Person — Process — Product

*. . . the more we scratch the more we want to scratch; the
more we define the more we shall have to go on defining the
words we have used in our definitions . . .*

— SAMUEL BUTLER

IN THE FIRST HALF of the twentieth century, creativity research
suffered from the assumption that creativity was largely a function of intelligence, definable by the intelligence test. Therefore
creativity received little separate attention. It was presumed
that one could cultivate intelligence, but reap creativity. Although reports appeared which suggested that extreme intelligence and creative giftedness were not identical, the idea was
not given serious consideration in the area where such notions
count: the schools. Their massive machinery in thrall to the
intelligence test, their teachers afraid to trust their own observations, their textbook writers bewitched by a cheap scientism,
school systems ignored the important implications of these
studies. Until this decade the intelligence test maintained its
power to define giftedness, while the doggerel of rote learning
and the litany of mass response stifled the creative gifts of millions of schoolchildren.

The ability to reason, dream and imagine, a superior aptitude for learning, and the unique forms of human love and
consciousness are essential to the human condition. In the same
sense, creative potential exists to some extent in all human
beings of average intelligence. Unlike a light bulb which com-

monly is either on or off, creativeness is not an all-or-none faculty, something you either have or lack. Like intelligence, creativity is inherent in the biological birthright of our species; like intelligence, or the light bulb operated by a rheostat, creativity varies in degree, in kind, and in the extent to which its potential is actually expressed by individual members of the species. No more than people are equally endowed with intelligence, or athletic ability, no more than students are equally apt in their studies, is creative ability evenly distributed throughout the population. We all begin life with innate differences.

The relationship between intelligence and creativity is still a source of confusion. High intelligence, a quality related to the intelligence quotient but not precisely what standard intelligence tests measure, is to be expected in those extremely gifted individuals whose creative contributions are unique and of value to society. It has been estimated that most creative scientists have IQ's of 120 or above. Other studies, based on biographical material, suggest that few men in history of outstanding ability had intelligence quotients of less than 120. However, intellectual brilliance alone is no guarantee of a creative mind. Whether "general intelligence" — at the moment a much maligned and highly unfashionable concept — accounts for creativity, or whether there are two kinds of intelligence, the one characterized by the creation of original ideas or products and the other by logical and analytical mental powers, is still a fundamental problem in creativity research.

Definitions

Many people still associate creativity with the production of a tangible product. Many regard it as the special province of the artist dwelling in the garrets and "pads" of bohemia, or the romanticized inventor tinkering his way to fame and fortune. This narrow view makes no provision for creativity in thought: in science, philosophy, law, religion, government, business administration, and most important, in human relations. On the other hand, the meaning of creativity has mistakenly been attenuated by the overzealous to include weekend therapy for the battered spirits of our contemporary lock-step existence. The modern conception of creativity admits the kindergarten child, the housewife, the salesman, as well as the genius. But creativity is neither a hobby, nor form of occupational therapy, nor is it synonymous with virtuosity, talent or genius.

Virtuosity may be defined as "great technical skill in the practice of the fine arts." Talent, a more ambiguous term, is a superior natural aptitude or faculty, generally confined to a specified activity such as exceptional musical or mathematical ability. In spite of considerable technical skill, a painter's work may be imitative rather than original and creative, whereas in the absence of unusual aptitude or "special talent," it is widely accepted today that a person may nevertheless be creative. Accordingly, the young child whose primitive artwork bears the genuine stamp of his personal vision, is considered creative, despite his lack of training or even artistic talent. Both talent and genius are believed to be determined heavily by individual genetic factors, although talent is more amenable to training and discipline. Musical talent, for example, may be developed through practice, instruction, and perseverance, but so far no amount of training or determination has produced a Mozart. "Doing easily what others find difficult is talent; doing what is impossible for talent is genius."

What is genius? William James once called it "the faculty of perceiving in an unhabitual way" and Albert Szent-Györgyi has aptly described it as "seeing what everyone has seen and thinking what no one else has thought." Genius is defined as exalted intellectual power, transcendent natural ability, and most important, "unusual power of invention or origination of any kind." Genius is, therefore, the highest form of original creative power. Excluded from this definition are the self-appointed "geniuses" of the cosmetic or public relations industries, of the keyboard and the tightrope, as well as those who have received the title as a reward for running out front in the IQ stakes.

At the height of the creative firmament, the purest, most brilliant stars of genius are easily recognized. Aristotle, Alexander, Leonardo, Shakespeare, Beethoven, Newton, and Einstein, to mention only a few at the pinnacle of human achievement, are secure in their glory. Gradually, as we descend from these sublime regions through the suffused glow of noble, but humbler lights, we encounter less exalted forms of genius, and eventually the threshold between genius and exceptional creative power becomes indistinguishable.

The genius, by definition, is creative. Within the framework of the definitions given here, his talent is usually, but not necessarily of an equivalent order. Picasso is an example of a genius with great artistic talent; Thomas Mann a genius with great literary talent. But Thomas Wolfe was once called "a genius without talent," implying that he lacked the literary craftsmanship, perhaps even the discipline required to give effective form to the raw wealth of his creative vision — a failing for which his devoted and talented editor Maxwell Perkins helped to compensate. The creative individual is only rarely a genius and need not possess talent, whereas the talented person may not use his powers creatively. These oversimplified distinctions are suggested as useful but provisional guidelines. Their tidy, but arbitrary borderlines often blend and blur when theory is confronted by the baffling complexity of real human beings.

Should you wish to be a genius, you must arrange to inherit the correct combination of rare genes from suitable forebears. Or you might importune some unknown mutagen, perhaps a stray cosmic ray, to glow with beneficence upon the genetic template which carries your design so that, marvelously and specifically altered, it will insure the development of exalted gifts at the time of your birth. Having been born a potential genius, you must now fulfill your genetic promise. Whether genius is a purely genetic phenomenon and its appearance due

to chance, or whether the genetic machinery requires some unusual environmental stimulus to summon it into action, is a
question for which there is no precise answer.

Thus far our approach to human creativity has been indirect.
We have attempted to clarify its meaning in current usage by
examining briefly those concepts which although related, are
not identical. At this point it is appropriate to provide a definition of creativity. Unfortunately, as has been wryly observed,
the most impressive fact about the subject of creativity is the
chaos in this field and the variety of opinions held by those
devoted to its study. Not only do definitions of creativity vary,
but even the meanings of component words such as new, novel,
original, useful, valuable are subject to debate.

True artists, said Plato, are those "who bring into birth some
new reality." Webster defines creativity simply as "the process
of making, or bringing into being" — a definition too broad
and too vague to be pertinent to an analysis of creativity.

There are numerous other definitions of which the following
are but a representative few:

The production of "a novel work [or the communication of a
novel idea] which is accepted as tenable or useful or satisfying
by a group at some point in time."

"The disposition to make and recognize valuable innovations."

"The ability to see (or to be aware) and to respond."

"A process extended in time and characterized by originality, adaptiveness, and realization."

Creativity has also been described as "a successful step into
the unknown," and "the encounter of the intensely conscious
human being with his world." Although a few authorities
would restrict the use of the expression "creative" to rare and
remarkable contributions, the majority propose different levels
of creativity. These range from the spontaneous, expressive
drawings of the young child, where skill and the quality of the
product are not considered, to the works of genius. Some investigators would exclude the contributions of genius from this

theoretical structure, suggesting that genius is not merely a difference in degree, but in kind. Finally, there are those, oriented toward the creative person rather than the created product, for whom the word includes the general creative abilities of all healthy, intelligent people.

It is significant that the criterion applied in most definitions of creativity is new or novel, as opposed to original. An original work or idea, as used in this context, generally suggests the creation of genius and other exceptionally gifted individuals whose contributions are unique to society. Margaret Mead has said that "to the extent that a person makes, invents, or thinks of something that is new to him, he may be said to have performed a creative act." This definition expresses an attitude prevalent among many contemporary psychologists and educators. It is important because it eliminates a social judgment of usefulness or value, and recognizes the creative process in the more prosaic experience of millions of people who have not previously thought of themselves as creative, and whose contributions are not likely to advance the general culture. The child, toying with his spoon at the dinner table, who discovers that triggering it against his finger he can use it to launch a green pea through the air, earns a quick reprimand from his parents. Nevertheless, their creative offspring has invented a primitive catapult, even though the principle of the tension-powered weapon is a very ancient discovery, and the dining table is, indeed, not a launching pad. Newton's discovery of the calculus was the creative contribution of a genius even though another genius, Leibniz, working independently made the same discovery.

The sample definitions offered here, although good in themselves, raise as many questions as they resolve. The birth of kittens and crocodiles fulfills Webster's requirements. Is the subjective and private experience of "encounter" sufficient to qualify as creativity? What is meant by valuable? By novel? Operational criteria of value and novelty, although essential in scientific studies of creativity, are extremely difficult to establish. A new work is one which departs from what already exists, but as members of the patent office know, the criterion of novelty is not easily defined.

From these definitions it should be apparent that creativity is a general term which, depending upon one's frame of reference, may refer to the creative person, the creative process, or to the product which results from this process. Without the process there would be no product; without the product there is no evidence that the process has occurred or that the person is anything more than potentially creative. Yet the product by itself is no proof of its creative origin. A visitor from a distant planet could not tell merely from looking at a single pencil or a single mousetrap whether the pencil is the prototype of its genus or one among legion; whether the mousetrap is an ordinary mousetrap, a better mousetrap, or a copy of the latter. A little human history is required. Art, wrote Jacques Maritain, "is the creation of objects to be made." An original masterpiece and a clever forgery or a skillful reproduction may all communicate the identical idea and provide the same aesthetic pleasure. The essential difference between the original and the copy is intangible: not what they say, but what they stand for. The masterpiece is a work which originates in the ideas of a great original artist and represents as closely as possible his creative vision. The reproduction merely copies the masterpiece — or re-represents the creator's ideas. The source of art is the artist, not his art. This is the truth we honor when we distinguish an original work from its replica.

The problem of defining creativity and of recognizing it are reciprocal issues. Unfortunately we cannot identify creativity by seeking the trail of the creative process within the cells and circuits of the human brain. The specific cerebral mechanisms of the creative act remain invisible and unknown.

Product

To identify the creative person by judging the product invites the difficult task of evaluating creativity. The most valuable creations, however, the works of genius, are those which go a step beyond the existing order. Lonely outposts of the future, such pioneer contributions often appear either evil or absurd to contemporary judgment. Stendhal's works were not considered "worthwhile" until nearly half a century after his death. Gregor Mendel's discoveries in genetics were disregarded for thirty-five years, and works of art once condemned and scorned are priceless museum treasures today. Objective evaluation of the creative product is a worthy goal, but as someone once observed: who evaluates the evaluators?

Finally, there are eminent psychologists who maintain that although the external judgment of society is not to be ignored, the value of the product must be established by the creative person himself. "Have I created something satisfying to *me?* Does it express a part of me — my feeling or my thought, my pain or my ecstasy?" is a fundamental condition of creativity as postulated by Carl Rogers. "If to the person it has the 'feel' of being 'me in action,' of being an actualization of potentialities in himself which heretofore have not existed and are now emerging into existence, then it is satisfying and creative, and no outside evaluation can change that fundamental fact." The exploration of latent human potential is an important new dimension in creativity research, but as a practical means of evaluating creativity, the subjective criteria of "me in action" has severe limitations. The concept of "me in action" does not preclude the possibility of a noncreative "me in action." One can build a bookshelf, set a new track record, help a friend and be both pleased and satisfied by the expression of what one regards as a real me, without being creative. Furthermore, not many people are sufficiently free of social pressure, or possess the honesty, courage, and self-knowledge to know whether they are expressing the real me, because they do not know who the real me is.

Person

A third approach to the identification of creativity is to consider the creative person. The study of personality variables in creative behavior is, somewhat unexpectedly, proving an extremely fruitful expedient. Traditionally, studies of creativity, or of what more accurately should be called problem solving, were conducted by "learning theorists," who stressed the cognitive functions — the so-called higher mental processes — and emphasized the emergence of a product of distinguished caliber. Curiously, the personality of the problem solver was ignored. Recent work indicates that the means by which man apprehends his environment and learns to deal with it is influenced by the unique pattern of traits and attitudes which distinguishes him as a person, and indirectly therefore by subtle social considerations. Emotional and motivational factors not only accompany the artist to the studio, but the scientist to the laboratory. Ernest Hilgard and investigators at Stanford University reported that the solution of even simple laboratory problems, which seemed at first to require almost purely cognitive powers, was significantly affected by the personality of the problem solver. For example, whether the subjects in this study chose to redesign the problem, restructuring its parts in order to solve it, was not primarily a matter of how "smart" they were. "Male orientation" (aggressiveness, daring, independence), although not necessarily male chromosomes, seems to have been the decisive factor.

The study of human personality has a distinguished history. Once a subject for the speculative genius of Hippocrates, Plato, and Aristotle, it remained for many centuries the province of the philosopher and the theologian. Since the end of the nineteenth century, personality theory, as it is now called, has emerged as a vast and sometimes recalcitrant domain within the general field of psychology. In its popular meaning, the word personality is generally equated with social skill, or with the dominant impression a person makes on others. One has a good personality or a bad personality. Certain people have "no personality," while others *are* personalities. Should attendance at charm school or the ministrations of a guidance counselor fail to improve the ailing personality, it is assumed that the individual will muddle through life with his negative personality, or get along without it altogether. Personality, in this sense, is regarded as a fascinating but relatively simple matter: a useful, but noncritical aspect of the total person. Personality theorists know otherwise.

There is at present no single valid theory of personality, and attempts to integrate the conflicting strands of the various theories which propose to order human behavior are considered premature. Even the psychologists' definitions of personality, of which almost fifty were once counted, vary with the particular theoretical system in which they are rooted. Unfortunately, oversimplification has been a temptation to which personality theorists, from Freud to the stimulus-response theorists, have frequently succumbed. There is a scarcity of empirical research and the ostensible "facts" are often ambiguous and subject to conflicting interpretation. One cannot construct a general theory of human behavior on the foundations of animal or abnormal psychology.

Personality theorists are still searching for answers to such fundamental questions as: the relative importance of conscious and unconscious determinants in behavior; the significance of genetic or hereditary factors; the part played by environmental influences; the role of reward and pleasure in directing behavior; the role of the self; whether the learning process or the acquired learning itself is the key to behavioral phenomena; the importance of early childhood experiences as opposed to events taking place in later stages of development; the number of motivational concepts presumed to be at the basis of human behavior, ranging from theories employing one or two motives, to those which hypothesize a conceivably unlimited number.

Reflecting their initial formulation of a personality hypothesis, theorists differ in how the individual should be studied. There are those, at present a minority, who assert that the nature of scientific investigation demands that the individual be analyzed in segmental studies, whereas others declare that it is necessary to study the total functioning person within the context of his environment, lest vital processes be suspended or lost.

> *Our meddling intellect*
> *Misshapes the beauteous form of things: —*
> *We murder to dissect.*

Should each person be studied as a unique human being, or is the individual more properly understood in terms of different patterning of variables common to all human beings? Finally, psychologists ask: which is more important to the development of personality — objective reality or the individual's subjective perception of himself and his environment? Again, there is no accord.

This brief listing of the Herculean labors which confront psychologists is merely intended to indicate the paucity of knowledge concerning fundamental aspects of human behavior. If we are to consider theories specifically formulated to examine and elucidate the creative personality, we must keep in mind the context of uncertainty and theoretical conflict in which they occur.

The psychologist who wishes to study the creative person is confronted by the baffling and sometimes embarrassing task of first identifying him — a challenge politely referred to as "the criterion problem," and somewhat less chivalrously, as "the criterion mess."

One study based on interviews of 166 physical scientists, working at Air Force Research centers, produced 150 criteria of scientific productivity and creativity. According to Quinn

McNemar of Stanford University, these criterion measurements included "everything except success at turning on a kitchen faucet." Statistical acrobatics eventually reduced this enormous list to fourteen categories. "Likableness," "status seeking," even "membership in scientific and professional societies" were among the final criteria. Further studies of 107 of these scientists yielded a "whopping total" of 130 potential predictors of scientific creativity.

Another form of criterion-based study uses as its subjects individuals rated as the "most creative" by their peers, or their supervisors. Although this seems a sensible procedure, such studies may be distorted by the judges' understandably complex notions of who is creative, and equally important, who is not. Considering past errors of contemporary judgment, one does not like to think of those who would not have qualified: Jesus, Copernicus, Van Gogh, of martyred saints and dishonored prophets, or of Socrates either, overlooked for his failure to publish, or eliminated from consideration due to lack of "consensus" among the experts. The range of criteria established in these studies and then used to predict creativity in others, is at best restricted by the nature of the original group. If, for example, you study a very select group of people — the forty most creative architects, or the top one percent of a group — it is possible to conclude that "intelligence has little or no relationship to creative performance in arts and science," and to present data as proof. But the data are deceptive. Of what significance is a low statistical correlation between creativity and intelligence in a group which is to begin with both highly intelligent and highly creative?

Psychologists who attempt to eliminate this source of bias by devising tests to detect and measure creativity, encounter other kinds of obstacles. Typical creativity tests are scored for the novel response or solution to problems designed to simulate various aspects of the creative process. But as Paul Torrance, the designer of many creativity tests, cautions, you cannot identify outstanding jumping ability by measuring how high an individual happens to jump. You must "create situations that motivate and/or require jumping." It is simpler, however, to construct controlled situations which require jumping than to devise those which elicit creative behavior. Even then, we might suppose that the jumper performs best when he jumps for his life or when his jumping occurs at an actual track meet. Without long, follow-up studies, one cannot be certain that the "creativity" measured by the test is related to creative performance in real life. The test criteria may also fail to separate truly creative persons from rebels, beatniks, delinquents, introverts, and other nonconforming types.

No more than life can be explained by the isolated properties of its molecules, can the creative mind be observed in its discrete functions: in measures of originality, fluency, and flexibility, or in answers to a Product Improvement or Figure Completion Test. The human being is a complex living system whose unique characteristics are provided by the interaction of its parts. The parts must first be identified. Ultimately the scientist must explain the relationships between the parts. He must discover the integrating mechanisms which coordinate the activities of complex components, whether his subject is cell life or creative life.

Fortunately, the problem of defining creativity is not insurmountable. As biologist George Wald once observed, you may not be able to define your wife, but you have no trouble recognizing her. It is essential that one agree that certain phenomena are illustrations of the subject under consideration, and then keep in mind the built-in limitations of this method. Definitions, said Samuel Butler, "are like steps cut in a steep slope of ice, or shells thrown onto a greasy pavement; they give us foothold, and enable us to advance, but when we are at our journey's end we want them no longer."

The Art of Living

Creativity as the production of a new entity is sometimes called "special talent creativity." Aptitude, training, and practice, as well as social and economic factors, play a part in establishing this variety of creativeness. Many psychologists now delineate another form of creativity which may exist in the absence of special talent. The precursor of all specific innovation in art and thought, it need not manifest itself in the tangible evidence of a product or an idea. This incipient type of creativity, called "self-actualizing creativity" by Abraham Maslow, the "creative attitude" by Erich Fromm, and "openness to experience" by Carl Rogers and others, is actually a loose constellation of personality traits which may be expressed in the everyday experience of living. Within one's genetic and constitutional limits, one can in this respect "create" one's own life without a special talent for painting or describing it, or for providing scientific explanations of its phenomena. What is required is the disposition and courage to encounter the world directly, rather than through the shopworn thoughts and stereotyped emotions of others, to originate one's own acts rather than to perform by rote and habit, and to feel rather than think one's own feelings.

As far as we can determine, animals lack the brain and symbolic language faculties with which to reflect on their own existence. But the human being knows that he is alive, and despite the storms which rage around him, is sustained and propelled by a sense of purpose, by a profound, intuitive sense of his own powers, and by the delight experienced in their use. The child whose schooling has not undermined his natural powers, learns not merely for extrinsic reward — grades, approval, college entrance — but because the act of learning provides its own pleasures. The sculptor models his clay to give form to his vision, not to possess the statue, and the scientist labors a lifetime of obscurity at an occupation which in many

complex and subtle ways is its own reward. In song and dirge
the poet celebrates the moments of existence. Little children go
to bed reluctantly and arise the moment their eyes are open,
and for all our unpoetic burdens, most of us know well this
sense of expectation and delight, not in miraculous experiences, but in the experience of living. Even the gloomiest European existentialist seeks deliverance from a life which he believes to be meaningless, through the act of living.

To think our own thoughts, to speak in our own accent,
rather than recite the clichés and half-truths of a prepared
script, assumes that we know who we are and that we participate directly in our own experience. Unfortunately secondhand
experience is the hallmark of our age. People go to the movies
to "read" the book. The concert is "almost as good as the recording." Baseball is "much better on television than in the
ballpark." Decorators "create" rooms with a "lived-in" look —
presumably for spirits who live out — and unabashed, art gal-
leries offer "original reproductions" for sale.

It is a common lament today that there is "no time to think."
Yet when granted the opportunity for quiet reverie, many people discover that they have forgotten how to think — and are
afraid to try. It is not so much time which is lacking, but habit
and courage. In this country leisure is coveted by the very people who would be quick to stamp it out with busywork, or with
the strange compulsive pastime, often more work than work,
known as play. Moreover, it may require considerable courage
for doubt-ridden twentieth-century man, afflicted with the me-
grims of spiritual nonbeing, uncertain whether he is a genuine
person, inviolable, and distinct from everyone else, to search
for and encounter his true self.

In his reluctance to encounter, alone and unaided, "the
perils of the soul," to chance the high seas of despair in the
hope of discovering more solid ground upon which to construct
his life, modern man commands sympathy. The atomic age has
been described as an age in which the ordinary man, not just
the philosopher, has caught a fleeting glimpse of nothingness.

The quest for identity, the posit of personal, subjective experience, rather than conceptual systems, as the source of truth, and the importance of real experience rather than its reflection in some form of mass art or rhetoric are central concerns of both existentialist philosophy and the existentially flavored psychology of creativity.

In 1925, from the little castle of Muzot in Switzerland, the great German poet Rainer Maria Rilke wrote to the Polish translator of his *Duino Elegies* that it is man's task "to stamp this provisional, perishing earth into ourselves so deeply, so painfully and passionately, that its being may rise again 'invisibly' in us." In celebrating the supreme importance of man's "creative" or "real" existence, Rilke expressed an existentialist theme which anticipated a major precept of modern creativity research. Man is frail and imperfect. His consciousness is divided and finite, and his life is but a spark between eternities. Yet it is through his power to shape his physical universe and to re-create and transform the external world in his mind, that he succeeds in transcending his own death. If the bitter prerogative of human consciousness is suffering, then certainly creativeness is among its most sublime gifts.

A creative attitude, or what Paul Tillich calls "spiritual creativity," is considered an essential characteristic of the productive, unalienated, fully functioning human being, and at times seems almost synonymous with mental health. A person who neglects his destiny, whose life ticks on without enthusiasm and a staunch appetite for living, who has never been enchanted by his own passions and desires, is cut from defective cloth. His condition may be attributed to mental illness or, etiologically, the disease of the spirit may be lodged in his social environment. Such an individual merely exists; he does not live. Expanded from the rare gift of the great artist or thinker to a process immanent in nature and in human nature, the modern concept of creativity has begun to permeate the airless chambers of our educational system, and is intimately involved with the emergence of a new, optimistic science concerned with the exploration of human potential and the expansion of human ability.

One cannot help wondering, however, whether the distinction between "special talent creativity" and creativity as a personality trait may not ironically turn out to be a false distinction. The expression "special talent" refers to the specific inborn gifts of individuals such as the artist, musician, or mathematician. It does not apply to personality traits such as perceptiveness, curiosity, a sense of humor, "openness to experience," as well as to that enigmatic bundle of emotions we call motivation.

The generic biological equipment, with which the human species originated, enables each individual to encounter his environment directly and personally. Man is endowed with a sensitive, flexible brain, relatively uncommitted to preset patterns of behavior. We are free to learn, discover, and think, and we possess an elaborate form of consciousness which provides each of us with our cherished sense of "I-ness" as distinct from those we call "you." But in these automated materialistic times, when the individual is invited to become a well-accoutered robot in exchange for his sometimes precarious human condition, many will accept, but some will decline the invitation. We do not know that these most human qualities (perceptiveness, awareness, integrity, a sense of purpose and self, even the potential for moral courage) are not at least in part an inborn "special talent" — a talent for living, upon which the future may well place a premium.

This question is raised here lest we assume prematurely that perseverance, a sense of humor, or motivation are definitely known to be attributes of a different order from the ability to handle numerical concepts or to render likenesses on canvas. Not everyone, for example, responds equally to motivating stimuli. The capacity to be motivated, although nurtured by the environment, has, we are beginning to learn, a genetic basis. At this time not enough is known about human personality to permit us to assign human faculties, particularly the complex components of creativity, to permanent categories.

Blue People

The nascent creativity with which most of us begin life, is readily observed in the art, play, and speech of the young child. Curious, imaginative, and still passionately close to his feelings which, however charming or savage, are at least his own, the child is an authentic person. Observe him at work with his crayons. Fully absorbed, pressing down hard on the paper, he makes his drawing mean what he wants it to mean. Despite the gleam of pride in his parents' eyes, he is not at this point an artist. His skills are primitive, his ideas immature. He may be surprised, even annoyed, to discover that he has failed to convey what is obvious to him. This is a picture of a man with no eyebrows! But he does express a sense of joy and enthusiasm, a spontaneity and intensity of feeling which adults admire and envy. The untutored child possesses two qualities which are always preserved in the mature artist: imagination, and the ability to encounter his own feelings.

All too soon he will learn to draw "the right way." Learning to distinguish one's private world from the public domain is an important part of growing up. For all its charm, the childish scribble is insufficient. Once in school, the child willingly heeds his friends and his teachers when they tell him: "That's not how you make a man." "Where's his other eye?" "People are pink (or brown), not blue." But the lessons go too far. The culture he absorbs, absorbs him. Eager for acceptance within the group, these quondam kings and queens of the parental roost are only too willing to renounce their autonomy for the privilege of imitating each other. For a while, to his parents' dismay, a puzzling double standard may persist. At home the child draws whatever comes into his mind; in school he draws whatever comes into his best friend's mind. Soon the child's

drawings are emptied of their own meaning, and art is reduced
to a ritual performance. Figures will appear in either left or
right profile, or in front view; faces and fish will congeal in the
stereotype acceptable to the severe art critics of the grade
school, and for the rest of his life, the apt pupil will draw — if
he draws at all — as he was taught. His vision is frozen. His
heart has been dismissed. The two-way elephants, dilapidated
dinosaurs, and rakish kings are gone, and the marvelous blue,
one-eyed people appear no more — except in the works of a
Picasso.

What is it we wonder forlornly that the adult has lost? He
has lost the ability to react to his own experiences. His world,
seen "through a glass darkly," is two-dimensional and flat, and
he is too. Children know how to look at flowers. They touch
them, taste them, and are foolish enough to grieve when the cut
bloom wilts and dies. To the young child the flower is a unique
event which he must explore personally. It is his "happening."
Adults, even adolescents, know all about flowers. They are
beautiful, fragrant, colorful, and so forth. Their fate in a vase is
so obvious it is not worth thinking about. What the sophisticated adult or world-weary teen-ager expresses, however, is not
what he feels, but what he *thinks* he *should* feel. To revive
jaded sensibilities, to restore desiccated feelings, some will turn
to the bizarre stimuli of the Way-Out and the Way-In — un-
derground movies, antic dress, psychedelic art, or the drug experience. In popular connotation a caterpillar is a stupid, unat-
tractive grub; a promised butterfly. The child who takes his jar
of newly collected caterpillars to the movies with him "because
they might feel lonesome at home," is not much of an entomol-
ogist and is a semantic innocent. But for all his ignorance, we
must respect his rich capacity for empathy, for tenderness and
compassion.

Our ingenuity betrays us. Articulate language enables the
human being to bind the discrete events of daily experience in
relatively stable patterns, to "tell" his thoughts to himself and
to share them with other human beings. An animal's life, on the

contrary, is a series of disjointed activities dictated by impulse, mood, and biological need. Dormice and pussycats, monkeys and moles have achieved a distinguished place in our literature, but animals themselves do not compose biographies. Without the shorthand of a symbolic system of language and number, the intricate level of learning and thinking attained by the human being would be impossible. If each time we wished to speak of even such relatively simple ideas as caterpillar, flower, or snow, we had to list everything we attributed to these terms, communication would swiftly grind to a halt. Ironically, we pay a high price for the convenience of language. Words are name tags which save us the trouble of thinking about the objects or ideas which they represent. Here exactly lies their capacity for mischief.

We do not have to see snow to deal with it mentally, and we can say "it is snowing" without further describing the weather. The very young child, still learning to speak, is forced to use his curiosity and intellect to invent definitions to describe new experiences. Everyone is familiar with the refreshing, sometimes disconcerting insights of guileless innocence. True, the child cannot respond to problems of the national budget. These involve abstract concepts for which his knowledge and experiences are still inadequate. But by the time either the budget or the nation becomes his concern, he may have lost the inclination to contemplate them except through the thoughts of others. As he acquires the vocabulary and built-in attitudes of his culture, the child's imagination is in danger of being shackled by the conventional and static concepts he inherits. Clichés and trite expressions substitute for true thinking, and mass-produced emotions replace genuine feeling and response. Gradually, thoughts are frozen in the words which embody them and the child learns to shuffle symbols — ambiguous packages such as nature, justice, or patriotism — which are dangerously divorced from the uncertain ideas they represent.

Weather reports now become succinct. "It is snowing," says the child. But he is a prisoner of his own progress. He may

never again "see" the snow. Once he learns that snow is a manifestation of "weather," the clever child, like his parents, is
likely to consult the weather bureau rather than his window to
find out if it is snowing. The forecast, couched in the militant
jargon of meteorologese, may report advancing weather fronts
and pressure systems in the remote corners of his continent, but
may have little to do with conditions which prevail at his front
door. Poets and painters, like very young children, still "see"
the snow.

> *White as a white cow's milk,*
> *More beautiful*
> *Than the breast of a gull.*

They know its power to mute man's shabby encroachments on
the landscape. They know the landscape "drawn in pearly
monotones." They have seen glistening frost flowers and smoke
puffs of powder snow, and occasionally, with the warming sun,
they rediscover its close kinship to water.

In a passage in *Modern Painters*, the English author and
critic John Ruskin wrote, "It is a strange thing how little in
general people know about the sky. . . . Who, among the
whole chattering crowd, can tell me of the forms and the preci-
pices of the chain of tall white mountains that girded the hori-
zon at noon yesterday? Who saw the narrow sunbeam that came
out of the south and smote their summits until they melted and
mouldered away in a dust of blue rain?" One wonders what
Ruskin would have thought of the modern air traveler, who
draws the shade on the drama of clouds and sunlight just outside the window of his craft and in martini and movie seeks
relief from the boredom of flight.

The philosophical quest to know things as they are, apart
from the bias of our senses and nervous system, has proved
futile. It was Immanuel Kant who wrote that through the use of
reason it is impossible to know the causes of our sensations, the
things in themselves. External reality, independent of our

knowledge of it, is unknowable. We know only what we experience and what the mind then orders in time and space. The reality behind the phenomena of existence is accessible neither to science nor philosophy.

Not only does objective reality elude us, as Kant attempted to demonstrate, but as anyone who has compared descriptions of an automobile accident reported by eyewitnesses knows, perceived reality varies with the perceiver. We are neither cameras nor tape recorders. Instead we operate the recording apparatus. Differing in our individual degree of artistry, each of us creates the world in his own mind. It is a world perceived and recorded with emotion, enriched by intellect, and altered by the passage of time. The ability to regroup the fragments of experience mentally in new and significant combinations, to move backward and forward in thought, to go where we have not been, to be where we cannot go, and to re-create even if imperfectly another person's feelings, is the supreme gift of our responsive, uniquely personal human brain.

If the props of experience were all that mattered, human memory would be burdened with an incredible clutter of meaningless, unclassified information. The creative act in its simplest everyday form is to separate a particular event from its ordinary context, and to relate it to other information in memory's warehouse, to endow the transient occurrence with meaning, and thus to grant it a small measure of permanence. Long before creativity became an official vogue, Walter Pater enjoined man to give "the highest quality to your moments as they pass." Writing about art, the cloistered Oxford scholar had described the art of living.

All That Glitters Is Not Creative

The depersonalized, mechanical structure of modern life is so sterile and boring that to many people to be "creative" means to do something other than what they are doing. The modern concept of creativity is broad, but not boundless. No more than creativity is a synonym for artistic talent, is it to be equated with everything admirable, satisfying, or useful in human behavior. Nor is creativity another word for production in the sense that to produce means to cause (he created a disturbance), or to make or manufacture. The development of a satisfactory theory of creativity may require that psychologists study not only those activities, such as learning, which are now understood to be within its province, but also delineate those which lie beyond. If you play tennis without the net is the game still tennis?

In an interview on the problems of automation, one expert mentioned the "need for creative work on all levels." He was quoted as saying: "The man who sees a job through from beginning to end, solves a problem, produces something that wasn't there before, is performing a creative act, whether it's writing a symphony or washing a car. Repairing a television set is creative compared to tending a machine in a factory."

Such well-intentioned, but misguided, dilution of the creative act is unfortunate because it cheapens the meaning of creativity. In addition it disregards other valuable, noncreative human activities. Repairing a television set is a useful, intelligent task, which in theory, if not always in practice, requires skill, application, and the ability to diagnose electronic disorders. Ordinarily it is not a creative act, nor if well done, need it be to earn our respect. The man who washes his car has indeed produced or caused the "cleanness" of his car, and certainly the automobile's appearance is altered, but we must distinguish between routine production and creative production. To wash a car is, as rightly suggested, "to see a job through." But it is in "seeing a job through" that the satisfaction derived from washing one's car may lodge: in the performance of a useful, responsible act, and in work which has meaning to the worker. Similarly, the housewife who bakes her own bread according to a recipe, sews a dress from a pattern, or tends her garden is doing useful, satisfying, but contrary to the women's magazines, uncreative work. Why must the encomium "creative" certify tasks which are for many other reasons worthy and satisfying? Among the variety of pleasures which may enhance noncreative work are pride in accomplishment, finishing something, economy, attendant fantasies (first prize in the flower show), the admiration of family and friends, the pleasure of doing the actual work, or perhaps a gift representing one's personal attention. The handmade and homemade are not in themselves creative. To do by hand what a machine ordinarily does is not a creative act.

It might require some element of creativity to wash a car if water were not available. It might be creative to repair a television set in the absence of standard parts, or should the instrument succumb to some unchronicled electronic disorder. The woman who designs the dress she sews, or bakes according to her own recipe, has a right to point to her modest creation. A degree of novelty is present in both instances.

This confusion between production and creation contributes to a more serious misunderstanding. The frequent prescription of so-called creativity as the remedy for the spiritual poverty of modern life may indicate the existence of a morbid social condition, but does not prove that its cause is a dearth of creative opportunity. A hearty dose of creativity is not the only possible cure for the problem of the fragmented "Teilmensch" — the factory worker or clerk, the business executive or engineer — who serves as a cog in a machine whose final product is so remote that he feels neither responsibility for, nor deep interest in, what he is doing. Deprived of the fruits of his labor, cynical, starved for dignity and meaning in his work, he toils in a plush-lined occupational desert. The experts say he feels no "involvement." He says he is bored. His reward is a high standard of living, a chance to be with his family, and the time and financial means to repair his atrophied self with his hobbies or in the doctor's office. The spiritually impoverished men and women, lured by advertisements or job recruiters offering the chance to do "creative work" are not all in need of creative work. Regardless of whether they work as garage mechanics, gem collectors, or biochemists, what they require is interesting, meaningful work where their specific aptitudes count.

The disaffected, cynical, but privileged college students who have at last begun to protest an educational system which is impersonal, indifferent, and as Paul Goodman has said, absurd; who are dismayed by the dreary occupational treadmill which awaits them if they want, as indeed they do, the amenities of affluence, are not all asking for a chance to be creative. Nor does the young woman who, having received a liberal arts education, yearns "to do something creative" express herself precisely. Her real problem is not so much the lack of creative opportunity, but the schizophrenic difference between what her education has told her she can do and the dull, mindless chores the workaday world will let her do.

It will take conviction and pluck if the young woman is to avoid being shackled to a typewriter, and it will take firm principles and strong motivation if the young man is not to succumb to the delusive security of a fringe-benefit life. These students want — as students have always wanted — an education which is relevant and meaningful, although what such an education should be is not necessarily clear either to the students or to their once-confident educators. After the school years they wish to be respected as responsible, dignified individuals. They would like the chance to identify with their work, to make a significant number of their own decisions, and, beyond a paycheck and prestige, the opportunity to serve not only the boss or the firm, but themselves. In the classroom, in the office and in the factory, they want to be men and women, not machines.

By now the ills of our materialistic culture are a familiar story. What is awry is not so much the lack of creativity, but the paucity of meaning and responsibility in the work people do. To spend eight hours a day, day after day, in a job the rewards of which are to be reaped in leisure or nonwork hours, is not a salubrious way of life. Thoughtful observers of contemporary society point out that eventually the corrosive effects of a hypocritical working life may poison those other cherished hours in which men and women have arranged to be human.

Neither the "good old-fashioned carpenter" who builds tables or bookcases, nor the hobbyist who constructs his own from a set of plans is doing creative work. Each is engaged in useful, responsible work. Satisfaction is a subjective experience, extremely difficult to measure. We must not assume that creative satisfaction is more satisfying — thus better, than noncreative satisfaction. The Monday-Friday carpenter and the Sunday carpenter may both derive as much pleasure and pride from their efforts as the creative individual who designs the bookcase he constructs. The reverse is not true. The creative carpenter would not be content to follow another's design.

What then is the origin of this personal sense of satisfaction? Happiness or a sense of well-being may depend upon a subjective equation between what is, and one's estimate of what could be. One's criterion of what might be attained, in turn, is based upon experience. Whether this mechanism of hedonic measurement is called a "floating aspirational level," the term used by psychologists, or the serpent in Genesis, in the final analysis, the pleasure one derives from work (or leisure) is related to intimate personal adjustments which are still little and poorly understood.

The individual who is himself highly creative is likely to assume that it is the creative component of the productive act which is the source of his satisfaction, as indeed it may be. Since the productive act, the act of "making something," is not without its own satisfactions, the person who produces an uncreative but useful and intelligent work may also be pleased and delighted with his efforts. There is also the possibility that this person may consider himself engaged in creative work, when actually he is not. The personal value of work may inhere either in production or in creative production, depending upon individual personality and aptitudes. In the case of the individual who fancies himself a second Dostoevsky, a purely internal evaluation is involved: not what he does, but what he thinks he is doing.

We still know very little, not only about the special physio-chemical mechanisms of creativity, but about the dense web of related processes — perception, memory, learning, thinking, imagination, emotion — whose neural patterns, mysterious and invisible, participate in the creative act. The knotty "criteria problem," fortunately, may be left to those who in their professional work are required to struggle with it. Nor is it our purpose to study the psychological profiles of creative architects or engineers, or to provide a concise formula for creative thinking.

At the present time, it is more profitable to look at creative man through a telescope, rather than a microscope: to observe him in the perspective of human history and biology; to examine creativity research, at least briefly, against the background of other scientific studies; and to consider the significance of the awesome power for which modern creative man finds himself responsible. In this manner, the nature, if not the definition, of creativity should gradually become apparent. If we become sensitive to the presence, either latent or expressed, of creativeness in ourselves and in others, and if we understand creative behavior as it relates both to our human status and to our personal human condition, we shall be well rewarded. To believe that man is the purpose of all creation and that the earth with its vast glories evolved for our pleasure would be hubris. But not to take pride in the godlike gifts with which our species is endowed, not to understand the power which has given us dominion over all the other creatures of this planet would be disastrous. For what we cherish and respect we will protect and cultivate; what we understand we may try not to abuse.

3. Creativity and Crisis

The real victim is the future.
— DAG HAMMARSKJÖLD

WHEN THIS CENTURY draws to a close and the historians of
tomorrow undertake the task of evaluating our times, it is possible that they will describe the twentieth century as one of the
great creative centuries in Western history. Like the seventeenth century, it is a time of "turmoil and transition" which
will dramatically alter the structure of our society and the patterns of our culture. As citizens of a scientific society, we live in
an environment equipped not only with the artifacts of science,
but one in which science shapes the national ethos.

Unlike other historical periods, however, the twentieth century is a time of unprecedented peril. Progress is doubtful, security an illusion, and peace a balance of terror. A slip here or
there, and man will pull the whole tent down on top of himself.
The real danger lurks not in the forest where the wolf prowls,
but in the air we must breathe; not on the bloody battlefield
where soldiers contend with one another, but in the staid and
sober laboratories of science and technology where the outcome
of modern warfare is now decided. The serious threat to our
future is not the diminution of our species through disease or
disaster, but ironically its successful proliferation. Estranged
from himself, man has become an exile in the bleak, mechanical world of his own creation — a world where acts of man

pose as awesome a threat as the "acts of God" which imperiled his helpless forebears.

Despite Arnold Toynbee's thesis that challenge and crisis serve as the stimulus through which man achieves new levels of creativeness, he also concluded that the interaction of "challenge and response" is subject to the law of diminishing returns. Civilizations have been defeated by a challenge which is too severe. In our hazardous times, courting crises is not recommended as a means of advancing civilization.

Creative Feedback

The current enthusiasm for the creative life has generated the unfortunate misunderstanding that creativity confers upon its possessor vague auras of intellectual superiority or moral virtue, and that noncreative pursuits are in some nebulous way, inferior. From the chemistry of single cells to the mechanisms of social systems, life is an organized and coordinated process, governed by the dual principles of conservation and innovation, of conformity and diversity. These opposed, but dependent, forces are found everywhere: in the metabolic cycle of maintenance and growth, in the physiological principle of homeostasis by which the body resists the forces of chaos and adjusts to changes in its environment, and in the pull and tug of the evolutionary process. As we have previously observed, the equilibrium between conservation and composition cannot be static if organisms are to grow and if life is to adapt to the contingencies of a changing universe.

Similarly, the development of society and culture depends upon a changing balance, maintained between those who innovate and those who conserve the status quo. Although innovation may be employed to maintain the status quo, the innovator generally alters it. Relentless, unchecked, and untested innovation would be a nightmare. If everyone were a "deviant thinker" or a nonconformist, principles of law, order, justice and morality could not have been established and society would not exist. The deviant thinkers would have nothing to deviate from. Those who uphold justice and keep the peace are as necessary as those who provide its rules. If repetition and rigidity are the dark side of the conservative coin, loyalty and stability are its bright side. With the dissolution of the Roman Empire, for example, and the withdrawal of Roman legions from Europe, tradition, stability, law and order also dissolved, and medieval Europe lapsed for a number of bleak centuries into a state of chaos and cultural torpor. Western civilization owes its recovery from this setback to the Church. Having stabilized its own organization, the Church not only preserved the legacy of the classical age, but provided the structure of a new order, rebuilding it upon the wreckage of the old. In the ninth century, an outburst of creativity in art and architecture, known as the Carolingian Renaissance, foreshadowed the glorious accomplishments of Renaissance Europe.

Moreover, it would be an oversimplification to suggest that the population is divided into those who conform and those who diverge. In our personal, occupational, and social functions and at different stages in our individual development, we play both roles. Even the most daring political leader must insist upon conformity to the group and must himself conform to these principles, lest the society he wishes to lead cease to exist. Teachers and parents must conform to the cultural definitions of their roles, at the same time that they advocate experiment and innovation. It has been pointed out that as individuals the astronauts are hardly conformist types; yet once they have volunteered for their jobs, they must adhere to a rigid program of training and flight procedure.

In all self-regulating systems, nervous systems (biological and electronic) or social systems, change is effected through the positive feedback of innovation. Feedback is the means by which an animal or a self-regulating machine such as a thermostat or an automatic pilot learns the result of its own behavior. Performance is controlled on the basis of actual performance rather than expected performance. Before the self-service elevator opens its doors to admit a passenger, it must check to see if the cab is really where it is expected to be, lest the trusting passenger tumble down the elevator shaft. Engineers, from whom the term is borrowed, describe feedback as either negative or positive. A thermostat whose goal is set at a given temperature, maintains that temperature with unswerving obedience until reset. This is an example of *negative* feedback. Systems capable of learning — heuristic machines such as chess-playing computers, as well as animals and human beings — which alter their objectives on the basis of past experience, illustrate *positive* feedback.

To keep track of itself and to adjust its goals to contingent events, a self-regulating system requires two-way communication channels. Suppose, for example, you wish to pick up an object such as an egg. It is not sufficient for your brain to fire a barrage of impulses over peripheral nerve routes directing the muscles of your hand and arm to obey its command. The extremity itself discharges a continual flow of "messages" informing the home office of conditions in biological exurbia. The brain then adjusts the pressure of your fingers against the eggshell so that the egg may be safely lofted, rather than crushed in your palm or smashed on the floor. Similarly, in the positive feedback of a democratic society elected leaders must be informed of the reaction of the electorate. When taping a television program, many performers consider a live audience invaluable because it serves as a gauge, indicating to the input (performer), the effect of its output (performance).

The role of the public in the process of creation should not be discounted. New ideas must be utilized and evaluated. Those which are chaotic or irrelevant must be discarded. It is not the conservative principle, but rather overdedication to conservation and conformity which is regrettable. Applying the principle of the wheel discovered by some forgotten genius, ordinary men not only tested its usefulness, but made the invention culturally viable. Eventually, other creative people freed the wheel from its axle and produced the spun potter's wheel and the free-turning cart wheel. Ideally, the quarrel between the creative individual and his society is, in Robert Frost's words, a "lover's quarrel." In any system required to grow and change, it is essential that these two principles be prevented from locking in deadly combat or in mortal stalemate. The conservative spirit has not been equally recalcitrant throughout history. The eras of classical Greece and the Renaissance are two periods in which a stimulating dialogue existed between those who created the revolutionary changes in art and a lively, although limited, public which came to gaze and comment.

If the conservative forces in a family, corporation, or government become so rigid that they no longer listen to the suggestions of their advance guard, the death knell begins to toll. If the forces of innovation are estranged from the reality they wish to alter then they too are doomed. The rare mutation which is successful is that which acknowledges the existing environment. Art, unlike daydreams, private fantasies or hallucinations, is the artist's encounter with reality or with some universal truth and the revelation of that experience to other human beings. Even the most creative research scientist must conform to the tenets of the scientific method and to the framework of his subject if his work is to be of value. Gradually, the conservative world of nature and man is altered by the innovations it absorbs. The continents of the earth are covered with grass and trees, instead of rocks and pebbles; and unimaginative, conservative men, not merely inspired dreamers, will tell you that the earth is round. Life, we say, has evolved; human beings have learned.

Although the noncreative, conservative forces in life provide a testing ground for creative offerings, it does not follow that their verdict is infallible. Generally, society judges a creation not by its intrinsic value, but by the usefulness or value of the product, or derivative products, to itself. Because the scientific method offers an objective means of measuring the validity of a new scientific principle, science is to a greater degree exempt from subjective judgment. Nonetheless, society still has the power to bestow laurels and funds upon those whose discoveries possess obvious utility and to ignore those whose work is so esoteric it lacks popular or political sex appeal. The creative process which produces a sword is the same as that which results in a scalpel; that which synthesizes a new medicine is no different from the one which yields a poison. The difference between a beneficial drug or a deadly poison may be only a matter of the dose used. Man's destructive weapons, from spears to nuclear missiles, have always been welcomed by those who, justly or unjustly, had need of them. Similarly, a painting may be valued as an investment or as a status symbol, and not for its inherent artistic properties. In the creation of civilization, society, therefore, plays the selective role which in the individual process of creation is left to the discriminatory powers of the artist or thinker, and which in nature is reserved for blind selection. Upon our collective ability to recognize and pursue those goals which subserve a sane and secure future, and upon society's exercise of its constructive genius depends the future happiness and well-being of mankind. One can only hope that as the author of its own destiny, society understands what it means to be a creator.

Power and Pace

In giving us godlike control over our destinies, science and its practical colleague, technology, have produced an awesome array of problems which in their complexity and range present an unprecedented challenge to the imagination, intellect, and moral fiber of man. These are problems which did not exist in the past — at least not to such an extent. A brief glance at a few of these issues should give us some idea, not only of the enormous task which confronts us, but of the nature of the creative effort and the stretch of creative imagination required in their solution.

It must be clearly understood that deliverance from the present morass is not a responsibility which can be left to the members of a ruling elite and to the experts who advise them. As political, scientific, psychological and economic considerations intersect, decisions become increasingly complicated, and the ordinary citizen, no longer able to follow the multiple threads of debate, goes home to mow his lawn. Intimidated by science, he swallows the too-glib suggestion that it is a subject permanently beyond his comprehension, a matter best left to "experts." But on election day, the ordinary citizen returns to the polls and votes. The leaders of a democratic regime must be sufficiently informed to interpret the advice of scientists and other experts, but they are also responsible to the citizens who elect them. Unlike the leaders of a totalitarian state, they are required to contend with public opinion and with the opposed interests of special groups, and must persuade a majority of the citizens to accept their decisions.

Writing about the education of citizens of a scientific society, the French scholar Raymond Aron has observed that the public must understand the actions of its rulers, and that public opinion, including the writers, journalists, and commentators who help to influence it, must be sufficiently enlightened to "permit" the leaders to listen to the advice of the specialists. An uninformed and alienated citizenry would be a tragedy. To cultivate one's own garden while the public gardens are consumed by the wilderness is to invite horticultural disaster. In "Answers to Hard Questions," E. B. White, when asked whether one should avoid becoming a father during the hay-fever season, declined to recommend abstinence on the basis of season or foliage. "The time not to become a father," he wrote, "is eighteen years before a world war." We too have hard questions and, one suspects, when found, hard answers.

As the horizons of man's knowledge expand, the possibility of mastering a limited portion of the environment increases. The cure of cancer, increasing longevity, direct chemical synthesis of food, and human genetic improvement are but a few predicted mileposts for an intelligent, rational society which eschews war as incompatible with survival. At the same time, the problems man must solve become more intricate and their solutions more elusive. Despite tremendous increases in the number of cars and roads, and in the size and speed of aircraft, this country faces a crisis in transportation. The hazards of science have overflown the laboratory. They appear in the air we breathe, in the food we eat, even in the drugs which cure now, but may kill later. Officials in government and industry have discovered to their dismay that in poking fingers blindly into the dense webs of complex, delicately organized systems, which are themselves constantly changing, they have snapped and snarled the threads of natural processes and violated the biological environment. Science has let a slippery genie out of the bottle and cannot get it back in.

If ignorance is not bliss, it is at least intellectually less taxing. Truth and goodness are not always interchangeable. Good and bad, right and wrong are not always clear. The beautiful truth which the scientist pursues in the laboratory may provide in other hands some ugly political realities. Is the thermonuclear bomb an instrument of the devil? Or is it a blessing in disguise — an ultimatum for peace? How long, asks one political commentator, does a deterrent no one dares to use remain effective as a deterrent? How many genetically damaged infants, another critic asks, are justified by the requirements of national security? Science is silent. These are moral or political judgments. For the modern physician, uncertain of the definition of life, or for the medical team forced by limited facilities to deal out life and death, the biblical injunction, "Thou shalt not kill!" becomes even more difficult to interpret. The risks to which human germ plasm have already been subjected are a serious concern. But the practical consequences, as well as the moral and ethical problems inherent in our potential power to alter our genetic heritage directly, are so formidable that few dare to speak these profoundly disturbing questions aloud. Fewer still have the courage to listen.

The control of human aggression, whether resentment or rage, delinquency or war, is an ancient problem in urgent need

of solution today. Sermons and systems of reward and punishment have a long history of failure. In our overcrowded nuclear
age, stoic resignation to the human capacity for beastliness
would be grave folly. We cannot afford to add fuel to the siz-
able fire of anger and frustration which was kindled long ago
when a self-centered and self-conscious creature began the
touchy business of living a communal life with other creatures
similar in nature. It is essential, say humanists and scientists
such as Aldous Huxley and Konrad Lorenz, that society with
the help of science find acceptable "safety valves" for channel-
ing man's violent and destructive emotions into satisfying, but
innocuous, outlets.

The scientific art of mind control, from scurvy television
commercials for children's toys, status-impregnated automobiles, and news reports which tell a credulous public what it
likes to hear, to the more exotic forms of brainwashing and drug
experimentation, presages frightening dimensions for the future. Organized persuasion and the "engineering of consent"
are subtle and sophisticated forms of their heavy-handed forebear, once known as propaganda. They are becoming insidious
arts, in which the persuaded fail to protect themselves against
infringements of their dignity and rights, either because they
do not recognize the means by which they are controlled, or
worse, because they do not regard such encroachments as noxious.

In the age of information overload, the dissemination and
interpretation of knowledge have emerged as a fundamental
concern. Increasingly, scientists and scholars find themselves
backed into the tight corners of their narrow specialties, unable
to speak intelligibly to one another. In the words of one authority on human problems, we are faced with a "proliferation in
knowledge" and a "contraction of understanding." More opti-
mistically, Willard Libby, recipient of a Nobel Prize in chemistry, suggests that the vast bulk of information will not be a
permanent obstacle. True understanding of various aspects of
nature will eventually lead to general conclusions and to new

principles which will enable us to discard the enormous baggage of substantiating literature which is summarized by the theory. "The value of a principle," said Emerson, "is the number of things it will explain." Both Newton's and James Clerk Maxwell's laws made it possible to state briefly information which otherwise would have filled libraries. At present, however, the problem of communicating scientific results quickly and efficiently not only among scientists, but to those in other fields whose work is influenced by scientific developments, is urgent and unsolved. Dr. Libby writes that "real inventions are needed in the use of rapid copying methods, in employing tape and television to communicate and coordinate scientific discoveries, and in developing library and educational techniques which would serve the rapid expansion of knowledge."

The modern university has become a "vital national resource," whose function is not only to transmit the past, but to participate in the solutions of the future. The unprecedented circumstances of our era require more than the reform of academic curricula and methods. It is necessary that we reexamine our educational goals and our idea of what constitutes a suitable education today.

Educators must decide what kind of education is required for men and women who are to live in the rapidly changing environment of a scientific society, who must learn to respect science without deifying it. How shall we prevent ordinary citizens, served by computers and an automated technology which they fear and misunderstand, from remodeling themselves in the image of the machine? What kind of education is appropriate for women whose dilemma is compounded by the fact that they inhabit a male-oriented world? Women receive more education and live longer than ever before, but, according to recent reports, are also unhappier than their male counterparts. How shall we educate political leaders whose psychopolitical decisions are rooted in scientific considerations or, conversely, scientists who can no longer ignore political and historical realities? The highly skilled and specialized physician who treats diseases, not patients, and the college professor who teaches subjects, not students, have become stock characters of the contemporary scene. A preeminent challenge to education today is to find, train, and encourage a corps of gifted men and women to serve as couriers between isolated specialties, and particularly between science and national policy. The broad approach of such "interdisciplinary generalists" would permit them to explore the human problems which flourish in the rear of scientific advance and to anticipate those problems which arise in the gaps between domains of delegated authority.

Since a dangerous game of crisis hopping appears, at least for the present, to have become our normal way of life, the method of dealing with existing crises as they arise is both maladroit and rash. It would be more prudent to study the genesis of crisis and to explore methods for managing critical situations in general before we tumble or blunder into a specific predicament. No more than the volunteer fire department is considered the most effective means of fighting fire, are improvised methods for extinguishing the flames of crisis expedient in our times. Obviously, the best time to handle an emergency is before it becomes one.

With so much at stake and the cost so high, it becomes an awesome responsibility merely to determine the direction of scientific research. It is impossible to foresee the future use of some seemingly esoteric category of research. Attempts to solve a specific problem by drafting detailed blueprints of scientific studies or by allocating funds only to the study of specific subjects are unwise and reveal a profound ignorance of the nature of creative discovery. If a cancer research project had been drafted before X ray or radioactivity was discovered, no funds would have been reserved for the exploration of their potential value, because, as Professor George Kistiakowsky of Harvard University writes, nobody knew they existed. Who could have known that the Curies would make a major contribution to the treatment of cancer? Who could have demonstrated that the

study of the microwave spectroscopy of the ammonia molecule
would lead to the discovery of the master and to a transatlantic
satellite communication system?

Our national computing power is doubling every year. As
unsleeping computers continue to spew oceans of data and par-
tially digested information, man must decide not only what is
relevant, but what is worth doing in the first place, lest he
drown in a flood of trivia. Wise use of the computer requires
that we distinguish the machine's work from work which demands human judgment, imagination, and innovation. Routine intellectual tasks such as memorization and computation,
once a major occupation of education, may now be left to the
machine, freeing man to concentrate on the more demanding
intellectual functions of generalization, synthesis, and the critical judgment of relevance.

If man fails to ask his machine the right questions, or if he
stuffs his computer's input with irrelevant data and false premises, the computer will only succeed in magnifying human error
— which without electronic assistance is large enough. There
is little advantage in speeding if you are headed in the wrong
direction. Moreover, the machine cannot by some internal
abracadabra resolve the discrepancy between our avowed principles and our actual goals. The computer is obedient; it does
what it is told. Computer technologists have a succinct expression for the close relationship between computer input and output. They call it GI-GO: garbage in — garbage out.

If we are to accept our responsibility for the problems created by scientific progress, mere awareness of their existence
will not suffice. The problems will remain lifeless abstractions
unless men are taught to care about what they do. Emotional
involvement is impossible, however, unless we are first able to
imagine the object of our proposed concern. The ability to
project on a mental screen, not merely the name of an experience (war, loss, love) but a film strip complete with a sound
track and a selection of accompanying emotions, is a uniquely
human faculty. The demands made on our powers of imagina-

tion are greater now than at any time in human history. Yet after a few bright childhood years, human imagination, in all but a few unusual people, is allowed to atrophy. It is a waste we cannot afford.

It is difficult enough for man to behave honorably on a man-to-man basis; national and international morality is still primitive. Consider the act of imagination required in the creation of the long-term morality which, if mankind is not to sprint toward extinction, must accompany a consciously controlled evolution, responsible for the well-being of generations yet to come. We are only now beginning to consider the issue of birth control seriously. Human imagination, with its traditional limits, is a serious obstacle to the success of this vital program. If men and women not infrequently shirk the responsibility for the welfare of their own children, how do they regard the welfare of a stranger's great-grandchildren? Or, as someone has observed, how do they imagine and feel concern for the child they deliberately decide not to have?

Insurance policies are sold because men accept their obligation to those they love, whose plight in the event of harm to themselves, is not difficult to picture. A threat to a neighbor or a friend is still within the scope of ordinary human imagination and, depending upon the individual, may trigger apposite stirrings of moral obligation. In the *name* of patriotism, freedom, or some other political or economic ideology, man can be enticed from his home and family in order to fight for an abstract principle, or for a territory he has never seen — something no animal can do. And only man knows the world to be a place which exists even without him.

Human imagination is remarkable. Nevertheless, it is biologically hamstrung. Our brain with its sense organs evolved as a superior instrument of survival in a world of saber-toothed tigers, not remote control war; of visible fire, not invisible fallout. In the intimate family life of cave dwellers, squatting around a common fire, man was not expected to feel kinship with those he had never seen. When he succeeded in projecting his thoughts and feelings through time and space, he used his imagination and memory to close the physical gap between his sense organs and their distant stimulus. The stranger was no longer strange, and the foreigner for whom he shed his own blood became a "brother." If our ancestors had seen electrons instead of wolves, wrote Albert Szent-Györgyi, we would be extinct. We continue to see the sun "set" and motion pictures "move," even though we know they do not. A considerable part of man's brain with its nervous system is no longer connected to the marvels it has created. How do we imagine the reality of destruction and death in a push-button war, which can be waged from the safety of an office building, whose outcome may be determined in the far reaches of a laboratory, and in which killer and killed never see each other. The man felled by your sword or gun leaves some record of himself in your brain. Even the sight of a battlefield is enough to remind men of what they are doing. But how does one comprehend the tragedy of half a million unknown people killed somewhere, whom you have never seen, but toward whose death you may have contributed?

Man's imagination has not yet learned how to deal with the extreme numbers, both large and small, and the remote possibilities which have become our way of life. We have begun to explore the immense reaches of the solar system, and we have descended into the genetic substructure of life and into the Lilliput of atomic subparticles. Yet very few of us have a sense of the size and time scales encountered in the macro- and microcosms. The average American can imagine the value of one dollar or a thousand dollars, and he rather likes to contemplate the idea of a million dollars. Much beyond this his imagination begins to falter. A megabuck scientific experiment has no relationship to anything he has experienced. He understands the difference between five and ten dollars, but the difference between five and ten billion dollars may be meaningless to him. Billions and trillions are unreal abstractions appropriate, as far as he is concerned, to the hyperbole of fairy tales. And yet megabuck spending is part of our culture. Similarly he comprehends a five-mile walk and a three-thousand-mile journey. The heat of fire is a concrete reality. But how far away is a hundred million light years? How hot is fifteen million degrees? How small is a hundreth of a microsecond?

Our traditional morality is based on a direct cause-and-effect relationship. Honest, law-abiding citizens do not kill each other — at least not directly. But when there is only a "probability" that an event will occur, and when that event may not take place for years or generations, a severe strain is placed upon the individual's imagination, without which his emotional machinery, his powers of reason, and ultimately his moral sense are crippled. In the absence of population control, a sane nuclear policy, safer automobiles, and curbs on air pollution, a certain number of people will suffer at an unknown time. Yet these impersonal tragedies fail to arouse the average citizen's sympathy and concern. You would not push your neighbor into an incinerator. Your direct participation in an abhorrent act condemned by our culture as murder would be obvious to you. But what is your moral responsibility if the fumes from your incinerator or your car contribute to the deaths of an unknown number of unknown people at some distant time?

We live in an age of statistical killing, but it has been observed we have failed to develop a parallel "statistical morality." None will evolve until we teach ourselves to care about the one tenth of one percent of a death for which we may be responsible. Large numbers, the statistics of probability, and a technology which extends man's irresponsible hand around the planet and forward upon the yet unwritten pages of history have transformed the quality of our environment. The creative task which awaits the average citizen and those who direct his education, is expressed by Robert S. Morison of the Rockefeller Foundation in the following counsel: people must learn to comprehend "the reality of action at a distance" and at the same time, they must be taught to experience "concern for that reality." To exploit science without understanding it, is to commit the dangerous sin of Moral Tourism: "going to new places with the firm expectation of proper accommodations and a readiness to blame the natives if it turns out not so."

The Responsible Creator

Confronted with a crisis in our political and social evolution, we find, moreover, that our historical timetable is antiquated and no longer relevant to the direction of future behavior. Not only are our problems fiendishly snarled, but the cultural conditions in which we must operate are unique in mankind's experience. Changes which once occurred in the leisurely course of centuries are now compressed into a generation. The killing power of the musket used in the Civil War was not much greater than that of the long bow invented in the Stone Age, yet the difference in the methods of destruction used in World War II and the nuclear weapon which helped to conclude that venture is staggering. In March 1945, 334 conventional B-29's bombed Tokyo, killing more than eighty thousand people. A few months later a single atomic bomb took the lives of more than seventy thousand people in Hiroshima. Students entering medical school today must learn at least four times as much as their teachers did two decades earlier, and by the time they finish their residencies — some eight years later — their knowledge of the basic sciences is already outdated. In such a world it becomes increasingly difficult to apply the lessons of the previous generation to the present, or to extrapolate the future from the past. If anything is certain, it is that the future is unpredictable and that tomorrow's environment will be dramatically different from today's.

Because innovation threatens the existing order, society, as has already been observed, traditionally resists change, assuming that bygone days and ways were better. In the recent decades of synthetic demand, planned technological obsolescence, even human obsolescence, constant unrestrained change is welcomed as an end in itself. Greed is our polestar. Innovation takes wings, but neither is there time, nor is it fashionable to ask if relentless, unchecked innovation benefits anyone but those into whose coffers the coins will tumble. One cannot help wondering what has happened to the restraining power of supposedly conservative society.

Confusing change with progress, we blindly pursue the new — whether it be an automobile, a fashion, an educational trend, or youth — firm in the conviction that the artifacts of the past, including people, are outmoded. The venerable past may refer to last year; a mere decade may separate hoary elders from the "swinging" young. The advertising industry is well aware of the persuasive power of such words as dynamic, up-to-date, young, growing, latest. Copywriters may struggle to distill their messages of enthusiasm in bright prose and snappy slogans, but the one word favored by advertisers over the years, is still the old word *new*.

The specific vocabulary of our era reflects yet another trenchant set of social values. Such words as alienation, apathy, disengagement, cool, and identity crisis signal that in the midst of plenty we remain in need. In all ages, the young have at some time felt themselves on the fringe of self and society. But there is evidence that, more than the passing affliction of youth, alienation may be a major theme in mature contemporary thought. Discouraged by an oppressive social system which tramples his dignity and his initiative, caught adrift in a mercurial world, without the comfort of values and ideals to sustain him, man is torn and sick at heart. No amount of material consolation, not even the little pills provided by medical science, are in the long run sufficient anesthesia for the dehumanizing operation.

Today, in middle-class America, children grow up and young adults mature in an environment where the older adult community implies that much is expected of the younger generation, but is itself too confused to define its expectations. The pace of social change, which follows in the wake of technological change, is so fast that parents no longer serve as satisfactory models for their children. Traditional values rapidly become obsolete, and new values cannot be formulated or old ones renovated fast enough to be of use. We are reminded that job commitment, long-range goals, "saving for a rainy day," and postponement of satisfactions, are ill-suited concepts in a world of changing job markets and constant inflation, where nuclear holocaust, rather than a rainy day, is the disaster for which we must prepare.

There is some indication that government, industry, and the complacent American public are slowly and belatedly beginning to accept the necessity for weighing the hazards of science, for putting a harness on its runaway technology, and for directing the course of social change which results from scientific advance. The almost un-American notion that the automobile may not be an unmitigated good, or the refreshing idea that our national resources should not become garbage dumps even in the sacred interests of industry and household plumbing, is beginning to occur not just to eccentric conservationists, but to a growing segment of the public. Gradually and painfully, people are being forced to realize that what appears to be free and natural may simply represent neglect on our part, and may not coincide with our long-range interests. Neglect and inertia are the soil in which blind decisions germinate, for the failure to make a decision is itself a decision.

The meaning of the word natural is capricious. Bertrand Russell once wrote that every advance of civilization was denounced as unnatural while it was recent. Those who oppose birth control or blood transfusion as acts "against nature" do not find it unnatural to wear clothing and eat cooked food. Urban life may not be natural, but neither is life on a farm, and if cavorting naked in the jungle is natural, it is also dangerous. Man differs from his animal relations in that from the time he left his apelike predecessors behind on the evolutionary ladder, he has refused to live according to nature's whim, but has tried to alter his environment to please himself. He has come as far as he has, not through acts of neglect, but quite the opposite

— by energetically, if carelessly, attending to his destiny. He is in trouble now because this destiny has expanded in time and space, whereas his powers of mentation have not been refurbished since the days when the Cro-Magnon hunter tried to forestall the pangs of an empty stomach or mitigate the perils of the hunt by painting his dinner on the walls of his cave.

To confuse the creative product with the wise and constructive use of that product is a serious error. As the first atomic scientists discovered to their profound shock, creation is not its own justification. Truth packaged in a product may be made to serve the baneful gods of wrath as well as gentler masters. Just as parents are responsible for their minor children, society is responsible for its creations. For neither children nor creations (ideas as well as things) have the judgment or power to guarantee that they will not be misused or exploited. It is man who determines whether the knife kills or cures, whether the computer is a wizard or a simpleton, and man alone decides whether in the name of the gods he has created, he sows love or wreaks destruction. No one, young or old, scientist or those who direct scientific policy, ordinary citizen or the elite who hold segments of public power, can afford to abdicate responsibility for the system any longer. Otherwise, those few who receive by default the management of human affairs, may not act in the interest of the majority; or a machinelike technology allowed to gallop along without a head, may convert us all to human machines.

Youth is traditionally the time of greatest flexibility and adaptability. But unlike the ape, who upon maturing loses his haunting resemblance to the human child, becoming difficult to teach, even brutish in temperament, man retains his ability to learn and adapt throughout most of his life. As the raw power of youth is ripened by the experience and perspective of maturity, the intelligent, well-cultivated human brain, far from wilting, bears the finest fruit of human endeavor — wisdom. A small band of human beings has always taken advantage of its biological potential. The others, after a brief fling at youth, have been content to grow prematurely old. This calamitous loss of human potential was less noticeable when man lost at an early age not merely his potential, but his life. Until this century, infant mortality was high, youth was often cut off in its prime through war, childbirth, and disease, and if one did survive, youth dissolved swiftly in toil and drudgery to old age. The task of maintaining the mind's growth during the long span of healthy, vigorous middle years was a problem few people enjoyed. The life expectancy of Neanderthal man is estimated to have been about thirty-three years. The average lifespan of the ancient Roman or Greek is estimated at about thirty years. As recently as 1900, life expectancy in the United States was less than fifty years. But in 1964, the newborn white baby could look forward to approximately seventy years of life, a twentieth-century bonus of two decades of added lifetime.

Although it is true that men live longer today, there seems to be more to do, and less time in which to do it. The first requirement for creative inspiration is a well-prepared mind. Important creative work does not sprout miraculously from an empty head. The muses cannot be heard in a vacuum. If we intend to advance the frontiers of art or knowledge, we must first travel to the existing border. In science, as well as other areas of scholarship, the journey to the limits of even narrowly specialized subjects is growing longer and more demanding. Today the length of educational apprenticeship required before a student is ready to do significant creative work may extend beyond the graduate work required for a doctoral degree.

The danger of postponing creative work until the student has mastered old fields of knowledge — which may soon be obsolete — is that during his laborious apprenticeship the habit of creative thought may be lost. Slowly, quietly, it is displaced by pedantic conformity and the mechanical assimilation of information and ideas. Somewhere on the road to becoming an "expert," the inclination to ask questions, the ability to accept complexity and to integrate apparently unrelated ideas, and a sense of fun and experiment, may succumb to attrition.

An important appeal of the Peace Corps, the Civil Rights movement, and programs for teaching handicapped and underprivileged children is that they offer students an escape from the grueling life of academic force-feeding, whose goal too often is not education, but the sheepskin passport to a job or a graduate degree. When college is "cash" and learning is earning, it is the student who is bankrupt. In social action young people find the opportunity to use their wits and their ingenuity to solve problems for which there is no text, and to seek creative approaches to new problems. They may do this with a minimum of preparation, knowing that their work is both relevant and useful.

In our fluid, unpredictable society, therefore, where men enjoy an extended life-span, but where the years of creative accomplishment may be displaced as much as a decade, the nurture of a creative attitude, the habit of creative thought, and an interest in the creative ideas and needs of others, become a lifelong imperative. It has been predicted that in an ideal society of the future, school and learning might occupy half an individual's day throughout his life. Insight into the nature of the creative process and into the way in which creative people interact with their environment should be part of a modern education. This insight is essential not only for those who wish to develop their own resources, but for parents and educators whose duty it is to prevent the blight of these fragile powers in the young; and for leaders in government, industry, and in centers of learning whose decisions today may be the unalterable realities of tomorrow. Parents, even in the midst of parenthood, and teachers while teaching must learn to create the changes in value and method young people require, and youth must be taught to esteem and cultivate its own creative powers. College deans, legislators, and industrialists cannot coast forever on the principles acquired in their formative years. These principles may have developed in an environment which no longer exists.

Addressing the class of 1971 in a pamphlet entitled "So You're Going to College," sociologist John Finley Scott writes:

Most advice you will get is one or more generations old and is therefore suspect. Your advisers mean well but, unless they are both well informed and really up to date on what is going on now, they may prove unreliable.

When your parents speak nostalgically of the good times they had . . . they may be recalling experiences which you will not be able to share. You probably are going to spend twice the time studying that your parents did.

We may recall, however, that novelty is not the sole prerequisite of creativity. Innovation incorporates some of the old modes; its roots, if not its bloom, are in the soil of precedence. If creativity is the production of a new entity, it is also true that the new entity must have form, meaning, and congruence with some aspect of reality. The splattered, remote fantasies of a disengaged mind do not qualify as true creations. Even while we attend the future, we must sift the past for those ideals which in modern guise might still prove viable and valuable. To lose our heads, to unship the past, may leave us drifting with neither rudder nor compass across the shoals and reefs of treacherous seas, without a beacon to light our uncharted course.

The day is past when the older generation can be held entirely responsible for the way things are, while the members of a petulant younger generation turn their backs on a world they claim they did not make. Neither did their young parents. The student revolutions on campuses throughout the country are a welcome sign that young men and women are abandoning their former appearance of apathy. Angry, often fumbling, but willing to ask the questions and provide the leadership their elders have shunned, these students have begun to rebel against the numbing burden of meaningless labor and a way of life which denies their individual worth.

Social scientists who have worked personally with members of this student generation regard the demonstrations at the University of California at Berkeley, and on other college campuses, as more than the sporadic explosions of fractious or delinquent youth. Student uprisings originate among an articulate activist minority of the students, but their message expresses the frustrations and the goals, not only of their silent classmates, but of a large segment of society beyond the campus. Protest is not enough. It is necessary to discover and implement the means of living in this "strange new world" no one seems to have planned. If the revolution, as it has been called, is to succeed in spurring educational reform, passion must blend with reason and experience. The students deserve the sympathetic support and wise leadership of the adult community. Those in authority have defaulted in their traditional obligation of nurturing the young, of guiding them toward the social and occupational world of adulthood, and have neglected to channel youth's considerable energy in constructive directions. Failure to contend with these problems has forced students to take matters into their own hands.

Who We Are — Where We Are

If we are to be enlisted in our own cause, we must understand our circumstances and our aims. We must know not only that the stork did not bring us, but that the angels have not adopted us. We are enjoined to examine the perplexities of human behavior in terms of the brain and the nervous system which direct it and to explore the brain's vast, untapped potential. Inasmuch as man is also a social animal, he requires a measure of historical perspective and some insight into the environmental pressures with which he is required to contend. Ever since Freud opened the gates of the unconscious and invited people to follow him and browse in the weird nether world he charted, the value of individual psychological understanding has been gradually established. Today the dire signs of an unresolved Oedipus complex are familiar to many, and the devious ways of the libido have been widely broadcast. The apostasy of an undernourished ego is called to account for all manner of foibles, and in the absence of guilt feelings, there are those who suspect they ought to feel guilty. However, we generally overlook the importance of understanding our biological foundations, our evolutionary history, as well as the broad social pressures which confront us not only personally, but as members of specific culture and era.

It seems curious that the subject in which the schoolchild receives the least instruction is himself. What too often is construed as science in the primary school instills neither the method nor the spirit of science, and in subject matter is a hodgepodge of clouds, magnets, planets, air, gravity, and seeds. With the exception of some dubious notions called "health habits," the study of man is consistently omitted. It is difficult to understand why the abstract subject of gravitational force should be more suited to the intellectual appetite of the fourth grader than his own natural history. Eventually children learn that the heart is a pump, and that the brain is responsible for intellect. How often are they taught that, although they may declare "I love you with all my heart," the residence of love (and hate) is in the brain? Children are told that their eyes are "windows to the world," but they do not learn that it is with their brains that they see — and see differently. They study "nature" without realizing that they are included. They study their neighborhood and their nation, the atmosphere and the exosphere, but not their natural home, the biosphere — the thin veneer of earth which is the natural habitat of all life on this planet. Children are taught to read and write, and they realize that failure to acquire these skills is a fatal handicap in school and in later life. But very few understand the advantage of semantic or human speech as compared to the grunts, growls, and squeaks of animal communication. Nor are they apprised of the potential treachery of words to which all their lives they will entrust their thoughts and beliefs. One reason animal studies fascinate children is that from an understanding of what an elephant or chimpanzee can and cannot do, they intuit what they are.

To consider ourselves educated, it is not enough to be acquainted with literary trends, Soviet-American relations, or the fact that not all the Dark Ages were dark. We must understand what it means to be human: how we became human, what it requires to remain human, and what the human being might yet become. It is a grave mistake to ignore our biological foundations, for everything man does, from eating his dinner to studying his own mind, is mediated through bone and flesh, muscle and nerve. Alone among all creatures on earth, man is able to accumulate a cultural inheritance and transmit this stored record to his fellowman and to future generations. Just as DNA transmits biological messages in the form of molecular code, the human organism uses symbolic language to communicate its cultural heritage. In growing chorus, geneticists and anthropologists remind us that our cultural inheritance is stored and applied by a brain and nervous system which are themselves biological instruments, produced each time we are born by our biological system of inheritance which also evolved under the selective stimulus of the environment. Evolution did not endow us with a sense of right and wrong, any more than it enables us to see viruses and atoms. "Nature," said Seneca, "does not bestow virtue; to be good is an art." Instead it provided the means of developing culture. It is within our culture that ethics evolve, that atoms and viruses are discovered, and it is by means of our culture that our concepts of ethics, atoms, and viruses are returned to our brain. Every time a human being is born, his brain, no different in kind from the one born some fifty thousand or more years ago, must be "wired" and "programmed" by other human beings to function within its own culture. How well the brain serves as an instrument of survival depends, therefore, on whether we succeed in making it understand the conditions of the environment to which it must adapt, and whether as the programmers of our own brain, we comprehend these conditions correctly.

In serving man by transforming the environment, science paradoxically has rendered the world in many ways increasingly difficult to live in. The question arises: What must man do to survive his creations? Great creative prima donnas, we have always pursued our "art" oblivious to its side effects. Now, we are warned, we must learn to live in the world we have unwittingly designed. Fortunately, it is still possible. At fashion's dictate, and to serve her vanity, a woman will cram her feet into shoes which were not designed to serve the structure of the human foot. But as long as a foot is a foot, no matter how willing the spirit, there are limits to its ability to adapt to conditions alien to its structure. Similarly, man cannot be expected to be malleable infinitely. The world has begun to pinch. There comes a time when man's essential nature, complex as that may be, must be respected or he ceases to be a man. When the foot fails, its owner knows immediately. When the human spirit has evaporated, its departure may not be recognized until too late.

At present we are at war with nature and out of balance with our environment. Powerful, brilliant, lethal, man is neurologically a creature, in Aldous Huxley's words, with a "lately evolved Jekyll-cortex associated with an immensely ancient brain-stem-Hyde." We are an anachronism: an old-fashioned, backward people daring for a few perilous moments to live in the world of the future. Pious talk, numbers, facts, logic, even threats of doom are nugatory as long as people read these ominous portents with a buttress of detachment and disbelief between their eyes and emotions. No amount of reward or punishment will enable a child to comport himself in the manner his society considers appropriate, unless he is first taught the mores of his culture. It is not sufficient to exhort modern man to behave himself "before it is too late." He may not know how.

A recently evolved relative of the apes who writes poetry and philosophy, and who hoards atomic weapons against an inclement season, has become the primary director of his own evolution. It is time to study the director.

We are concerned with creativity, not world crisis. Yet the two subjects are inextricably entwined. Man's creative genius contributed to the crisis; deliverance lies in the immediate creative efforts of a better informed, more humane and responsible humanity. Yet mere survival is not enough. Our present perch on the brink of a new evolutionary era may be precarious, but the view from there, if we can curb and control our destructive tendencies, is exciting. The limits of human intellectual potential are unknown and have only begun to be explored. It is estimated that human beings today use only a small part of their capacities. Summoning courage, imagination, and foresight, it is possible for man to use his reason and creative powers to establish a new age, unlike any he has known even in his most extravagant dreams. This is not to suggest naïvely that life will be perfect, that cruelty and violence will dissolve, that chance and tragedy will be abolished, and that we shall all be supremely happy. But the world of the intelligent and responsible creator would not merely be a world equipped with futuristic hardware — moving sidewalks, underwater cities, household computers — but would be one in which the expansion of knowledge has immensely enriched, rather than impoverished, the quality of human life.

Struggling in the quagmire of constant, rapid change, but within sight of the "sunlit uplands," we would be wise to pause and consider carefully who we are and where we wish to go, before hurling ourselves upon what may be an irrevocable course to disaster. Today, however, a mood of cautious optimism is justified. For the first time in his history, man knows enough to prevent serious mistakes. We need not guess what is happening in the next village or beyond the rim of the ocean. Nor, mistakenly believing ourselves to have been placed at the hub of the universe by an omnipotent deity, need we wonder whether it is through malice or oversight that we have been forgotten. The horizons of knowledge have expanded to the point where it is possible to hover above our planet, outside of it in space, beyond it in time, and to look long and carefully at what has transpired there during the past four or five billion years.

Balancing population and food supply, for example, has

been called the major problem the world faces today. People driven to desperation by hunger and privation will resort to war or riot. Unless the impending crisis of increasing population and decreasing food is prevented, our future on this planet is threatened. But it is now at least technically feasible, not only to control world birthrate, but to create an environment in which food resources, both natural and synthetic, are adequate to the demand. As Buckminster Fuller says, we know how "to do more with less." Lemmings may run down to the sea in suicidal emigration when home is no longer habitable, but man has devised more humane means to limit his number. When he looks at the sea, he confronts not a watery grave but a potential farm. Whether in the aquaculture of the future he profits from the mistakes of the agriculture of the past, whether he remembers the debt he owes the sea in return for its gifts, remains to be seen.

Science and machines are neither inherently good nor evil. If men so wish, science and technology are prepared to be heroes, not villains, in the human story. We now possess the knowledge and the means to manipulate powerful natural forces to benefit mankind; the scientific study of ourselves is thriving and genuinely exciting; and we are awakening finally to our grave responsibilities as conscious creators.

4. Fashions in Human Nature

. . . a boy's will is his life, and he dies when it is broken, as the colt dies in harness, taking a new nature in becoming tame.

— HENRY ADAMS

IN THE FIRST half of this century, social and behavioral scientists have championed such causes as IQ, "leadership," sexual fulfillment, motherhood, and life adjustment — although not in that order. The spotlight of attention has shifted and the broad subject of creativity — its nature and nurture — is at last enjoying its season of esteem. The concern is serious, overdue, and welcome. Unfortunately, the subject appears dangerously close to achieving the status of an educational fad, or to being reduced to a potent sales cliché. The contemporary middle-class American family lives in a house "created" by the real-estate developer, father devotes his weekends to "creative" do-it-yourself projects, mother's lipsticks are "created" by "geniuses" in the cosmetic industry, and their children express themselves with "Creative Paint-By-Number Kits," fortunately ignoring the numbers because they are too young to read. Moreover, a child's unsatisfactory grades in mathematics or "social behavior" are more palatable if the magic words imaginative or creative appear somewhere on his report card.

Efforts to determine — preferably before reaching so venerable an age — whether one harbors within oneself a latent Grandma Moses or attempts to lure children from the television screen back to their crayons are commendable and safe. Like money in the bank, creativity is generally conceded to be a Good Thing, and its cultivation desirable. But most people understand that the value of a bank account is its potential buying power or the prestige money confers. The inherent virtue of creativity is not so explicit. Good Things are rarely as innocent as they appear. If we are not to be misled by them we must ask: Good for what? And for whom? Obviously what is truly a Good Thing cannot be good for everything. Milk is a Good Thing, but not for the child who is allergic to it; and beauty, for all its goodness, will not feed hungry people. Creativity is neither an all-purpose panacea for the private wounds inflicted by modern society, nor is it a soothing poultice to be applied to the world wherever it hurts.

Before setting out in search of future Einsteins in kindergarten or on weekend adventures in self-expression, which ironically reflect someone else's "self," it would be wise to consider the nature of the undertaking. The study of creative man and the creative process is a fascinating and inspiring subject. Although there is a paucity of concrete information about the mechanisms of creativity, the subject has enormous entertainment value as the spice of popular magazine articles and after-dinner conversation, and as a stimulating topic for armchair speculation or fashionable but pedantic Ph.D. theses. Torrents of data and advice have already begun to flow through the popular press. Often the reporting is intelligent and sound. Frequently, however, by the time a concept, which was at its source a tentative or untested hypothesis, filters down to the home, the classroom, and the personnel office, it is oversimplified and distorted to the point where it bears little semblance to the original.

This deplorable trend is reflected in a popular magazine article which confidently announced: "There is every reason to believe that creativity in children and adults eventually will be as simple to diagnose as measles or the common cold." If we consider the plight of the patient whose common cold is in fact pneumonia, it is interesting to speculate what would happen if the "symptoms" of a full-blown case of creativity (independence, desire for solitude, tolerance for ambiguity, devotion to difficult tasks) are actually unruliness, morbid withdrawal, indecision, and devotion to impossible tasks — the "symptoms" of quite a different syndrome. Undoubtedly the author did not intend the distasteful metaphor literally. Nonetheless the unconscious comparision of creativity to a disease, with the implication that it must somehow be cured or controlled, is entirely consistent with the perfunctory attitudes of our push-button society. "Tests are being developed" the writer continues, ". . . which would identify creativity even as IQ tests are used to rate pupils' minds." This is an alarming prediction considering the failure of the IQ tests in exactly this respect. It is even more disturbing if we recognize that the problem of defining creativity remains a major embarrassment to creativity research. A British psychologist, writing on the problems of defining intelligence, made the alarming discovery that the word "definition" itself has twelve definitions. The validity of socalled creativity tests in predicting actual creative performance is still unknown, and even the experts are not certain what the creativity tests actually measure. One shrinks from the disagreeable prospect that valuable studies of the personality structure of creative people may be diverted in the long run to answer the fatal question: Does he test creative?

Motives and Methods

Many creative adults greet the prospect of a formal study of creativity with suspicion and vociferous contempt. It is absurd and pretentious, they maintain, to probe the holy provinces of inspiration or to presume to write a recipe for a profound, mysterious, and autonomous gift, which leaves its calling card but declines to provide even its possessor with an address at which it can be reached, or a schedule of its inconstant comings and goings. Writing about creativity one becomes familiar with the scornful complaint that the word itself is barbaric. It has been so cheapened by misuse that one applies it reluctantly to a quality which is the finest expression of the human spirit and the essence of life itself. Intuitively, creative people tend to agree with Whitehead's dictum that "creativity is ultimate." One does not attempt to explain first principles.

The creative person, however, particularly the artist, often regards the scientific dissection of his muse as fundamentally wrong and pernicious. He looks upon his interrogators with as much affection as the green lawn does the cleats of the football player. With a hearty sense of self-preservation where his gift — if not his purse — is concerned, the creative person gives the devil his due and, hackles up, prepares to elude his scientific inquisitors. For it is his freedom — his freedom to be himself — which the creative person treasures above everything, firm in his conviction that this fertile, potent, and independent self is the source of his powers.

As he watches scientific knowledge, channeled through the practical offices of technology, yield marketable products, the creative individual cannot help wondering in what form, and for whom, his human resources, once subdued, are to be marketed. Although his immediate pursuers may carry banners stamped with the classic goal of knowledge for its own sake, namely for the sake of understanding and the love of learning, experience suggests the banners are musty and limp. In the end, he fears, nature's secrets will be used to control and exploit his gifts for the profit of others. Unfortunately, his suspicions are justifiable.

The classic tradition of Aristotle and Aquinas, in which understanding is the goal of knowledge, has yielded to the Baconian spirit in which the fruit of knowledge is power and the "effecting of all things possible." From the start, modern science was close in spirit — if not in method — to its near kin, magic. In the scientific era, the wonders of magic were to be produced by a knowledge of natural causes rather than by the incantations and potions of the magician and alchemist. Instead of pursuing knowledge in order to illumine man's relationship to his environment, those who sponsor the wizards of modern science too often seek the "magic" facts and formulas with which to control and manipulate nature for less commendable purposes. The Baconian gospel of "bending nature to man's will," when unaccompanied by a good measure of understanding — in the old-fashioned, impractical sense of wisdom — may have disastrous consequences. As science, in its search for "useful knowledge," undertook the subjugation of nature, it became increasingly aggressive, leaving in its wake a disagreeable trail of waste and destruction. Moreover, nature, like the mythological Hydra, is a wily opponent. For every head of the monster severed, for every problem solved by science, new ones arise to take its place.

When Francis Bacon proclaimed that knowledge was power, he meant power over nature, not man. At that time, still two centuries before Darwin, man and nature were considered separate entities. Today we understand that man is part of nature. What happens when the nature to be so enthusiastically subjugated is human nature? And what happens when the power of knowledge, augmented by modern technology, becomes increasingly the power of the few to dictate the fate of the majority, including those generations as yet unborn?

Not only does the creative person distrust the motives of his pursuers, but he may be wary of their methods. There are, of course, responsible social and behavioral scientists who have labored in print and practice to correct the past errors of their professions. Unfortunately, changes in intellectual climate proceed slowly and behind the bright forerunners drags the unwieldy baggage of fallacious, outmoded practice.

Psychological diagnosis, as well as pedagogical jargon, is too often subtly destructive, having little respect for human dignity, but considerable concern for the preservation of its own superior position. There are teachers who speak solemnly of children who "achieve beyond their potential." They notice neither the immediate absurdity of what they have said nor, when faced with such a paradox, does it occur to them that if a child has mysteriously surpassed his predicted capacity, it may be the index of prediction rather than the child which is in error. Generally, this embarrassing discrepancy is accounted for by some such saving grace as "motivation" or "application," grafted like an epiphenomenon to the child. It is assumed that the "overachiever" pays a special price in excessively long study hours. In many cases this may be true, although it is difficult to understand why the capacity to concentrate and work should not be considered part of an individual's "potential." It is always easier, however, to manipulate the child to fit the theory than to adjust the theory to suit the child — provided, of course, one is very careful not to look at the child. It is quite true that children will not be able to read before the age of six if they are not taught. Those children who have pulled off the trick at five or even younger must be ignored. A mystique of "readiness" presides over such shenanigans. It is an attractive idea: if a child does not learn, it means he cannot learn, thereby absolving administrator, teacher, and child of further responsibility in the matter. The educational Establishment has only now begun to consider the heresy that one might do something about readying the readiness.

In such an atmosphere, the creative person is not entirely wrong in suspecting that rather than being explained, he may be "explained away." This sleight-of-hand is accomplished by a number of techniques. The first, *reductionism,* is the method of explaining one process by reducing it to another — then, step-by-step, all the way downhill until there is nothing left. Julian Huxley calls this the "nothing but" school. To say that man is *nothing but* a bipedal primate with an oversized brain infers that he is a deluxe animal rather than a human being endowed with an animal nature. Actually, it is the difference between what an ape is not and what a man is that accounts for the man. Similarly, if learning is nothing but "acculturation," if curiosity is nothing but "drive reduction," and if creativity is reduced to "compensation for personal inadequacy," or "regression in the service of the ego," then the rabbit trick is in process. "You cannot go on seeing through things forever," says C. S. Lewis. "The whole point of seeing through something is to see something through it."

Closely related to reductionism, in what might be called a triad of methodological sins, is *atomism*, or the analysis of a system into its elementary components. The analytic method is a sound scientific procedure, but it is misleading if it is not followed by synthesis. If for the purpose of studying man, we peel him down to his cell molecules, if we continue our dissection to the inorganic atoms of an ultimate protein particle, and in turn to its physicochemical processes, we still have not attained our objective if we abandon our investigation at this point. The interactions of matter and energy do not suffice to explain the phenomenon of man. As the eminent neurologist Judson Herrick said, "Vital processes face the other way about, forward not backward, and the key problems of biology are not analytic, but synthetic."

Bundles of instinct and reflexes do not account for the glory of man. Hope and fear, delight and ambition cannot be understood as the patterns of stimulus-response codes. The whole is quite different from the sum of its parts and in converting everything to the quantitative terms endemic to computer intelligence, no provision is made for the qualitative properties of life. The moment this is done truth slips out the back door. If hate is valued at plus five, and love at minus five, is the sum of hate and love zero? As Herbert Muller once observed, one dollar plus a thousand dollars is more money than a thousand dollars plus one dollar.

The third member of this unhealthy trio, *specialism*, is familiar to most of us as a major affliction of our society. Specialism is the consideration of a part of a system without reference to the whole to which it belongs: to treat a man's ailing heart but overlook his ailing marriage; to pursue school integration but ignore education; to plan round-trip excursions to the moon without considering whether the return voyage will be worth-while. Examples are legion.

> *I'm afraid you've got a bad egg, Mr. Jones.*
> *Oh no, my Lord, I assure you! Parts of it are excellent.*

To speak of a knitting machine or of a computer is to indi-cate the nature and purpose of these specialized tools. But man is not biologically specialized for a single purpose. His fingers have not evolved into knitting machines, nor is his brain solely a calculating machine. A "creative man" means a *human being* who is creative. Creative man's needs, his nature, and his des-tiny are only intelligible when examined within the context of a nature which is human, against the backdrop of human history, and in the prospect of a future hopefully in the human tradi-tion.

The implications of specialism for the study of human behavior are serious, because, as the highest integrative appa-ratus of the body, the human brain is understandably as intri-cate as the behavior it orders. In the world of push-button ma-chines which dispense everything from refreshments to nuclear war, man is also viewed as a complex machine, not too different in kind from one of his automated gadgets. The living brain is an unbelievably complex organ, and along its densely woven circuits cerebral traffic flows in a kaleidoscope of patterns and subpatterns, shifting endlessly in time and space. Nowhere within its deep folds does the brain maintain discrete offices for the administration of intelligence, memory, consciousness, emotion, or imagination, nor is creativity an autonomous func-tion. Its mechanisms, silent and invisible, require the critical guidance of intelligence, access to the storage vaults of mem-ory, and the power supplies of emotion. How the brain pro-duces our thoughts, ideas, and dreams or how it knows that it is a brain remains, even in this age of triumphant science, one of the deepest mysteries in the universe. Conclusions drawn from the necessary, but distorted, perspectives produced by the artificial division of the nervous system are frequently misleading. Now and then we must look up from our work and put the human being together again, in order that we may see what he really is.

From Doctrine to Dogma

Unfortunately, the thinking, feeling human being cannot be examined under a microscope nor will his drives and motives precipitate to the bottom of a test tube. Because human nature is deceptively accessible, and yet so unwieldy as experimental material, it is essential that we cultivate patience and learn to accept hypothesis and incomplete evidence for what they are. "Man is bound to speculate about the universe beyond the range of his knowledge," said Morris Cohen, "but he is not bound to indulge the vanity of setting up such speculations as absolutely certain dogmas."

Let us imagine that we wish to build an exact replica — a scale model — of a human being. However, we have not yet acquired all the necessary components: the mechanisms of consciousness and intelligence are still missing; the data on learning are unreliable; no one knows how to design the circuits of imagination; and assorted drives and emotions lie scattered on the workbench until someone determines whether to install them so that the model will be "born" with them, or to leave them out and let the robot acquire them after parturition. At this stage such a model would not be expected to function, because it is obviously incomplete. Yet where the living human being is concerned, we are not so reasonable. With hardly a pang of conscience or twinge of doubt, we prescribe for mankind as if these gaps in our knowledge did not exist.

Unfortunately, for the slapdash, irresponsible processing of the tentative information obtained in the sciences of man, living human beings, particularly children, pay a high price. No megabuck experiment in nuclear or space science is ultimately as expensive as those seemingly unsophisticated trial-and-error experiments by which theories of human behavior are tested. Neither cyclotrons, nor spaceships, nor seven-million-dollar computers are necessary: only a mother and her children; a teacher and her pupils.

When the "answers" are found, they must be understood as provisional, for absolute certitude no longer exists in science. That we "know in part, and we prophesy in part" is a curious bit of biblical wisdom which antedates modern scientific theories of probability and uncertainty. Funeral services for the rational, harmonious world of Aquinas and for the classic science of Newton were conducted at the opening of this century by the priests of modern physics. The simple faith in a changeless universe, eternally pursuing a fixed mechanical course, obedient to the immovable laws of nature, and the naïve belief that the secrets of such a world could be perfectly revealed through science have been shattered. The concepts of science are neither absolute nor enduring. The formulations of even so great a genius as Einstein provide not final certainty, but reduction in error; not perfect truth, but a closer fit with reality.

In theory, psychologists are aware that to an extent they are always controlled by the form of their experiments. They deal with the matter of science, but frequently are denied the advantage of its methods. Psychologists must extrapolate human behavior from the performance of laboratory animals — always a tricky procedure — or they must struggle with the multiple variables encountered in studies where human beings are the subjects. It is somewhat like rattling a box to determine its contents. The psychologist may not be able to overcome the limitations of an experiment, but unless he recognizes these restrictions, and remembers them as he interprets his data, it is a simple matter for him to find what he wants to find.

In the popular presentation of a theory, it is not necessary to state the premises of one's assumptions, or the conditions of an experiment, so that very quickly hypothesis achieves the status of necessary principle.

In the sins of dogmatism committed by behavioral and social scientists the gullible public becomes an accomplice. "Sentence first — verdict afterward" seems to be the way we prefer it. Sometimes, as in the instance of Freud, the limitations of the experimental study — its built-in prejudices — are not explicit even to the originator of the theory. Influenced by his biological orientation in neurology, and limited by the prudish, patriarchal culture of middle-class society in Victorian Vienna, Freud attributed to changeless biological instinct what subsequently has been ascribed to interpersonal relationships or the cultural milieu. Allowed to congeal too soon to the hard, unbending form of dogma, Freudian theory in the incompetent hands of self-appointed apostles, opportunists, and propagandists, who lacked their master's genius and integrity, became in many cases a bizarre gospel responsible for considerable misunderstanding and precious nonsense.

Similarly, all that was left of John Dewey's profound, if fallible philosophy of education after its flesh had been picked by the vultures of popular consumption was a crass, wasteful educational creed which gave progressivism a bad name and turned the teachers college into a catastrophe.

On a smaller scale, the quasi-comic misadventures of Dr. Spock's celebrated doctrine of permissive toilet training provide a useful illustration of the genesis of the so-called scientifically proven "laws" of child development. Taking his cue from Freud, from one of his own patients and a "few other pediatricians" interested in the problem, Dr. Spock stated in a book whose fame as a child-raising bible he never anticipated, that the "best method of all" was to allow the child to train himself. Eager to imitate others in the family, the child presumably would achieve this goal around the age of two. This was important and welcome relief from former rigid and aggressive toilet-training techniques, and Spock's contribution in this respect is not to be demeaned. Release parental pressure, said Spock in effect, and all will be well. This dictum, which was actually an untested hypothesis, prevailed until it finally became apparent to Spock himself that all was not well. Some of the children failed to perform as predicted. More serious, as Dr. Spock and a generation of parents ruefully discovered, an important premise had been overlooked in the formulation of the original theory: the release of excessive parental pressure is desirable, but it does not follow that the absence of all guidance is a greater good.

In areas which extend far beyond these concerns of the nursery, parents have payed dearly for the enthusiastic but uncritical acceptance of permissiveness as an unqualified virtue, and for the hasty assumption that permissiveness and "impulse-release" are synonymous with the unlimited indulgence of a child's whims. The blame lies not so much in the failure of the original theory as in the premature conversion to doctrine, and then to dogma, of a hypothesis whose verification would require years of trial-and-error testing.

In this brief collection of cautionary tales, the rise and decline of the IQ cult in the American schools during the first half of this century is particularly instructive. To a certain extent it is from the ashes of the IQ test's failure that the phoenix of "creativity" has arisen. The possibility of replacing IQ worship with a "cult of creativity" is an unpleasant but not unlikely possibility. One is reminded of a remark made by Alfred North Whitehead in 1945 to his friend Lucien Price. In the 1880's at Cambridge University, Whitehead observed that, like everyone else, he believed that nearly everything was known about physics that could be known. "By 1900 the Newtonian physics were demolished, done for!" said Whitehead. "Still, speaking personally, it had a profound effect on me; I have been fooled once, and I'll be damned if I'll be fooled again!" Whitehead was a brilliant philosopher and mathematician; he was also a very wise man. How many times we must be fooled before we learn, remains to be seen.

Although it had been suggested as early as 1898, and sporadically thereafter during the next forty years, that the relationship between creativity and intelligence might not be as close as assumed, this view remained buried in the professional journals of psychology. During this time, the intelligence test, originally designed in 1905 by Alfred Binet and Theodore Simon to identify feebleminded children in the Paris schools, and subsequently revised and standardized by Lewis M. Terman and his colleagues at Stanford University, became the crucial metric in the official designation of giftedness. The systematic study of the gifted child undertaken by Terman at the beginning of the century, although valuable in other respects, unfortunately resulted in equating giftedness with high IQ and labeled as "genius" any child with an IQ of 140 or over. It was arbitrarily assumed that "general intelligence" and IQ score were identical, and then to compound the error it was further supposed that giftedness and intelligence were synonymous. In the unassailable logic of the syllogism, the gifted child and the high-IQ child emerged from this bit of hocus-pocus one and the same. The creative child, however, belonged to a different category. He was the child who painted pretty pictures, played the piano, or wrote poems.

Actually, many psychologists are not certain what the IQ test measures. Even less understood is that baffling mental quality we call intelligence. To those who have lived through the shameful decades of IQ branding, it is cool comfort to learn that, for all practical purposes, intelligence may be defined as the thing measured by an IQ test.

As a predictive measure of "intelligence" the tests, in fact, inspect a narrow range of intellectual performance, placing heavy emphasis on the ability to recall, to recognize, and to solve certain kinds of problems, but ignore other, equally important aspects of intelligence: imagination, innovation, discovery, and the ability to recognize what is relevant. Furthermore, from the outset, the designers of intelligence tests have been haunted by the difficulty of producing a test which measures innate mental capacity — untainted by cultural background and education. Plainly, the intelligence test is a convenient label but an elusive measurement.

Despite the dubious nature of its fundamental assumptions, the use of the IQ score remained strangely immune to criticism and continued to serve as the sacred index of a child's native ability, from which the child might deviate only in the disconcerting and refractory form of the under- or overachiever. Other forms of human excellence, such as imagination, creativeness, sensitivity, concentration, curiosity, and moral courage which do not lend themselves to measurement on the psychologist's yardstick were simply ignored. When new intelligence tests were designed they were evaluated according to their ability to measure the same things the old test measured, thus propagating the original narrow concept of intelligence.

Second thoughts are now in order, and the neglected virtues have been summoned for long overdue consideration. The generation of high IQ "geniuses" has reached adulthood and it is painfully apparent that something is wrong. Follow-up studies of the 1,000 juvenile "geniuses" (IQ over 140) who participated in one of Terman's many studies of gifted children show that although as adults they are far superior to the average population in such matters as schooling, careers, income, health, and marital status, they have not as a group produced a single creative genius. These high-IQ children were indeed gifted, but the creative children had slipped through the net set for them. It was obvious that if they were to be found, the concept of giftedness would have to be woven of different mesh.

For the acceptance of theories of human behavior as articles of absolute faith, without attention to their credentials, we eventually pay a dear price. Concerned with its own rituals and ceremonies, and dedicated to unquestioning veneration of itself, the cult approach to human nature makes no allowance for ambiguity, ambivalence, or for subsequent revision. When the span of popular acclaim has ended, the period of recoil and recantation is usually so noisy and the hullabaloo so great as the scapegoat is trampled to death, that little sober thought is given to amending the theory to retain what is valid and what might yet be of use.

"IQ Tests Called Harmful to Pupil," announced the heading of a *New York Times* article reporting a creativity conference. In effect, the current "hot" product is sold at the expense of the old. This, of course, was not what the speaker said. The IQ test is in fact a useful tool and cannot in itself harm a child. The harm proceeds from the misuse and misinterpretation of the IQ score by a parent or a teacher. To shift the blame from human beings to a tool is the same as saying, "Axes Called Harmful to People" — as indeed they are when wielded by dangerous people.

Repeatedly, in far more serious situations, our trouble seems to be not merely that we cannot separate the signal from the background noise, but worse, that we cannot tell which is the signal and which is the noise. Adrift in the brilliant but brittle world of scientific magic, we have foolishly disregarded those traditional guidelines of ethics and values by which man examines his purposes and questions their meaning and significance, and without which it is impossible to discriminate what is of value to him and what is worthless.

Human Nature Is Out of Fashion

Creativity is the unique heritage of our species, the hallmark of human nature. Yet, ironically, we are committed to its cultivation at a time when human nature is out of fashion. Speaking during the first Industrial Revolution, Emerson spoke for the second — or Automation Revolution, when he said, "Things are in the saddle and ride mankind." Emerson little dreamed the extent to which man was to become a pawn in the service of the powerful "things" produced by human ingenuity and genius.

Psychological research is too often employed not to benefit human beings, but to exploit their resources: to maneuver people so that they will serve the production and propaganda gods of our material civilization and believe that they do so by their own wish. Singing sweet hymns of patriotism or progress, industry and government, assisted by their prophets in advertising and public relations, dangle the carrot of money and status in front of their victims, while behind they brandish the stick of fear — fear of the Communists, of the competition, or simply of not "keeping up."

The real tragedy in the case of the job applicant who, without so much as a whimper of protest, submits to a lie detector test given to determine whether he is "company material," is neither the cynicism of those responsible, nor the fallibility of the test itself, but that John Jones does not realize that his human dignity and worth have gone by default. When a man has been so thoroughly brainwashed by society that he accepts this invasion of his privacy, agrees to testify against himself, and acquiesces in the disfranchisement of his right to defend himself — in this case against the accusations of a machine, John Jones no longer exists. A living robot has taken his place.

Necessity need not be the mother of invention, but today invention becomes the mother of necessity. Our affluent society is preoccupied with the production and compulsive consumption of material goods we have been taught to want. Responsible economists and social critics have cried out against the evils of this ethic in which consumer demand is manufactured. It is an ethic so sinister that as its poison infiltrates our social attitudes, its followers ultimately "consume" each other. Cannibalism and human sacrifice are uncivilized. Yet our Western materialistic culture condones social cannibalism as a necessary sacrifice to society's collective appetite which, spurred by ambition and fear, demands that we devour whatever is proffered, even human dignity, in the sacred name of "the standard of living" or the so-called "national good." All that remains after this unholy feast is, once again, John Jones the living robot. Not everyone lives according to these principles, but they provide the dominant flavor of our contemporary ethos.

In such a milieu, an expressed concern for the cultivation of creativity may have little to do with creative people. More accurately it may be greed for the products of their efforts. A popular book on the subject of creativity entices the potential reader with the potent symbol of the dollar sign emblazoned on its cover, implying that the implementation of one's fortune is the foremost value of the creative life.

Industry, with its keen nose for fashions in Good Things, has also discovered creativity as a marketable resource worthy of patronage. However, the creativity promoted by those personnel directors or junior executives who tend the temple fires but could never light them is a sorry version of the "product." When originality is confused with speed or even facility, the creative potential of a job applicant may be measured by the number of words he can write on a given subject, in a given period of time, regardless of content. What a dismal prospect for poor Flaubert who took five years to write his slim masterpiece, *Madame Bovary*.

A supervisor may be asked to rate the creativeness of the employees in his group. If he confuses the term "creative" with the term "productive," the high rating will go to the person who "gets the most done." The daydreamer, whose imaginative ideas may include the suggestion that the problem on which he is working is not worth doing in the first place, will undoubtedly be tagged as lacking in "company orientation" and awarded the dunce cap.

In our mechanized society where thoughts as well as automobiles may be assembled in an automated factory, it is also, by some narrow logic, expedient to reduce children to those yes-no codes most easily processed by such a system. Life aboard the assembly belt proceeds smoothly when the child surrenders the human prerogatives of imagination, wonder, and doubt for concepts and ideas which conform to the simpleminded limits of the multiple-choice test, and when he submits to mechanized education in which prepackaged thoughts run the circuit from eyes and ears to tongue and hand, tarrying in the brain only long enough to be memorized. The final step in this bitter capitulation by the child, who is too young to understand what he has so lightly relinquished, is to promise to entertain only those hopes and dreams which can be classified, accounted for, and therefore controlled. When life becomes one giant data-processing system, the winners are those with the greatest aptitude for being data.

Are we sincere when we proclaim that we wish to cultivate the creative resources of our society? We maintain that we want forceful, imaginative leadership in our country, but politicians know that an election campaign is hardly the time to have original ideas. Lip service is futile. Dedication cannot be purchased, and creativeness cannot, any more than love, be bought outright for a sum of money or grown in the soil of empty rhetoric.

Consider the case of Tommy. His parents are delighted to hear from his kindergarten teacher that their son is a creative child and that he appears to have artistic talent. Aware of their obligation to foster their child's creative health, these good parents enthusiastically set out to nurture Tommy's nascent but genuine talent. Tommy is provided with equipment, encouragement, and eventually with instruction. In the middle of his first year of college, Tommy comes home and announces that "college is a waste of time!" What he really wants to do is go to art school, perhaps see the world a bit, and then settle down to paint seriously — and incidentally, as his stunned parents see it — starve seriously. It is too late to offer a caveat to these unhappy people. They are suddenly disillusioned with the lovely, but vague notion of creativity to which they have so innocently subscribed, and are appalled by the practical reality of cold pads and bearded hippies. "Oh Tom, that's not what we wanted for you," pleads Tommy's mother. "My God, son! How can you do this to us?" sputters his father. The frolic is over and the screws are about to be put to Tommy. Eventually Tommy may win an art scholarship or marry a girl who will support him, but as far as his parents are concerned, he is a dropout and a disappointment.

Tommy's parents have looked at human nature as a malleable commodity, tied to the procrustean bed of society. Stretch it out if it is too short; crush it if it is too long. The ancient Greek mythmakers, however, acknowledged that for Procrustes' victims the treatment hurt. Devoted to an ideal of creativity, Tommy's parents have not been devoted to Tommy, the creative artist and the human being. He is *nothing but* a reflection of his parents' needs, which in turn mirror the demands of society. The child is indeed father of the man, for ironically it is to the child that his parents' deepest emotional needs are entrusted, while they, for their part, need only provide art lessons, a comfortable home, and faith and understanding so frail they vanish at the first strain. It is a strange and bitter bargain.

While it is easy enough to ridicule such hypocrisy, there can be little pleasure in it. We cannot ignore the predicament of these unfortunate parents. Having been enticed into the cultivation of a commodity for which there is no appreciable "market," they now lack the courage to swim against the tide.

Tommy's creative talents are an attractive adornment. They are to be courted only as long as his status and economic security derive from occupations accounted respectable, and his artistic endeavors are confined to the safe role of an avocation. In this country the general public is suspicious of the artist and grants him status and solvency only after he achieves fame — a condition more easily fulfilled posthumously. Eric Gill, the artist and critic, once observed ruefully that in this century man can only be human in his spare time.

Irresponsibility where human welfare is concerned is immoral; blind faith as a euphemism for ignorance is dangerous. Serious attempts to nurture the creative resources of a human being while denying his human condition are not only absurd, but doomed to failure. If our endeavors are not to become an expensive abortion; if Tommy, his parents, and society are to be reconciled for their mutual benefit, major changes must occur in our public and private attitudes, and in our educational methods. Anything less is whistling in the wind. One has a responsibility to Good Things — to the magic wishes granted by the Good Fairy, to knowledge, and to one's native gifts. Otherwise, mankind's creative policies, either by sudden disaster or the slow atrophy of the human spirit, may terminate in "accidental suicide." It is essential that we understand the full meaning and significance of human creativeness, and that we recognize our responsibility to a biological heritage which has made man, second only to God, a creator of the universe.

5. The Birthright Lost

THROUGHOUT THE MILLENNIA of his existence, man has altered this planet with his creations, erecting in the wilderness the vast edifice of civilization and projecting upon the trackless expanse of time the dimensions of mind. Man is an animal who can examine his own thoughts, who awakens each day and creates the world in his imagination, and who knows that world as a place which may exist even without him. Having discovered himself, he is driven to know himself. In this century of doubt and spiritual anxiety, suspecting that his very existence may be absurd and meaningless both on earth and in heaven, he is challenged "to create what he is" — to give meaning to his existence, and thus to create meaning from nonmeaning.

Several thousand years before the concept of "creative man" received the blessing of formal scientific recognition, and long before man learned to subject his assumptions to the critical examination of his intellect, the tradition of creative man appeared in ancient myth and legend. Although an irrational, emotional, even visionary means of apprehending the phenomena of experience, the source of the true myth, before its elaboration in art and literature, lay in actual experience. Ancient man seems intuitively to have grasped the basic creative faculty of his species. Often subordinated to other themes in mythological literature, man's creative power is nevertheless implicit in the many creation myths which recount the theft of divine prerogatives and man's subsequent appropriation of creative powers.

In Mesopotamian mythology it is Ea or Enki who becomes

man's benefactor; in later Egyptian mythology Osiris, the patron of civilization, plays the role familiar to most of us in the Greek story of Prometheus. The creation of mankind, according to one version of this well-known Greek myth, was delegated to Prometheus and to Epimetheus, his scatterbrained brother. Epimetheus bungled the job. He endowed the animals with speed, strength, protective covering, courage and then discovered that there was nothing left for frail, short-lived man. He appealed to his brother for help. The wise Prometheus fashioned man erect like the gods, stole the forbidden gift of fire, and taught man how to use it in various practical arts and crafts. For his refusal to submit to divine will, for usurping divine control over nature, and for teaching man to use his practical intellect in the management of his affairs, the proud, disobedient Prometheus was chained to a high crag in the wastes of Scythia where he bravely endured the penalty of his pride until eventually he was set free.

Zeus punished mankind by his catastrophic gift of Pandora and her fateful casket of plagues and sorrows. But even the king of the gods could not undo what had been done. Man, foresighted, ingenious, defiant, and creative remained the beneficiary of Prometheus's gifts, as well as his spiritual descendant. It is significant that although man received godlike power to control the forces of nature, the wisdom to make good use of his gifts was not provided. The ancient chroniclers of the human scene seem to have been correct in their observations, if not in their explanations.

It seems particularly felicitous that the great biblical epic of divine creation also relates the story of the birth of human creativity. It was not the purpose of the authors of Genesis, whose mission was of a moral nature, to mark man's acquisition of creative power. Creative man is largely a modern concept. But the description of man as a creature who behaves creatively is nonetheless firmly embedded in the opening chapters of the Bible.

Regard for the theological significance of the disaster in

Eden and regret, perhaps, for the lost delights of Paradise, tend to obscure the further implications of the biblical story. If that fateful day in Eden marks man's disobedience to divine injunction and his subsequent punishment, then it also records man's unique triumph. Upon eating of the forbidden fruit, Adam and Eve acquired not only knowledge of good and bad, but its twinned gift: the power of creative invention. Although the Bible does not state it explicitly, we are told that having recognized their nakedness, Adam and Eve took matters into their own hands and invented clothing: they sewed fig leaves together to make "aprons" or loincloths. Installed in Paradise to tend and keep it, these primeval gardeners had usurped divine powers, and docile no longer, proceeded with conscious purpose to alter the design of their creator. God punished the erring couple by expelling them from the Garden of Eden before they could steal the other divine prerogative, immortality. Nevertheless the parents of mankind had become in this sense more godlike than Yahweh-Elohim had created them. Moral considerations aside, the great tradition of the Bible describes primal man as erring, but also as intelligent, imaginative, deft, and creative.

Although the biblical emphasis is on knowledge, interpreted not as information, but as awareness, or "the full possession of mental and physical powers," it is implied that the awareness of the existence of a problem (nakedness) suggests the urgent need for its solution (clothing). Conversely, before man could become a creator, his eyes had to be opened, for there are no solutions to problems which have not been recognized and defined.

True to his biological tradition of motor response to a stimulus, man ordinarily responds actively in deed and thought, with muscle and mind, to the demands of his environment. Unlike his animal relations, man has the imagination and conscious control to postpone satisfaction of his short-range needs in favor of long-range needs. But our impatient species still has little affinity and less gift for that more sophisticated form of action: conscious, deliberate nonaction. Once man is aware of a problem whose solution lies within his practical intellect, he feels impelled to accept its challenge. If it is possible to go to the moon, he will go. How to go, not whether to go, is the question he prefers to answer. To "not do" something he wants to do, to exercise restraint, is not known to be one of man's outstanding faculties.

It appears from mankind's subsequent history that having embarked upon a repast of stolen fruit, man's misadventure in Eden ended too abruptly. One cannot help wondering where, or in what other fertile garden grew the fruits of self-control and wise restraint which man would require in his long journey from loincloths to moon suits, from the gates of Paradise to the arid wastes of Mars.

The Self-Employed Stone-Ager

In the allegory of Eden, Paradise was lost and human history began. As Paleolithic man set forth to make his way in the hostile, difficult world of the Old Stone Age, stripped of armor, hide, fangs, wings, the arboreal gifts of his near relatives the apes, and lacking the automatic instincts which serve the beast in the absence of higher mind, he was in a sense the most naked creature that had ever browsed the earth. But not the most helpless; for within the expanding cortex of his brain he carried what was to become nature's supreme, if most perverse accomplishment: the human brain. Many of the ancient inborn patterns of reflex and instinct had been "erased" from this unique, custom-designed organ. No longer committed to pre-set patterns, the brain was free, as it had never been before, to invent its own behavioral patterns, and to compose its own destiny.

The millennia passed and man remained true to the broad spirit of his birthright. The level of his productivity, creative or otherwise, was of course low. Old Stone Age man (Paleolithic man) devoted most of his time and energy, as well as his imagination and intelligence to the struggle for survival. He lived by his prowess and his wits, made his own decisions, and solved his own problems. Self-employed, the Old Stone Age hunter fished, hunted, chipped flint, dug roots, and made clothing as the need arose. Except for some part-time specialists in ritual and magic, in art, and occasionally in certain craftwork, there was almost no occupational specialization. The records of prehistory are thin and imperfect; much of what is written about the life and times of early man is at best enlightened guesswork. Nevertheless as Lewis Mumford observes, to the Stone Age hunter a life in which day after day, all day long, one man made all the clothing, another all the tools, and still another all the decisions would have been intolerable — and still is today to primitive people. With few exceptions the nomadic life of the Paleolithic hunter was restless, dangerous, and inefficient, but it was neither routine, nor, within its own primitive context, meaningless. Even today, as if summoned by some ancient atavistic trait in his nature, modern man in the duck blind, in the cornfield, upon mountaintops and on the sea, heeds the "call of the wild" to seek self-renewal and the illusion of an integrated life in primitive hand-to-hand encounter with nature.

The vast stretches of the Old Stone Age, shrouded in time and ice, seem almost endless when compared to the time which has since elapsed. During this period, when creeping glaciers advanced and retreated across the earth, changes in man's way of life were so slow that for a long time progress is almost imperceptible. For several hundred thousand years Paleolithic man had lived precariously as nature's guest — careless, wasteful, but content with nature's bounty in her own season and at her own convenience. Then suddenly in a few millennia the New Stone Age (Neolithic Age) and the Agricultural Revolution brought man to the outskirts of civilization. The Neolithic Age, which began about seven to eight thousand years ago, lasted a mere two thousand years in Europe; no more than three to four thousand years in Egypt and Mesopotamia where it began. Archaeological "ages," it should be noted, do not refer to universal periods of time, but rather to the materials used for making cutting tools, and thus to the economic development of a culture.

In the great valley of the Nile, on the fertile flood plains between the Tigris and the swift-flowing Euphrates, and along the waters of the snow-born Indus, our Neolithic ancestors began to create an artificial environment, altering nature's design to suit their own needs. Man invented the "biochemical processing plant" known as a farm, and gradually made his food supply, animal and plant, grow where he lived instead of pursuing it in its own habitat. The excitement and physical freedom of the huntsman's way of life were sacrificed, but in the relatively comfortable routine of sedentary village life the long expedition of creative man to and beyond the gates of civilization began to accelerate. Ironically, this journey has terminated for many on the assembly line and in the office cubbyhole.

Man's numbers increased enormously, property and traditions began to accumulate, and for the first time in his perilous history he knew a measure of security and stability. Undoubtedly there was some increase in the specialization of labor, but for much of this period the major division remained the ancient separation of tasks between man and woman. The shaman, the priest, and the artist-magician continued to practice their specialized crafts; there is also evidence of Neolithic flint miners who exported their wares, and individuals gifted in handicrafts must occasionally have been employed by their neighbors in return for a payment of grain. The division of labor was still rudimentary, however, and each household in the self-contained Neolithic settlement could produce all of its needs including all forms of craftwork. Community tradition, however, rather than individual imagination and inspiration dictated the design of most of the craftwork produced by these household industries. The Neolithic housewife made and decorated her own pottery and probably derived considerable satisfaction from the dramatic production of form where none had been. In her work she expressed not her own creative imagination but the collective imagination of her village contained in the rules and rituals which she in time would transmit to her daughters, and they to theirs.

In the twilight of prehistory the hunter who had come home from the fields to turn farmer, rested briefly on his laurels, enjoying the benefits of a food surplus, dependent upon outside communities only for luxury articles or for an occasional bride. The intimate village life of the small, isolated Neolithic hamlet nurtured the customs and traditions, forerunners of legal and moral codes, which made it both practical and possible for man to use his creative imagination to improve the manner and style of his life.

It is difficult for us, imbued with the anthropocentric legacy of classical Greece and Renaissance Europe, to imagine how Stone Age man must have conceived of himself. The birth of ego had occurred very much earlier when, after eons of mindless time in which no creature had ever known itself as distinct and separate from the rest of creation, a strange, upright being with a large head looked out upon the timeless oblivion of the animal world and sensed vaguely that he was apart from it. As the tenuous concepts of I and You began to form, as time was shaped and sectioned by mind, as man began to think about "tomorrow," conjuring its apparition in his imagination, hope and human aspiration were born.

But the modern preoccupation with the question of identity — who am I? — was not the concern of Stone Age man. The Neolithic peasant, like his Paleolithic forebear still felt himself psychologically committed to the welfare and greater reality of his tribe or clan. The tribe itself was a powerful entity which, with little regard for the boundaries of time, included the living and the dead, totemic animal kin, ancestral ghosts, and the hovering spirits of the animate and inanimate world. Image and reality, past and present — all concepts of his own invention — were intermingled. As yet he had not established clearcut boundaries between these different regions and moved freely among them with the vivid imagination of an artist still on intimate, subjective terms with his creations. No longer identified with the animal world, he easily reidentified with that world in art, in the dance, in magic, and in his relationship to the common ancestral spirit he and the animal shared. Although the needs of his clan and community were foremost in the consciousness of primitive man, paradoxically, when one considers the plight of modern man, each member of the Neolithic community appears to have led the meaningful life of a complete Neolithic human being. Barbarian that he was, he was at least an unfragmented barbarian, not a skilled collector or probe, not an educated button-pusher or dial-watcher.

As the New Stone Age drew to a close and man arrived at the brink of recorded history, the rate of change, which had already accelerated within the stable forms of village life, began dramatically to gain momentum. The birth rites of civilization some five to six thousand years ago were attended by an outburst of invention which with comparative speed created sophisticated urban societies where not so long before the simple village life of the farmer had been the custom. The plow, the loom, the wagon wheel and the potter's wheel were invented. Oxen were put to the yoke, the power of the wind was harnessed to the sailing ship, the method of smelting copper ores was discovered, and the solar calendar was designed. With the invention of written language, mortal man transcended the oblivion of time and achieved a measure of immortality.

The Farmer Comes to Town

The advent of civilization coincides with the development of a metal technology and the rise of the cities of the Bronze Age. Etymologically the word "civilization" refers to an urban society. Characteristically the city — even as we know it today — is a community of sophisticated specialists, unable to survive without the services of others, both within and beyond the community, but who together are capable of elevating the collective level of existence and of enlarging the horizons of human life. The archaeological records and concrete remains of this period are few and fragmentary. It is always difficult to point to specific beginnings, for what the future will one day designate as a beginning was at the time merely a transition from the past. By the time evidence of civilization appears, its ill-defined, modest formative stages are already lost in the veiled foredawn of history when growing Neolithic towns evolved the physical and cultural foundations of Bronze Age cities.

It is believed that on the alluvial plains of the great river valleys in Egypt and in Lower Mesopotamia, groups of Neolithic farmers united to drain marshes, restrain violent flood waters, build dykes and platforms, and to clear the jungle fringe of the wild beasts which lurked there. In a tremendous cooperative undertaking they succeeded in wresting rich farmlands from reedy swamps and dense wilderness. Attached to the land which their toil had created, but which now rewarded them with fine pasturelands and bounteous harvests, people lived and thrived for many generations in permanent Neolithic communities.

As the scale of social cooperation and the need for an accumulated food surplus grew, as population and prosperity increased, so did the need for more complex and effective methods of administration, control, and protection. Gradually these thriving communities began to expand and alter so that elements of the village culture, and outside it as well, were eventually concentrated in one region and reorganized in the new unit of urban culture. The armed stronghold and the shrine — power and magic — which often were separately located were now united in the heart of the evolving city. Men left their isolated, self-contained agricultural villages and came to dwell in the large, heterogeneous communities which provided in one area the diverse elements which had once been scattered throughout the entire region. In addition to leadership, housing, work facilities, a water supply, and access to important waterways, the city provided a marketplace for the exchange not only of grain and goods, but for civilization's most valuable commodity: ideas.

A surplus of food created by nature's munificence and man's ingenuity began a chain of events which ultimately resulted in the release of surplus human energy. Artistic and intellectual experiences which had once been reserved for special occasions became daily events; avocation became vocation in the new style of urban life. Released from the exhausting bondage of satisfying his animal needs, of catching and cultivating his dinner, and stimulated by the lively traffic in foreign ideas brought by the outsider and the stranger, urban man was at last free to express his dreams and fantasies in art, literature, dance, and music, and to cultivate his mind and tend its long neglected gifts.

But the "comforts of civilization" were achieved, as they still are, at a cost which became dearer as these comforts increased. The price of the vast mobilization of power and the greater efficiency and vitality of the new urban mode of life was, for all but the privileged classes, the gradual loss of a varied, unspecialized way of life. For the first time in his sojourn on earth, man was restricted to a single lifetime occupation. Civilization did not originate with the discovery of a metal technology or the invention of writing. It was founded by a social invention: a complex machine whose thousands of precision parts were human, and whose divine operator was conveniently represented by his ministers in the priesthood. Vast armies of men, from priests to porters, worked under central leadership to accomplish magnificent feats of civil engineering — a triumph not only of administrative genius, but of sheer manpower and perseverance. The largest and oldest of the pyramids of Gizah was built before either the wheeled cart or the pulley was invented, with implements of stone and primitive machines such as the lever, the roller, the ramp and, of course, an expendable supply of human life.

In time, society was stratified by caste, class, trade, craft, and profession. There arose a class of professional and full-time specialists who neither tilled the soil nor hunted, but lived instead on the surplus food which others produced. Biologically, man is an adaptable creature whose chief specializations, a large brain, dexterous hands, and eyes in front of his head, underwrite his biological freedom by enabling him to design and construct tools instead of growing them as permanent physical appendages to his body. But, ironically, in the interest of greater efficiency and skill, he began to perform as a tool. What he had gained biologically, he began to relinquish culturally.

Five to six thousand years ago there occurred a momentous event in man's history. The art of writing was invented. In written language man's ephemeral thoughts and dreams found permanence; past and future were joined by means of an enduring bridge of written words. In the small Neolithic hamlet it was possible for the shaman or priest to keep track of the business transactions of the community, and cultural records were easily stored in the minds of the village elders, transmitted from one generation to the next by oral tradition. As the community grew in size and complexity, as strangers came and went, unprecedented problems arose and the old system for storing the community experience no longer sufficed.

Before writing was employed in the lofty service of literature and philosophy, it was used to administer man's practical affairs and to keep the economic ledgers of the gods. In both Egypt and Mesopotamia the priesthood and the temple precinct played an important role in the commercial transactions of the city. The origins of this tradition were rooted in a past which was even then remote. The relationship between the Stone Age tribe and its local spirit or godling had always been a contract of mutual benefit. The spirit was expected to look after the needs of the "tenants" who occupied his region; they in turn provided the food, supplies, and sacrifices which were the spirit's due. From the beginning the gods were landlords, represented in their material affairs by their earthly spokesmen: the primitive magician and the witch doctor, and later the sophisticated temple priests. As a result, in Egypt and Mesopotamia written records were at first kept by the members of the priesthood and the scribes of the temple. In Egypt the highly complex art of writing was actually retained as an official secret. Eventually the written record, originally invented to facilitate bookkeeping, would be used by those who possessed its art to expand the horizons of intellect and ambition, to record ideas and emotion, and to recount the glory of the gods and not unaccountably of their ministers on earth.

Writing was only one of many privileges the priestly class monopolized. Charged with the leadership of the community, the priesthood was quick to recognize that the harsh toil and manual labor required to supply man's basic animal needs were not conducive to reflective thought and to the nurture of the creative spirit. In the early civilizations of Egypt and Mesopotamia, man's creative birthright, as well as many other resources, was gradually usurped by a small group of specialists — the king, his royal retainers, and the priesthood — whose growing power rested in the ignorance of the populace. While the majority of the people labored, the ruling classes, released from drudgery, provided administrative leadership and appropriated the leisure required for creative effort. In this way human resources which were theoretically the right of many, now vastly expanded in form and scope, came in actual practice to reside in the few.

In the gloomy myths of Mesopotamia, man's lot is quite specifically described: he was created as a servant of the gods. The Mesopotamians believed that in the beginning the gods had toiled at harsh manual labor; it is no surprise that they found their existence loathsome and intolerable. In the magnificent Akkadian creation epic, *Enuma elish,* it is recounted that the gods, wearied by the tremendous exertion of wresting the cosmos from chaos, were at last freed to lead the good life by Marduk, the God of Babylon.

> *Verily, savage-man I will create.*
> *He shall be charged with the service of the gods*
> *That they might be at ease!*

As the centuries passed, the conforming, ritualistic way of life prescribed by the despotic priesthood and tyrant kings in Egypt and Mesopotamia in the persuasive name of "national interest" sealed its own doom. For it swallowed not only the small people, but the great, including the king, and ultimately the priests themselves. Creative endeavor and the search for truth cannot long survive in an atmosphere in which self-expression and self-development are discouraged as dangerous, and where dependence on God's mercy has replaced human enterprise.

We must understand, however, that mankind's creative birthright was not suddenly stolen, but was surrendered slowly and willingly by the people to the kings and gods they had themselves created. The Egyptians who lived at the time of the Old Kingdom were a vigorous, self-reliant, individualistic people. In Mesopotamia the earliest political pattern had been a primitive form of democracy. Gradually in Mesopotamia the "good life" became the "obedient life," and in her sister civilization "submissive silence" was the spirit recommended to those who wished to find favor in the eyes of the gods.

It has been suggested that as civilized man learned to control natural events over which his ancestors had no control; as he reclaimed land from marshes and swamps, and began to command the great river routes; as he accumulated surplus property which required protection, and as foreign conquest became both an enticement and a threat, he became increasingly dependent upon the administrative, magical, and divine powers of his chieftain or king. Investing the ruler with greater secular and sacred powers, he inevitably diminished his own. In this way the social will of the people was expressed in the king whose expanded privileges gave him further power to impose his own will on his people.

Among the nations of the ancient Near East, Israel's government was unique. The initiative and final authority for the selection of Israel's leaders were left to the people who decided how and by whom they were to be ruled. Jewish judges and kings ruled not by divine right but by "divinely imposed responsibility." The king was responsible to his people and was expected to use his office for their benefit and not for his own profit. The leaders of Israel were mortal, their lives transient and, like Moses, they were subject to human failings. When the people forgot that it was the Lord who was their ruler, the prophets reminded them of their traditional prerogatives, affirming the principle that the king was subject to the same ethical standards as his humblest subject. In condemning the rulers of his time, Ezekiel proclaimed, "Woe unto the shepherds of Israel that have fed themselves! should not the shepherds feed the sheep?" The principle that the monarch was merely the servant of the Lord persisted throughout the history of the ancient nation, in hope, in ideal, and for a time in its institutions. The tradition of local self-government, of individual participation in public affairs, and of the sovereign rights of the people, developed in the hills and valleys and the desert wilderness of ancient Palestine, endured through centuries of dispersion helping the uprooted Jews to surmount the shock of exile. As the people of God, a god vastly different from the deities of other nations, Israel never succumbed to the menace of kings.

In Egypt and Mesopotamia man had gone forth to tame nature, but ironically in the process he had subjugated himself. What man did not know, and even now is slow to recognize, is that he is part of nature: in altering nature, he too must change. Divested of the proud, independent heritage of its predecessors, a society of wretched spectators found vicarious pleasure in the emerging personality and glorious achievements of its monarch. Although he had surrendered his right to live the fully human life of an integrated individual, the ancient subject of the despotic Oriental state could at least look up to the pedestal upon which he had set his king and see there a fine example of a resplendent, free-standing individual, no longer submerged in the group, but a god himself or the chosen of the gods. Thousands of years would pass before men would claim as their own that which in the formative years of civilization they had created in the single person of the king.

A Creative Society

As the once-magnificent empires of the East lay stagnant and dying, in the steep mountains and small, sheltered valleys of ancient Greece which lay then at the western fringe of the civilized world, there arose and bloomed a radiant civilization, the like of which had not been known before. Throughout the world of the East a miserable and suffering populace eventually learned to endure by denying the importance of the external world: by retreating, as in Egypt, to the world of the dead, or by turning inward to the unseen realms of the spirit. The tradition of Western civilization, with its concepts of freedom and human dignity was born in Greece a number of centuries before the birth of Christ. An inspired fusion of the older spiritual inheritance of the East with a new rational spirit which was to become the way of the Western world, produced an efflorescence of genius in art and thought which has not since been surpassed and which has shaped the mind and spirit of man from that time to this very day. For several glorious centuries in ancient Greece the creative potential of a people was entrusted not to a chosen few but to the citizenry itself. The domain of the intellect and imagination was no longer reserved for a jealous priesthood but was the responsibility of all the Greek citizens.

Greek "democracy" was of course limited. The institution of

slavery conveniently released the Greeks from dull, routine tasks, from the drudgery of manual labor, and provided the measure of leisure necessary for creative and intellectual pursuits. Moreover, in Athens the privileges of first-class citizenship were enjoyed by less than one in seven individuals — women being among those excluded. In this sense we must regard the Athenian citizen as a member of a privileged, elite group.

The strict division of occupation which had appeared at the dawn of civilization was for many reasons avoided in Greece. Socrates was a stone cutter by trade; the poet Hesiod was a poor farmer; the great dramatist Sophocles was a skilled wrestler, ball player, and musician, as well as a general, a diplomat, and a priest. In Athens, the greatest of the Greek cities, and the one about which we know the most, the responsibility for private and civic functions was constantly rotated so that the Athenian citizen led the integrated life which had in Egypt and Mesopotamia been reserved for royalty and the priesthood. The ordinary Athenian citizen was expected to provide military service and jury duty, to represent himself in the law courts, to participate in public business decisions and in the affairs of state which elsewhere were conducted by tyrants or paid officials. He took part in athletic competitions, expressed himself in aesthetic matters and joined in the common pursuit of knowledge. Participation in the arts was considered a citizen's duty. A man who at one time entered a dramatic competition as an author, might at another time serve as an actor or a judge. A considerable portion of an Athenian audience, therefore, consisted of former participants — a highly critical and receptive group of spectators. The great playwright Aeschylus, who wrote at least seventy dramas, was also an actor, a costume and scene designer, and a producer. Between 480 and 380 B.C., two thousand plays of superior quality and five to six thousand equally select new musical compositions were written and produced in Athens. Yet it is estimated that at its height there were no more than forty thousand full-fledged citizens in Athens.

Many factors are thought to account for the sudden flowering of genius among a few million people within a period of less than two centuries. The Hellenes, as the Greeks called themselves, were a people in whose blood mingled the disparate biological stock of the warlike Dorians, the vigorous Achaeans and the autochthonous peoples of Mycenae and Crete; whose culture fused the traditions of the heroic Achaeans, of whom Homer sang, with elements of the earlier artistic and highly civilized Aegean culture. The exhilarating climate, the luminous blue skies, the radiant sunlight of these enchanted islands of the Aegean summoned men to action and deed. Propitious waters and winds favored the sailor and as the arts of navigation developed, commerce and trade prospered. Undoubtedly the mountainous configuration of the land helped to shape Greek character and Greek concepts of political independence. Vast military and bureaucratic machines were not required to defend these intimate village communities. Protected by steep mountain strongholds, the Greek village could easily be held by a small group of courageous, high-spirited men. These proud warrior peasants and sailors were inclined to a rugged individualism and naturally put a premium upon self-reliance and freedom.

The leisure and personal independence enjoyed by the Greek citizen were afforded, not merely by the system of slavery which existed everywhere in the ancient world, but by the nature of the land which freed the Greeks from the materialistic obsessions of the powerful and wealthy Egyptian and Babylonian empires — and of those all too familiar in our present affluent society. If the Greek peasant lived frugally, his natural surroundings guaranteed him a minimal living and released him from a life of unremitting toil. Leisure, not material wealth, was the gift of the land to its people. Unlike the Egyptian or Assyrian community which was capable of producing an economy of abundance but remained a slave to the whims of the river it was required to control, and in turn to massive military and bureaucratic organizations, no such opportunity existed in the sparsely settled, isolated communities of the rocky Aegean Islands and the rugged Balkan peninsula.

The heroic tradition of the Greeks, alien to Eastern culture, but so familar to those of us in the West, was succinctly expressed in the Homeric ideal: to strive for excellence and to surpass all others. For the first time in recorded history, the individual was recognized as a supreme entity and his attainments honored. Man was expected to think for himself, to live in his own way, and to serve his state as a willing servant, intelligently, directed by inner discipline and not in blind obedience to external constraint. In Egypt the monarch had been deified while individual attainment was inhibited. In Greece where, according to Protagoras, man was the measure of all things, the gods were conceived in human scale, while man was enjoined to be godlike. One of the injunctions graven in the shrine at Delphi was: know thyself. One would not have found such advice inscribed in a Babylonian or Egyptian temple.

For those of us who are concerned with the nurture of creativity in modern life, it is significant that the monumental outpouring of Greek genius occurred in an atmosphere where the glory of human, not divine, achievement was celebrated; where a varied, responsible way of life was esteemed above the colossal power and material comforts achieved in other civilizations at the expense of disabling specialization; in a society which was itself creative, and in which the creator was cherished above his creations.

A Gift of the Gods

The self-aware individual, respected for his own worth, "the rightful lord and owner of his own person," had at last emerged from the blurred fabric of group consciousness. Many centuries would pass before the specific details of this image would accrue and before man would be both mature and bold enough to create the concept of "creative man." We cannot consider the development of man's attitude toward his own creative powers, however, without first understanding his concept of nature's creative force, for what he believed about himself was patterned by what he understood in nature.

Because primitive man's welfare was intimately tied to the annual renewal of fertility and life in the barren earth, he was quick to recognize the creative power of nature. At first the creative and reproductive forces of the earth were worshipped directly. Eventually in many cultures these attributes were incarnated in a mother goddess, often accompanied by a young male god. In Mesopotamian mythology, for example, the passive, procreative power of the earth was embodied in an earth goddess, Ki or Ninhursaga, while the active creative force was personified by Enki, or Ea, god of the sweet waters. In the devious, unpredictable, but seemingly purposive ways of the "waters which wander in the earth," the Mesopotamians innately recognized the essence of the creative force.

Descending suddenly from the heavens and disappearing into the soil, arising elsewhere in cool springs, brooding in deep lagoons, flowing out over the earth in swift rivers, water seemed to possess a will and intelligence of its own. And wherever water went, the land was blessed with life; fields, plowlands and orchards flourished, and man prospered. It was natural that the god of these waters should acquire the characteristics of cunning, of imagination, and of superior intelligence. Eventually Enki's creative domain extended from nature to human behavior. For it was the spirit of Enki which manifested itself in the production of all new entities — in the inspiration for "wise counsel," in the solution of problems by new methods of action, and in the work of artists and craftsmen.

Ancient man was a dependable observer. But as he began to speculate about the mechanisms of nature's forces he was more entertaining than reliable. In a time when neither the spirit nor the method of science yet existed, when human credulity was high and miracles abounded, before it was known that the processes of life and growth are controlled by natural mechanisms, man relied on his own experience to interpret the forces of nature. What was human was regarded as normal or natural. What deviated from the normal, and therefore could not be explained, was considered extra-human or supernatural. Thus each spring the earth, dormant and barren, incapable of effecting its own resurrection, awaited the indwelling gods for deliverance. At first this miraculous creative force was believed to reside within nature itself. In Hebrew and later Greek thought, however, God was relocated outside of nature. No longer immanent in the world he had created, God became a transcendent deity who dwelled above and beyond nature. Sun and moon, thunder and rain, once gods themselves, were now but reflections of his glory.

In this orderly plan, man was privileged, but dependent upon his omnipotent creator. Neither his design nor his behavior was ever to be altered and there was little room for the manifold demands of human life. The scientific and intellectual revolutions which followed from Darwin's work in biology and Einstein's in mathematical physics destroyed the closed mechanical order of the world, substituted a system of change and growth, and allowed for man's human qualities. Once man recovered from the hearty shock to his self-assurance incurred in the discovery that he, like his animal relations, was bound by the laws of nature, that he no longer was the culminating glory of creation, he found that his own powers had been enormously expanded. Being part of nature, subject like lions and daffodils to the same laws of change, growth, and development, man was capable in some measure of understanding the forces which ruled his life. No longer God's chosen servant, he was at least his own master, free to chart his own destiny.

Reluctantly, man had come to understand that the myriad species which populate the earth evolved slowly over eons of time, one from the other; that the "new ideas" in animal design, which are the raw material of the evolutionary process, are random genetic accidents and part of nature's process. It is neither immanent nor transcendent divine purpose, but the sys-

tem itself which is fount to the magnificent stream of life which
has proliferated upon our planet.

By the time man became consciously interested in the origin
and meaning of his creative powers, the conception of creativity as a miraculous gift "added on" to the normal complement
of human characteristics had long been an established tradition. No more than man could explain nature's creative force,
could he account for his own powers without resorting to the
idea of supernatural intervention. Furthermore, he may have
sensed the inherent creative potential of his species, but daily
experience made it quite apparent that creativity was by no
means a commonplace occurrence. The power to create may be
our human birthright, but our creative resources are not distributed in even measure among all the members of our species,
nor even in the well endowed do they necessarily come to frui-
tion. Those whose gifts are superior — who are genetically
chosen, and for whom the combination of environmental and
emotional factors is favorable — do indeed stand forth from
their fellowmen.

From earliest times, therefore, men observed the manifestation of imagination and creativeness in select individuals, distinguished by outstanding ability, by exceptional status or
privilege, and by what appeared to be a private line to the spirits and the gods. We may recall two of the early specialists: the
medicine man or shaman, whose trances were attributed to a
visit from the spirit world, but whose endowments of intelligence, imagination, and dramatic talent must have been considerable; and the Paleolithic cave artist whose fusion of
practical magic and spiritual impulse culminated in a brilliant
efflorescence of artistic genius. It would not have been unnatural to conclude that creative power, like magic and religion
with which it was so often allied, was a miraculous and transcendent gift, bestowed on rare occasions by the gods upon
chosen mortals.

Even the word "genius," which comes from the Latin word
meaning "to beget," had from the first a divine connotation.

Originally it applied to the guardian deity which presided over the destiny of a person, a place, or an object. The "guardian angel" and "evil genius" are superstitious vestiges of this primitive religion which still haunt our modern vocabulary. Eventually, the resident spirit disappeared and the word was extended to individuals — or periods of time — possessing exalted creative or intellectual ability.

More than two thousand years ago the philosophers and poets of ancient Greece had already begun to speculate about the nature of the creative process. It is not surprising that this subject attracted the interest of these remarkable people whose passion was knowledge, and to whom the arts were a matter of high seriousness. It was characteristic of their genius that they sought to understand the nature and origin of knowledge itself — a subject about which men still ponder. Having cut their gods in the human image, and having designed the human image on a heroic scale, the Greeks did not hesitate to ascribe to man certain creative qualities ordinarily associated with God. Despite the magnificent creative achievement of Greek civilization, the Greeks placed a limit on man's role in the creative process. According to the tradition of Plato and Aristotle, man was confined to the reflection or imitation of nature or, upon inspiration with what Socrates called "divine madness" (*furor divinus*), to serving as the mouthpiece of the gods. Plato regarded the artist or poet as an inspired madman who, in the old Greek sense, is "possessed by a god." It is God himself who speaks through the words of the poet.

Not only was creativity a rare gift, divine in origin, but for many centuries after the fall of Graeco-Roman civilization, the use of the word create was restricted to the works of God. In the austere Middle Ages it would have been blasphemous to ascribe to man that power which was reserved for God alone. In the materialistic culture of contemporary society, this impressive word is commonly used to adorn the image of various organizations and activities which are expected to profit by exploiting the current mystique of the term. Tasteless travesties such as a

Creative Steel Rule Dye Co.; "creative cooking," in which the end product need not be edible; "creative thinking," which in the present jargon implies that "uncreative" thinking (old-fashioned learning) is a decadent occupation, make one long for a return to a measure of medieval humility.

The great artists and craftsmen of the Middle Ages produced their works of art — often anonymously — not, as we might expect today, to express themselves but to illumine God's meaning as he revealed it through his chosen. Even so, their efforts sometimes earned the wrath of saints and churchmen who denounced the great cathedrals as evidence of worldly pride and as distraction from meditation on God. *"Creatura non potest creare"* ("the creature cannot create") wrote St. Augustine, and similarly St. Thomas Aquinas affirmed that man imitates and produces; only God creates. In the sense that man can produce something which did not exist before, by devising new combinations of existing material, he imitates God's creation; but to create "something from nothing" (*creatio ex nihilo*) is the work of God alone. The doctrine of creation from nothing appears in St. Augustine, who maintained that the world was created from nothing and that God created not only its form but its substance. *Creatio ex nihilo* was not the classical Greek view found in Plato's *Timaeus* where God arranges pre-existing material. In the book of Genesis this concept is blurred and obscure. Although Jewish scholars have interpreted Genesis 1:1 as an argument for *creatio ex nihilo*, there are others who disagree. In the Egyptian and Mesopotamian creation stories, the creator-gods themselves first emerge from primordial chaos upon which they then impose form and order. Self-created, the gods separate light from darkness and redistribute the formless waters. The primeval abyss, however, was there from the beginning — "Outrageous as a Sea, dark, wasteful, wilde."

The Middle Ages was a time of sharp paradox and violent contradiction in which man was taught that he must both respect and loathe himself and that, created in the image of God, he was nevertheless wicked and depraved. It was an age of faith and piety, cruelty and greed, of order and anarchy, of saint and barbarian. Medieval man may have been lusty and exuberant, but the Church regarded him as sinful. In the Renaissance the emphasis shifted. The discovery of the classical traditions of individuality and self-sufficiency provided authority for a revolt against the devout mood and hierarchical structure of medieval life in which the primary virtues were faith, humility, and obedience, rather than personal accomplishment, self-expression, and original enterprise. Not until the Renaissance did man have the temerity to acknowledge his creative powers. Man, the "free and proud shaper" of his own being, was at last free to transform and fashion himself as he chose. For the first time artists began cautiously to speak of themselves as creators and to refer to their works as creations. The greater part of the vocabulary of creative art and literature which we take for granted today derives from this period. The German genius Albrecht Dürer describes the painter as one who "creates in his heart . . . new shapes of men and other creatures the like of which was never seen before"; and a sixteenth-century English critic, throwing medieval piety aside, compared the poet to God, claiming for man the power to bring into being, by means of his imagination, that for which no previous pattern existed.

Yet the artists and writers of the Renaissance were somewhat amazed by their newly discovered talents and were not entirely comfortable in claiming them. Even Leonardo da Vinci avoided the word "create" in his writings and maintained that painting was a science rather than a "creative" pursuit. The distinction, as we shall later see, is significant. Creativity implied original invention by divine or superrational inspiration, whereas science was understood as the mere copying of fact. Only in the romantic idealism of the nineteenth century, with its credo of freedom and self-expression, did the poets and thinkers of this period — men such as Goethe, Fichte, Carlyle, Coleridge, Emerson, Wordsworth — finally popularize the concept of "creative man."

Man's attitude toward himself had undergone a profound change, yet the inspiration for extraordinary achievement remained, as it had from ancient times, the responsibility of God — or Satan — depending upon personal and historical perspective. With the growing knowledge of biology and genetics in the nineteenth century, the physical spirits were exorcised, but many still believed that such unusual powers if not supernatural, were at least biologically superhuman. In his own time Michelangelo had been hailed as *divino* by contemporaries who believed literally that secular genius presupposed sacred inspiration. Today when we praise the "divine" singing of the opera "diva" we echo this earlier tradition of celestial sponsorship and inspiration from "on high." The frustrated creator who blames his muse for lack of inspiration, fails to recognize that to the extent that there is a muse, she resides within himself and is not a fickle, transcendent creature cavorting through the heavens, deaf to his call and blind to his need.

Beginning with the sixteenth century the prerogatives of genius were dearly bought. According to Panofsky, "the rise of man to the status of 'genius,' however, was in a sense a second Fall from Grace." Man became "creative," but unfortunately creative man's sanity was threatened. The basis for the concept of genius which evolved during the Renaissance had been established many centuries before this time. Epileptics and lunatics, saints and prophets — often one and the same — had long been considered divinely possessed and were regarded with sacred awe. Plato had said that secular genius owed its inspiration to "divine madness," a form of passionate psychic energy, which the modern reader must not confuse with insanity. In the *Phaedrus*, Plato has Socrates explain that there are two kinds of madness: "one produced by human infirmity, the other . . . a divine release of the soul from the yoke of custom and convention." The classical concept of genius was now embellished within the context of late Neoplatonic thought, which by the fifteenth century had become a strange philosoph-

ical brew compounded of the classical ideals of Greece and
Rome, and an uneasy fusion of magic, astrology, and mysticism.

To the earlier image of genius, the Renaissance scholar appended the more exotic, but less salubrious concept of "melancholy" which Aristotle had already foreshadowed. A person
who possessed unusual gifts was expected to pay for them with
a divine, but terrifying melancholy which elevated him above
his fellowman, but left him balancing dangerously on the brink
of insanity. The philosopher and the poet, and somewhat later,
the artist, were admitted to the exclusive group of saints, seers,
and madmen, free to exercise the exalted privileges of those
who possessed celestial "connections," but condemned to the
suffering presupposed by such high ambition. In the famous
paired poem, *Il Penseroso*, the young Milton celebrated the
gifts of melancholy.

> *But hail thou Goddess, sage and holy,*
> *Hail divinest Melancholy,*
> *Whose Saintly visage is too bright*
> *To hit the Sense of human sight;*
> *And therefore to our weaker view,*
> *Ore laid with black staid Wisdoms hue.*

Almost two centuries later, in the beautiful, visionary lines
of "Kubla Khan," Coleridge provided a fine portrait of the bewitched, somewhat daft prototype of the genius still familiar to
us today.

> *And all should cry, Beware! Beware!*
> *His flashing eyes, his floating hair!*
> *Weave a circle round him thrice,*
> *And close your eyes with holy dread,*
> *For he on honey-dew hath fed,*
> *And drunk the milk of Paradise.*

Misunderstanding Science

Although the serious rift between science and humanist philosophy and art did not occur for several centuries, by the end of the sixteenth century there were indications of the incipient divorce. Leonardo was among the first to distinguish between "creativity" and "science"; and, according to Panofsky, the Italian Quattrocento fought for intellectual recognition of the visual arts under the aegis of science rather than creativeness. Art theorists argued that mathematics enslaved the spirit; Petrarch, among other humanists, looked with disdain upon those who were interested in nature's phenomena; and Erasmus ridiculed the natural philosopher and the mathematician as dull, plodding, uninspired pedants and was not interested in the revolutionary discoveries of his age. The feeling was reciprocated. Francis Bacon referred to humanism as "delicate learning" — a point of view still prevalent today.

Truth was revealed to the creative mind by irrational inspiration. Science, parting company in the sixteenth century with magic and religion, sought objective truth by means of the rational intellect, by mathematics, and eventually by experiment. Men believed that creativity involved the creation of something which had not existed previously, whereas science was limited to the reproduction of fact and to the discovery of the "laws of nature," which — like America, discovered by Columbus but created by God — were regarded as God's original handiwork.

Despite the scorn of the humanists, the pioneer scientific geniuses of the sixteenth and seventeenth centuries were regarded with awe and wonder, and their powers were ascribed to supernatural forces, either divine or infernal. The term genius by definition implies an exceptional mental endowment specifically of a creative kind. Today the word is commonly misused in referring to people who have great talent, facility, superior intellectual ability, or an upper-bracket IQ, but whose original contributions may be negligible. The prophets of the new spirit in science and the brilliant philosophers who introduced the Modern Age, men such as Descartes, Hobbes, and Locke, were among the most creative men our world has known. Ironically their contributions were not considered "creative."

As the gospel of the scientific method spread, as science was purged of the exotic contaminants of magic, religion, and mysticism, there evolved one image of the scientific man and another of the creative man. Both concepts persist today, not without some justification, as popular fallacies. It was assumed that art is the exercise of irrational emotion and inspired intuition, whereas science is the exercise of logic and reason; furthermore, that creativity is not logical, but that science, since it merely copies fact, is not creative. Inherent in this formulation are two fundamental errors:

(1) The craftsmanship, the discipline, the aesthetic logic, and the high order of the artist's intellect are overlooked. Without these qualities art, literature, and music would be nothing but formless outpourings of feeling: dabs and daubs of unrestrained fantasy, verbal vegetable soup, a kaleidoscope of sound — secret communications from the artist to himself.

(2) In its complexity and compartmentalization, in its smug sense of superiority, in its growing dependence upon monster instruments, and its proliferation of specialized jargon, modern science, like modern art, has become increasingly inhuman and mechanical. Yet buried beneath the elaborate, clanking machinery of the System and the Establishment, breathing life into the scientific behemoth, lies the ephemeral creative act — that unique and mysterious synergy of imagination, intuition, emotion, and reason.

Both art and science have always had their industrious laborers and inspired pedants who toil over the designs of the "master architects," who follow where others lead. "Many small make a great," said Chaucer. That every scientist is not in the vanguard of his profession is no reason to debase the value of the conservative, dedicated foot soldiers without whom scientific conquest would not be possible. Nor, however, is this reason to slight the essential creative act by which the individual scientist wrests from chaos a vision of the universe which would otherwise remain as devoid of shape and meaning as the clay in the sculptor's barrel or the paint on the artist's palette.

At this point, therefore, let us consider some of the reasons for the distinction between "creative" and "scientific." They are significant beyond their historical context, for they express a fundamental but common misconception not only of the nature of scientific discovery, but of the creative act itself.

Rules and Recipes. If we compare the creative act in science and in art, one important difference is apparent. A scientific discovery is an abstract idea; it is not a product you can touch. In its final form the long creative genesis of the idea is eliminated, lost in the recesses of personal memory, consigned to the trash pail, buried and forgotten in the pages of scientific history and biography. What remains at the end of the scientific quest is a magic formula: a few drab letters, a set of impersonal symbols capable of summoning the stars or devastating the earth — rules and recipes which serve as solutions to problems which no longer are problems. The scientist's struggle to dispel not only the murk of error and confusion but to transcend the cultural beliefs of his times, his foolish questions, his private metaphors, his discarded hypotheses, and all trace of his personality are absent when the end product — a concise theorem or a quantitative expression — makes its public debut.

Despite what we learn in school, the experimental or mathematical proof of a scientific theory, for all its logic and elegance, may have nothing to do with the origin of the theory. It may have been provided afterwards by the discoverer, or by someone else. Every schoolchild learns the formal geometric proof for Pythagoras's theorem (the square on the hypoteneuse of a right-angled triangle is equal to the sum of the squares on the remaining sides) as given in the first book of Euclid's *Elements*. But how many students understand that although this is one means of verifying the proposition, it is not the means by which the theorem was discovered. Probably the equivalent rule, known as the "rule of the cord," had been familiar to the early Egyptian "Rope Stretchers," the primitive surveyors who reestablished the land boundaries after the periodic flooding of the Nile. It has been suggested that Pythagoras, or a member of the Pythagorean Brotherhood, may have discovered this relationship by observing the patterns of squares and the play of sunlight and shadow while pacing the colored tile floors of some ancient Egyptian temple.

Galileo, the fiery gentleman who invented the telescope and trained it upon the mountains of the moon and the satellites of Jupiter, is often hailed as the genius who launched the "scientific method." In the history of science, both the nature and the means of Galileo's accomplishments are the subject of considerable controversy, for as a transitional figure who stood between the Middle Ages and the Modern Age of Science, Galileo understandably did not express a consistent viewpoint in his writings. Galileo was indeed a careful observer, yet for all the balls he rolled down inclined planes, or the weights he is said to have dropped from the Leaning Tower of Pisa, the great physicist was not the careful experimenter we today might imagine. The crude conditions of his experiments could not have produced such exact laws as the celebrated law of falling bodies. It is believed that Galileo devised his theories by a combination of reason and imagination, first imagining the consequence of experiments rather than observing them directly. The experiments served as a rough check on his theories and as a demonstration of their validity. In his own words, the causes of effects were not to be found in experiments.

The story is told that when Newton was asked by the astronomer Halley how he knew that the theory of planetary motions he had just described was true, Newton is said to have replied, "Why, I have calculated it." Halley knew from this that Newton had already worked out the theory of gravitation. Unable to find his calculations, Newton promised to write out the theorems and proofs, and later sent Halley two different proofs. Encouraged by Halley, who also paid the costs of publication, Newton began work on the *Principia*. It is debatable, however, whether the difficult geometric form of the *Principia* represents the mental processes by which Newton made his discoveries.

Michael Faraday, the brilliant, visionary physicist who postulated the theory that light is an electromagnetic radiation, nevertheless had no knowledge of mathematics beyond the simplest elements of arithmetic. According to the physicist Helmholtz, Faraday postulated his theories by a "kind of intuition, with the security of instinct, without the help of a single mathematical formula."

In relating tales of well-known geniuses, it is necessary to add that care must be taken not to give undue credence to their own highly subjective accounts of how they made their discoveries. Vanity, lapses of memory, and self-deception are afflictions of the genius as well as of lesser men, and the scientist who has become a public figure may quite easily come to believe in the myth of himself.

Society, however, does not need the record of the creative scientist's art, nor is it necessary to understand the means and the spirit of science in order to exploit its accomplishments. We can use our television sets without understanding Clerk Maxwell's equations, and the electrical engineer who is heir to Maxwell's knowledge can apply the equations without appreciating their creative origin. The polio immunization is as effective for those who merely bare their arms, as for those who understand the basic principles of immunity, not to speak of the nature of the creative vision by which Louis Pasteur discovered these principles.

A work of art, on the contrary, is a tangible product which reveals the qualitative nature of its subject. As in scientific creation, false starts and the genesis of the idea do not appear in the completed composition. Because qualities and attributes cannot be summarized in a universal numerical code, the work of art demonstrates part of the process by which it was created. In science the means serves only until the end is achieved; in art the visible part of the means becomes the end.

At present those who are concerned with the philosophy of science and with its implications for human life suggest that the nature of the scientific enterprise — "what science does and how it does it" — may hold a deeper meaning for men than the actual knowledge and the exploitable products these conclusions yield. The laws of science are not ultimate truths; they are working approximations of reality. J. Bronowski has observed in a perceptive essay that the values of science which derive from its method and from its spirit of exploration are more important than its specific discoveries. This does not contradict what has been said about the creative process in science, but emphasizes the need to understand the scientist, his problems and responsibilities.

We can describe a conversation between two people by saying, "He proposed" or "They had an argument." But only the actual conversation or a skillful literary approximation can capture the essence of the event. To know the Mona Lisa we must see the original painting, or at least a good reproduction of it. "Mona Lisa by Leonardo da Vinci = Famous Painting of Woman with Enigmatic Smile" would hardly suffice were one to hang it, framed, on the wall. "Art is life seen through a temperament," said Zola. For this reason we cannot "use" — appreciate or understand — a work of art without responding to it with our own emotions and intellect, thereby re-creating a personal version of the artist's creation. In the case of avant-garde art, or art outside of our cultural experience, the act of appreciation may require the effort of education. Because the domain of art is subjective human experience, and not the abstract world of anti-matter or noncircular circles, art is expected to "speak to us" on first acquaintance. If the language of the novel or the musical composition is not immediately intelligible, the work may be rejected or condemned with a self-satisfied sniff of disapproval. No sensible person expects to judge whether a chemical formula is good or bad — thus right or wrong, without first studying chemistry.

On the other hand, the truth of mathematics and the physical and biological sciences is easier to judge for it can be measured or stated numerically and tested in the impersonal laboratory of nature where, in theory, personal and subjective tastes are not involved. Because the symbols employed by the artist are subjective and concerned with the attributes of things, there is no absolute standard against which the "truth" of art may be immediately evaluated. To the chemist, water is H_2O; the painter has as many ways of saying *water* as the eye and mind have of seeing. For the same reason that human experience cannot easily — or safely — be reduced to numerical quantities, the postulated verities of the behavioral and social sciences, like those of history, medicine, or the stock market, remain highly fallible.

The Logic Machine Fallacy. The popular concept of the scientist as a cold, mechanical reasoning machine from which the contaminating forces of emotion have been rigorously excluded is not true. The belief that the scientist is a super-squirrel who diligently hoards facts from which he then induces inevitable conclusions, or conversely, that the scientist starts from given premises and plods forward step-by-step deducing necessary conclusions is also false.

Had Johann Kepler, for example, persisted in the task of calculating all the possible *circular* orbits for the planet Mars, a lifetime of work would have been in vain. In terms of traditional cosmic geometry the problem was insoluble. Since the time of Plato and Aristotle, men believed that the heavenly bodies moved in circular orbits, at uniform speeds, their motion conveniently provided by an "Unmoved Mover" or God. The laws which governed the earth, furthermore, were not thought to operate in the sublime heavens. To entertain the shocking idea that the velocities of the planets varied and to imagine that they traveled in the distorted orbit of an ellipse required a major revolution not only in Kepler's science, but in his spiritual outlook. Kepler was a devoutly religious man, inclined as well to Pythagorean mysticism. The solution to the astronomer's problem, and the concept of gravitational force toward which he was groping, required thousands of pages of tedious calculation, but was also inspired by a mystical analogy between the behavior of the sun and its planets, and God and the Holy Ghost.

Just as a knowledge of harmony cannot in itself produce original music, the exercise of logic alone cannot generate new ideas. The road to discovery begins in hard, methodical work, and ends in logical verification, but at the crucial moment of insight it must traverse the mysterious, subjective realms of intuition and imagination. Great mathematicians and physicists — supposedly the most "scientific" of the scientists — reveal in their own writings a romantic, mystic, even religious conception of their craft. Guided by instinct, intuition and by aesthetic emotions such as a sense of beauty and a delight in harmony, they are certainly more kith to the artist than kin to the computer. Newton, the "Monarch of the Age of Reason," left an extraordinary collection of unpublished works concerned with esoteric theological matters, mysticism, alchemy, and experiments in magic. Kepler's mathematics and respect for scientific observations were rigorous enough (at a critical point in his calculations he discarded six years' work because his calculations departed by eight minutes of arc from actual observations), but the speculative, irrational flights of Kepler's imagination and the ecstatic joy which illumines his writings, while delighting the poet and the mystic, would give a computer electronic apoplexy.

Among scientists themselves, one often encounters the smug individual who believes that to science alone is vouchsafed the truth. Convinced of the superiority of his discipline, he looks with scorn upon those whose mental processes or work bear the unfortunate taint of emotionalism and subjectivity. Religious faith is regarded as the refuge of the weakminded and the unenlightened. Yet it is the great scientific mind, not the small, which feels no need to deny the realm of the spirit, and which with the humility born of knowledge accepts the limitations of the rational mind with both logic and grace. Norbert Wiener has observed that science is itself founded on an act of supreme faith: the fundamental belief that nature is subject to law. This premise can never be proven or demonstrated, but must be accepted on faith by all scientists. In a now famous aphorism, Einstein said, "Der Herrgott ist raffiniert, aber boshaft ist Er nicht" ("The Lord is subtle, but he isn't mean"), by which he meant that if a scientist succeeds in unraveling one of the secrets of inanimate nature, the rules of the game will not arbitrarily change just to thwart him. In the trenchant words of the physicist-philosopher L. L. Whyte, "The mystic believes in an unknown God, the thinker and scientist in an unknown order; it is hard to say which surpasses the other in non-rational devotion."

The Laundry List Fallacy. Not only must a scientific theory be simpler than the facts it summarizes, but it must reveal a pattern or a hidden unity, making it possible to predict events beyond those given in the original situation. No more than a poem is an assemblage of words is science an assemblage of facts expressed in the mnemonic of a formula.

If I go to the window and record everything I observe: that it is raining, that there are clouds in the sky and puddles on the street, that it is 9 A.M., that the windowpane needs washing, and so forth, I still cannot predict with accuracy when the rain will stop and what the weather will be tomorrow. Theories do not emerge full born from collections of data. First, the scientist must have some idea of what kinds of facts are relevant to his problem. Later, the working hypothesis may have to be altered should it provide a false trail.

Similarly, it has been pointed out that for all its meteorological instruments, its tables and charts, its vast collections of data, the science of weather is still in its infancy. It awaits its Galileo, its Newton, or its Darwin to impose law and order upon the millions of recorded observations; as Clerk Maxwell said, to recognize the "principles amid the endless variety of their action." With the exception of some general understanding of weather trends and phenomena, our method of dealing with the weather remains relatively crude. If the weather forecast is for rain, we may rely on this prediction and behave accordingly, or we may carry an umbrella all day to make certain it does not rain. To the man on the street — and he is the one who gets wet — science and superstition still appear to be equally effective.

The creation of meaningful patterns from confusion, and the discovery of what Coleridge called "unity in variety" is not a task for a computer, either electronic or human. Genuine creations of the imagination and intellect, scientific laws, like traffic laws, do not exist until the scientist creates them from the chaos of experience. The eye sees only disorder; it is the mind which creates order.

The "Laws of Nature" Fallacy. The belief that the scientist merely discovers the "laws of nature" mistakenly assumes that such laws exist. In the eighteenth century the laws of nature were regarded as real laws which God had created and which nature was required to obey. Originally, God set the planets in motion and having "turned on" the Law of Gravitation and the other laws of motion, his work was done. Henceforth, the universe could be left to operate like a perpetual-motion machine. As Alexander Pope confidently wrote:

> *Nature and Nature's law lay hid in night:*
> *God said, Let Newton be! and all was Light.*

In the twentieth century a sadder and wiser Hilaire Belloc wrote his answer to Pope:

> *It did not last: the Devil howling, "Ho!*
> *Let Einstein be!" restored the status quo.*

Mathematical and physical principles are the means by which we understand nature and deal with its forces, but they are neither summaries of actual fact, nor direct representations of things as they "really are." The law of gravitation is not a physical entity which causes things to fall; it is a formula, created by Newton, which states *how* they fall. The *force* of gravity, which Newton used to explain the changes of motion of a body, and which expresses the attraction between these bodies, actually does not exist in the sense that a force is something which pushes or pulls. Similarly, *mass,* which as Einstein discovered can for better or worse be converted into energy, is not something we can touch. It is a concept which describes how objects behave. The laws of nature are, in fact, the laws of man.

A major effect of twentieth-century theoretical physics has been to stress that the so-called laws of nature are not absolute rules, but are general principles which describe not what will happen in a given case but the probability that an event will occur. Science provides not final certainty, but reduction in error; not perfect truth, but a better fit with reality. If science and absolute truth were synonymous, we would not have fashions and factions in science. Moreover, the belief — beloved to the television commercial — that scientific proof is the equivalent of truth is naïve. One can get to the right place for the wrong reasons. From headache pills to relativity, experimental tests at best confirm the prediction of a given theory, not the absolute validity of the theory itself. A person may be helped by a new drug, but if the same results are achieved by a placebo, the drug is indeed proven effective in achieving its purpose, but for reasons which may have nothing to do with its chemical formula.

Scientific imagination is generally underestimated by those whose acquaintance with science is limited to the formidable pages of a school text, or even worse, to the unintelligible blackboard squiggles which in the popular media are intended to indicate that "science is going on here." Far from being a minor faculty, scientific imagination may actually be required to transcend the evidence of the senses. In the long history of scientific thought it is a striking fact that not all "foolish questions" are asked by fools and that the counsels of so-called common sense are often a fertile source of nonsense and error. Things are not what they seem. The lifeless rock which lies so quietly in your hand, like the star "painted" on the dome of the evening sky, is actually a hive of ever-changing, whirling atoms. In a hundred years, or a million years, the form of both the rock and the star will be different.

Just as the great writer or artist finds meaning and inner beauty in the commonplace — the fly on the wall, the loaf of bread on the table — so the creative scientist may find significance in what others dismiss as self-evident. It has been said that one aspect of Einstein's genius was his childlike inability to understand the obvious. Einstein did not merely solve the problem of relativity; it took many years to discern what the problem was. For seven years he struggled to determine the velocity of light. Finally, according to his own account, he asked himself what turned out to be a crucial question: Did he really understand what he meant when he said that two events were *simultaneous* — if they occurred in two different places? To his surprise he discovered that he did not. Five weeks later, while holding his job in the Patent Office, Einstein completed the Special Theory of Relativity.

For centuries "common sense" demonstrated that the sun revolved about the earth, which itself remained stationary. For Copernicus, and his precocious predecessor Aristarchus, to consider a heliocentric hypothesis required a tremendous act of imagination and speculative thought in which aesthetic motives and a deep faith in the mathematical harmony of the cosmos played a considerable role. Copernicus did not arrive at his theory by measuring the movements of the earth. For example, stellar parallax (the shift one would observe in the apparent position of the stars if the earth moved) was predicted, but not observed until the nineteenth century. Eventually science succeeds in educating common sense and ideas which appear irrational at their inception become models of reason and good sense. Although many of us still find it difficult to believe that motion in a straight line is the physical equivalent of rest, as Galileo discovered, or that a rubber ball and a lead ball dropped from a height will hit the ground at the same time (assuming the absence of a resisting medium), no one today believes that angels transport the planets about the earth.

Modern theoretical physics appears to have stretched the human imagination to its old-fashioned limits, demanding that the mind acquire new dimensions if it is to make its way through the weird landscape which lies on the other side of the looking glass. In this world, space is curved, an electron behaves at the same time as a particle and a wave, and it is possible to predict the behavior of minute particles of matter which no physicist has ever seen, and to manipulate an atom which cannot be pictured as a concrete object in the imagination. For, after all, the atom is not "just like a little sun with its planets whirling around it." Interestingly, the new generation of scientists, not required to *un*learn the old model of man and the universe, adapts itself more readily to the rarefied abstractions of modern physics than did its predecessors.

In sweeping rapidly across the millennia of history and prehistory, it is impossible to account for the swirls, eddies, and countercurrents which churn beneath the advancing wave front of a general historical trend. Nonetheless, it may be said that in the broadest sense, until quite recently, the so-called ordinary man was spared the tainted gifts of the gods, but was in turn eliminated from the ranks of the creative. The scholarly bookworm with his musty intellect, and the "nonhuman" scientist with his stainless-steel mind, lost their creative prerogatives, while upon the artist, no matter how mediocre or uninspired, devolved the blemished crown of creativity. It would not be until the second half of the twentieth century that science and the humanist tradition would restore to Adam's descendants the birthright which was first surrendered or usurped, and subsequently misunderstood.

Is it necessary, we may ask, to understand the meaning of

creativity? Does it matter whether or not we label certain behavior creative? The great medieval artists, who would not
have dreamed of calling their work creative, nevertheless produced glorious masterpieces of religious art, and the actual
creative contributions of the scientist, thinker or artist exist no
matter what men choose to call them. A name is, among other
things, a definition and a symbol to which we entrust our
thoughts. It reflects our cultural values and in turn affects our
attitudes and ideas. What we define as *good, patriotic,* or *creative,* and designate as desirable goals, influences the behavior
of those who aspire to these conditions, or who are in a position to encourage or reward their fulfillment.

If creativity is acclaimed as a Good Thing, but the nature of
creative behavior is not understood, a young man may accept a
position as a "creative scientist," only to discover that he must
instead produce, publish, or perish. A young woman may answer an advertisement seeking "Creatives," only to find she is
wanted as a typist and errand girl in the hallowed precincts of a
publishing firm — at a salary diminished in return for the dubious perquisites of toil near the outposts of a creative environment. On the other hand, outstanding creative talent may atrophy or be corrupted in a society which misunderstands its
gifted children and misuses its gifted adults. If we applaud creativity, but disapprove either of the creator, or of the form in
which his gift manifests itself, then the creative, but nonconforming child may find himself in the bad graces of his elders,
and the talented composer may go unsung and unpaid.

In an era noted for its affluence, but notoriously bereft of
other major human satisfactions — noncreative as well as creative — those who have neglected or ignored their native gifts,
and whose way of work, or way of life has been reduced to dull,
mechanical computation, fail to comprehend what the Greeks
understood so brilliantly: that an abundance of spirit and intellect, not jingling coins, is the more enduring form of wealth.
The most sublime creation of the human spirit is neither a symphony nor a statue, but an original, authentic human life. Such

individuals will never know what Einstein called "the deep shudder of the soul in enchantment," but will certainly experience the tremors of the soul in emptiness and sorrow.

In the end, as members of society, we all pay the toll for those whom we have directly disfranchised, and for the disaffected and disenchanted who have unknowingly surrendered the inalienable birthright of our species: the right to create.

6. Psychology Goes Scientific

*I mean he'd keep telling you to unify and
simplify all the time. Some things you just
can't do that to.*

— J. D. SALINGER

TRADITIONAL RELIGION may struggle to redefine itself and uneasy theologians doubt and debate, but science and education
have for some time been welcomed as new gods in the American pantheon. Among those who worship at these shrines, it
matters to very few whether the reigning spirits are in residence. Their business is with the high priests of the cult. Their
devotion and respect are inspired by the material trappings of
faith: edifices, ritual equipment, and ceremonial jargon. What
they revere is neither learning nor science. Instead, they embrace a primitive faith in the magical power of "scientific research" to bestow the grace of truth even where none exists; of
"universal education" to testify to their democratic intentions;
and a naïve trust in the academic diploma to confer the keys to
the Kingdom of Success.

In the last quarter of the nineteenth century the two cults
merged. Education, in the slow process of becoming free, compulsory and universal, and afflicted with a variety of growing
pains which have yet to subside, beheld the exciting young science of psychology and found it fair indeed. For its part, experimental psychology looked up from its rats and puzzle boxes
and cast a covetous eye upon the copious supply of "human

young" cooped up in the classrooms of the expanding educational system, and happily nodded assent. Education and the immature and insecure science of psychology promptly eloped. It is not surprising that educational psychology, the offspring of this hasty union, was for many years as unwholesome a creed as the dogmas of its unstable parents, but one which now enjoyed the veneration due the scion of two major national divinities. Subsequently psychoanalysis immigrated to this country and offered to help about the nursery. That it was welcomed, then garbled and misused, added new dimensions to the debacle.

During this period experimental and educational psychology produced theoretical grotesqueries and sponsored unseasoned "laws of learning" which not only made no provision for imaginative, creative, and nonconforming behavior, but which unintentionally furnished the growing academic bureaucracy with precise methods for extirpating all but the most tenacious samples of the creative spirit. To make things worse, the definition of "giftedness" failed to include the creative child. One went to school to acquire the traditions of the past, not to explore the unknown. The ideal primary school pupil was, and still is, predictable, docile, neat, credulous — and preferably female. Since technically the gifted child meant the high-IQ child, studies of giftedness overlooked many creatively gifted students who had failed to win laurels in the IQ stakes. The concept of giftedness was limited to the metric of IQ, to the display of academic talents admired by the schools, and to overall academic performance and class standing. Many students who could not meet these requirements, but who would later to everyone's surprise make creative contributions, were effectively excluded from these studies. Also eliminated were so-called "late bloomers" — Winston Churchill being a classic example — and students whose gifts were unevenly distributed: the "peak-and-valley" student, brilliant in mathematics, a simpleton in French. The failure to recognize the creative child was partly to be charged to the early studies of giftedness which centered on the classroom, which also supplied the criteria for identifying giftedness.

The denial of creativity and the construction of learning theories which accounted for knowledge but not discovery, for memory but not innovation, was inherent in the rapid, haphazard, and premature development of psychology and education as new sciences. At the same time, social, historical, and economic pressures lured all but a few educators into the trap of brittle scientism.

Mass education, committed to the democratic but difficult idea of education for everyone, genuinely welcomed the assistance and authority of scientific psychology. Perennially defensive about its status as a profession, education eagerly donned the mantle of "science" and emerged as the dignified Science of Education, self-consciously devoted to measuring, counting, classifying, correlating, testing, comparing and "objectifying" all that came within its sweep.

Experimental psychology, aspiring to rank in the scientific "big time," concluded that it could not afford the embarrassment of a "mind" which still bore the ancient taint of that scientifically even more abhorrent entity, the soul. Eager to discard its country-cousin look, a major sector of experimental psychology jettisoned the mind, and with it the ingredients of the creative process.

In its early years experimental psychology was a science of *conscious* experience. Until Freud excavated the buried realms of the mind and forced the public to recognize the power of these subterranean precincts, a major storehouse and processing center of creative thought and imagination, familiar to Schiller and Goethe, to Wordsworth and Coleridge, was overlooked by the official science of the human psyche. The concept of creativity which in its historical odyssey had already acquired the stigma of nervous affliction, was eventually smuggled into psychology through the back door of neurosis and mental derangement — a distortion which is only now being corrected.

Finally, the spread of political democracy, the rapid development of industry, and the military needs of governments which were to wage two world wars within a quarter of a century, generated a political and social climate which bestowed collective freedom and human rights at the expense of personal freedom and individual rights. A compulsory public school system is an extraordinarily effective instrument for molding the children poured through its machinery to suit the nation's purpose. With some exceptions, the schools ignored, rejected, and systematically annihilated the creative birthright of the students under its jurisdiction. The progressive education movement which offered the creative child his only hope failed to deliver its promise. Afflicted with fatal uncertainty in its values and goals, in the absence of explicit methods for implementing its ideas, progressive education wobbled and finally miscarried. By the time the Progressive Education Association was dissolved in 1955, progressive education had become a term of contempt used to condemn educational innovation in all its forms.

It is unjust, however, to throw the entire blame upon the beleaguered public school system for buying educational theories and marketing an end product designed to please the taxpayers. We may scold educators and score learning theorists, but the schools of this period were only the instrument of a society which sponsored mass man and average woman, which praised adjustment and conformity, and which had neither funds, nor time and patience for what was single, unique, unpredictable, and creative.

"Creativity came close to being a lost cause in American education," wrote George Stoddard, Dean of the School of Education of New York University. The neglect of creativity during psychology's early development in this country, and the tragicomic misadventures of learning theory in the classrooms of this nation are not mere historical curios. Psychology today is broader in scope and wiser, but the social and economic forces which submerged the creative powers of millions of schoolchildren have substantially increased. From nursery school to graduate school the *word* creativity now titillates and delights. If, however, our "right" to create is to be recognized in practice, not merely in principle; if we hope to preserve the creative potential of our own and our nation's children, we must resolve the conflict between the creative individual and our educational philosophy.

Body and Soul

From its inception modern psychology carried about its neck the albatross of that ancient philosophical dualism, known as the mind-body problem.

> *What is mind? No matter!*
> *What is matter? Never mind!*

The brain, which Sherrington called a "great ravelled knot" of nerve cells, is a physical structure of atoms and molecules governed by the laws which govern all matter. Every nerve cell operates like every other nerve cell. Electrical impulses traveling along the highways and byways of the nervous system are standard stock, differing only in speed and intensity. The nerve cells of a mouse are not much smaller than ours, and among adult human beings the absolute weight of the brain is so variable that it is not a reliable guide to intelligence. The brain of a genius does not differ in appearance from an ordinary brain, and no one, thus far, has been able to demonstrate a difference in the basic structure of average and exceptional brains.

Without the brain our mental processes are inconceivable. Yet we do not know how electrical impulses in the brain are converted into the color, tone, and content of our emotions or thoughts, or even for that matter, into the images we see. We can trace the path of a nerve impulse bringing an inverted image from the retina, by way of the optic nerve, to the visual center in the cerebral cortex. But no one knows how an electrochemical disturbance occurring within the brain, buried beneath a vault of bone, is mysteriously projected beyond the surface of the brain and body to a point in space where it is perceived and recognized as a tree.

The distinction between mind and matter, postulated by Plato and solidified by Descartes, persists to this day as a profound, unsolved problem of science, and a perpetual headache to the science of the mind. Before Plato, Democritus, one of the founders of Greek atomism, in an attempt to explain the world without resort to unscientific notions of "purpose" or that future event known as "final cause," offered a straightforward, mechanistic theory in which one event is caused by another event which in turn is caused by an earlier circumstance. The atomists' theories bore a remarkable resemblance to those of modern science. The skeptical Sophists, on the other hand, had come to the seemingly irreverent conclusion that nothing could be known with certainty and that knowledge and ignorance were therefore indistinguishable. Plato, a philosopher in whom logic and mysticism were intermingled, criticized both the mechanical principles of the atomists, and the assertions of the more cynical of the Sophists.

Influenced by the ascetic Orphic mystery cults, Plato and his successors cleft body and soul, producing a dualism of mind and body in which the lowly body received the worst of the bargain. Split man, his immortal soul incarnate in a perishable container, set out on a long journey through philosophy, religion, and science, until no longer a philosophical curiosity, he eventually became a commonplace in popular thought. Plato would have thought them absurd, but today there are psychic researchers intent upon photographing the "human aura" in the process of transmigrating from its expendable body.

The Platonic soul as it appears in Plotinus and other Neoplatonists was an invisible, detachable, and immortal entity in which Ideas or Forms existed independent of the body and of experience. The world of the senses, so important to the empirical spirit of an earlier, more cheerful Greece, was relegated to the perishable body, which although tolerated, was regarded as an obstacle to truth. True knowledge of reality was not to be found in the misleading immediacy of physical objects and experience — in sight or sound, in pain or pleasure — but was revealed in contemplation. In his distrust of the physical world, and his denial of experiment and observation as a source of truth, Plato rejected that noble rationalism which had been the special genius of Greece. Science had no sooner awakened in the ancient world, than the Neoplatonists put it to sleep.

To the levelheaded, scientifically oriented Aristotle, the high-flying Platonic soul which appeared to get along better without its body, was a bizarre apparition. Although he continued to distinguish between mental and physical processes which now included mind as well as soul, Aristotle limited the authority of the soul. Practical reason was restored to the body and only "creative reason," which was immortal, remained in custody of the soul. Unlike Plato, Aristotle included movement and sensation in man's psychic life and welcomed the senses as an important source of knowledge. Aristotle's scientific approach with its attempt to reinstate the banished senses was premature. The dualism of mind and body which has haunted Western thought since antiquity was destined to deepen still further before its repair might begin.

Neoplatonism dominated the thought of the Middle Ages. As Greek civilization decayed and the chaos and misery of the Dark Ages descended upon Europe, a philosophical arrangement which promised eternal happiness upon release from the bondage of the wretched flesh must have appeared especially attractive. Ministering to a poor and illiterate populace for whom the world offered little cause for rejoicing, the Christian church fathers developed a psychology which denigrated the human body and denounced the wicked world it inhabited. The moderate asceticism of Plato's body-soul dualism was elaborated in the writings of the church fathers who vehemently abjured the sinful flesh. Perishable body and immortal soul were opposed. The realm of the body was relegated to the

Devil's jurisdiction, whereas the soul, the repository of mind, was assigned to God, whose will the faithful did not question. The mind, therefore, was not considered an appropriate subject for study. With the revival of Aristotle in the twelfth and thirteenth centuries, philosophical thought and Christian doctrine turned once again to the study of man's nature. But the Platonic dualism persisted, only to be further extended in the seventeenth century by Descartes, the great Renaissance philosopher and mathematician.

A devout Christian, yet a genius imbued with the new scientific spirit of inquiry, Descartes, with slight exception, denied all interaction between mind and matter. Ultimately, the Cartesian system provided two independent and parallel worlds which operated like clocks. Wound by God, the two clocks kept time with each other. Mechanical acts, controlled by physical laws, were left in the charge of the body which, without the mediation of mind, responded automatically to stimulation by means of reflex action. The mind attended to rational acts of judgment, choice, and will, and was overseer of imagination and feeling. The soul, whose point of contact with the body Descartes located in the pineal gland, buried deep within the recesses of the brain, was an inconsistent concept since events in the pineal gland were exempt from the otherwise ubiquitous laws of mechanics. Eventually the soul was eliminated by Descartes's followers.

Compared to Plato, Descartes's concept of a "rational act," or of thinking, is startling. Love is an act of reason, said Descartes, and depends upon one's calculation of the pleasure the beloved object may bring. Perception, which Plato rejected as misleading and which he unceremoniously dumped into the realm of the body, was restored to respectability in Descartes's system by the simple expedient of removing it from control of the deceptive senses. According to Descartes, perception was no longer "an act of sight, of touch, nor of imagination . . . but an intuition (*inspectio*) of the mind." It is through our powers of judgment that we see with our eyes.

Western thought has suffered from Descartes's decision to divide the house and move so much of our mental furniture exclusively into one room. But to Descartes's empiricism and ruthless commitment to a mechanistic hypothesis, we owe the initiation of a psychology based not on past dogma, but on direct observation of reality. Henceforth, thinking would involve not only reason, but all conscious processes, including sensation, perception, emotion, and will. True knowledge is given by God, said Plato, and — later — the church fathers. True knowledge derives from observable fact, said the skeptic and scientist Descartes, who began his philosophy by doubting everything he could possibly doubt and concluded in his famous *cogito* that the proof of his existence is inferred from the knowledge that he thinks.

After Descartes, philosophers would deny either man's soul or his substance, and some would attempt to straddle both terms of the antithesis, but there was now a new concern with the problem of how we know what we know. Moreover, the Cartesian separation of unanswerable metaphysical questions, such as the real nature of ideas, from those which could be profitably investigated by science, encouraged the advance of sensory physiology.

By the middle of the nineteenth century, philosophy and physiology converged upon studies of sensation. Encouraged by physicists who had discovered the relationship between stimulus and sensation, between sound waves and sound, physiologists were occupied with measurements of reaction time, of "sensation intensities," and with investigations of the stimulus-response mechanism in simpler mental processes. The triumphant progress of nineteenth-century science and technology engendered enthusiastic faith in "scientific fact" as the basis for human knowledge, and a disdain for all beliefs which lacked scientific credentials. It was inevitable that men would attempt to apply the extremely successful experimental and quantitative techniques of the laboratory sciences to the study of the human mind, previously the concern of the philosopher and theologian.

Experimental physiology, a scientific forebear of the new psychology, had made remarkable progress in studying the brain and nervous system. Studies of heredity, race, environment, especially the theory of evolution, emphasized that man, like monkeys and microbes, was an appropriate subject for science, and stressed man's psychological as well as his structural affinity with his prehuman relations. In the optimistic discipline of chemistry, scientists, employing John Dalton's atomic-theory recipe, were enthusiastically mixing and stirring their atoms and molecules with profitable results. Psychologists, following a parallel course, began to study the *elements* of conscious experience and the laws according to which these elements combined. Now psychology underwent a second housecleaning. The theoretical content of psychology was left undisturbed, but the method of armchair reasoning was abandoned. Squirming slightly, psychology embraced the methods and standards of science.

Psychology literally means the study of the soul or mind. To the founders of experimental psychology who antedated Freud, the mind they presumed to explore was the conscious mind. The word "mind" was disconcerting to a young discipline, seeking admittance to the prestigious circle of the natural sciences. Incorporeal and intangible, lacking size, shape, motion, and mass, the mind was not a proper subject for scientific inquiry. Upon discovering a ghost in his laboratory, the scientist elects either to ignore it or to redefine it, and proceeds to study its more accessible manifestations. In practice, therefore, psychology is the study of behavior and experience from which mind is then inferred. The major schools of psychology are actually distinguished by their assumptions concerning this elusive entity. Whether the mind is an assemblage of pulsing nerve cells, a process, or in some mysterious way more than any of these, the general problem of "mind," like that of "life" in biology, and "force" in physics, is not profitably investigated.

Auguste Comte, who founded the "science" of sociology, refused to admit psychology to his classification of the sciences, insisting that introspection — the technique of looking inward and describing one's own experiences — was not a suitable method for studying mental phenomena. The mind cannot think, and at the same time think about its own thoughts, said Comte. Therefore, there can be "nothing like scientific observation of mental phenomena." Comte's objection was fundamental. Referring to "the New Psychology," the great American psychologist William James described it as "a string of raw facts; a little gossip and wrangle about opinions." "This is no science," wrote the eloquent and humane James, "it is only the hope of a science."

In the late Victorian era, at a time when Freud was still a medical student, psychology declared its independence of philosophy and set out to establish itself as a branch of the life sciences. The first formal laboratory for experimental psychology was founded in 1879 by Wilhelm Wundt, a physician and professor of philosophy at the University of Leipzig. Wundt determined to free psychology of all metaphysical assumptions and to provide the purified discipline with the much-admired method of science. While the industrious Wundt was bent over his metronomes and flashing lights, the mind-body problem slipped into the laboratory behind his back. Its specter has remained there, to the consternation of generations of psychologists. Wundt's pioneering work in experimental psychology was primarily devoted to the study of conscious experience, and specifically to sensation, which the German professor confidently equated with "mind." Wundt considered sensation to be the only mental function capable of being reduced to the quantitative terms required for laboratory work. Pedantic, hardworking, and humorless, Wundt fussed over the details of his new science, providing it with coherence, rather than bold new theories. An indefatigable worker and a prolific writer, Wundt trained so many of the pioneers of the new science during his long life, that it has been said that much of the history of psychology consisted of rebelling against the limitations Wundt had established.

Across the seas in America, William James, the brilliant and urbane philosopher who taught the first course in experimental psychology at Harvard, had little sympathy with Wundt's limited notion of mental life and with the tedious Germanic tradition of using introspection to dissect "molecules" of conscious experience into "elements" of sensation. The scope of psychology, to James, was not to be reduced to describing in detail the taste of lemonade or the sound of a metronome. James was a scientist altogether remarkable for his integrity, compassion, and generosity of spirit. Despite his desire to be scientific, and at the expense of erecting a consistent psychological system of his own, James refused to give logic priority over human dignity, nor would he deny ethics or sacrifice part of human experience in return for the dubious security of a harmonious scientific system. More clearly than his successors, James understood the enormous difficulty of applying scientific standards to the study of human experience. Psychology as a natural science, he wrote, "means a psychology particularly fragile and into which the waters of metaphysical criticism leak at every joint."

William James wrote toward the end of the age of rationalism, intellectualism, and traditional piety. Just across the border lay the modern era, the age of irrationalism and determinism, of existential anguish and computer logic. Unfortunately, James's germinal work in the psychology of consciousness was destined to be overshadowed by the dramatic revelations of psychoanalysis — whose author James admired — and by the explosive pronouncements of American behaviorism. Even more regrettable was the smug disregard of a rare spirit of humility and creative courage, of a psychologist who refused to distort human nature in order to cram the rich diversity of mental life into the pigeonholes of a theory straining to remain consistent. Even the exact science of physics has managed to function with such inconsistent theories as the wave theory and the quantum theory of light. James preferred to leave his theories tentative, even contradictory, rather than to force that "foolish consistency" which Emerson had called "the hobgoblin of little minds" — a most felicitous attitude in a callow science. It is worth observing that endowed with a wide-ranging, flexible intellect, an ability to tolerate ambiguity and unanswered questions, and to refrain from imposing a premature and frangible order upon his subject, William James vividly exemplifies qualities of temperament characteristic of creative individuals.

Among the pioneers of modern scientific psychology, however, James was unique. No sooner had Wundt proclaimed psychology a science than the infant discipline found itself wrestling with the mind-body dualism inherited from its philosophical forebears. In an age which esteemed science and in which the foundations of orthodox piety and faith wavered, modern psychology felt that it could not tolerate an old-fashioned soul which mocked the laws of Newton, or human purposes which bore the opprobrium of divine or spiritual origin. By the first decade of the twentieth century, Wundt's experimental method of introspection, dependent upon the subjective reports of a mind observing itself, had fallen into disrepute. Likewise, James's once popular concept of the "self," so important in current studies of creativity, was quietly buried by hardheaded psychologists too insecure to admit an idea which somehow suggested a disembodied spirit.

To escape the blemish of the humanist's unscientific concern with value, and to avoid identification with religion, the unfledged science concluded that to be admitted to the select circle of the natural sciences, it must comport itself like the older members of the family. In its desire to express itself in the language of mathematics and statistics, to be quantitative and objective, and to discard the method of introspection, American psychology, for the most part, devoted itself to problems which permitted measurement in the laboratory, which could be displayed in overt behavior, and which, so it was believed,

could be objectively observed. Obviously, the danger of following these guidelines is that if exact quantification is a fundamental criterion, then those problems become important which
permit quantification. One might add that if consciousness was
to be ignored as unscientific, and if the experimental subject
did not have to talk about himself, crib and cage provided ideal
laboratory material.

With the eclipse of James and the decline of the broad-
minded spirit he represented, independent, unpredictable creative man was banished from the new science of psychology. For
the first part of this century studies of creativity were either
discouraged or obscured by a narrow, methodical psychology
which maintained that learning was simply conditioning or the
establishment of rigid chains of reflexes; that human motives
were "intra-organic stimuli," and that man was a collection of
particles which obeyed the laws of motion. It is ironic that at
the very time when physics and other branches of science had
come to the conclusion that the cosmos was not a machine, psychology assumed that man was.

Rats, Cats, and the Human Young

During the early years of this century, experimental psychology gave rise to two major schools of psychology, opposed to
Wundt and to each other. Behaviorism and Gestalt psychology
protested Wundt's method of introspection as unreliable and
unscientific. Both objected to Wundt's narrow preoccupation
with morsels of sensation, yet quarreled among themselves like
naughty children. The militant behaviorists pretended that the
Gestaltists did not exist. Classical Gestaltists returned the com-
pliment.

The early leaders of behaviorism, Edward L. Thorndike and
John B. Watson, proceeded to study conditioning and stimulus-
response behavior in babies and animals. Thorndike, whose
animals occasionally succumbed to unorthodox subjective
states such as annoyance and satisfaction, was a behaviorist in

emphasis, if not in allegiance. Watson was the movement's flamboyant promoter. Fashionable, bombastic, and arrogant in its conviction of scientific objectivity, behaviorism dominated American psychology, distorted "learning theory," and several decades after overstaying its welcome, lingered as a blight in the classrooms of this nation.

To Comte the mind-body problem was a hurdle which psychology could not surmount. Psychology cannot be a science because a mind cannot make a scientific study of itself. Conscious experience is not a proper study for science, agreed the behaviorists. We shall not depend upon the unreliable, subjective reports of human beings. Instead, psychology shall be confined to the study of *behavior* which, being open to public inspection, can be observed and measured in the laboratory. The words "mind" and "mental" were anathema to Watson, who eventually deserted his mindless psychology of conditioning for a career, not too illogically, in advertising. With this pronouncement, consciousness, that is, the "mind," from which Descartes had deduced his existence, was consigned to the realm of myth along with those other metaphysical undesirables, soul and spirit.

By starting with the double-entry system of mind and body, and then discarding half the book, the behaviorists did not solve their problem; they merely ignored it. Mental phenomena resistant to laboratory study do not disappear simply because they are unwelcome. Behaviorism, it is true, produced fruitful studies of the conditioned responses underlying many of our complicated learned acts, but mulish and misguided, it refused to concede its limitations. States of mind were not merely caused by bodily movements; they *were* bodily movements. Thinking was no longer the association of ideas, but a complex system of stimulus-response connections. Speech movements, rather than ideas or even speech, became the elements of thought. Someone observed that psychology, having first lost its soul, was now losing its mind.

Behaviorist principles, adopted by educational and child

psychology, flourished in a psychological climate which was already congenial. As early as 1900 American psychology expressed the national proclivity for practical results and its impatience with the more leisurely European tradition of reflection and speculation. The development of IQ testing and its associated statistical methods — for use in schools, clinics, and in the armed services — grew so rapidly that psychologists paid little attention to the nature of intelligence. Influenced by Darwin and Galton, then by James and Dewey, American psychology was concerned with the measurement and testing of individual differences and with objective studies of how individuals adjust and adapt to the environment. In a sad travesty of natural selection, however, "adapting" was soon to be equated with "giving in" and "giving up"; with conforming to the herd rather than altering to meet the vicissitudes of the environment.

Flavored with the pragmatism of Peirce and James, psychology was practical in its orientation. Enchanted by statistics and tests, psychology neglected the more subtle human endowments such as personality and independent behavior, thinking, imagination, and creative ability. It was willing to simplify mind and the design and purpose of laboratory experiments in the interest of scientific rigor. Imagination and originality are not likely to be found in studies of rats and pigeons, who, among other things, lack a history of creative achievement, nor will such qualities appear in objective tests not designed to elicit them.

Eventually the ardor and theoretical excesses of the early behaviorists were tempered, and today few psychologists adhere strictly to any one of the original psychological schools. Although behaviorism declined as an "ism" among psychologists, its more extravagant ideas, nevertheless, were by then deeply embedded in the school system where fossil doctrines often enjoy a busy and perverted afterlife.

The Return of the Mind

In the 1920's, with the tardy arrival of Gestalt psychology on these shores, American psychology received a transfusion of fresh blood. Gestalt psychology was founded by Max Wertheimer in Germany around 1912. Wertheimer's ideas, and those of his younger colleagues Köhler and Koffka, did not become fashionable here until the thirties, when the leaders of the movement, fleeing the Nazis, sought refuge in the United States. By that time Watsonian behaviorism with its stimulus-response jargon and its antiphilosophical bias was firmly entrenched.

The Gestaltists restored man's mind and dignity. Thinking and understanding, however inconvenient, were once again respectable occupations, and it was accepted that man might possess higher mental processes not present in animals. Gestalt animal experiments, based on the premise of a thinking, perceiving mind, enlisted the services of the most intelligent non-human animal, the ape. These experiments, like those of the behaviorists, were prejudiced in favor of the postulates they purported to test. But if we are required to use animals to help write human psychology, rather a cogitating chimpanzee than a maze-running rat — and preferably a psychologist who is neither.

The behaviorists had asked: How does the organism act? The Gestaltists asked: How does it perceive? How does it detect meaning? And finally: How does it think? The word Gestalt means *form* or *configuration*. The Gestalt psychologists maintained that the parts do not determine the whole, but on the contrary that the whole determines the parts. We perceive an entire configuration first, and only then its individual components. A song is identified by its melody, not by its specific notes. Transposed to a different key, where the notes are certainly different, the song is still recognized by the relationship of the notes to one another. Similarly, the illusion of movement in the motion picture is not present in any of the separate frames of the film.

In a larger sense, Gestalt psychology was a protest against atomism, the explanation of wholes by their constituent parts, which since the time of the pre-Platonic philosophers had served successfully as the method of science. To the Gestaltists it was immaterial whether the despised "irreducible bits" or "atoms" of experience and behavior were Wundtian "bundles" of sensation, or the chained reflexes of the behaviorists. According to Gestalt doctrine, psychology must proceed from the complex to the elementary, studying patterns of behavior and experience, rather than their single elements. In its rejection of analogies with outmoded atomic theory, and in its stress upon understanding the whole structure, the Gestalt psychologists had at last brought psychology abreast of trends in modern field physics and biology. Interestingly, Wertheimer was a friend of Einstein's, and Köhler, who had been a pupil of Max Planck, was always proud of his knowledge of modern physics.

Gestalt psychology tended to ignore the role of learning and memory in organizing the patterns of perception and was more successful in the area of visual perception where it had originated. Furthermore, if the behaviorists found their patron in Democritus, the Gestaltists eventually delivered themselves into the philosophical embrace of Plato. In trying to dodge the linked associations of stimulus-response theory, Gestalt psychology assumed pre-given, primary models of reality — *Gestalten* — which are not acquired by learning, but are latent in the human brain. Plato's metaphysical Forms had returned.

Gestalt psychology was never accepted in this country as a final system. However, once it had battered down the stronghold of behaviorism, its ideas were enthusiastically adopted by other psychological schools — including the behavioral. Gestalt concepts provided the necessary leavening for stimulus-response theories, and were finally incorporated into contemporary "cognitive" psychologies which are more interested in man's inner mental processes, than in his outward acts.

Despite theoretical imperialism and internecine squabbling, psychology gradually began to recognize the scope of the task it had undertaken in studying the enigmatic, singularly endowed creature who knows who he is, but does not know how he knows it. Freud's explorations of the irrational, unconscious mind could no longer be ignored. Cultural anthropology returned from its forays into primitive cultures beyond the European pale with evidence that much of what is considered inalterable human nature was the result of local fashion and social environment. Finally, psychologists discovered modern physics. Relativity theory pointed out that observations are relative to one's frame of reference. Field theory suggested the fallacy of neglecting the environment. Not only does the environment help to shape behavior, but in the absence of the natural environment, experimental results may be spurious. Tests of individual differences, for example, are an important part of our social machinery. Yet they are valid only to the degree that they represent the actual environment. Except in the contrived world of the laboratory, cats do not escape from boxes by licking themselves or by pulling pieces of string. It has been observed that in real life food is not always found to the right or to the left, nor does a reward always appear when you press the right lever. When a young child throws a penny into the wishing well and his wish comes true, he believes the good fairy inside the well is responsible. When a rat collects a tidbit of cheese because it has successfully operated a series of levers, the good fairy this time is the psychologist.

Learning Theory

The highest form of learning is the discovery of something new. Yet creativity was excluded from the learning theory which paraded from the behaviorists' laboratories and confidently installed itself in the classrooms of the growing public-school system. The excesses of Watsonian behaviorism are behind us, but more sophisticated behavioral theories of learning

thrive, and the educational problems conducive to their acceptance continue to increase.

Learning and its preservation as memory are the raw materials from which the previously stored input of the brain is
summoned and rearranged to reveal relationships which for the
thinker are new. It is not necessary that we be conscious of the
logic underlying our conclusions, or even that our thoughts be
reasonable and our reasoning logical. The flow of images and
feelings through our dreams, and the dissolving, kaleidoscopic
patterns of fantasy or idle reverie are also forms of thinking.
Whether puzzling over mathematical problems or spinning
dreams, a problem may be solved, a discovery made, or memories are sorted and selected to produce fresh designs. Much of
what we consider thinking is not thinking at all. Instead of saying, "I can't think of her name," it would be more accurate to
say, "I can't remember her name," for in this case there is no
arrangement of memory, only the recall of a fact.

Although words play an important role in expressing our
inner thoughts, not all thinking, or even reasoning need be
verbal. Some people are primarily verbal thinkers; others may
rely on complex visual or auditory symbols as well. A study of
the working habits of creative mathematicians, conducted by
Jacques Hadamard, revealed that at the crucial stages of their
creative work, the mathematicians did not rely on mental
words, or on any form of precise mathematical symbolism.
Visual images, vague auditory signs, or even muscular sensations were commonly reported as their units of thought. Referring to his own scientific thought processes, Einstein once told
Max Wertheimer, "I very rarely think in words at all." In reply
to Hadamard's query, Einstein wrote that "more or less clear"
visual images and muscle sensations were the psychical entities
involved in the "combinatory play" of his thought mechanisms. Hadamard himself observed that the advantage of such
visual pictures is that being naturally vague, they "lead . . .
without misleading." For whenever a thought is captured in
words, a precise, inflexible backbone penetrates the rich, in-

choate blur of imagination's art. Hoisted on its convenient mast, the idea can be grasped, examined critically, and shown to the world. But in the process, part of the idea may be lost. Sometimes it is the residue which contains the truth.

Not all thoughts expire the moment they are set in words. The thought may be honed and shaped in the conversion to tangible form; or the idea may be immanent in the words which carry it. Moreover, the higher primates, particularly man who is endowed with articulate speech, also learn by thinking. The child may learn by a process of trial and error that fire burns. Next he learns that the word "hot" symbolizes the disagreeable experience. Later when informed that although they may emit no flame, the radiator and stove are also "hot," he concludes without further experiment that they are to be avoided. In this case the conclusion drawn from the reasoning process, by which cause and effect are related, is itself the lesson learned.

What is "learning theory"? As yet, no one has seen the multiplication tables entering the molecular storage vaults of a cerebral nerve cell; no one has observed a habit recording the pattern of its trace along the neural highways of our nervous system. Since we cannot observe directly the process by which we learn to hold a pencil, to kiss, or to recognize a letter of print no matter how varied its typeface, learning must be inferred from modifications in behavior. The learning theorist then develops a hypothesis to explain the invisible transactions responsible for the observed behavioral changes.

Psychologists generally define learning as a change in behavior due to experience. Not included in this definition are activities attributed to inborn responses, maturation, or temporary influences such as drugs and fatigue. The need to deduce learning from performance, a practical laboratory requirement, arbitrarily excludes from learning those experiences which do not reveal themselves in some form of action or expression. Referred to as "latent learning" and "incidental learning," these dormant learning experiences are familiar to psychologists and have been studied experimentally. Latent learning in a rat may consist of knowledge of a maze which is not revealed until the animal has good reason (food) to hurry from entrance to exit.

Whereas it is expedient to infer learning from behavior, it is an error to identify learning with behavior. Failure to perform when tired or intoxicated does not prove that the individual has not learned, or has forgotten what he will clearly remember when he has recovered. On the pedagogic scene, for example, the concept of latent learning was, with rare exception, either unknown, unwelcome, or regarded as unserviceable.

The child who reads a book but who has no chance to demonstrate what he has learned has not learned anything according to the definition which insists that learning *is* behavior. The proof of learning is the examination, the recitation, even the mindless "research" report copied from the encyclopedia. The science student who has digested his textbook and his lecture notes and who presents a laboratory manual filled with correct answers is presumed to have "learned" science and is rewarded with a good grade. All too often what the student has really learned is not science, but a lesson in expediency. Science, he is led to believe, is concerned with the verification of accepted truths, rather than the discovery of new truths; science is drudgery and skillful cheating; experiments rarely work out the way they are supposed to and should there be a discrepancy between the textbook and his own data, the latter are never to be trusted. This gratuitous lesson is not what his instructors had intended to teach. Yet the proof of the perverted lesson is demonstrated only when the disillusioned student turns his back on the dreary subject forever. By that time his teachers are busy teaching the wrong lessons to new students, unaware of the nature of their spurious achievement.

Not only does the learning theorist infer learning from behavior, but in many experiments he is compelled to deduce human behavior from animal behavior. The outskirts of the solar system, the interior of the atom, and the floor of the ocean, are more accessible than the living organ each of us carries locked in his skull.

Since science requires systematic, verifiable information, artificial laboratory study is necessary. Life in its natural state is too complicated, and human behavior is subject to a vast assortment of slippery variables difficult to control in an experiment. The laboratory is, however, an unnatural environment, and the tangled, troublesome variables — interest, anxiety, stress, ambition, values — represent the circumstances which have brought one creature to the laboratory in search of knowledge and left the other in the experimental cage. Theories which prosper in the hothouse atmosphere of the laboratory may not survive outside. Laboratory animals can only be induced to perform on command — running mazes, pecking circles, operating levers — in return for a reward. Because internal motives such as curiosity or pleasure in learning do not easily lend themselves to laboratory study, it appeared that the motivation for learning is external. In transferring theories based on animal experiments to children in the nursery and classroom, the architects of learning theory myopically assumed that children think and act like laboratory animals — and in the case of the behaviorists, not very bright ones. Referring to Harvard behaviorist B. F. Skinner's two influential books, *The Behavior of Organisms* (1938) and *Science and Human Behavior* (1953), Hilgard writes, "neither title betrays that the precise data derive largely from experiments on rats and pigeons." For all its haunting resemblance to us, the ape's intelligence does not exceed that of a four-year-old child, and no one has ever taught an ape to talk. The gap between man and even the most intelligent beast remains formidable and irrevocable.

The behaviorists and stimulus-response theorists regarded learning as the acquisition of rigid chains of reflexes. They found support for their theories in the bar-pressing, circle-pecking talents of hungry or confined rats, cats, and pigeons, despite that in a less absurd environment, these animals do not "solve problems" by operating levers or pulling strings. Left to their own devices, pigeons have better things to do than play table tennis or the piano — and they do them better. The Gestaltists, whose theories postulated an act of knowing and thinking, entrusted the burden of their experiments to the highly intelligent chimpanzee. In comparing the work of the American stimulus-response king, Edward Thorndike, to that of the German Gestalt man, Wolfgang Köhler, Bertrand Russell once observed, "Animals studied by Americans rush about frantically, with an incredible display of hustle and pep, and at last achieve the desired result by chance. Animals observed by Germans sit still and think, and at last evolve the solution out of their inner consciousness."

The two leading brands of learning theory are *stimulus-response* theories and *cognitive* or field theories. In addition, several theories have been postulated which do not fall into either category. There are, however, no learning theories which can be taught with confidence. From the time a stimulus arrives in the sensory area of the brain informing us that we are hungry to the departure of another impulse from the motor region, resulting in a trip to the refrigerator (or a decision to refrain in deference to diet), the cerebral proceedings are veiled in mystery. How the psychologist explains the unknown cerebral events — thinking, or something like it — determines the learning theory to which he gives his allegiance.

Stimulus-response, or "switchboard theory," hypothesizes that the brain acts as a telephone exchange, providing rigid connections between the incoming stimulus and the outgoing response. Cognitive theory, an extension of Gestalt psychology, utilizes the field concepts of physics, and infers a flexible process which integrates the hunger-refrigerator (or no-refrigerator) sequence. To the cognitive psychologist the essence of understanding is not mechanical, but involves an intelligent act of knowing. Whether we begin at one end of town or the other, we find our way home, says the cognitive psychologist, because we *know* where we live. The switchboard school says we get home by *trial and error*. The cognitive psychologist maintains we learn facts, or "cognitive structures." The stimulus-response psychologist insists we learn habits.

Learning theorists differed not only in their definitions of what is learned, but they bickered about the way the learner solves a new problem. The characteristic explanation offered by stimulus-response psychologists is that problems are solved by trial and error. Stimulus-response partisans are not discomforted by the complex behavior the cognitive school attributes to "knowing." The stimulus-response problem solver finds the answer to an algebra problem, or is propelled home from the outskirts of town, by means of the chained links of habit patterns appropriate to his task. If these fail, he constructs new habit patterns using slow and fumbling trial-and-error procedures. The trial-and-error learner attempts many solutions, discards those which are unsuccessful (providing life and limb are not lost), and retains the adequate solution in his repertoire of habits. Through repetition and practice we learn to walk and talk and to tie our shoelaces, and it is in this way that our conditioned reflexes and habits are formed, including the unseen linkages which are probably the origin of prejudice, irrational fears, and many of our inexplicable intuitions.

Learning by *insight*, or "understanding what to do," is central to classical Gestalt and other cognitive psychologies. Essentially, this is a method in which the subject, when necessary, restructures the problem according to his understanding of its basic requirements. He then summons pertinent experiences and arranges them in new and useful relationships, assuming, of course, that such relationships exist. A rat required to press a lever in order to feed itself, cannot sit back and "figure out" what to do, because from the rat's point of view, the solution to the problem is enormously difficult. Arbitrarily designed by the experimenter, it has nothing to do with the causal world of rat experience. In this case, as the Gestaltists were quick to point out, the rat is forced to use trial-and-error methods until it stumbles on the psychologist's secret.

Learning by insight can be very rapid, and is facilitated by the use of language which permits man to lock complex thoughts and ideas in the symbolic form of words. The ability to perceive resemblances is fundamental to the process of thought, from its most primitive to its most exalted levels. The ape climbing on a box it has pushed underneath a bunch of bananas hung high out of reach has discovered the sticklike "reaching" properties of the box, which does not otherwise resemble a stick. Galileo, observing a lamp swinging in the Cathedral of Pisa and thinking of the oscillations of a pendulum, and Darwin, pondering the Galapageian finches and Malthus's essay on population, solved their respective problems by discovering the resemblance between ostensibly unrelated concepts. In an extraordinary scientific insight, Einstein pointed out the relationship among such seemingly disparate phenomena as matter, energy, motion, and time. The moment of insight, the bright idea or brainstorm, is sometimes called the "Aha" or "Eureka" experience — the latter in honor of Archimedes, who according to legend discovered the solution to the problem of measuring the amount of gold in King Hiero's crown while watching the water level rise in his bath as he sat down in his tub. Having found what he sought, he ran naked through the streets toward his home shouting "Eureka!" The flash of insight, however, is no indication of superior intelligence since the solution may be wrong.

The relationship between learning by insight, or inductive inference, and the clumsier trial-and-error method is not always clear, nor is the distinction between the two as absolute as their proponents believed. Frequently the methods combine. Mistakenly identifying trial-and-error with conditioned-reflex theory, classical Gestalt theorists rejected the hit-or-miss method of learning. The behaviorists presented their animals with problems which were too difficult, forcing them to employ trial-and-error techniques. The Gestaltists, on the other hand, chose tasks which were but a step away from solution, thus suggesting that problem-solving by insight occurs in a single flash of understanding.

Learning processes are actually a combination of understanding and habit formation. The moment of insight may be preceded by many trials, whereas trial-and-error learning may involve the manipulation of thoughts as well as physical objects and may be controlled rather than blind. The trial-and-error learner is not simply bumping around in the dark. The chimpanzee makes several tentative attempts to move the box before discovering the correct solution; the artist makes preliminary sketches of his work; the writer writes and revises, and even the genius experiments with possibilities. One need only recall Kepler's years of misery, travail and blunder. Edison's trial of one substance after another in his search for a filament for the incandescent light bulb was not a random search. The careful testing of a scientific hypothesis may require controlled, planned trial-and-error methods.

The muscle-gland psychology of orthodox behaviorism overshadowed the work of the cognitive theories, although both Watson and his doctrines were considered controversial. Having purged psychology of its mental paraphernalia and of its philosophical ambiguities, behaviorism produced a learning theory which dismissed man's capacity for thought, and denied the right to create. According to Watson, just as the rat manipulates variables until it solves its problem, the poet manipulates words "shifting them about until a new pattern is hit upon." Watson insisted that neither rats nor poets, painters or dress designers, have a "picture in mind" of what it is they wish to achieve.

In the more sophisticated behavioral systems of Skinner, Guthrie, and Hull, creativity is still explained away or dismissed. Like Watson, Skinner, who is famed for his theories of operant conditioning and for the application of his doctrines to the teaching machine, considers problem solving a matter of manipulating variables. Guthrie regards originality as a lucky accident and therefore beyond the sphere of science. According to Clark Hull, the difference between man's accomplishments, including his verbal and mathematical productions, and those of lower animals, is one of quantity rather than quality. In this view human beings are just bigger, busier rats.

With its slick jargon, its trumpery predictions, and its optimistic but innocent faith in science to remodel human affairs, behaviorism during its heyday in the twenties made sparkling copy for journalists and delighted the general public. Watson had dismissed all instincts except for that enduring trio — sex, anger, and fear. A devout environmentalist, he retained the fatalistic idea of heredity only to the extent that the genetic system was required to assure our physical presence, including the muscles which had become mind. A younger generation of psychologists, mesmerized by the gospel of science, succumbed to visions of a new scientific era in psychology. Watson had boasted that given complete control over its environment and conditioning, he could train a normal healthy infant to be anything from a doctor to a thief, "regardless of his talents, penchants, tendencies, abilities, vocations and race of his ancestors."

Heady with the magical power of science, psychology had lost its head.

7. Adventures in Education Land

*Those who cannot remember the past
are condemned to repeat it.*
— GEORGE SANTAYANA

Learning Theory Goes to School . . . and Fails

THE AMERICAN SCHOOLS of the nineteenth century, dominated by Calvinist traditions, were thoroughly dedicated to drill, rote learning, and to breaking the child's will for the good of his soul. It was assumed that the untutored child's nature was undesirable and that childhood was totally without virtues of its own. Children were regarded as wicked and wild, and at the same time, as passive receptacles for the teacher's wisdom. The teacher's task was to "mold" the child to the prescribed form. Dickens, Carlyle, and Rousseau are among the many authors who have described the miserable plight of children fallen prey to vicious tyrants and drumbling, brokenhearted pedants. But education was then relatively haphazard and much of it was optional. Before long, mass compulsory education, vested with the authority of science, would affect a majority rather than an elite group, and would become a more powerful and cogent factor in shaping the national character.

In the tumultuous years which followed the Civil War, our expanding industrial nation rapidly outgrew its decrepit school system. The struggle for free public education, begun in the Jacksonian era, dramatically accelerated. As a result the character of the schools, except in the agricultural South, was basically altered. Despite the opposition of the upper classes, of business, and of angry churchmen who railed against "godless" schools, the needs of a growing urban, industrial society could not long be denied, and resistance to free primary and secondary schools dissolved. Industry required literate workers. Waves of immigration brought to America the poor and oppressed of other lands, swelling the population and increasing the number of children who had to be assimilated, educated, and processed as citizens. The extension of suffrage, the fight to abolish child labor, and general humanitarian and democratic sentiment contributed to the ultimate triumph of compulsory education at public expense.

It soon became apparent that public education was neither a menace to the moral and American foundations of society, nor a threat to capitalist enterprise. The public schools preached sound morality and reverence for the American flag, extolled the virtues of democracy and the mores of the business world, and emphasized the general needs of the community and the nation. In science and economics controversial issues were avoided. The curriculum tiptoed around Darwin and his uncouth apes. Civics and mathematics, history and music were not taught for their intrinsic value, but as a means of training future citizens to "deal with life" — specifically American life. Art and music were cultural fripperies and literature was proper and polite. The "recitation method" of rote learning — memorization and reciting answers in class — was the standard means of instruction. The authority of teacher and text was absolute, and obedience, politeness, and neatness were then, as they still are, cardinal virtues. Teachers who encouraged independent thinking and free inquiry were the exception; the aggressive mind, being disruptive, was unwelcome.

With the passage of compulsory education laws and child labor statutes, high school enrollment began to double every decade. In 1870 there were approximately 80,000 students in public high schools; in 1900 over half a million. In 1930, four and a quarter million students were enrolled in high school, approximately the number of students attending college in 1964. Accustomed to educating an aristocratic group destined to enter select occupations, the schools found themselves in the unenviable position of teaching children regardless of their ability to learn or their desire to be in school. The dropout rate soared. That schools were increasingly isolated from the life for which the young supposedly were being prepared did little, as John Dewey recognized, to inspire students with delight and devotion to their studies.

To meet this crisis educators concluded that the antiquated school system required thorough reorganization in accordance with the rigorous criteria and efficient methods of science. Obviously an alliance with the psychologies of learning and child development would be advantageous. Not so clear, however, was the means by which education was to convert to the stringent requirements of scientific discipline. Born of need, enthusiastic and ambitious, the new science of education suffered from an embarrassing shortage of scientific method and a dearth of reliable information about how children learn. This serious defect was quickly buried beneath mountains of statistics, data, charts and other measurements disguised in mathematical-statistical double-talk.

For nearly half a century Edward Lee Thorndike, the energetic precursor of behaviorism and the father of stimulus-response learning theory, reigned as the high priest of American education. As one of the founders of the scientific movement in education, and not a man to shilly-shally, Thorndike tackled education's problems with straightforward good sense adulterated nonetheless with grievous fallacies. Despite the rise of competing theories, America's classrooms were dominated first by Thorndike's mechanical trial-and-error learning concepts, and later by a bizarre hybrid which resulted when Thorndike's learning theories were crossed with a bowdlerized form of progressive education. In his forty years at Columbia University's Teachers College, Thorndike trained the vast ma-

jority of the state school superintendents and a large propor-
tion of the urban school superintendents. Thorndike's success
may be attributed in part to his remarkable drive and enormous
productivity, but equally to the presence of a national market
ripe for his labors.

Thorndike made important contributions to the psychology
of learning, but to the cause of creativity in education his theories were a blight. The American psychologist was a contemporary of Ivan Pavlov, the celebrated pioneer of modern learning
theory. Pavlov regarded conditioning as the fundamental principle of learning and the conditioned reflex as the basis of all
higher neural activity. The stern, unbending Russian physiolo-
gist, however, scorned the "zoopsychologists" for their unscientific point of view, ignored the subject of motivation, and forbade the use of psychological terms in his laboratory. While
Pavlov was ringing bells to make hungry dogs salivate, Thorndike studied conditioning and stimulus-response behavior in
animals and came to somewhat similar conclusions. Unlike
Pavlov, however, whose bailiwick was the digestive system and
whose experiments dealt with involuntary physical functions,
Thorndike and the psychologists who followed him were concerned with conditioning the purposeful, motivated behavior
involved in solving problems. Classical (Pavlovian) conditioning, as opposed to *operant* conditioning, an extension of
Thorndike's theories, is an experience which "happens" to the
subject. The animal or person is passive and the response (salivating when a bell rings; applying the brakes as the light turns
red) is acquired without any effort on the part of the subject.
Thorndike's animals, on the other hand, worked for reward,
participating actively in the laboratory games invented by their
master.

When Thorndike made the transition from problem solving
in animals to the learning problems of the two-legged subjects
chewing their pencils in the nation's schools, he casually dismissed millions of years of cerebral evolution. Required to
solve synthetic laboratory problems, Thorndike's animals, we

may recall, proved rather stupid pupils. Presumably the babies and children in Thorndike's research were destined to blunder through life, opening and closing doors, learning spelling and geography with nothing better than cats' brains in their heads — and not even the respectable faculties of good mouse-hunting cats, but the insulted cerebral organs of poor, silly puzzle-box cats. Thorndike's conception of a science of education, therefore, although practical and efficient, was seriously vulnerable.

To a school system supported by public funds, under the control of local communities, and required to account for itself in regular so-much and how-much reports, Thorndike's statistical science of education was a blessing. It facilitated the measurement and presentation of its pupils' progress in tidy form, eliminated the teacher's subjective evaluation, and provided the certification of "scientific research" for its methods. Polite, obedient children who could spell, write a neat hand, and recite poems, dates, and the multiplication tables provided a clear and visible answer to parents who asked: What are we getting for our money? The youth who questioned the catechism of American history, the precepts of American business, or who muddled through school like Darwin, Bismarck, Einstein, Franklin Roosevelt, or Churchill, would not have appeared a profitable investment to the ordinary taxpayer.

Committed to the noble and democratic idea of educating everyone at public expense, mass education was also dedicated to economy and to mediocrity. The classroom was geared to the average student, while the bright, the creative, as well as the backward student suffered. The extensive use by the military services of group IQ testing, as opposed to individual testing, furnished a precedent for the schools. In the indiscriminate rush to apply the magic test numbers to all sorts of decisions involving children, the intelligence quotient was sadly abused. The culturally deprived or culturally different, the emotionally disturbed, the nonverbal, the creative, the slow or reflective were all penalized by the test which presumed to measure innate capacity.

The new science of education was greeted enthusiastically by members of the teaching profession. Prior to this it was assumed that anyone could teach school provided he or she had nothing better to do. Teaching, occasionally art, was more often underpaid drudgery, and teachers, particularly the ladies who presided over the primary schools, were held in low esteem. Their salaries the target of public penny-pinching, their professional and even their private lives, subject to public prejudice and caprice, teachers were delighted by the improvement in their status when they became educators. Their once plebeian occupation was now embellished with the impressive patois of science and statistics. Unfortunately their command of argot and methodology was superior to their knowledge of the subjects they taught.

Harassed and overworked, teachers were understandably grateful for assistance in the difficult task of handling the academic and disciplinary problems of unwilling or bored students. They welcomed teaching methods and classroom attitudes sanctioned by "scientific research" and were thankful for tests which helped to winnow the smart from the stupid. Age and grade standards were established, educational testing accelerated, and increasingly, essay questions were replaced by objective-type examinations which could be "standardized," "validated," and scored by machine.

A one-man educational industry, Thorndike was the answer to the average teacher's prayers. He supplied learning theories, laws of learning, textbooks, word lists, handwriting scales, dictionaries, methods for teaching arithmetic and spelling, vocational guidance tests, and intelligence tests. His output was prodigious, his energy extraordinary, and as the dean of American educators, his influence vast. Thorndike's contemporaries, Charles H. Judd at the University of Chicago and Lewis M. Terman at Stanford University, and their students in turn helped to carry the gospel of scientific education to schools and educational departments throughout the country.

The Laws of Learning

Impressed by the methods of the physical sciences, Thorndike enunciated the "specificity doctrine," which states that the educator must know specifically what he is doing and must then verify his results. Since, according to Thorndike, learning consists of forming specific stimulus-response connections, the teacher must know exactly what is being taught, and the pupils must demonstrate clearly what has been learned. Otherwise the practice required to form habit patterns may strengthen the wrong bonds and praise or censure may be misdirected. At the command of a ringmaster, whose wisdom he was not to question, the student was required to demonstrate the result of the learning venture in recitation, reports, and examinations. The dutiful student memorized what was taught, never wondered what was withheld, learned to quote rather than to think, and studied in order to pass tests and earn high grades.

The specificity doctrine applies to laboratory experiments, and is effective in teaching spelling, word definitions, and basic computing skills in which the answer is always the same. The mechanical concept of specificity is useless, however, in teaching such subjects as creative writing or literary criticism where there is neither a single "correct" answer nor a specific blueprint for obtaining the result. Specificity is also seriously misleading in the case of the student who attempts an imaginative and valid solution to an algebra problem, yet obtains a wrong answer.

Inherent in this doctrine is the repressive lesson that tests, college entrance examinations, intelligence and aptitude tests, are not the occasion to question the questions or to experiment with original thinking, because the System recognizes the correct answer but makes no allowance for the quality of the thought processes involved. By the time pupils emerge from twelve years in the dark tunnel of school, little is left of the bright gifts they brought with them on the day they entered. Imagination has atrophied, curiosity and the love of mental adventure are suppressed. Rather than learning to ask meaningful questions about things they do not understand, the timid conceal their ignorance in silence, while the artful and adept learn to ask questions designed to impress the teacher or to show off what they already know.

When the classroom is converted to a giant laboratory in which students are required to demonstrate that specific behavior which is regarded as the only valid proof of learning, then learning shrinks to memorizing facts, acquiring mechanical aptitudes and parroting information provided by the teacher. Most children comply all too easily with this formula. Independent thought demands effort and motivation and the child's natural impulses are easily inhibited. In a rigidly conceived science of learning there is no room for exploration, experiment, and innovation. These qualities can be encouraged, but they cannot be programmed and controlled. Science is precise; education imprecise. With blinkers on their eyes, the new educators went forth in smug pursuit of "scientific objectivity." As a result they overlooked the various forms of latent learning. The unspoken lessons of the classroom — attitudes, values, style — and the unclassified knowledge obtained through play and exploration may not be expressed immediately in measurable behavior. What could not be tangibly demonstrated did not exist.

Thorndike's conception of the role of reward and punishment in learning was distorted by his animal experiments and his myopic preoccupation with the proprieties of scientific rigor. In his famous Law of Effect, Thorndike anticipated the principle of reinforcement, the keystone of subsequent conditioned-response theories, and a principle fundamental to the development of "programmed learning" and the teaching machine. The Law of Effect states that the strength of a connection is increased when accompanied by a "satisfying state of affairs," and decreased in the presence of an "annoying state of affairs."

That people will repeat behavior for which they are rewarded is hardly a sparkling discovery. But, according to Thorndike, kind words and food pellets affect all nerve cell connections, including those which merely happen to be in the vicinity of the rewarded bond. Furthermore, this neural "goodwill" is achieved directly and mechanically, unmediated by ideas. Thorndike's external rewards helped the child to distinguish the right from the wrong performance but, beyond this, bore no inner relationship to the activity concerned. Bypassed and snubbed, the individual existed only as a housing for his stimulus-response circuits. Later the word "reward" with its quaint aroma of subjective pleasure was replaced by the no-nonsense term "reinforcement." The more extreme behaviorists eliminated the fuzzy idea of motivation altogether.

No one doubts that learning improves when it produces a "satisfying state of affairs." Jerome Bruner observes that the real issue lies in where one locates the reward or reinforcement. To Thorndike and his followers, reward was a bonus appended to the work. External rewards — high grades, diplomas, college admission, praise — are not the only incentives to performance. The range of Thorndike's vision was blocked by the basic premises of his own theory. A psychologist devoted to a learning doctrine which insists that learning proceeds by stamping-in arbitrary habit patterns is not likely to discover that learning is not in itself sterile, but is capable of generating its own motivation and rewards. Interest or pleasure in what one is doing is a satisfaction only to be found in work which has meaning to the worker.

Behaviorist learning theory strangled creativity in the harsh rigging of its constructs. It overlooked important positive internal motives and drives such as curiosity, the urge to explore, joy in learning, and the desire to achieve competence and to emulate a model. Classical Gestaltists also used external rewards in their experiments, but the Gestaltists regarded behavior as intelligent striving toward a meaningful goal and not as an exercise in "need-reduction." During the first part of this century, however, educational practices were dominated by imperious behaviorist doctrines which denied that the child's mind participated in the learning process, and to which the idea that learning might yield its own rewards was entirely alien.

Thorndike and the behaviorists regarded the motivation for learning as either external or nonexistent. In the nineteen thirties and forties other psychologies, including the Freudian, reinforced this gloomy portrait with the assumption that the motivation for all behavior was negative: the diminution of stimulation and excitement and the reduction of biological drives. Life was a joyless struggle toward some bland, tensionless oblivion.

Since 1950, studies of curiosity and exploratory drives have compelled psychologists to revise this lugubrious estimate of human and animal nature. It is suggested that in addition to external pressures we learn because we require information about our environment, and because clashes between processes in the central nervous system demand it: we learn because we must. A hungry rat will pause in his pursuit of food to investigate a novel feature of its environment, and a bird will risk its life to satisfy its curiosity. Animals appear to seek experiences not to make obvious use of the information, but simply to have the experience. There may be an intrinsic motive for learning, such as Bruner's "will to learn," whose reward inheres in its own exercise. Play, exploration, taking things apart, listening to music, and doing crossword puzzles — as puzzle addicts know — are self-rewarding activities. For many people it is more fun to run than to arrive, to pursue than to possess. The struggle for financial success, the act of writing a book, and the excitement of scientific exploration may be equally or more rewarding than the consummation of the goal.

Thorndike's theory of learning transfer through Identical Elements constituted an additional roadblock not only to the creative child, but to education in general. Boys and girls are sent to school with the expectation that what is learned there will be transferred to situations beyond the classroom. But how does this transfer of learning occur? The answer to this question determines the response to the two central issues of education. What should students learn? How should it be taught?

According to the doctrine of "faculty training," widely accepted in Thorndike's time, the mind resembles a collection of mental muscles. Just as a boxer strengthens his legs by running, a child can strengthen his reasoning faculties by studying arithmetic and his memorizing powers by commiting poems to memory. Some people believed that it made no difference what a child studied — it might even be unintelligible — as long as it was difficult. Challenging this notion of "training the mind" through formal discipline, William James demonstrated that practice in memorizing poems did not greatly improve one's ability to memorize other poems.

Thorndike, who had been a pupil of James at Harvard, pursued the study of transfer in greater detail. From his animal studies he came to the conclusion that human beings accomplish this transfer of learning by means of those *elements which are identical* in either the *substance* or the *procedure* of the new and old lessons. Reading, writing, and oral expression, useful in various classroom activities as well as in later life, illustrate a transfer of identical substance. Looking for information in dictionaries, cookbooks, and mathematical handbooks involves the transfer of identical procedures. It is for this reason, undoubtedly, that the tedious drill of alphabetizing is an exercise so highly esteemed in the primary schools. Aside from its value as busywork, its charm is that it is an uncontroversial task which with precision and elegance satisfies the theory of Identical Elements and the postulate that learning is specific, never general. Whether destined to search learned bibliographies or to file insurance papers, the child who has learned to alphabetize his spelling words has mastered an indispensable technique of literate civilization. Thorndike's theory of transfer, on the other hand, led to the conclusion that the study of mathematics or French was a waste of time if the child were not going to use these skills in later life — an idea which progressive education, for quite different reasons, found attractive.

Intelligence in Thorndikian terms does not, as we might suppose, represent understanding or the individual's ability to discern general principles analogous in two situations, but rather the accumulation of habit patterns mechanically triggered by specific stimuli identical in the new and old situations. Accordingly, the skill of alphabetizing requires practice and repetition in order to stamp upon the circuits of the nervous system the pattern of seeking first "A," then "B." The child is not expected to grasp the idea of alphabetical order, any more than he need understand the meaning of arithmetic functions in order to fill in the answers to arithmetic problems. The intelligent child, therefore, like the intelligent cat, is rich in his possession of stimulus-response connections and well endowed with useful habit circuits.

Thorndike did not actually deny ideas or insight; he simply regarded them as the natural outcome of applying habit patterns acquired through repetition and drill. Critics of Thorndike accuse him of disregarding the importance of *how* people use their habit resources and of failing to consider that even when the same bonds or connections are involved, the way a problem is presented or perceived affects the ease with which it is solved. Gestalt experiments suggest that an individual's ability to solve a problem is limited by the way he perceives it.

Far from expediting the transfer of learning, the presence of identical elements in a new and an old problem, as well as the magnetic attraction of the earlier solution, may actually obstruct the solution to the new problem. Sultan, one of the stars of Köhler's celebrated study of anthropoid intellectual capacity, learned to stand on top of a box to retrieve a piece of fruit hung out of reach in his cage. For several weeks Sultan performed experiments involving stacking and climbing on boxes. Then in a new experiment the familiar box was left in the cage, but the fruit was placed on the ground *outside* the bars. Although a stick was also available, the ape stupidly dragged the box to the bars of the cage opposite his prize, climbed on top of it, and then still puzzled went off to fetch more boxes. Sultan's absurd error was the "after-effect" of a formerly successful solution. Ordinarily, a chimpanzee would not behave so foolishly. Are we to conclude that the ape which originally discovered how to use a box as a tool is more intelligent than the ape which now ignores the stick and insists upon dragging a cumbersome box to its cage? Learning to be stupid is education's gift to apes as well as to children. Köhler mentions the similarity between the crude stupidities of the chimpanzee arising from the mechanization of habit, and the repetition by human beings of certain meaningless, moral and political clichés, long after the context of events in which they arose is forgotten.

Familiar procedures are practical, chary of time and effort, and understandably attractive to the problem solver. To escape the hypnotic effect of a deep-rooted mechanized response, it is advisable to set aside a stubborn problem permitting time and a change of scene to dissolve a focus which has become rigid, thereby restricting the perceptions and thoughts our cortical circuits will tolerate. Later when the fixated patterns have dimmed and we return to the problem relaxed and with a fresh approach, we may discover, for instance, not the elusive word required to repair an awkward sentence, but that the problem is best solved by rephrasing the entire line. Archimedes was unable at first to solve the problem of measuring the volume of gold in the king's crown because conventional methods of measuring the volume of irregularly shaped objects required the physical destruction of the crown: melting it down and pouring the liquid into a measured volume, or hammering it into a regular geometric shape. Freeing himself, in this case by an act of genius, not merely from a personal mental rut, but from the rule of tradition, he finally abandoned the idea of measuring the crown directly. Instead he substituted an equivalent volume of bath water which could be poured and measured without risk to the king's crown or his own head.

Just as learning may be inhibited by the presence of identical elements in dissimilar situations, stereotyped behavior may result from a form of training known as overlearning. Overlearning refers to the extra repetition of a response required to learn a lesson, not merely for immediate recall, but to fix the response for long retention. Spelling, memorizing telephone numbers, swimming, typing, and bicycle riding are overlearned skills. Perfected by practice, these responses are in some way deeply etched upon the nervous system, and despite considerable neglect, tend to endure.

Obviously, the retention of skills and information through overlearning is a valuable adaptation to the exigencies of living. But overlearning also has undesirable consequences. Once established, mechanized habits persist in spite of punishment, even when they lead to inanity and error and are no longer useful — a phenomenon for which psychologists have yet to find a satisfactory explanation. The process of overlearning blinds the learner to unfamiliar relationships, to new possibilities of solving problems, and appears to destroy initiative. The animal or individual either cannot perceive or cannot seek new means of solution.

We are all familiar with our preference for certain artificial procedures learned during childhood. Patterns such as the order of dressing, or the route traveled to a certain destination, may endure long after they have ceased to be logical. Rats overtrained to use a path which includes a jump prefer the familiar path to more direct routes. After years of doing arithmetic problems in the style drilled in during his childhood, the adult may be perplexed by the new mathematics, which his children, who have no overlearned barriers to overcome, grasp with ease. Like Sultan, the adult has difficulty disentangling himself from his earlier commitment. It appears that the mere presence of a well-drilled habit is sufficient to smother curiosity, curb imagination, and inhibit the urge to explore. One possible explanation for this type of fixated behavior is that the overtrained activity becomes an end in itself. The practice of putting on one's shoes before one's trousers becomes a separate goal with precedence over the sensible observation that fashion having narrowed the trouser leg, the shoe-trouser sequence is illogical.

Man is endowed with a uniquely flexible and adaptable brain. Compared to man, animals are provided with a relatively large inventory of inflexible instincts and reflexes. Animals can learn less, but have less to learn. More than any other animal, man is free both to create and solve his problems and to establish the rules by which he governs himself. It is prudent, therefore, to be fastidious about the habits and conditioned responses we introduce to our neural circuits. Our biological freedom to think, choose, and innovate must be protected from the encroachment of forces which have the capacity to destroy or cripple those sensitive cerebral faculties upon which our survival as individuals and as a species depends.

Although today cognitive psychologies which welcome creative behavior and divergent thinking flourish, and enlightened educators criticize rote learning and question the meaning of grades, the past excesses of behavioral learning theory are still relevant. At the same time that concepts of creativity prosper, theories of conditioning are also fashionable. Thorndike's principles have been succeeded by more elaborate conditioning theories, particularly *operant conditioning*, the "behavior-shaping" doctrine, of Harvard's B. F. Skinner. With its love of statistics and measurements, and its conviction that the focus of teaching is on behavior, rather than the student, behaviorism is admirably suited to the mass bookkeeping of universal education and to the automation of the classroom and the teaching process.

The "Unfinished Revolution"

While behaviorists devoted themselves to the elimination of what Watson called the "intangibles and unapproachables," to "methodological considerations," and to the principles of drill and habit formation, John Dewey and the progressive education movement offered a radically different solution to the educational crisis of the post-Civil War years. Progressive education regarded children with affection rather than distrust, with respect rather than alarm. An educational movement no sooner born than betrayed, progressive education was the first to offer encouragement to the creative child.

Influenced by his own permissive upbringing, Dewey fused the strands of several educational philosophies and espoused an educational doctrine which established the child and his needs as its central concern. After World War I, Dewey's ideas were seized by reformers and applied in a great revolutionary movement which was called progressive education, but rarely was. Dewey's criticisms were relevant to the conservative, obsolete school system in which they evolved. Whether teaching love of God and country by singing, or preparing students for vocations by offering outmoded manual training for jobs which would soon be obsolete, the schools were sadly divorced from the real needs and lives of their students. It was never Dewey's intention to pander to juvenile caprice as it subsequently became convenient to believe. Rather, Dewey limned the existence of the child's needs, in contrast to adult-imposed needs. If Deweyan education was "child-centered," it was because the child himself and the inner growth of his mind and spirit were ignored by those to whom his welfare was entrusted.

Dewey believed that by closing the breach between events in the classroom and in the world outside, between school and experience, education would no longer be regarded as an alien, abstract exercise in tedium required of students in the name of "preparation for life" — an imaginary life to be lived in some nebulous future. It is a dreary fact that education is still divorced from its pupils' interests, if not exactly from their "needs." Students, both the cynical and the sensible, quickly abandon the idea that education is concerned with learning. The purpose of education is to have had it. However empty and absurd, education represents income, status, even draft deferral; to others it means escape from the ghettos of poverty and discrimination. The knowledge of future rewards may sustain students at their labors, but it does not mitigate their boredom, or diminish their hostility to the system in which they are trapped.

Dewey's educational philosophy was a humane and dignified creed which stressed the recognition of individual differences, and stood for the "expression and cultivation of individuality" as opposed to the subjugation of the individual. Rather than preparation-for-life, education was to provide an "acquaintance with an ever-changing world" through actual experience (learning by doing). Blind acceptance of the thoughts of others and acquisition of isolated, meaningless skills and techniques by drill and rote were repugnant to Dewey. Finally, Dewey believed in group experience obtained in school as the basis for a future democratic community.

Unfortunately, Dewey's philosophy contained the seeds of its own defeat. Not only were some of its concepts vague, but progressive education failed to implement its admirable ideas with practical teaching methods, inviting the rapid perversion of Dewey's principles. By contrast, Thorndike had provisioned his educational theories with a full battery of teaching techniques. The quantitative, statistical nature of Thorndike's science of education facilitated the development of mass educational methods so familar to us today. Because progressive education treated students individually rather than statistically, and because it recognized curiosity, imagination, and discovery in the learning process, it was at a grave disadvantage in providing the average teacher with explicit instructions for applying Dewey's precepts in unadulterated form. The volatile, changing atmosphere of a Deweyan classroom required secure, sensitive, artful teachers well trained in group dynamics and in subject matter.

"Cultivation of individuality" is a worthy objective, but as Paul Torrance indicates, it is difficult to recognize individual differences unless you know *"what* individual differences are important in individualizing instruction and *what* individual differences in mental functioning, motivation, and personality are brought into play in various ways of learning." Studies of the learning process suggest that the roads to learning are diverse: regal and pedestrian, direct and devious, swift and leisurely. Children learn best when teaching methods are tailored to their past experience and to individual abilities and motivations. The child with a poor visual memory may profit from a heavily phonic approach to reading. Other children, at least for a while, may require the encouragement of "really reading" afforded by the "look-say" method of memorizing key words in the first year primer, before they are ready to undertake the more demanding task of "sounding out" syllables and analyzing word structure. Children also vary in creative endowment and in their ability to handle frustrating tasks. Highly creative boys and girls enjoy the demands of "open" tasks, but may be bored by carefully planned and controlled lessons. Less creative children may be more successful when their lessons are carefully organized and their work closely supervised.

The hypothesis, entrenched in progressive education's "object lesson" and "project method," that we learn best when satisfying an innate curiosity about an authentic situation, although commendable, is seriously fallible. No matter how great his interest, the schoolchild cannot "learn by doing" unless he receives intelligent direction and is taught the skills of research. Furthermore, the stress on activity so well suited to the primary grades is less appropriate in the secondary schools. Endowed with a thinking, reasoning brain, and the gift of human imagination and symbolic language, high school students may be expected to manipulate abstract ideas — to count pennies without holding them. Finally, the assumption that the child will have no difficulty learning material as long as it interests him, disregards a critical factor in the learning process, namely, his expectation of success or failure. For all his interest in learning to read, write, or to tell time, the child who anticipates failure and eschews an emotional drubbing, may sensibly conclude that painting and block building are what really interest him.

An aggressive campaign to "sell" progressive education to the public was launched by resolute entrepreneurs in the movement. The spirit behind Dewey's words was ignored, and his words, notably ambiguous, were misunderstood. Watson, who had been Dewey's pupil and who had been influenced by Dewey's pragmatic philosophy, remarked years later that he had never really understood what Dewey was talking about. Apparently, Watson was not alone. Mediocre teachers milked the doctrine for its more attractive concepts. "Learning by doing" and "freedom of expression" became ends in themselves, and the "object lesson" was vested with magical properties and sprinkled throughout the curriculum even when glaringly inappropriate. Dewey, with good reason, distrusted teachers and textbooks, preferring experiment and the laboratory as a means of discovery. But Dewey never intended the laboratory experiment to be a cheap, mechanical imitation of science in which the student knew ahead of time what he was supposed to find.

Whereas Dewey personally understood that method could not be separated from content, his emphasis of the "supremacy of method" led others to conclude that method was an alternative to substance. In revolt against this distortion of the original progressive credo, disillusioned educators and an alarmed public eventually demanded a "return to subject matter." This slogan is indeed hollow, for no sensible person would wish to restore the educational dark ages of the nineteenth century. While it is true that method must be sustained by content, content without method is also absurd.

Infected with popular misconceptions of Freudian beliefs in the emotional benefits of a permissive environment, "freedom of expression" ceased to be a means to an end, but became an educational goal in itself. Freedom of expression is ludicrous if the student has nothing to express. In the absence of formal subject matter, educators finally discovered that the student could, nevertheless, express "himself." A philosophy of education once dedicated to the real needs of real children degenerated to the proposition that what children really needed was the opportunity to "unfold" their own personalities to suit themselves — although apparently no one else. Progressive education became permissive education, fully justifying the scorn of its critics. After reaching its zenith of popularity in the thirties, progressive education, intellectually bankrupt and torn by factionism — except in a few private institutions — retreated in disgrace, an educational catastrophe. Yet what was wise and valuable in Dewey's educational philosophy was never given a chance; only what was tawdry and wrong.

Misalliance

Despite the conflict in the educational philosophies of Thorndike and Dewey, Thorndike and his followers grafted tenets of the progressive program — life adjustment, pupil needs — to their own educational creed, producing a mongrel doctrine which contained the worst of both. Permissiveness was now added to the "scientific movement" in education. This farrago of nonsense was too much for Dewey, but not for his followers who gobbled the scientific bait of Thorndike's "laws of learning," heedless of the theoretical hook on which the laws were hung.

Influenced by progressive educators, Thorndike decided that it would be easier to hammer his stimulus-response bonds into children when schoolwork was conducted in an atmosphere of "zeal," by which he meant the expectation of reward or success, and when instruction was related to children's natural purposes. What these were, however, was not clear then, nor even now. Originally concerned with devising a curriculum relevant to the interests of schoolchildren, progressive education floundered in Dewey's turbid prose and came to the fatuous pronouncement that schoolwork must derive *directly* from the children's immediate interests or purposes. In the twenties and thirties the search for these elusive entities led educators a merry chase. To their chagrin, they discovered a long list of things in which children were *not* naturally interested, ranging from the projects on which they were actually working to their future jobs. Under the influence of pseudo-Freudian concepts, natural purposes were eventually interpreted as "drive-reduction," and "impulse-release," and were expressed in the educational doctrines of permissiveness, spontaneity, life adjustment, and democracy — the latter being a euphemism for conformity.

While Thorndike was softening his harsh doctrines with progressive bonhomie, progressive education pounced upon Thorndike's Laws of Learning and snipped off what was useful. Concerned with the divorce between schools and life, and battling the doctrine of training the mind through formal discipline and mental exertion, progressive education found Thorndike's theory of transfer alluring. Children learned singing from singing, not discipline or patriotism. The theory of identical elements, moreover, postulated that to be worthwhile, training must be directly related to what children would do in later life. The progressives conveniently disregarded what should have been repugnant to them, the concept that the Thorndikian transfer of learning was entirely mechanical. Thorndike's identical elements "recognized" each other without the intervention of the child's thought processes. Enthusiastically and uncritically, a second generation of leaders in the progressive education movement, no longer the intellectual peers of its founders, utilized Thorndike's "scientifically proven" theories to support progressive methods. Dewey shook his head in despair, turned his back on both Thorndike and his own followers, and lived to see the educational landscape overrun with the weeds and tares of his own intellectual seed.

Among the more dubious contributions of the new science of child psychology was the belief that children were not reliable sources of information about themselves and that in the interest of science they were best ignored. Laws of learning and so-called laws of child development, no matter how precarious and scientifically uncertain, helped to eliminate uncertainty from teaching. Scientific "findings" removed the onus of responsibility for educational achievement from both teacher and child, which if nothing else, brought sunshine to the classroom. Studies of intelligence and child development dictated what children were able to learn and at what age they could learn it. In practice progressive education may have been "child-centered," but the child it centered on was an abstraction, and not the living, growing child teachers were taught to look at each day without seeing.

The disintegration of authentic progressive education to a vulgar caricature of Dewey's educational philosophy was a serious blow to creative education. Respect for his ideas, and the opportunity to seek his own answers are essential to the nurture of a child's creative powers. But creativity is not haphazard self-expression, nor does it thrive in an atmosphere of self-indulgence or permissiveness. Critical control and discipline, as well as fundamental knowledge are essential to the creative process. Regardless of familiar tales of sudden insights in strange places — bathtubs, cathedrals, taxis, and dreams — great ideas do not fall as gifts from the gods into unprepared minds.

In the creative process, analysis and organization must be preceded by exploration. The time for a child to clean his room is after he has played with his paints and blocks, not before. The writer who prematurely subjects his imagination to the blue pencil of his critical intelligence, may find himself with nothing to edit. We are reminded of what Holden Caulfield said about the Oral Expression teacher who yelled "Digression!" every time a student departed from his point to discuss something more interesting. To the suggestion that this unpleasantness might be avoided if he selected the subject that interested him first — and then stuck to it, the young hero of *The Catcher in the Rye* observed, "Lots of time you don't *know* what interests you most till you start talking about something that *doesn't* interest you most." Eventually we must tidy our rooms and our thoughts, but if the rigidity of the housekeeping discipline is imposed prematurely, there may be nothing in the house worth keeping.

Wafted on the crest of the Freudian cult, permissiveness infected the attitudes and values of the outlying social culture where, for the young recipients of adult indulgence, it became a bitter recipe. The hands-off policy referred to adult responsibility and not to youth's obligation. Children were expected to resolve a permissive upbringing with a decidedly nonpermissive attitude toward the goals in their lives. By midcentury, permissiveness, belongingness, conformity, scientism, and an emasculated curriculum, the shambles of what Paul Goodman has called an "unfinished revolution," were widespread. Vague and inadequate, Deweyan progressive education, moreover, was not creative education. It placed more stress on critical and analytical thinking than on original problem solving.

While cleaning up the theoretical and applied debris of this compromised revolution, let us not reject the dream of educational reform with which the progressive movement started. We have yet to devise education which is not only physically, but morally and intellectually humane; we must still bridge not the gap, but the growing canyon between school and work, between the education of the middle-class child and the slum child, and betweeen the attitudes and values we preach and those we actually practice. Its theories revised and expanded in terms of newer studies of learning, its spirit adapted to the realities of chronic poverty, undeclared hot and cold wars, moral uncertainty, and the insatiable demand for skill and knowledge, the canons of progressive education remain a precious legacy. Furthermore, the chronicle of the movement's failures and disappointments should serve as a valuable Baedeker for the modern educator. In its respect for the rights of children and for the virtues of childhood, and in its recognition of the individual's need to grow and to achieve his potential, progressive education supplied a foundation for what might yet evolve into creative education: education which is neither propaganda nor play, which is undertaken for the sake of learning, and which, inspired and inspiring, nurtures rather than diminishes the child.

World War II began and the storm broke. The general educational goal of producing literate workers and loyal citizens, and developing youthful personality failed to meet the specific requirements of modern society. While opportunities for unskilled labor diminished, the nation faced a shortage of engineers, scientists, technical specialists, and other skilled workers. With the advent of the cold war and the onset of scientific and technological jousting, it became apparent that henceforth manpower would have to be converted to brainpower, and that the educational system held the key to survival in the age of the Bomb and the computer. When in October 1957, Sputnik danced around the earth beeping its way into public consciousness, suddenly the "gifted" child, like the gifted baseball player, became a national asset. Atom-splitters and stargazers were courted in their laboratories and observatories; brains were in fashion.

Concern for national security coincided with new perspectives in creativity research and with disturbing returns from the American classroom where gifted students were discovered to be wasting their time, and where many who were gifted went unrecognized. If an academic diet of drill and grill made Jack a dull boy, the more exotic fare of extreme permissiveness was just as unwholesome. Education was shoddy, and the plight of the ghetto child was to become a national scandal. In addition to their other obligations, educators began to recognize the effect of the teaching process on the intellectual and emotional life of the child. As a result, there were heard impassioned, if not always sober, demands for a reappraisal of the techniques and aims of education.

The call for a reevaluation of the "methods and objectives" of education suggests that at some point there existed a measure of accord among educators as to the purposes of education and the means of achieving them. Unfortunately, there was no such accord. Reappraising and redefining the "techniques and aims" of education is a perpetual occupation among the higher echelons of the teaching Establishment, perhaps because education has never possessed a clear statement of its purpose or of how to achieve it. Notwithstanding continual debate about the results education ought to achieve, despite a dearth of reliable information about how we learn and how to teach, education goes about its affairs as if it had such matters tidily in hand. The "science of nonthought," as Jacques Barzun has called it, has become a major scientific and commercial enterprise, refusing to concede that its ideas are vague and its underpinnings frail.

Compulsory universal education may have many deficiencies, but power over children is not one of them. Although subject to innumerable oppressive restrictions, the public school system has considerable authority to apply tenuous learning principles and to mass-test flimsy hypotheses. Conversely, it can use its power to suppress innovations which do not serve the interests of those in control. A radical change in policy will be unmercifully resisted and opposed by those who prefer consistency to truth, and conviction to uncertainty. Whole generations of schoolchildren may be compelled to participate in what are actually ill-conceived and badly conducted experiments. The parent whose child is required to learn a different method of working division problems or of adding fractions with each new teacher he encounters is naïve if he assumes that this is necessarily "new math." The older generation of nonreaders is now being followed by a generation of sophisticated mathematical illiterates. The various modern mathematics curricula, for example, were urged upon the nation's schools before being thoroughly tested, and before teachers were prepared to handle the new concepts, with the result that today children memorize the new mathematics instead of the old. If they cannot solve problems they can at least impress their elders with the glossary of set theory or chant the logical proof of addition.

Ultimately there is no way of testing educational theories except in the environment of the real classroom. For this reason, the intellectual standards as well as the personal principles and integrity of those in charge should be of the highest quality. Once entrenched in the school system, inane textbooks and inept reading programs are not easily dislodged. The educational countryside is still littered with concepts and teaching methods which have been officially retired. Bound by the cumbersome bureaucratic machinery and by vested economic interests, the public school system is a lumbering behemoth fed on abstractions and funded by private and federal foundations. In a small-scale enterprise a skillful teacher may improvise, override a poor curriculum, and tailor instruction to the needs of real children rather than statistical norms. The "laws" of learning may collapse and psychologists may concede, as Thorndike did, that they were wrong, but the recall of the massive educational armies launched in the premature commitment to error or oversimplification is a formidable and expensive task. After an educational program is initiated, many years may pass before the results are appraised and the truth known. Undoubtedly there is a price we must pay for innovation, but when schools and teachers grope, children are their partners.

Throughout the ages children have been the beneficiaries of adult devotion, not necessarily to their needs, but to what the older generation piously refers to as its duty. From the day they enter kindergarten, children constitute a captive audience required to consume the education provided by their elders who by virtue of experience and judgment are presumed to know what is best. Whereas formerly, religious and moral authority sanctioned adult prerogative to break the child's will, trammel rebellion, and exorcise devils, the manipulation of the young now proceeds under the respected auspices of science.

Children are neglected and confused in the name of "impulse-release" or "self-fulfillment." In accordance with irrefutable laws of learning which regard teaching as "behavior-shaping," pupils are drilled, conditioned, and indoctrinated to acquiesce in the criteria of mediocrity. They are provided with "research-tested" methods and materials, tethered to an inflexible curriculum, and then rated and regulated by mass-produced and mass-administered mental tests. They are taught the safe but dreary rhythms of the academic lockstep; they learn to submit to boredom, and to fear their classmates' success as much as their own failure.

Consistent with this trend, toys are sold with the implication that unless tea sets and fire trucks have learning value, they are a waste of time — and by insinuation that the products of a manufacturer who understands that the home is a "powerful laboratory for learning," and that play isn't really play, are superior. Accordingly, parents are offered "cause-and-effect toys," "manipulative equipment" and playthings which afford "first experiences with academics." Toys provide "sensory-motor experiences," dramatize "family customs and mores," and "develop spontaneous verbal and physical dramatizations which clarify and extend information." One would hardly surmise that this lyric prose refers to nothing more remarkable than rattles, paints, and dollhouses. Lest old-fashioned parents cling to the innocent notion that the purpose of play is to have fun, they are warned that according to "scientific findings," the lack of a planned learning environment may cost the child precious IQ points which "can mean the difference between a semi-skilled and a professional career." That the promotion of toys intended by the manufacturer for "creative play" should stress an increase in the child's IQ, a measure which has been the bane of the creative child's school life, suggests either ignorance or irresponsibility in the interest of a potent sales pitch.

Children are alternately coaxed and frightened into accepting the bit and harness of a secondhand life, or are required to submit to the clumsy meddling of those more devoted to the spurious laws of child development than to children. Schools are no longer inhuman penal institutes. Although fear still poisons the school atmosphere and the teacher's power to make children miserable remains, teachers are at least expected to be kind to their pupils and to like them. But if school today is less a prison, it has become a laboratory where children are the guinea pigs. It is a sloppy laboratory unable to distinguish between science and superstition, but one which has attracted the barons of the "knowledge industries" with the pungent aroma of government and foundation money.

The science of learning is primitive. The bureaucratic machinery with which even the most talented and devoted teacher must contend is unwieldy. Finally, the cynicism and ignorance of peripheral industries whose business is Business, not learning, and which do not hesitate to pander to parental anxiety and public credulity, are threats to a vigorous and robust educational apparatus. It is imperative, therefore, to protect children from exploitation in this most peculiar and unscientific laboratory.

8. Machines

What is technically sweet will be produced.
— J. ROBERT OPPENHEIMER

THE HANDICRAFT STAGE in education has now come to an end, and to mixed choruses of woe and acclaim, education has embarked upon its own industrial revolution. Sponsored by various public and private grants, "cognitive" machines (computers, teaching machines, talking typewriters) and their older audio-visual cousins (television, videotape, film) have begun to invade the nation's schools. The application of technology to instruction and the automation of the classroom promise exciting educational opportunities. On the other hand, educational engineering portends an unholy alliance between a specific technology which regards education as a multi-billion-dollar business opportunity and an educational system which desires to do its job professionally and scientifically, but is uncertain what that job is.

We are dependent on the technical decisions of the experts who inhabit Education Land. The intelligent layman, however, has an obligation to discern the areas of confusion and to penetrate the professional mumbo-jumbo which shrouds trivia, confused ideas — or the total absence of ideas — in the charisma of science. Although we are spending more money on education than ever before, we still face a critical shortage of basic information about the learning and teaching processes.

More than half a century ago, Whitehead remarked that the

reason for most of education's difficulties is that "necessary technical excellence can only be acquired by a training which is apt to damage those energies of mind which should direct the technical skill." Cultural and educational attrition and personal neurotic problems account for a vast loss of human creative potential. It would be tragic if the growing demand for technical skills were to result in an increase in the proficiency with which we destroy our creative powers.

As a means of "behavior control," conditioning and response-reinforcement techniques are particularly well suited to the thriving field of educational engineering and will be used increasingly in the decades to come. One predicted Orwellian refinement of response-reinforcement technique is reinforcement by direct electrical stimulation of the cerebral "pleasure centers." By implanting electrodes in the subject's brain, it will be possible to reward or punish selected patterns of behavior. The use of a computer to monitor the procedure would automate the entire undertaking. No longer will the student be dependent on the reinforcing smile of his teacher or on pleasurable feelings induced by knowing he got the right answer. Instead, a precise electrical caress will be delivered directly to his brain.

A culture which has learned to program electronic "thinking" machines, not illogically considers the possibility of programming its human thinking "machines." As a courier of the "knowledge revolution," the teaching machine or, stripped of its hardware, simply programmed instruction, is one of the most impressive applications of response-reinforcement theory. Based on a modest hand-cranked machine designed by psychologist Sidney Pressey in 1926, the auto-instructional device, as the teaching machine is sometimes called, is a controversial innovation, damned by some and lauded by others as the most exciting invention since the medieval tradition of oral education succumbed to the printed book. To covet blindly such equipment, and to regard as modern and progressive those schools which have installed learning laboratories and electronic study centers are corrosive trends. We must understand that teaching machines, programmed learning, computer-assisted instruction (CAI), scrambled books, "tutor texts," and other programmed books are the offspring of that mechanical brand of learning theory which maintains that to think is to give the correct response.

Hardware and Software

The most popular teaching machines today are the evolutionary issue of the "Skinner box," used by the Harvard learning theorist to train rats and pigeons to do tricks. Unlike Pressey's "teach-test" machines and others on the market which employ multiple-choice questions, Skinnerian machines require the student to compose his own answers.

Programmed teaching devices vary in complexity, in design, and in cost. Some programs are simply paper texts, either linear or branching in design, costing a few dollars. The most elaborate are glittering computerized systems which answer the student's questions, analyze his errors and "decide" what further help he needs. In addition to the computer, the student console may be equipped with a variable package of audio and visual learning aids, including color television, tape, records, film, light pens, and teletypewriters. The mix-and-match array of components from which educators must choose is itself dazzling and confusing. But whether the price tag is $5 or $150,-000, essentially the auto-instructional device functions as a friendly private tutor which teaches by making succinct statements, asking questions, and correcting each answer as it is given.

To write a learning program, the designer must first reduce the material to its smallest stimulus-response units or "frames." The appropriate size of the individual frame, however, is a source of controversy. Progressing through a sequence of graded steps from the simple to the complex, the student is cautiously ushered through his lesson. In a typical learning program the student is given a brief statement of facts. He then answers a simple question and checks immediately to see if he is right. If the answer is correct — and it usually is — he continues to the next question. An elite teaching machine, harnessed to a computerized typewriter, may reply: "Right you are" or "Sorry, try again." With less sophisticated hardware, the student simply compares his answer to the one appearing in the answer window, or he may press a button and wait for a buzzer or light to signal approval.

Unlike a conventional textbook, the programmed lesson is responsible for its students' errors. The criteria of many programs require at least ninety percent of the students to pass the final test with a high grade. Otherwise the learning program, not the student, is considered a failure, and the program is revised. Brighter students complete the work faster. The questions in a conventional textbook oblige the student to organize the material he has learned. They are designed to test the student's academic mettle and to teach by exposing error and misconception. To the programmed lesson, error is quite literally against its principles. Its questions are designed or "cued" so that the right answer is almost obvious. Encouraging the correct response to a stimulus by means of a well-placed "prompt," or by asking a question to which the answer has just been given, creates an opportunity to reward the student and to reinforce the specific stimulus-response bond or question-answer linkage. As a drillmaster, therefore, the teaching machine differs from the conventional drill in that its repetitive exercise is organized in a systematic, cumulative sequence.

Skinner's response-reinforcement technique is a refinement of Thorndike's Law of Effect, which stated that we tend to repeat an action which leads to a satisfactory result. Thorndike's cats received their rewards only after solving relatively difficult problems by means of trial and — in the beginning — much error. There was no one to coach them as they fumbled toward freedom or food. Skinner reduced the guesswork, streamlined the conditioning process, and provided a ringmaster. To shape learning behavior directly and efficiently, Skinner concluded each correct response must be immediately reinforced. Skinner's performing animals, accordingly, earn a food pellet each time they make a correct move. Furthermore, their trial-and-error efforts are carefully supervised and controlled to lead them toward the correct response and to diminish error which is considered a waste of time since it is not the occasion for a "reinforcing" tidbit of food. For this reason the programmed lesson also informs the student immediately whether his answer is right or wrong. If he is wrong, the program supervises the necessary repairs. If he is correct, the desired response is presumably reinforced by the immediate satisfaction of knowing he is right.

Encouraged by his achievement, the compliant student can be led step-by-step along the reinforcement trail of programs which range from table setting and roller-skating safety, to chess, calculus, and memory training; from service station management and oxyacetylene welding to poetry. There are those who regard the electronic nurture of our future Miltons and Shakespeares as a melancholy prospect. They may comfort themselves, however, with the hope that perhaps genius will be among the refractory ten percent who either prove unamenable to the machine's tutelage, or express their disapproval by pulling its plug and jamming its keys.

The technique of instruction used by the teaching machine is frequently referred to as the Socratic method, a claim both presumptuous and inaccurate. It is true that programmed instruction uses the dialectic method, but there the resemblance to Socrates ends. The theoretical roots of programmed learning are in Pavlov and Skinner, not Socrates. The dialectic method was used by the ancient Greek philosopher to correct faulty thinking and to promote consistency in the analysis of matters about which something was already known. The Socratic method is most effective in checking illogical thinking and in preventing an irresponsible thinker from having his way on both sides of a question. It is unsuited to an empirical science which strives for enlightenment and wisdom in virgin territory.

Participants in the Socratic debates may be guilty of errors of logic, but the ability to think, logically or otherwise, is assumed. Unlike the shrewd Socratic questions designed to trap the student in his own errors, the programmed questions are carefully cued to condition the component responses of *new* learning in a student whose behavior is the only criterion of his success or failure. Manufacturers of teaching machines are pleased to invoke the name of the Greek paragon of wisdom, whereas they are understandably reluctant to promote their wares under the banner of Ivan Pavlov, master of salivating dogs and father of conditioned-reflex theory.

The teaching machine is an ingenious device for training rats to play pinball and for teaching preschool children to read. It is useful for instructing the retarded and the disadvantaged and for teaching reading to illiterate adults. It is also effective in imparting mechanical skills and for preparing adults for specialized education. The armed forces have exploited response-reinforcement techniques for training technical experts, and industry has discovered in the teaching machine a valuable tool for increasing the effectiveness of the individual as a well-greased cog in a mass-production system. Whether an apprentice mechanic understands solid-state physics is not important as long as he can be trained quickly to assemble and repair transistorized equipment, and retrained should his specific skill become obsolete. Innovation in design must await those whose teachers did not demand unquestioning acceptance of their instructions. It is quite another matter, however, to assume that for the average student there is no purpose or advantage in knowing ahead of time what one is searching for or trying to achieve.

Programmed instruction as used in the schools is intended merely as a teaching aid, to be integrated with other forms of instruction — group discussions, reading, individual guidance — and monitored by a teacher who welcomes the machine, yet understands its limitations, and who knows how to operate it and when to turn it off. Nevertheless, as long as the student is seated at his learning console, we cannot forget that his "teacher" is a machine which adheres to the behaviorist principle that only behavior is real and that information which does not result in behavior or which cannot be programmed does not count. The exercise of logic which so concerned Socrates is no problem to the student whose logic is provided by the programmer who also does his thinking.

Spoon-feeding

A major advantage of programmed instruction is that it permits the student to work actively, by himself, and at his own speed. The fast learner may advance as rapidly as he wishes; the slow learner may work at a more deliberate pace, exploring supplementary material provided by the more sophisticated branched programs. Neither bored nor embarrassed, the student receives the undivided attention of a machine which does not scold and never loses its temper. In a conventional classroom the student may have to wait until his homework or test papers are corrected to find out what he does not understand. Meanwhile class lessons continue on the assumption that earlier principles are understood by everyone. The teaching machine, on the other hand, will not permit the student to take new steps until he has mastered the old. Teaching machines combined with recording equipment are particularly effective in foreign language instruction. Working actively and in privacy, yet under the tutelage of an expert, the student can practice his pronunciation without blushing, matching his skill with that of a teacher whose speech and idiom are authentic.

That students are kept busy, however, does not mean that their time is well spent. Obviously, the teaching machine is only as good as the design and content of its software. Many educators were bitterly disillusioned when, in the mid-fifties, the market was flooded with slatternly programmed and inadequately tested teaching machines. Responsible people both in education and industry agree that it is not the hardware but the software which is their most serious problem.

The premise of the much publicized "individualized instruction" is that in all cases and for all students learning proceeds best in solitude, when the learner competes only with himself and administers his own reward. It is implied that the stimulation of other pupils and the teacher is undesirable and negative. The elimination of the unpredictable, two-legged intelligence sometimes referred to as the "teacher variable" may be an advantage in controlled research studies. But in the ordinary classroom the menace of human judgment and imagination and the peccadilloes of human emotion are risks we must assume lest we also eliminate the "student variable," replacing the splendid diversity of the human mind and spirit with regiments of drones.

As computer-driven teaching machines in full "aural-oral" regalia apply in growing number for work in the classroom, the question inevitably arises: Will the machine replace the teacher? Although the most ardent supporters of programmed instruction insist that the machines will never eliminate the teacher from the school system, it should be noted that enterprising publishers have already programmed the entire high school curriculum, including those imprecise subjects which must be twisted and mauled before being submitted to the rigors of programming. Mass instructional techniques — such as television, film, and audiovisual tapes — combined with automated individual instruction will make it possible, at least in theory, to eliminate not merely the teacher but the entire school system.

Conditioning, rigidly controlled drill, and the highly structured self-correcting Montessori techniques have been used effectively with severely deprived or disadvantaged children. Certain schools of psychotherapy recommend conditioning as a therapeutic technique. It is significant, however, that the area in which response-reinforcement and programmed instruction are most fruitful is in animal training, in supplying lessons which involve mechanical drill, or where the individual, for genetic, social, or emotional reasons, is unable to function with the complement of mental powers normally provided by a human brain.

The "discovery method" of learning, favored by progressive education, rewards the student with the sudden experience of insight. But insight is not inevitable. Culturally deprived, or otherwise academically crippled children, as we have already observed, may never catch on, or, anticipating failure, may refuse to try. Creative performance presupposes certain basic requirements which include curiosity, the ability to concentrate and observe, to think and handle symbols, and a significant measure of self-respect. The mentally stunted children of the slums learn to stay out of trouble by not thinking, by not asking questions, and by tuning out the thrum and din in which they are constantly enveloped. Nevertheless, for children who have been trained to fail, the programmed lesson, even with its guarantee of consistent success, hardly seems appropriate. Confused, frightened, and inarticulate when restricted to the formal vocabulary and language patterns of the middle-class schools, these children need the warmth and attention of a real teacher rather than the impersonal anodyne of a machine, or a machine-like teacher.

The conventional middle-class nursery school, oriented toward the child's overall development, emphasizes group activity, imaginative play, freedom, and independence. As an educational model, however, the middle-class nursery school is inadequate for the disadvantaged child who is deficient in learning skills middle-class parents automatically give their children, and who already suffers from disastrous intellectual malnutrition by the time he arrives in school. The controversial Bereiter-Engelmann method drills preschool children as if they were soldiers in verbal, logical, and arithmetical concepts. Bereiter and Engelmann, professors at the University of Illinois, attempt to compensate for the cognitive handicap of the disadvantaged child by means of rigid training procedures designed to give the slum child a "head start" which will not dissolve as soon as he confronts the real work of the first grade. The proponents of this method offer a carefully structured and controlled set of rote lessons in conjunction with rewards and suitable punishments. Middle-class prerogatives generally permitted a child, such as expressing enthusiasm, relating personal experience or interjecting his own ideas, are to be discouraged or tolerated only at the teacher's discretion. Bereiter and Engelmann assume that the slum environment offers ample opportunity for the expression of enthusiasm and other "childlike" forms of affect. If the disadvantaged four-year-old is to succeed in the first grade, he cannot afford to waste any more time being a child.

That the poor child, even in the interest of expediency, must acquire the missing cognitive skills at the sacrifice of the personal and creative development considered vital for the middle-class child does not seem a palatable solution. Children force-fed by means of a drill and rote-learning method which stresses obedience and conformity may demonstrate superior performance on standard achievement tests, but it is sad to think that this narrow goal — a dubious educational aim for the "advantaged" child — is the best we can offer. All children deserve respect and all are entitled to know themselves as worthwhile individuals whose feelings and ideas are valued. Whether they live in the slums or the affluent suburbs, children must learn to organize their thoughts, to consider alternatives, and to make decisions. A child who is drilled in his music class, as the song goes, to "think when the teacher says 'Think,' " or who is discouraged from relating personal experience or interjecting ideas irrelevant to the teacher's presentation may display "appropriate schoolroom behavior" and may quickly learn to read above grade level, but such children are being cheated. They are learning to submit to external control rather than to develop true self-control; to perform well on school tests, rather than to integrate knowledge and to consider the consequences of their thoughts.

Culturally deprived children are also socially and emotionally deprived and such shortsighted techniques compensate for deficient intellectual skills by depriving the child of essential developmental experience. It does not seem right that any child, poor or rich, must catch up in language or number concepts by means of techniques which suppress natural curiosity and thinking, which discourage him from making his own decisions, or that he must surrender his creative potential in order to repair his neglected reasoning and linguistic faculties.

The verbal inadequacies of the disadvantaged child are an obstacle to his creative development, and yet it is a mistake to conclude that the disadvantaged child cannot communicate. The slum child is at a disadvantage in school, but not in the street. The imaginative, spontaneous language of the under-privileged, rich in simile and analogy, stands as a testament to the innate creative potential of this sector of society. Our current everyday language has been enriched by words such as *bread* (money), *dig* (understand), *jazz* (worthless talk), *cool it* (take it easy), *pad* (room), *shades* (eyeglasses). In his lack of semantic rigidity, in his imaginative use of words, and in the ease with which he combines language with such nonverbal means of communication as gestures and pictures, the disadvantaged child resembles the creative person. It has been observed, however, that if the educational system fails to provide a constructive outlet for the creative potential of the culturally deprived, their creative talents are apt to be used destructively or in the service of delinquency.

Undeniably, programmed instruction has certain advantages. A good program presents material efficiently and releases the teacher from the role of drillmaster. Relieved of time-consuming mechanical chores which drain the energy and spirit vital to good instruction, the teacher is free to provide individual guidance and lively, informed instruction in the unprogrammed world of learning beyond the machine's jurisdiction. This assumes that the teacher will not be required to fritter away the time adjusting earphones, nursing recalcitrant equipment, and returning students to automated tutors they have deserted. There is no guarantee that it will not be necessary to prevent children from filching the machine's knobs, monogramming its expensive hide, or devoting their perverted ingenuity and creative energies to dismantling and dismembering their electronic teachers. The grim facts of public school life, familiar to teachers and principals, are far removed from the rhapsodies of sales promotion literature. Vandalism and theft are grave afflictions of the urban public schools. Textbooks are mutilated, television sets and slide projectors lead a perilous existence, and anything which is not bolted down soon disappears. Many schools have found it necessary to install costly burglar alarms as a deterrent to pupils who would spirit away everything, including the bricks and mortar if it amused them. What is not deliberately defaced or stolen is sooner or later "fiddled" to death. It is quite realistic to suppose that for every child who brings his teaching machine an apple, there will be another who commits assault and battery or provokes an electronic nervous breakdown. Programmers and manufacturers may boast of products which are "teacher-proof," but they have yet to design equipment which is pupil-proof. Ironically, our closest approximation to this goal is still the sensitive, resilient, living teacher who not only can withstand considerable assault, both physical and spiritual, but who, in spite of abuse, persists in trying to reach children who would not hesitate to reduce a computer to a rubble of transistors and wires.

Psychologists and educators studying the learning process are among the unexpected beneficiaries of programmed instruction. The construction of a learning program, advancing in graded units from elementary to advanced principles, requires thoughtful analysis and organization of the subject matter. Although the adaptation of instruction to the individual differences of children is currently the battle cry of educational crusaders, there has been little organized research on the best way to individualize instruction. Reading is one of the most popular candidates for programming, but one educator frankly observed that we do not know how to teach reading to students who cannot learn by the methods we use. The learning program serves as a "learner-tracking system," which provides a complete record of the steps taken by the student in the process of learning — or more accurately, when learning by this method. Should the student fail to understand the material, the written record is tangible evidence of where he has lost his way, or why what appears logical and obvious to the teacher, does not to the pupil. The learning program may then be revised according to this insight, and in the long run should result in improved teaching and curriculum design.

The chief objection to programmed instruction is that it discourages imagination and creative thinking, has no tolerance for doubt, and distorts its subject matter by squeezing the material into the arbitrary format of questions whose answers are unequivocally right or wrong. The student cannot speculate on solutions which did not occur to the designer of the program, nor can he entertain ideas which attract because they are vivid or intuitively compelling, not because they are next in sequence. Once severed from its author and inserted in the machine, the paper program is insensitive to the vagaries and evanescent notions of a mind which is capable of ranging broad patterns as well as absorbing details. "It was programmed for a certain thing — but I'm not," complained a college student, worsted in an argument with a pedantic teaching machine.

Just as experimental psychology once ignored modern field physics in favor of an outdated mechanism, educational behaviorism still has an embarrassing proclivity for discarded concepts. In comparing the treatment of informational processes by computer designers and behaviorist psychologists, David Hawkins observed that machines designed to classify complex data function more efficiently if they are programmed for "nondirective" exploratory behavior. Yet programs written for human beings assume that learning advances one step at a time toward a single goal. Side trips, when provided, are for remedial purposes. Exploration is discounted, the intricate network by which constellations of ideas are related to one another is ignored, and the endlessly shifting patterns and subpatterns which provide human thought with its unique depth and brilliance are dismissed.

Programmed instruction assumes that mistakes are of no value and that learning is best accomplished when attended by a minimum of error. This axiom may pertain to practicing the violin or learning a foreign language, but it is not apposite to problems which require insight and versatile behavior. Failure can be a great teacher. "When we return from error," said St. Augustine, who spoke from personal experience, "it is through knowing that we return." Throughout the centuries the world has profited from the errors, accidents, and laboratory mishaps of its geniuses. The discoveries of roentgen rays, fermentation, penicillin, and America are classic examples of brilliant achievements emanating from original blunders. Moreover, the systematic pressure to give the right answer may suppress the student's natural inclination to ask questions, and destroy his tolerance for mistakes — his own as well as those of others. Education in credulity and conformity leads in the end to mental bankruptcy. The risk of error must be calculated in the cost of truth.

Spelling, vocabulary development, multiplication facts, and mechanical skills such as map reading are suited to programming. Much of the curriculum, however, cannot be programmed without insult to the material. The appreciation of a poem is a subtle aesthetic experience involving complex subjective processes which cannot be reduced to questions and answers. The exaggerated stress on detail inherent in learning programs which spoon-feed material fragmented into bite-size units may actually obstruct understanding of the problem.

Whereas it is generally agreed that the teaching machine is a useful tool for presenting factual material, it is alarming to discover mathematics and physics listed among examples of "factual" subjects which can be safely entrusted to programmed instruction. Although these subjects lend themselves to presentation in objective questions with *right* or *wrong* answers, the student whose mathematics teacher is a machine or a programmed book acquires a set of well-reinforced stimulus-response connections, but little insight into the nature of mathematics. He is taught literally to "do" mathematics. The electronic teacher is a machine addicted to logic, incapable of wonder and delight, or intuition and inspiration. It has never had a "premonition of things unknown," and it has never imagined itself wrong. Its pupils are at best mechanics, not mathematicians.

In programming the student with information as if he were a machine, we encourage him to become a machine. The unintended pun in the expression "teaching . . . machines" becomes a bitter truth when the student is regarded as a mechanical input-output system, and learning is reduced to "wiring in" or conditioning desired responses. The term "self-" or "autoinstructional" device, often used when referring to programmed learning, not only denigrates the achievement of those men and women who were truly self-taught, but demonstrates the fuzzy jargon which uncritical educators use to sell half-clad ideas to themselves as well as to the public. The student does not teach himself, any more than computers and teaching machines "think." The real instructors are those who write the learning program, who provide its content and organize its presentation. The student merely administers the lesson to himself.

When students use a computer to solve intricate problems or to simulate real-life situations in computer-controlled games, the machine serves as a useful tool, a junior partner in the learning venture. But when a computer is programmed to program robots attired in skirts and trousers, the machine is no longer partner, but master. The student is not working with the machine; the machine is working on him.

Silent Lessons

Writing about methods of behavior control, Gardner Quarton mentions that some techniques are in a sense irreversible, and then in a caustic aside cites as examples destructive brain operations and college educations. That the teaching machine is not a creative instructor should not in itself be a serious shortcoming. There are still sufficient classroom tasks involving practice and drill to justify the machine's hire. Nevertheless, the extensive use of a fashionable teaching tool which supports the mechanization of habit raises additional problems for which there are no satisfactory solutions.

First, we must ask what is the effect of programmed instruction on the young person's latent creative potential? What is the influence of response-reinforcement training on his powers of perception? How does the machine affect his capacity to apprehend existence beyond the man-made realm of words and symbols, or his ability to imagine what he cannot perceive?

Habits and overlearned or conditioned behavior are important adaptations to our environment and essential to the survival of a gifted, impetuous animal meagerly endowed with inborn responses. Once a chain of conditioned responses is established, the behavior pattern becomes automatic and life is both simpler and safer. But how does the presence of a habit "pathway" affect the formation of new circuits of response? A faulty golf swing cultivated over the years is not easily repaired, and the music student who has dutifully practiced wrong notes and incorrect fingering will have difficulty recovering his investment in carefully drilled errors. Our nervous system prefers overlearned or well-drilled responses, and habits tend to discourage alternate forms of behavior. The act of committing certain behavior patterns to the automatic circuits of habit, therefore, must not itself be automatic and mindless. It is necessary to distinguish those skills and lessons which are clearly improved by mechanization from those whose future growth and flexibility may be seriously impeded by the early installation of rigid habit formations. Precision and consistency may be virtues in learning arithmetic skills, but the child who is introduced to mathematics through the effective technique of conditioning may no longer be "open" to more venturesome concepts and may have incurred a lifelong bondage to routine.

It is still too soon to tell whether children taught by programmed instruction learn more than those using conventional methods, but if teaching machines are as effective as their proponents maintain, then we must consider the possibility that they may teach too well. Neural circuits which have been too deeply stamped with the linked components of a skill may block the emergence of new responses. Thus, the student may become resistant to new techniques and modes of perception even when the old ones are inadequate. It has been suggested that the presence in the brain of entrenched sets of behavioral rules might actually inhibit original thoughts by obstructing or paralyzing the higher cortical centers ordinarily in charge of mental spring-cleaning and creative speculation.

The mechanisms of fixated, stereotyped behavior, as previously observed, have not been sufficiently studied. The persistence of error is an enigma which psychologists have yet to explain and whose solution lies deeply embedded in the living, pulsing nerve cells of the elusive and inscrutable brain. At this time we do not know enough about the neurophysiology and chemistry of learning and thinking to answer the question raised here, but neither does present ignorance justify the oversight of the adverse effect of conditioning on the individual's creative powers and on his tolerance for ambiguity, for the unfamiliar, and the unknown.

We come now to a second problem. All animals, even protozoa and lowly worms clustered at the foot of the evolutionary ladder are capable of learning. Not only does man learn more than any other animal, and make better use of what he has learned, but the special genius of his species is its ability *to learn how to learn*. More than any other animal, man uses not one or another method of learning, but integrates various styles in subtle and adroit combinations.

In the course of his early vocal experiments, should the infant stumble on the combination "ma-ma," he will be rewarded immediately by his mother's smile. Encouraged by her attention and approval, the baby soon learns his first word: Mama. Observing the important role of well-timed reinforcement in shaping the infant's early behavior, Skinner concluded that we can learn to do calculus in the same way. However, the student who invites the teaching machine to shape his "reading behavior," also submits, willy-nilly, his "learning behavior" to the authority of an instructional process which, although benevolent, has no high regard for his intellectual powers.

In the traditional classroom, bored or unhappy students inadvertently learn that learning is acquiescence, memorizing, ruthless competition, flattery, and shrewd dishonesty. But we must also question the new silent lessons the child absorbs when his instructor is a mild-mannered but arbitrary response-reinforcement machine.

The human brain is born incomplete. At the age of three years the brain reaches two thirds of its full size and after this initial burst, it continues to grow slowly. The weaving of the invisible neural pathways of learning progresses throughout most of adult life until in the intricacy of its design and the wealth of its interconnections, the brain surpasses anything we might build or imagine. Human speech and symbolic thought enable man to rehearse his problems in his head, to summon the past, and to extrapolate the future. The powers of his unconscious mind enable him to intuit truth and to know what has been never known. It does not seem reasonable, therefore, that the crude method by which the inarticulate infant is led forth from the timeless blur of animal existence and conducted toward the sharp light of human self-consciousness, should be appropriate for the high school or college student.

How does the systematic denial of his power to reason and think, to form independent opinions, to sustain doubt and tol-

erate ambiguity, affect the student's learning powers? So-called
"trial-and-success" programs "structured" according to the
"tested principles of educational psychology" to encourage the
child to give the correct answer, suggest smooth promotion
rather than valid science. Certainly, it would not be improper
to ask: *what* tested principles? What is a child actually learning when he answers questions carefully cued to prevent him
from flirting with error, when "if" and "sometimes" are virtually eliminated by the tight construction and circumscribed
content of the lesson, and when in the machine's artificial environment success is divorced from genuine effort. In life there is
ultimately no success except that of our own making, for even
chance, as Pasteur said, favors the prepared mind.

Is it true, as programmed instruction implies, that in the
world beyond the machine's domain, answers unattended by
reward or a "pleasant effect" are incorrect? Is the converse
true: that a feeling of satisfaction indicates a correct answer?
In the words of Emerson, "Truth is beautiful. Without doubt;
and so are lies." A wrong answer, unrecognized as such, is capable of delighting its author. For many centuries men were
pleased to believe they lived on the back of a tortoise, that God
had hung their planet in the center of the universe, and that
when one sneezed, out went the soul and in rushed the devil.
For that matter, correct answers dishonestly come by, must be
cherished for reasons which appear in a quite different emotional account book. Although some type of behavior is indeed
reinforced, as a tool for shaping behavior response-reinforcement is a relatively unrefined and imprecise technique. Assigned the task of reinforcing arithmetic learning responses,
the leash-and-biscuit technique may be hammering in an automatic fill-in-the-blank-space response. Teachers and parents, of
course, are not innocent of this practice, but the elite cadre of
teaching machines is premised to be faster and more effective
in achieving its goals — whatever these may be.

We do not know how a child inured to the spoon-feeding of
the programmed lesson, in which he is not required to follow

complicated instructions, to scan material or to hazard a guess, will react to the more stringent demands of unprogrammed lessons and their attendant anxieties. Genial, mechanical, and carefully controlled, the programmed lesson is relatively undemanding. Thinking, as the active pursuit of insight, is hard work. The student must concentrate, formulate problems, and organize and analyze material. He must be taught to construct a logical argument, and at the same time must learn to generalize from specific examples. He must know how to observe and what to observe. He must cultivate the art of the shrewd guess and the quick perception.

> *Come forth and bring with you a heart*
> *That watches and receives.*

In all but exceptional individuals, living thought is too fragile to endure in the presence of a less demanding alternative. Its existence is further imperiled when the child is seduced by a choice which bears the sanction of those who tell him they know what is best, and distribute rewards and punishments as proof. Recalling Sultan's preference for absurd overlearned solutions, or the difficulty we have in freeing ourselves from methods and attitudes carefully reinforced during childhood, we must consider that a child "overtrained" to learn by programmed instruction may resist learning by other less efficient, more demanding means, not because he prefers his teaching machine, but because his nervous system does.

The use of teaching machines in industry and in the military services may be justified by the shortage of qualified instructors and the constant need to teach new skills. Adult students have specific goals and have already experienced a variety of learning methods. The character and opinions of the young child, however, are still unformed, his mind is sensitive and malleable. His future vocation and interests are unknown. By virtue of youth and inexperience, he is also singularly vulnerable. The perspective of maturity permits the adult to embrace expediency while yet evaluating its potential for mischief. The defenseless child, on the other hand, absorbs the lessons in learning untempered by the critical judgments which protect his elders.

One wonders what kind of scientists, teachers, composers, and stockbrokers children will become if denied the opportunity to develop the inner discipline and intuitive faculties essential to the function of an independent, untrammeled mind. Civilization is indebted to those men and women who, warmed by faith and nourished by courage, devoted their lives to the search for empires, bacteria, and stars, as well as to the pursuit of moral and aesthetic visions. In many instances the only "reinforcement" society had to offer was the negative assurance that they were quite mad. Programmed instruction is suited neither to all subjects, nor appropriate for all students. But if response-reinforcement techniques are not a felicitous choice for everyone, how are we to determine which children shall be submitted to behavior-shaping and which are to be spared the conditioning machine that one day they may take their place behind its controls? There is no answer to this rather ugly question. In view of the muddled predictions of mass-produced aptitude and intelligence tests, any proposal that an objective test might serve as arbiter is repugnant. It is imperative that educators, program designers, and those who subscribe to programmed instruction understand the perils of programming as well as its convenience.

Behavior manipulation is an issue which arouses strong and acrid emotions. Sound evaluation of behavior-control technology and prevention of its abuse are possible only when predicated on theoretical understanding of the underlying assumptions and mechanisms. Programmed learning has been called the most promising development in education since the turn of the century. It derives, however, from the somber behaviorist doctrine, more suited to cats than children, that learning is conditioning and behavior-shaping. There is no guarantee that the behavior-shapers know what is good for us and that they know how to achieve it; that teachers are properly introduced to their new aids and know how to use them to advantage. It is assumed that we can rely on the integrity and talents not only of educators, but also of the foundations and government agencies which subsidize the education profession and the education industries.

The Knowledge Market

The machines are here to stay. The real problem, as usual, is not what the machines can or cannot do, but what we do with the machines. Advocates of programmed instruction qualify their support with the provision that the teaching machine, like other artifacts of instruction, will prove a boon to the schools if it is *properly used* and its *capabilities and limitations are fully understood* — a modest, but nonetheless ominous, stipulation. Pollution, poison, devastation; death on the highways, hanky-panky in the drug industry, simian antics on the television screen, and a space industry whose lifeblood is fear and war, represent industry's commitment to its stockholders, not to public welfare. The application of the recondite arts of psychological conditioning and indoctrination in the mass media, indiscriminate use of tranquilizers in hospitals for the mentally ill and the aged, and the electronic assault on our privacy are omens of what we may expect from the new barons of the knowledge industries.

The teaching machine has been hailed as an educational advance as valuable as intelligence and aptitude tests. This is hardly a reassuring testimonial when we recall the perversion of these tests in the schools and the neglect of the theory behind the tests by those who adopted and adapted them. The abuse of objective testing, and the misuse of the project method and the science laboratory, of reading programs, team teaching, and educational television are further reminders that the proper use of educational tools and techniques is not inevitable. Many a method described as a "fluid situation" is often about as fluid as a vat of freshly poured concrete.

Intended as an aid to the teacher, not as a replacement, the teaching machine ironically is frequently neither. The machine does not begin to purr the moment it is installed in a classroom. If the teacher growls at the newcomer, the gadget may be doomed to gather dust, or may be relegated to an incidental or occasional role. To assure effective use of equipment and the correlation of classwork with machine instruction, teachers must be trained to handle both the mechanical and pedagogical demands of their new assistants. Misunderstood and forsaken, high-priced teaching machines stand broken or idle in school basements and in government-supported research centers because funds were allocated for the purchase of equipment, but not for the training of those who would use it. The vast waste of money, time, and effort associated with language laboratories and educational television is attributed not only to the deficiencies of software and to the conservatism and hostility of teachers, but to neglect in providing teachers with the knowledge they require to use their junior partners wisely.

The educational system is regarded simultaneously as the nation's scapegoat and savior. In response to urgent demands that we hurry up and win the space race, that we teach not merely the "whole child," but that we teach him *something*, and more recently that we inject advantages into our disadvantaged children, educators have embraced gimmicks and enlisted in crash programs. They have swung from no work to overwork, from extreme permissiveness to extreme pressure. Scrambling to climb aboard the audiovisual bandwagon, school administrators with little understanding of either the theory or the limitations of programmed instruction became the victims of slick packaging and glib salesmanship. Many learning programs on the market have not been adequately tested in typical school systems, nor has there been sufficient long-term study of how programmed instruction interacts with other components of the teaching process to warrant the mass adoption of these costly techniques. Bad decisions which cost millions of dollars are not easily disposed of, particularly if they are congealed in hardware and organizational changes. We shall go on living with our expensive mistakes and our children will continue to be taught by them.

Representatives of the education equipment industry offer the specious argument that they can be trusted to sell "a product of high intellectual quality," inasmuch as their customers are "intellectuals." This standard of quality may be valid when selling equipment to the physics and engineering professions where the criteria of good performance are known. But education is a science by proclamation, not fact. The criteria of a product of high intellectual content are vague and controversial. When a spokesman of a large educational corporation states, "I know of no market in which a constant orientation to the needs of the customer is more vital to success," he subtly skirts the real issue, namely, that the buyers are not knowledgeable. Educators disagree about what is needed; they are divided about *what* to teach and *how* to teach.

The public school system is not a vast monolith but is actually a variegated patchwork of school boards, administrators, teachers, children, and taxpayers. Although the mechanisms of the learning process are still obscure, the budget for educational research remains a pittance. Despite the recent increase in federal funds and the contributions of private foundations, the amount and quality of educational research are inadequate. Less than one half of one percent of the nation's outlay for education is devoted to research and development, compared to ten percent in other major industries.

Expense, bureaucracy, a conservative preference for familiar procedures, and the intertwined economic interests of peripheral industries have obstructed innovation in the schools. It has required heroic effort to rout the archaic "Dick and Jane" readers. The primer's electronic counterpart may prove equally unyielding. The development of a good learning program is costly. The expense of purchasing hardware and software, of alterations in classroom design and facilities, and of changes in school administration and curriculum, justifies fears of a frozen commitment to specific programs and devices. Who will have the courage to tell a school board or a foundation committee that the choice of a particular learning program or machine was a mistake? And who will understand that such mistakes are inevitable? If the education industries are financially successful, who will dare to say that a particular course is inadequate, that a curriculum which is commercially sound is academically unsound, or that a theory of learning requires serious revision and that the equipment in which it is incarnated deserves to be scrapped?

Publishing companies, computer research groups, and electronics manufacturers are concluding corporate "arrangements" to develop learning center systems and multi-media learning packages dedicated, they say confidently, "to help teach people how to know." One admires their enterprise and enthusiasm, but in those divisions where company policy — not advertising copy — is composed, let us hope there prevails a degree of modesty and some awareness of the paucity of valid principles of learning. As one educator remarked recently, "It is unreasonable to expect a manufactured product to do what both parents and teachers have great difficulty doing."

No more than we would be so naïve as to wish to do without the benefits of the computer or to restore the bucolic delights — drudgery, disease, and hardship — of preindustrial society, is it reasonable to deny education its industrial revolution and to ignore the advantages of quantity production and quality control. But hindsight and historical perspective serve as grim warnings against the development of academic slums and intellectual blight. One measure of progress may be our failure to repeat all the mistakes of the past.

As the prospering technology of education prepares to exploit raw learning theories and as the computer and its minor brethren advance upon the classroom, we are again reminded of the amplified power of all automated procedures to magnify error as well as to augment knowledge. The automation of ignorance is quite likely to be a next step in the vaunted learning revolution. The power of an incompetent teacher is limited to the students he personally encounters. A poor textbook may be offset or ignored by a good teacher who modifies the official curriculum to meet students' specific needs and injects standard material with the distinct flavor of his personality and style. But an incompetent computerized learning program will shape the mentality of large masses of students. The "teacher-proof" learning program, designed to resist the teacher's meddling, is not only insulting, but is a chilling educational concept: a dangerous step toward letting the machine stamp in the behavior chosen by a remote author without the firsthand judgment of the classrc: cher to edit its instruction.

Many educators fear that, like educational television, mass-produced learning programs, films, and video tapes threaten the local school system's control over what will be taught. Commercial interests and the educational foundations already exert significant influence on instruction and on the content and development of school curricula. Powerful centralization of control in the offices of a foundation, a film producer, or a publishing company may promote uniformity and damage the highly individual interaction of teacher and student. The classroom teacher is reduced to a technician who administers a "fully-tested teaching system" which dispenses a mass-produced package of conventional wisdom. In such a stultifying, clinical atmosphere, the interesting, intuitive teacher who is directed by an inner creative impulse and who regards teaching as an art will find something better to do, leaving the profession to those who enjoy monitoring machines.

Hailed as "individualized instruction," programmed learning is more precisely described by one of its important sponsors as a means of individualizing the *presentation* of the curriculum. The pressure on corporate giants to market a product which meets the competitive claims of rival manufacturers leads to dreary standardization and imitation, whether the products are breakfast cereals and television programs, or textbooks and curricula. Because of the origin of the teaching material, programming imposes an unbecoming conformity on the curriculum. What professes to be mass individual instruction becomes individualized mass instruction: the mass-instruction porridge is served in portions suited to the student's needs, to be ingested as rapidly as he can or as slowly as he must.

The feedback of information about the learning process and suggestions for improving future programs are considered major advantages of programmed teaching. But as slipshod, inadequately tested programs flood the market, critics within the field warn that economic considerations may encourage a tendency to congeal the form of a program once it is adopted and paid for. There is a regrettable temptation to sell machines of a specific design before companion software has been written and tested. If a school invests in such equipment, it may find itself heavily mortgaged to those programs which work for the machine, if not for the pupils. The valuable feedback from the programmed lesson is meaningless if the expensive hardware cannot accommodate itself to revised software.

While school boards and professional administrators, teachers' organizations and parents engage in a blustering struggle for control of the schools, there is a serious danger that large segments of educational policy may be determined eventually by the manufacturers of educational equipment: by products, not problems. If educators default in handling their own affairs, industry will gladly assume the mandate. Decisions must not be left to the education industries or to any group which seeks its own advance through control of education and whose vested interests encourage it to represent self-interest as the child's welfare.

Children are compelled by law and constrained by economic and social pressures to attend school. There is a high risk, however, that educational technology will refine the technique of smoothing the rough angles and sharp corners of individuality, and that it will accelerate the process of packaging children to meet short-term national goals.

The child under the close surveillance of a teaching machine is deprived of a time-honored means of resisting the full force of his education, namely wool-gathering or simply failing to learn. For the child seated in front of his little "black box" is required to work actively and to learn what is being taught. The machine tracks his progress and tattles on command. Even the privilege of failing or of not understanding is denied him because programmed instruction is so engineered that the student must learn what is being taught. Certainly not every child staring out the window is a Wunderkind, and failure ordinarily is not to be recommended, except as a protection against schools which are themselves failures. Freedom to oppose regimentation, to remain unconvinced, to shun a degrading, destructive education, and the right to tune out selectively without dropping out of school provide pupils with an essential escape hatch.

In a positive sense, the more society and educational technology narrow the student's chance to escape the full impact of his schooling, the more urgent it becomes to make school a salutary experience. We must cherish the right to exercise what Bertrand Russell called constructive doubt, to remain open to various methods of learning, and we must safeguard the child's potential freedom to serve society by leading it instead of following it. The youth who is trained to fill today's job will be unemployable tomorrow, and those who have been required to memorize the world as it is will never create the world as it might be.

It is unjust, however, to put the entire blame on the educational system for its failure to serve the community, when the community fails to serve itself. The schools cannot be expected single-handed to prevent riots, eradicate poverty, and rescue our dying cities. The public must examine its own conscience, its crash-program mentality, and its persistent demand for answers which are simple to problems which are not. The present educational crisis cannot be alleviated by sticking Band-Aids and slogans on the system, or even by patching it with money. We must expedite the schools' task by demolishing the festering slums which pour their damaged children into the choking schools, by providing training for jobs which really exist, and by offering the poor and the powerless a genuine place in society.

Creativity in education has several meanings. It refers to imaginative, innovative teaching. It also suggests the cultivation of individual artistic and intellectual talent, and the nurture of the student's power to perceive and respond in his own accents. In a more profound sense, however, creativity in education implies a new role for the schools in society: creative rather than conservative, open rather than closed. It has been the custom of education to prepare children for the future by indoctrinating them with the wisdom of the past, and by encouraging obedience, conformity, and obeisance to orthodox dogmas.

In America, moreover, public education's primary mission was to facilitate industrialization and to fire the melting pot. Now that a heterogeneous mass of immigrants has been transformed into a homogeneous nation, we are in danger of being boiled down still further into abstractions. Today our problem is not how to expand industry and build cities, but how to live in these cities, how to resist the compulsions of bigness, automation, affluence and the mass media, and how to preserve what is unique and inviolable in each of us. The educational system must therefore be sufficiently bold and flexible to veer from its traditional conservative course in order to foster the lavish diversity and hybrid strength upon which our greatness depends.

As the pressures for conformity mount, and the population itself is increasingly standardized and regimented, education must not serve as a bludgeon for promoting national uniformity. Vital, imaginative, varied, and courageous, it must become instead the instrument for opposing the coercions of a way of life in which rebels march in regiments and "wild ducks" fly in the same direction. Education is enjoined to sponsor a free, pluralistic society, and to encourage diversity and promote individualism. Above all, it is imperative that education resist its own standardization. It must abjure those incursions of its integrity by which learning becomes indoctrination and guard the rich and fertile soil in which innovation thrives from the ravages of forces which would reduce it to a wasteland.

9. In Old Vienna

THAT THE CREATIVE PERSON is both privileged and cursed is an ancient concept. It was elaborated within the context of sixteenth-century Neoplatonic philosophy and then glorified by the moody romantic writers and thinkers of the nineteenth century. This notion still thrives in the minds of those who believe that the price of genius is a measure of madness; that the cost of humbler creative talent must be a degree of mental aberration. The myth of the sick artist resembles the stereotyped image of the "gifted" child as a pale, maladjusted myopic weakling. As a statistical composite, the gifted child is healthier, more robust and energetic, and better coordinated than the average. Before the romantic movement, however, reference to the artist or genius as "mad" implied that he was inspired, idiosyncratic, and unconventional. It did not mean that he was mentally ill or insane. The relatively unalienated artists of ancient Greece, although possessed by divine frenzy, were never considered sick, and neither the sanity nor the virility of the Renaissance artist was questioned.

Romanticism was an exuberant and often contradictory movement. In the broadest sense it opposed the dry classicism and gelid rationalism of the eighteenth-century Enlightenment. With a Faustian longing for a rich, boundless experience of life, the romantics scorned the "gray and ashen" perfection of science in which the world was conceived as a machine, to pursue what Santayana called "the cry of the heart." They glorified the emotions, stressed the tradition of the individual, and exalted sentiment and the imaginative powers of the irrational mind. Goethe who embodied the romantic ideal of abundance and freedom, nevertheless despised the sickly cult of the romantics. Loyal at the same time to the Greek canons of balance, clarity, and reason, he attempted a synthesis of romanticism's rich humanity and the classical ideals of order and control. As a movement, romanticism was riddled with ambivalence and tension. Jubilant and brooding, revolutionary and reactionary, its moods were expressed in the pessimism of Schopenhauer, Kierkegaard and Tennyson, in the idealism of Hegel, in the optimism of Carlyle and Emerson, and in the assorted forms of gloom and idealism of Wordsworth, Shelley, Coleridge, Byron and Dostoevsky.

In this atmosphere of morbid subjectivity, egoism and self-indulgence, the artist and genius were looked upon as victims of mental illness. Max Nordau proclaimed the artist a mental degenerate and Cesare Lombroso declared him a pathological freak, ascribing his condition to the abnormal enlargement of the cerebrum. "What the world calls 'genius'," wrote Poe anticipating this ugly diagnosis, "is the state of mental disease arising from the undue prominence of some one of the faculties." Mysteriously alienated, eccentric, and exotically doomed, the brooding romantic poets were saved from the earthquake of complete insanity, as Byron wrote, by the eruption of imagination.

The unwholesome privilege of the creative individual acquired philosophical sponsors in Hegel and Carlyle, who contributed the cult of genius according to which the genius was hoisted atop a lonely pedestal. Left at these Olympian heights, the genius was worshipped, but condemned to exist apart from ordinary mortals. That the artist was bound to know sorrow and suffering was not an invention of the nineteenth century. Prior to this time, as Herbert Muller observes, the artist usually knew why he was unhappy. The romantic writer, however, epitomized by the melancholy Byronic hero, was afflicted with a nameless disease of the spirit which had neither palpable source nor cure. Pursued by unrelenting furies, a stranger and an outcast, the poet regarded his fate — which incidentally afforded him considerable narcissistic pleasure — as punishment for some ineffable, but awesomely heinous sin.

Because creativity involves the rejection of the established order, the creative person is likely to appear rebellious, eccentric, even "crazy." As long as society respects his vocation, his madness is not taken too seriously. But if, like the modern artist, he is estranged from his culture, it may be expedient for both society and the artist to identify disaffection with mental disorder and to equate rebellion with neurosis. To the bourgeois morality of the nineteenth century, dominated by the ethos of the business and industrial community with its devotion to work, social ritual, health, and hygiene, the artist's bohemian life appeared depraved and unhealthy. Writing poems or painting pictures did not qualify as responsible, virile occupations to the citizens of a utilitarian society loyal to the injunction that man must earn his cottage or castle through hard work — honest or otherwise. It also followed that those who scorned the middle-class proprieties must, like the irresponsible grasshopper, pay for this privilege with suffering.

Creative man, as personified by the artist, was therefore exiled to the periphery of society. His social status and livelihood became increasingly dependent upon his ability to accommodate his work to the tastes of a growing middle-class public — a gift in which Byron and Sir Walter Scott excelled. On the other hand, the scientist, inventor, and engineer, whose useful, "realistic" work provided the foundation for nineteenth-century material progress, unless wildly eccentric, escaped the stigma of neurosis. Unlike the unstable "creative" spirits engaged in the genesis of fantasy, entertainment, and cultural luxuries, the scientist was regarded as a sober, respectable citizen occupied in productive work. Now that the scientist has become a pillar of twentieth-century society, the myth of the mad scientist has all but died, ironically at the very time when society's collective madness may turn out to be its blind faith in the power of science.

Caught in the tension between the values of a drab, material-istic society and his own artistic values, the artist cooperated in establishing the popular stereotype of himself as the recipient of divine gifts, separated from the common herd not merely by his talent but by his abnormal behavior and the special quality of his suffering. It was a pact of mutual contempt and suspicion, admiration and dependence. Artists in the past have rebelled against their society, but in the romantic era the artist became a flamboyant creature beyond the pale of the society he had appointed himself to improve. Writers disdained the values and taste of the public which bought their works in increasing num-ber, but failed to take them seriously as prophets and guardians of Culture. The romantic writers proudly concluded that like the ancient prophets and half-mad seers, they too had been "called" to serve in an exclusive priesthood. With enthusiasm and self-conscious dedication they nourished those differences which distinguished them from an audience of philistines.

Although the relationship between art and truth is far from clear, both the artist and the public accepted mental derange-ment as the price the artist must pay for his powers of revela-tion. This rationalization, as Lionel Trilling observes in a trenchant essay on creativity and neurosis, enabled the ambiva-lent public to cast the artist in the role of prophet or idiot, to condemn his moral turpitude or to admire his divine sponsor-ship. The primitive beliefs in disease as an instrument of knowl-edge, in affliction as a source of strength, and in the benefac-tions of mutilation were particularly well suited to the "no pains, no gains" spirit of the Victorian age. In truth, the crea-tive artists of this period were a highly neurotic breed, alien-ated and aloof, as the Greek and Renaissance artists had never been, from the standards and mores of their times. Undoubtedly the artist's growing estrangement and hostility to his society contributed to his genuine problems of adjustment. For its part, society dealt him generous portions of suffering and an-guish and was quite capable of making him physically and mentally sick.

To the romantic myth that "great wits are sure to madness near allied," Freud now brought the sanction of science. Psychoanalysis, particularly oversimplifications of Freud's earlier ideas, provided scientific reinforcement for the popular theory which accepted mental illness as the foundation of art and genius.

Sick . . . Sick . . .

For forty-six years Sigmund and Martha Freud lived in a large, comfortable flat on the first floor of the massive stone house at number 19 Bergasse in Vienna. A butcher whose first name was Sigmund kept shop on one side of the main portal; on the opposite side the other Sigmund had attached his medical shingle. During most of this period Freud's office and study adjoined his family quarters, so that in the few minutes between fifty-five-minute analytic sessions Freud could leave his rug-hung consulting room and slip into the family quarters to refresh himself with the latest household news.

Each morning at seven Freud arose, took a cold shower, and by eight, attired in a dark suit, stiff white collar, and bow tie, was ready for his first patient. At one o'clock he sat down to a substantial lunch with his wife and six children, after which he enjoyed his daily constitutional. Generally, he returned to his consulting room at three for steady work until nine when he joined his family for dinner. The unvarying routine of Freud's working year in Vienna was punctuated by carefully planned, idyllic summer holidays with his family. These cherished vacations in the Alps away from the Vienna he hated were devoted to collecting mushrooms and wildflowers and to long tramps through the pine forests. This restful phase of his holiday was usually followed by more sophisticated travel abroad. Significantly, Freud maintained a sharp seasonal and geographical division between work and play, business and pleasure.

Freud was a devoted son, a loving husband, and a kind, indulgent father. His adoring wife, Martha, was a superb manager who saw to it that the well-run household revolved about her husband's comfort and convenience. According to Ernest Jones, the atmosphere of the Freud household was "free, friendly, and well-balanced," pervaded by a remarkable spirit of harmony and tranquillity. This warm, serene family life was in strange contrast to the savagery of the events which took place behind the heavily curtained double doors of Freud's consultation room, and in the adjoining sanctum of his book-lined study. Long after the family had retired for the night, Freud would sit at his desk to confront with undaunted courage the ugly demons of the irrational mind. In elegant prose, distinguished for its grace and clarity, this puritanical, chaste son of the nineteenth century wrote of hostile urges and primitive lusts, of infantile sexuality, and of the dark night of the unconscious mind. The father of a new century, he remained the son of the old.

The striking disparity between the even tenor and predictability of Freud's personal life and the barbaric mental life he probed symbolizes the central paradox in Freud's work. Called a "romantic mechanist" and the "last pre-Freudian rationalist," Freud produced a fatalistic system infused with a Christian sense of original sin, in which guilt, that indispensable partner of sin, was cast in a principal role. Loyal to the utilitarian morality of nineteenth-century industrial Europe, which regarded work as duty and sex as a means of procreation, Freud, according to his critics, created a reductive, pessimistic psychology which tethered man to his primitive instincts and which in its theories, if not its therapeutic technique, slighted man's unique biological assets, will, reason, choice, and creativity.

Originally Freud had hoped to construct a quantifiable science of the mind in terms of the laws of the conservation of energy, according to which energy is never lost but is instead converted into some other form. Neurosis, according to Freud, is caused by the damming up of sexual energy. Terms such as resistance, repulsion, attraction, and repression make psychoanalysis sound like a project in hydroelectrical engineering. Intensely rational himself, a man who believed that the irrational squalls of the unconscious could be controlled by the analytical powers of the rational mind, Freud was at the same time an imaginative genius who pursued hunches, intuitions, and whose early theories were indebted more to hypnosis than to orthodox psychology or medicine.

Although Freudian theory maintains that man is chained to his brutish instincts, Freudian therapy assumes that man is free to heal himself through understanding and reason. In the long run, the ambiguity of Freud's work, resulting from his own ambivalence, contained the seeds of a psychology which would attempt to heal the Cartesian rent in the human psyche and which through the reintegration of reason and instinct would restore creative man to health and respectability.

Attired in the frock coat of nineteenth-century morality and eighteenth-century Enlightenment, this fastidious Victorian patriarch opened the gates of the mind and descended heroically into its cellar. Freud was not encouraged by what he found there. He occasionally misinterpreted what he encountered and there was much he never discovered. With genius and indomitable courage, impelled by a need to know the truth, Freud explored the family nightmares and sexual gorgons of neurotic Europeans caught in the cultural and social upheaval of modern urban life. It was an age which saw the breakdown of traditional religion and morality, the emancipation of women, and the transition from the rational ideals of the Age of Reason to the irrational and often nihilistic attitudes of modern times.

Freud did not discover the unconscious, an honor he specifically reserved for the literary masters. In his *Notebooks*, Coleridge had already written of the "twilight realms of the mind," and even used the term "psycho-analytical." The unconscious mind was, however, primarily the metaphysical province of the writer, philosopher, and theologian. By dramatizing the power of unconscious mental processes in subverting conscious mentation, Freud made the unconscious public property and the concern of medicine. He issued scientific statements about its architecture and appointments, and forced people to examine the grotesque contents of the inner mind in order to understand their neurotic problems. Where once there grew the rare flora of imaginative insight and irrational thought, Freud installed the common, although not necessarily authentic, fauna of biological instinct. The psychic realm of veiled feelings and exalted inspiration became, as well, the mean abode of tragic drives and mental illness.

Plato had sketched the mind-body division; the Cartesians performed the surgery. The Enlightenment esteemed the rational powers of the conscious mind, whereas the romantics, standing on the opposite side of the mental schism, championed emotion, passion, and the dark, intuitive powers of the irrational mind. When science confronted the mind-body problem, the behaviorists in a brash attempt to construct a psychology which qualified as a natural science, simplified their task by discarding the mind. Freud, who also aspired to the objective standards of science, maintained the traditional philosophical dissociation of the mind, but brought to it the blessings of science and the dimension of a spurious biology. Freudian determinism is based on the inexorable dictates of instinct — and to the horror of his outraged contemporaries, sexual instinct. Man was offered, on the one hand, a determinism of no-mind, and on the other, a determinism of a mind dominated by innate instincts and by the patterns of behavior acquired in infancy. For all his devotion to science, however, Freud accepted the challenge of studying the mind, and more remarkably, the unconscious mind. Psychoanalysis, as a result, was not a quantitative science. Freud continued to hope that one day it would be, but to the credit of this testy, dogmatic genius, he was honest enough to recognize that his original goal had eluded him.

What Freud in his time and place could not see, others did. Modern perspectives in creativity research are radically different from classical psychoanalytic theories. Nevertheless they are profoundly indebted to the genius whose conception of a natural science of the mind, although unable to reconcile the opposed parts of man's nature, at least retained all the parts. But before psychology could undertake the restoration of man's creative birthright, before man's will and reason would be returned to him, Freud's theories were to reinforce the ancient association between creativity and mental aberration.

The spirit and purport of modern creativity studies are best understood if examined against the background and premises of classical Freudian tradition. Contemporary positive concepts of creativity have arisen within the context of psychologies which do not share Freud's concern with the vicissitudes of instinct. Unavoidably, abridged accounts of Freud's work present psychoanalysis as a static system, an impression which is erroneous and unfair. During his long and productive lifetime, Freud's theories underwent a gradual metamorphosis, becoming less raw and didactic as their author aged and mellowed. An idealist at heart, Freud was eventually discouraged by the intrinsic tragedy and pessimism of his work and hoped that it would be replaced by a more sanguine formulation of the human condition.

Located on the banks of the Danube and surrounded by the fabled Wiener Wald, Vienna at the turn of the century was a city of laughter and culture, of music and literature, the home of Bruckner, Mahler, and Richard Strauss, of Schnitzler and Hugo von Hofmannsthal. But beneath its charm and levity stirred the uneasy tensions which heralded the political and social cataclysm of the twentieth century. Freud was a physician, disposed by training to a biological rather than a cultural or environmental orientation. To his Viennese consulting room came sick and disturbed patients tormented by the strident discords of a highly competitive, materialistic society already beset with the dry rot of alienation.

Many of Freud's theories, therefore, contained the built-in bias of his highly selected evidence. It is not surprising that he returned from explorations of the disturbed unconscious with pathological trophies or that, almost inevitably, his view of the human psyche was pessimistic and negative. Lacking contact with so-called normal individuals, limited in his understanding of behavior in primitive cultures, Freud increasingly stressed constitutional factors as central to his theories and underestimated the influence of social forces and interpersonal relationships in the development of personality. He thus founded what he believed to be a psychology of universal human nature on the quicksands of Victorian hypocrisy and on the unhealthy ambivalence of European attitudes and mores. After poking about in the dirty laundry of patriarchal European family life, including his own, Freud proposed the Oedipus complex as an inevitable and fundamental biological instinct. Anthropological studies of matriarchal or primogenital non-European cultures do not support this conclusion.

The Ego Sandwich

Freudian mental topography carves the mind into three realms: id, ego, and superego. The id, whose unconscious forces are obscure and inaccessible, is a wild terrain of primitive instinct. The ego is the domain of conscious perception, of reason, and the control of motility. It is sandwiched between the demons of the id which storm it from below, and a stern, oppressive superego which, as the authoritarian representative of society, is the source of "conscience" and therefore of guilt. Parts of the ego and superego may also be unconscious. A buffer state, hemmed in between the warring dictators of an unbridled animal id and a conscience-pinching superego, as well as a third tyrant, the outer world, representing reality, the feeble and bruised ego finds itself in a cruel predicament. It may spend much of its time in anguish and agony, and much of its energy in building defenses against the corrosions of its nasty neighbors, or in trying to negotiate a truce which would guarantee its right to exist. With the onset of civil war in the psyche, the stage is set for tragedy.

The antithesis of id and ego is a scientific incarnation of the ancient mind-body dualism in which instinct and reason are

opposed. In the biological morality play as described by Freud,
the flesh and the unconscious emotions are cast as potential
villains. To encourage the wishy-washy ego to resist seduction
by the tempestuous id — which among other things is a cauldron of sexual drives — the superego, in which Mama, Papa,
Church, and Society are bundled together, stands guard to make
certain the victim is appropriately wretched should he fail to
keep the lid clamped on his bestial nature. Were the harsh, unbending superego to have its way we would all be saints. Freud
appears to have disapproved of the contents of the cruel superego, and once described man's moral conscience as an "uneven
and careless piece of work."

To Freud instinct and reason were predestined antagonists.
In order that reason, which he equated with culture and "reality," may dominate, the demands of the primitive id must be
sublimated and man's instinctive nature restrained. The cure of
neurosis was effected through the analysis of unresolved psychic conflicts. Accepting the reality of his predicament, and
having acquired insight into its nature and origin, the patient
gradually learned to control the destructive and regressive con-
vulsions of the irrational mind. Ambiguity and confusion in
Freud's own attitude toward the opposed aspects of man's nature are responsible for pungent debate in interpreting the prescriptions of psychoanalysis. At the one extreme, Freud's work
has been construed as a franchise for the release of man's instinctive nature from the shackles of social convention, or even
as a warrant for sexual license, and at the other, as a formula
for adjustment and conformity, and as expensive instruction in
the art of "coping." Freud himself wrote that education must
steer its way between the Scylla of giving the instincts free play
and the Charybdis of frustrating them.

Unfortunately, the Freudian ego was inadequately equipped
for its role as mediator and was deficient in positive virtues of
its own. At best it received an arsenal of defensive machinery
for protecting itself during the bloody skirmishes between uninhibited drives and the lacerating pangs of conscience. The

Apollonian rule of reason, the polestar of Western culture, was usurped by the primitive Dionysian forces of the irrational mind, to which Freud accorded superior power in dictating the patterns of behavior. Whereas he did not flinch from pursuing the pleasure-seeking animal id into its lair, Freud was at heart an old-fashioned rationalist who accepted the id but had little admiration for it. He entrusted his long-range hopes for mankind to the restoration of reason's jurisdiction, and based the design of his immediate therapeutic technique on the curative powers of intellect, analysis, and understanding. "Where id was there shall ego be." Hope for the future lay with the rational mind which by its very nature "would not fail to concede to human emotions . . . the position to which they are entitled." We must be careful to distinguish the target of Freud's moral judgment. More than anyone, Freud helped to free people from Victorian prudery. It was the primitive instincts of which Freud disapproved, not the people possessed by them.

Getting Nowhere

The price of civilization, according to Freud, is the subjugation and renunciation of our ignoble instinctive drives and a heightened sense of guilt. High on the list of mournful axioms in the Freudian primer of speculative biology is the postulate that we are born with a "death instinct." Freud believed that the energies of this innate drive toward death — destructiveness and aggression — are inherent in human nature, rather than possible reactions to a malignant environment. Forced to account for the inconvenient evidence of man's positive behavior and for the obvious fact that most of us choose to stay alive, Freud gloomily theorized that our positive behavior is merely a substitute for the negative behavior.

Eventually Freud offset the death instinct with a life instinct to which he gave the name eros. The life instinct is composed of two drives: a rather anemic ego or self-preservation drive, and the drive for procreation known as libido (sexual energy). The

Freudian life instinct got its author out of a tight theoretical corner by modifying the awkward conclusions demanded by an inborn drive toward death. In offering us a chance to live, however, it offers little joy in the prospect. According to Freud, we thwart the death instinct, at least temporarily, by turning its energy outward in the form of aggression or by balancing it with erotic aspects of the life instinct. Sadism and masochism are the unsavory results of eroticizing the death instinct.

Freud neglected the full significance of man's will to live, although his own rich, creative life stands as a testament to the psychology he never wrote. During his long painful battle with cancer, Freud refused until almost the end to take drugs, including aspirin, to ameliorate his suffering. He once told Stefan Zweig, "I prefer to think in torment than not to be able to think clearly." Concerned primarily with his sexual libido theory, the sacred core of psychoanalysis, Freud for many years ignored the other face of eros, the drive for self-preservation. Custodial care and protection from outright annihilation by its unsympathetic mental neighbors, the id and superego, were all Freud offered his feckless ego. Concentrating on the sexual etiology of neurosis, Freud failed to comprehend that the preservation of self involves the nurture of its more profound needs: growth, fulfillment of its potential, and the integration of its dissonances.

Freud lived in a highly competitive era ruthlessly devoted to the attainment of material progress. Darwin's "survival of the fittest" was literally interpreted by the aggressive, materialistic Victorians as a dog-eat-dog contest. In this puritanical view, those who were poor deserved to be; work was identified with "reality," which was in turn unpleasant; and the high cost of civilization, like parenthood, was sacrifice and renunciation. Art might be appreciated, but the artist's way of life was not. Indulgence in fantasy and creative enterprise which denied the claims of reality was not considered a serious occupation for the responsible adult.

Influenced by the attitudes of his milieu, Freud invested

human nature with his cultural prejudices and drew a distorted portrait of the human condition. According to his critics, Freud explored the pathology of sex, but ignored the pleasures of love; he slighted the value of play and fun, and disregarded the joy of learning, striving, and creating. The Freudian child is born a potential prisoner of biological necessities, and before many months, inevitably becomes a victim of his parents' nurture. Life consists of treading the tightrope between brute and saint and getting from one end to the other with a minimum of pain. Freud believed that the ideal course lay somewhere between "unrestrained sexual licence and unconditional asceticism."

The nature of the aggressive drive is still poorly understood. A controversial subject, aggression has attracted the attention of ethologists studying its role in animal behavior and of worried Americans who fear that aggression may have become the hallmark of the age. The post-Freudians maintain that Freud did not distinguish between destructive aggression driven by hatred and a desire for power, and the normal self-assertion and aggressiveness which is essential if a plant or an animal is to grow and master its environment and if eventually a human being is to know himself as unique. The pondweed which races to the surface of the water in a fight for sunlight and survival; the child who struggles to walk; the man who refuses to be absorbed by the petty dictates of company policy; the woman who asserts her own identity as a distinct individual: all living organisms responding to their genetic potential are not merely subverting the death instinct, but are fulfilling the demands of capacities which insist upon a chance to function.

The individual who fails to make full use of his faculties may be consumed by the noxious poisons of a life in the process of decay. Disagreeing with Freud, Jung and Rank postulated that man's need to express the positive aspects of his nature might result in neurosis if denied. Violence and destructive aggression may result from the frustration of one's urge to *live*, rather than from instinctual drives whose purpose is to keep the unrelenting death instinct at bay. The "energies" of the Freudian instinct system were conceived as fatal inevitabilities rushing inexorably downward, like a cataract pouring over the falls, unless checked or diverted. Whereas Freud ascribed cruelty to a universal instinct, many contemporary psychologists propose that cruelty may be learned by a child who has been badly treated by life. The man who jumps from the bridge, takes his life, according to Freud, because his aggression — the mechanism assigned to monitoring the death instinct — can no longer be directed outward. Now it is suggested that he may destroy himself because his attempts to live have been unbearably thwarted. A failure in his relationships with other human beings may be the fundamental cause of his suicide, and a desire to punish those who appear to have failed him may provide additional motivation.

If we turn from the human psyche to the principles which operate in nature, it becomes apparent that the process of synthesis is primordial, and thus far, victorious. The positive and constructive direction of life is evident in the mysterious organizing principles which support life in a single cell or a complex system; in the body's ability to transcend its own death by reproducing; and in the potential for variation and invention inherent in the genetic system. Death is not so much the destruction of the organism, as the disintegration of its vital coordination.

According to the law of entropy, in a complete, closed or isolated system chaos increases and order decreases. Despite entropy and the prospect of personal death, in an open system such as organic evolution the tendency to deteriorate toward disorder and sameness decreases. There may be local enclaves of death and degeneration, but in general, natural processes lead toward greater variety and specialization. Cruelty, destruction, and decay are part of nature's pattern. The strong prey upon the weak and there is a life cycle which concludes in death. Nevertheless, as far as we know, life — reproduction, growth, harmony, change — appears to be the primary principle of nature's dominion. The profusion and diversity of living creatures which have evolved upon the once harsh wasteland of our planet attest to a universal generative force, and to the triumph of life.

Death and disintegration, the blind sieve of natural selection, even nature's "mistakes" are not ends in themselves, but in the long run appear to operate in the interest of life and creation. For the plant cannot flourish unless the undergrowth is cut away; there can be no creative act, either of nature's kind or of man's, without abstraction, simplification, and the rejection of those possibilities — animals or ideas — which are unsuitable. In a timely death we make room for life.

"To be an error and to be cast out is a part of God's design," said William Blake. The extravagant waste in nature which brings grief to individual creatures and species, demonstrates the heroic scale of nature's "imagination" and the lavish vitality which is the source of novelty and the unforeseen. Perfect efficiency and overly meticulous planning lead ultimately to the construction of closed, unchanging systems which, lacking intrinsic creative power, are indeed destined to a fatal rendezvous with the law of entropy.

Freud's discoveries were a beginning, not an end. Intuitive and daring, yet rational and dogmatic, a proper Victorian who advanced a theory of sex in the cradle, Freud was a pioneer whose work was at war with itself. Not unexpectedly, Freudian man was afflicted with a severe case of the duality disease: a profound and irreparable crack running through the middle of his psyche. To Freud the irrational forces of the mind, although a source of energy and pleasure, were at the same time a serious liability. Man's wretched instincts were regarded as negative, primitive, and of no value to civilized society or personal growth. As L. L. Whyte observed, Freud failed to provide an effective integrating principle between the forces of instinct and reason. In slicing through the mind of disassociated Western man, he did not discern that the split might be only a partial division, and that beneath the incision there was potentially a single entity, "unitary man." Even though the cerebrum of the human brain is sectioned anatomically and functionally into two relatively independent hemispheres, neural circuits provide communication between the cerebral lobes and the lower centers of the brain.

After an initial fight for acceptance, Freudian tradition with its vivid language and imagery became deeply entrenched in our culture. There were many, both of the profession and the laity, who believed that the gospel of human nature was given during Freud's lifetime and the subject forever closed upon the death of that formidable Viennese genius. For those who have lived during the revolution in thought produced by Freud's discoveries, it has not been easy to maintain his contribution in proper perspective. Those guardians of the sacred relics of Freudian belief, or the partisans of any single "school" of psychology who are under the impression that they alone have been vouchsafed the only authentic version of the truth, seem unaware that they have halted at a partial understanding of the human mind. The advance of knowledge is due to those who are brilliant enough to propose new hypotheses, but who first are brave enough, not to defend, but to challenge the old.

Defectors

Following several decades of fierce loyalty to orthodox Freudian doctrine, the young science of depth psychology began to move beyond the long shadow of Freud's influence to develop new psychoanalytic concepts. Some of these ideas were, in fact, latent in the writings of Freud's later years. Ironically there is now growing appreciation of the work of the first generation of Freudian defectors, Adler, Jung, and Rank, who were exiled from the psychoanalytic movement for their heresies — to the ultimate loss of all concerned.

The first to risk the master's wrath and to leave the Freudian camp was Alfred Adler, best known for his doctrine of the inferiority-superiority complex. Adler objected to Freud's exclusively sexual explanation of neurosis, and in an act tanta-mount to sacrilege, replaced sex with the search for power. The former general practitioner of medicine postulated striving for superiority, the need for self-realization, and the drives of the ego as the dominant influences on personality.

Primarily holistic in his outlook and concerned with the "style of life" and total personality of his patient, Adler took the first step toward the construction of a psychology which went beyond illness. Both in theory and therapy, Adlerian psy-chology was founded on respect for the individual person, for his goals and personal wishes, and regard for him in his present situation, including the cultural pressures to which he was sub-jected. These concepts were later developed by Karen Horney, one of the many heirs to Adler's thought. Although Adler is accused of superficiality and oversimplification, the influence of this first of the renowned Freudian apostates, particularly in the field of parent-child relationships, has been broad and pro-found.

Whereas Adler's work is marked by its rather bald simplic-ity, Carl Gustav Jung's psychology is abstruse and metaphysi-cal. The Jungian unconscious is an exotic abyss, containing many levels, but no ground floor. Beneath the ego and the per-sonal unconscious, which resembles the Freudian unconscious, Jung postulates a collective unconscious, which has some paral-lel in Freud's later concept of racial memory. Buried in the collective unconscious are fossil memories: traces of major events in the past experience of the human species, as well as contributions from man's animal ancestors. This ancient com-mon legacy is inherited by the individual as a biological poten-tial and is believed by Jung to account for latent fears and de-sires, and for the myths and symbols shared by members of our species. Unlike the disagreeable Freudian unconscious, the col-lective unconscious is an honorable place, a valuable museum whose archives contain the collected wisdom of the human race. A visit to one's collective unconscious promises rewarding con-tributions to self-understanding and self-development.

To reject or tamper with the Freudian theory of libido was to commit the one cardinal and unforgivable sin. Like Adler, Jung refused to accept sex as the sole foundation of human behavior — and misbehavior. After converting the libido from pure sexual energy to a more general psychical energy or life force, Jung too left the fold. Jung's psychology resembles Adler's in its concern with the integration of the total personality. Despite his fascination with mankind's primal past, Jung also believes that man is at the same time guided by the future: by his goals and aims, and by his need to affirm his own destiny.

According to Jung, personality development involves the act of realizing one's potential, a creative process in which the self acts as a symbolic goal. From his explorations of the tensions between parents and children, Jung concluded that education tends to repress not only forbidden instincts, but to suppress or mask many positive attributes of the child's personality which have the misfortune to conflict with society's interests. The role of interpersonal relationships and the pressure to conform to the cultural blueprint were to become dominant themes in the work of Erich Fromm and Harry Stack Sullivan. Today these themes have become the leitmotiv in the study of the creative personality.

Otto Rank, the youngest of the three, and the last to depart the Vienna circle, began as a close and devoted disciple and became in the end the most radical of the heretics. Brilliant, creative, broadly cultured, Rank alone in the psychoanalytical movement was Jung's equal in his breadth of historical and cultural knowledge.

Rank's "will" psychology endows man with the potential existential power to will or create himself, rather than saddling him with the burden of repairing the botch nature has made of him. The conscious powers of the mind have regained their thrust and force, and man is offered the chance to determine consciously what he will become. Although afflicted with conceptual haziness, the Rankian will, as an integrating principle in the personality, is close kin to the Jungian self. Essentially a defensive weapon used to prevent the individual from submitting to the will of others, the will battles the direct external pressures of parents, spouse, even the therapist, as well as the internal compulsions of one's own instinctive nature. Plowshare as well as sword, however, the will may be employed as a constructive tool in the service of a common good. The mature, independent, but not alienated, person may decide to affiliate his will with the will of others. Rank considered it the therapist's task to liberate the patient's will and to free him from the lacerations of guilt which ensue when his behavior deviates from the expected pattern.

In all of his work Rank was deeply and sensitively concerned with the problems of the artist and the creative person. Rank insisted that the creative artist could not be understood on the basis of Freudian theory whose negative testimony causes the artist to doubt himself, to question the motives for his concern with art, and which destroys the wellsprings of creative inspiration. To Rank the artist is not a neurotic, nor do his creations represent the sublimation of scurrilous biological drives. Creativity is regarded as a manifestation of health and the artist emerges in Rank's portrait as a hero whose work expresses mankind's dormant or suppressed will.

Rank casts human personality in three molds. The *normal* or *adapted* man is the person who unconsciously avoids the challenge of discovering his self, who accepts his culture, and who in Erich Fromm's words "escapes from freedom." Although he is comfortable with himself, and even useful to society, Rank had little admiration for him. The *neurotic* is the individual who attempts self-encounter, fails, and is left to suffer in the unresolved impasse between society's demands and his own needs. The artist manqué, an example of abortive creative development, is an "artisan of technical skill," who has lost his original creativity. An imitation artist, he lives like an artist, looks like an artist, even suffers like one; he has a talent for the life, but not for the work. The *creative individual,* by contrast, rejects the conventional ideology and through creative growth and conscious effort successfully encounters and accepts himself. His will is his to give or to withhold. Freed of self-doubt, guided from within, a unique and autonomous being, he is at peace both with himself and with others.

Rank's concept of self-affirmation makes better philosophy than therapeutic practice. Self-assertion has been interpreted to mean freeing oneself from a false self-image by examining one's assets and defects, or as the right to be as one is — an argument for rebellion, self-indulgence, and nonconformity for their own sake. The self one defines as true may be as much an illusion as the self one rejects as false. Nevertheless, Rank's theory of human nature is important. The freedom to create one's own destiny becomes an intrinsic human right, and man's creative powers are at last, not merely respectable, but are focal and potent forces in the pursuit of this goal.

Deviating from Freud, yet differing with one another, these early rebels began even in Freud's lifetime to reassemble what their Viennese colleague had put asunder and to suggest an affirmative psychology premised upon respect for the individual and faith in his creative power to encounter life and endow it with meaning. In contrast to Freudian theory and to the romantic concept of human nature which insisted upon a fundamental antagonism between the individual and civilization, Adler, Jung, and Rank no longer regarded civilization as man's inevitable enemy. Man is a communal animal whose mental life has evolved from the beginning within the context of his social life. Between society and the individual psyche, they proposed fundamental unity rather than predestined antagonism.

The present is influenced not only by the past, as Freud had shown, but by man's hopes and goals, by his sense of purpose, and his need to grow, create, and to use his native gifts. For there is hope as well as memory, and dreams project the future even as they return the past. Man's unconscious drives and animal instincts may be a source of concern, but the value of his conscious aspirations may no longer be ignored.

Today there is a heartening movement in major sectors of modern psychology to end the wars of instinct and reason and to dissolve the harsh dichotomies by which man is riven. Sorrow, guilt, frustration, and conflict have not been abolished and the depressing themes of modern life — alienation, anxiety, conformity — abound. Man is not in the sentimental sense born free. But neither is he handed a one-way ticket to doom. Creative, moral, and intelligent, his will and dignity restored, he is offered a chance to contend with his afflictions and to triumph over the inner strains and spiritual discontents of his times. In the words spoken by Goethe's Faust, "He only deserves freedom and life, Who is daily compelled to conquer them."

10. The Birthright Restored

WHEREAS FREUD expounded a psychology rooted in illness and conflict, the trend today is toward a psychology of health, harmony, and growth. Studies of creativity and prescriptions for its nurture are being contributed by psychologists and psychiatrists of diverse schools, as well as by philosophers, theologians, and existentialist writers. Despite differences in theory and technique, these schools share a common approach which distinguishes their members from adherents to the behavioral or classical Freudian psychologies. Called a "third force" by Abraham Maslow, these affirmative, humanistic psychologies, in their own words, are more concerned with constructive self-actualization than reductive self-dissection; with psychosynthesis rather than psychoanalysis. To the principle "Know thyself," underlying Freud's thought, the humanistic psychologies add the injunction: Become thyself.

The self, "partly known and partly knower," the long-neglected Me and I of William James, has finally been rehabilitated and restored to the psychological lexicon. Psychologists who adhere to this holistic concept of human nature recognize the value of man's conscious sense of identity, the virtue of his will, and the importance of his ability to perceive, think, imagine, and to strive for those goals he considers worthwhile. Piaget and his followers emphasize that the methods by which the human mind imposes logic and order on experience, and the means by which it transcends the fleeting patterns of immediate sensory information, are as important to an understanding of

the human mind as the study of its crippling emotional conflicts.

Down Below in the Freudian Cellar

Since Freud's safari through the thickets of the unconscious, psychologists have continued to explore the sunless
caverns of the unconscious mind and its vestibule, the preconscious. In his later work, Freud pointed out that unconscious-
ness is not an exclusive characteristic of the id. Parts of the ego
and superego are also unconscious. For those who regarded the
subterranean vault of the unconscious as a crypt infested with
vermin, crammed with vile longings, and with the unbearable
refuse of nightmares, it is heartening to learn that the unconscious is more than the trysting place of demons.

Not only does the unconscious record drives, instincts and
their associated memories and wishes, but it also preserves attitudes and emotions, stores the neural patterns of skills and
habits, and directs the performance of our internal organs. The
unconscious is a receptacle for material too painful or dangerous to be admitted to the presence of the conscious mind. But it
is also a quiet chamber in which are preserved fragile symbols
of beauty, humor, and personal truth, recorded not in the impersonal clichés of the outer world, but directly as experienced
by the individual himself. In the refuge of the unconscious
mind delicate aesthetic images, perceptions of truth, morsels of
wit and fantasy, and dense clusters of thought and emotion are
protected from the harsh censure of the conservative, opinion-
ated outer world, which has established a branch office in the
individual conscious mind. Often this material is not repressed
or actively buried, as in the case of forbidden or painful experiences; it is simply forgotten or suppressed, as Jung discovered,
in the process of meeting the realistic, unpoetic demands of
daily life. If the unconscious is a prison, it is also a sanctuary.

As Freud himself cautioned, the literary metaphors employed in descriptions of the unconscious may be deceptive. The unconscious is not a place which can be located on a map of the brain. It is, first, a form of memory: specifically those recordings of instincts, drives, and experience which are not ordinarily available for recall. According to Freud, the preconscious, or what James called the "fringe of consciousness," is an intermediate station containing mental phenomena which, subject to censorship, are capable of reaching consciousness. It differs in this respect from the deeper, darker unconscious which surrenders its material reluctantly, if at all. The levels and dimensions of the unconscious vary in the blueprints of its numerous independent surveyors. To avoid confusion, the term "unconscious" as used here, refers to all the content of the mind beyond the spotlight of awareness.

The unconscious also denotes a process which sorts the overlapped meanings of ideas and the nuances of emotion, integrating fragments of stored experience in significant patterns. Whereas the conscious mind assembles the raw data of conscious memory in a process we call thinking, the unconscious mind retrieves and assorts unconscious raw material to form thoughts which remain beneath the surface of awareness. Entrusted to the coded signals of words, conscious thought processes are relatively precise, logical, and chronological, but at the same time, slow in operation and shallow in meaning. Unconscious thought processes transcend the literal restrictions of conscious language. With incredible speed and economy, they scan the ever-changing flow of buried experience, sorting fragments of feeling, condensing images, toying with analogies, juggling and shuffling patterns whose validity exists beyond the thin zigzags and conventional dots and dashes of conscious thought.

Here in the unconscious lie the roots of creativity. More than a burial ground for unacceptable ideas and wishes, the unconscious is the spawning ground of intuition and insight, the source of humor, of poetic imagery, and of scientific analogy. Sometimes for reasons which we still do not understand, unconscious thoughts are forwarded to the conscious mind, appearing suddenly in the form of a bright idea or that quick instinctive feeling or perception which we call intuition or hunch. Just as forbidden impulses may break forth in the symbolism of the nightmare, forgotten perceptions and strands of emotion may rise to the surface of the conscious mind in the form of the inspired dream or the precious moment of insight. Given the other conditions required for creativity — temperament, motivation, intelligence, knowledge, a gifted hand or ear — the critical faculties of the conscious mind review and evaluate these naked insights, converting them into artistic and intellectual creations.

The steps in the creative process may be described as preparation, incubation, insight or illumination, and verification. The first intimations of the creative process may appear in what Whitehead called a state of "imaginative muddled suspense." Below the surface of the conscious mind, in what Henry James called the "deep well of unconscious cerebration," safe from the clumsy, critical interference of consciousness, occurs the key process in the act of creation: the genesis of inspiration and of creative insight. The gifts of the unconscious are sometimes terrifying, but they are also delightful, useful, and on occasion sublime.

The province of the unconscious is also the abode of the inner core of the private self. Contrary to Freudian theory and theological dogma, the humanistic psychologies maintain that the essence of man's nature is neither good nor evil, but is either neutral or antecedent to such judgments. One's public self, on the other hand, consists of that part of the unique inner self which may be safely displayed, plus the surface or conscious self which has gradually formed in accordance with the mores of a particular culture. The edited version of a life published for the outside world is considered valid only to the extent that its author has access to the original personal truths stored within the subterranean precincts of his mind.

Once childhood is over, these hidden sources are not easily

repossessed by the conscious mind, for the unconscious will not display its wares upon command. In the process of growing up, the child is buried within the man. The original self, egoistic and somewhat wayward, begins to retreat behind a more subtle and devious outer structure, better suited, however, to the realities of life. But as we lose contact with our spontaneous, ungroomed nature we indiscriminately cut ourselves off from the treasures hoarded there. If a person seeks the gifts of the unconscious, he has no guarantee that he will not encounter its goblins; if he would discover the delights and the creative truths of the nether regions of the mind, he must be prepared to meet and accept his true self. Obviously, one's inner identity is never entirely revealed, but it is necessary to leave the secure enclave of one's public image and venture into this uncharted wilderness with sufficient honesty to face private reality. The creative person has never broken diplomatic relations with his inner identity, and has never lost the way back to these potent wellsprings of joy and humor, of imagination and inspiration. His gift, as Coleridge said, is to "carry the feelings of childhood into the powers of manhood."

The kinship between child's play and the playful, experimental stage of the creative process is striking. Children play with toys; adults toy with ideas. Both the child and the creative adult are characterized by their openness to new experience; delight in fun, fantasy, and jokes; and an intense absorption in work, which obliterates the summons of the outer world to come home for dinner or to go out and earn it. Far from marking time, or wasting it, these early free-wheeling years of play and experiment on the child's own terms and for purposes which are intrinsic to what he is doing, are essential training in a way of perceiving and thinking which in our competitive, verbal culture are ordinarily short-lived. Childhood, with its limited stage, is the time when we can afford most gracefully to be impractical, absurd, imaginative, honest — and wrong.

The progressive selfish intrusion, therefore, of adult purpose on the child's world of fantasy and play must be viewed with dismay by all who wish to prevent the tragic attrition of the child's creative endowment. There is a growing tendency to extract additional educational mileage from the child's life by infiltrating indiscriminately his playtime with adult work values. Although we are labeled a youth-oriented society, the children we admire will soon be sad travesties of authentic children. Adults shower children with toys, wear their clothing, sing their songs, and rather wistfully recall the halcyon days of their own "unstructured" childhood. Yet very few of these frenzied, joyless adults entirely approve of the child at play or can resist meddling with him as he goes about the business he knows best. Having driven our wildlife into a few remaining corners of the earth, we appear determined to render the vitality and élan of childhood extinct.

The children of our affluent society are increasingly spared the early necessity of working for a living. Although they are told that leisure is to be their heritage, they see little of it while they are young. When we entice a three-year-old into an early-reading program, or when we crush an adolescent with a burden of homework which would offend a respectable labor leader, we are in fact stealing his childhood. More than a sentimental trespass on the "land of lost content," we usurp those fleeting hours in which the child must master the most elementary lessons of creativity. If he is to retain his incipient creative endowment, and if he is to mature as an independent, creative adult, the child must be permitted to serve his creative apprenticeship in its appropriate sequence. He is unlikely to succeed if the natural order of this development is violated. The monsters of the unconscious mind are a sturdy tribe, but its good fairies, unfortunately, are ephemeral and easily routed.

Dionysus and Apollo

As religious faith declined and as traditional values collapsed in the latter half of the nineteenth century, men gradually turned inward to the self in search of meaning in life itself.

God had become remote and impotent, his person destroyed and his essence as an ideal equivocal. The vast universe, man learned, was not designed as his home. Science was a treacherous friend. To his dismay, man discovered that he was serving the social system which was originally intended to serve him. Shivering in the cold winds of a universe which had no special love for him, the erstwhile rational animal with the immortal soul, in the process of losing both his soul and his reason, attracted not only the philosopher, but the artist, theologian, psychologist, and psychiatrist to his sickbed.

The doleful philosophy of existentialism and the optimistic psychology of creativity may appear at first glance to have little in common. One should not overlook the creative courage with which the existentialist plumbs the dark irrational night of human existence, prepared to construct his life upon the very ashes of despair. Neither should one misinterpret the optimism of the "open" psychologies which offer man freedom to seek his own salvation, rather than a nepenthe for anguish and uncertainty.

The roots of existentialism are ancient. But in the nineteenth century, led by Nietzsche and Kierkegaard, and in this century by Heidegger, Jaspers, and Sartre among others, existentialism became a major philosophical movement. There are limits to human reason, insists the existentialist, and therefore a rational view of an unpredictable, irrational universe is absurd. Disillusioned by the terrible unreasonableness of rational men, and by the public and private acts of insanity supported by rational arguments, the existentialist rejects the *abstract* rationality of the Enlightenment: the faith that there is no problem that reason alone cannot solve, or that rational men cannot handle. The existentialist quarrel, as William Barrett emphasizes, is not primarily concerned with classical, godlike reason, which in ancient Greece was never divorced from feeling, or with the genuine role of intellect in subduing the forces of cruelty and injustice. The main target of existential protest is that insidious form of rational control which has pervaded our way of life to

the point where it has become a substitute for genuine thinking, and in which human feeling, experience, and insight are
no longer summoned to check the rhetoric of rationalism.
There are sources of truth, says the existentialist philosopher
— and the existentially inclined psychologist agrees — which
can never be reached by intellect.

According to Jean-Paul Sartre, the brilliant if somewhat
morbid exponent of one branch of modern existentialism, the
essence of man's nature is not a ready-made entity, but derives
from his existence. Man creates himself, says Sartre. American
psychologists, aware of the effect of genetic and constitutional
factors on behavior, are reluctant to grant man an entirely free
hand in the undertaking. Instead they refer to the creative enterprise as self-discovery or self-actualization. The more radical
contemporary existentialists such as Sartre differ from their
predecessors in their belief that man's existence — the source
of meaning in life — is itself meaningless. Summoning the
"courage of despair," man's task is to affirm his self even in its
meaninglessness, for in so doing, he gives meaning to his existence. Sartre asserts that life has meaning only in a commitment
to action and in personal involvement in society.

Despite criticisms of negativism and despair, existentialism
has been a remarkably creative movement. The artistic expression of existential anxiety has produced such masterpieces as
Kafka's *The Castle* and *The Trial,* Eliot's elegant, cultivated
poem *The Waste Land,* Sartre's *No Exit,* and Camus's *The
Stranger.* The authors of these works presumably have transcended the Sartrian nightmare of nonbeing through the creative expression of their despair. Similarly, modern art, dance,
and music — bleak, discordant, and abrasive — have rejected
the rational canons of Western intellectual tradition and turned
with fervor to the exploration of other forms and ideals, particularly those of primitive and Oriental cultures. By testifying to
man's spiritual poverty and to the absurdity and contingency
of his existence, modern art achieves a powerful triumph of the
spirit. While nuclear scientists and world leaders flirt with the

production of nothingness, the portrayal of nothingness has become a serious creative task for the artists who depict our age.

American psychologists and psychoanalysts, who in general decline the extremes of the more somber European philosophers, have found an exciting stimulus in existentialism. Existentialist thinkers, for their part, have borrowed heavily from psychology. The quest for identity, and the influence of growth and possibility in shaping personality are themes common to both. Subjective experience and intuitive judgment are extolled at the expense of abstract conceptual systems and verbal, analytical reason. Each discipline acknowledges passion, vitality and the drives of the unconscious as integral to a nature which is whole, human, and authentic. "The heart has its reasons which reason does not know." Without the focusing power of emotion, brittle reason would clatter along like a sterile calculating machine, fragmented, disorganized, and lacking purpose or direction. For it is human emotion, unkempt but magnificent, which is partner to reason's triumph, even as it is unrestrained, morbid emotion which corrupts reason and makes men unreasonable.

It was the mark of Greek genius to have understood this. Delight in the energetic use of the body was as much a part of the Greek way of life as respect for harmony, balance, and rational order. The Greeks worshipped Apollo, the civilized god of reason and lyric poetry, yet they also revered Dionysus, the God of the vine and of tragic poetry. The splendor of Greek accomplishment in art and thought derives from its magnificent synthesis of Apollonian form and order, with the passion and surging vitality identified with the Dionysian spirit. For a few immortal moments in the history of the world, mind and spirit were united, and reason and emotion reconciled as never before and never since. In the words of Edith Hamilton, "the truth of poetry and the truth of science were both true."

Existentially oriented psychology attempts to fuse the Dionysian and Apollonian elements in man's nature and to dissolve the severe dichotomies according to which reason and emotion are inevitably opposed, and in which creativity, depending upon intellectual fashion, has been mistakenly identified with one or the other side of the breach. In the act of creation the individual heals the rent in his psyche. Imagination and form are merged through the integration of unconscious and conscious thought. Sober reason acquires the wings of imagination and the energy of passion, whereas the Bacchanalian virtues of the instinctive, earthy wine god are tempered in the golden clarity of Phoebus Apollo, the quintessence of rational enlightenment.

The feeling of ecstasy and elation, or that sense of luminous consciousness, experienced at the moment of creative insight is the result of a momentary union of conscious and unconscious levels in the personality. As the individual transcends the warring forces in his nature, emotion, will, and intellect merge and fleetingly he experiences himself as a total person. The ecstatic or "peak experience" is common not only to the creative act and to the process of self-actualization, but to the mystic and aesthetic experience, as well as to love and childbirth.

As man learns to understand and accept his ungroomed, irrational nature and to embrace his inner self, he escapes the stranglehold of doubt, inhibition, and fear. As Maslow observes, he wastes less time and energy protecting himself from himself. Energy and enthusiasm wax as conflicts diminish. He becomes more perceptive, spontaneous, efficient; softer and yet stronger. Suffused with vital warmth and imagination, his powers of reason and logic flourish. The wintery numbness of alienation melts and he feels freer, more human, less afraid, and more fully alive.

Looking Backward

Throughout his long professional career, Freud was fascinated, yet repeatedly baffled, by genius and creativity. On numerous occasions he attempted to psychoanalyze the genius of such artists and writers as Michelangelo and Leonardo, Goethe and Dostoevsky — an undertaking somewhat marred by the absence of the subjects themselves. Long-range psychiatric diagnosis continued the questionable nineteenth-century practice of deducing a celebrated author's medical ailments from his writings. Pathography became a favorite pastime of the Vienna Psycho-Analytic Society and of heavy-handed psychoanalysts after Freud who went to work with zeal, and little awareness of where the ice grew thin.

Despite his valuable studies of dreams, wit, fantasy, and Greek tragedy, Freud never provided a systematic theory of creativity. Psychoanalysis has enhanced our understanding of specific works of art, but Freud's pronouncements on the more general subject of genius and creativity are confusing and lend themselves to misinterpretation. In his study of Leonardo's homosexuality and stunted sexual development, Freud made the curious statement that he did not consider Leonardo a neurotic, presumably because Freud regarded neurosis as a universal cultural affliction. The practical concept of illness depends on the degree and severity of the neurotic symptoms. The neuroses, according to Freud, originate in a "*conflict* between ego and sexuality." In *Civilization and Its Discontents* Freud described man as a "prosthetic god," who is not yet happy in his godlike character. "When he puts on all his auxiliary organs he is truly magnificent; but those organs have not grown on to him and they still give him much trouble at times." In the same book Freud wrote that the love of beauty is related to sexual feeling. Yet he admitted that, like the science of aesthetics which had failed to explain the nature and origin of beauty, psychoanalysis also had scarcely anything to contribute to the subject. "Before the problem of the creative artist," Freud stated, "analysis must, alas, lay down its arms."

Although he insisted that psychoanalysis could not explain the *origin* of the creative gift, Freud suggested that like other forms of socially useful behavior, creativity results from the sublimation of unacceptable predispositions deriving from libido, and that it serves as a substitute gratification for unfulfilled drives and longings. The severity of Freud's earlier ideas in which art was conceived primarily as a neurotic form of expression was mitigated in his later works where he distinguished between the neurotic and creative use of unconscious material. The neurotic person suppresses the material buried during childhood in the morgue of his unconscious mind, whereas the creative individual, endowed with a certain "flexibility of repression," accepts these "freely rising" ideas and elaborates them in creative achievement.

Freud appreciated the playful quality of the creative imagination. He recognized the artist's innocence of perception, his delight in humor, wit, and fantasy, and ultimately esteemed the artist as an intuitive psychoanalyst who obtained his insights from exploration of his own psyche. Nevertheless, Freud's interpretation of creative behavior was grievously infected by his puritanical bias and was distorted by the romantic portrait of the moonstruck genius. The creative life, according to Freud, was a continuation of childish insouciance and a retreat from duty and reality. As a means of solving oppressive unconscious conflicts, creativity may be superior to painful and paralyzing neurosis, but its status remained vaguely unhealthy. Bordering on pathology, never respectable in its own right, creativity, in the reductive literature of classical psychoanalysis, acquired a lengthy list of unwholesome aliases: oral, anal, or intestinal fixation; sadistic, masochistic, or narcissistic compensation; sublimation or regression, voyeurism, exhibitionism, and oral eroticism. Poetry according to Brill, is *nothing but* the "chewing and sucking of nice words and phrases," and the spectators in a museum viewing the "drive discharge functions" of Giotto and Rembrandt, Picasso and Grandma Moses are soothed and consoled by what Freud called the "mild narcosis" of art.

The object of classical Freudian psychoanalysis is to teach the individual to adjust to the world and to accept the unpleasant demands of reality. Since the creative person, in Freudian terms, escapes from reality and fails to adjust to its fatal inevitabilities, he is almost by definition denied a comfortable niche in Freudian theory. For the creative person is precisely the individual who possesses sufficient independence of intellect and character to ignore tradition and social pressures; who quarrels lovingly and constructively with aspects of the reality others accept. Creative people are absorbed in work of their own choice and may not be the best wage earners, husbands, wives, or parents. Often they are sustained by a sense of destiny or calling and may be defiant, immodest, selfish, and at the same time enormously credulous. A person endowed with Keats's "negative capability," who is "capable of being in uncertainties, mysteries, doubts, without any irritable reaching after fact and reason," may not endear himself to those who confuse open-mindedness, a tolerance for ambivalence, and the ability to lie fallow, with sloth and indecision. Dedicated, passionate, and endowed with tremendous drive and energy, creative man is not a conformist nor is he "adjusted."

Neo-Freudian psychoanalysts elaborated the Freudian distinction between the unconscious and the "System Preconscious," shifting the responsibility for creativity from the unreasoning id to the reasonable ego. According to Ernst Kris, creativity is "regression in the service of the ego." Although an improvement in its public image, humanistic psychologists argue that creativity in this conception is still a reversion to primitive and infantile modes of thought. Kris postulates that just as the conscious ego or self regresses in sleep, fantasy, intoxication, or in severe mental illness, it is also capable of voluntary abdication of control in the interest of creative enterprise. While the ego withdraws, temporarily relinquishing the psychic helm, primary mental processes are uncaged and briefly permitted to frolic and romp. Once useful contributions from the preconscious and unconscious have been collected, the adult ego reasserts itself and the revels of the primitive mind are ended.

Looking Forward

In a more radical delineation of the mind's organization, Lawrence Kubie draws a sharp distinction between the unconscious and preconscious, thereby separating the symbolic sources of creativity and neurosis. The roots of creativity are assigned to the shallows of the preconscious, whereas distorted and repressed symbols which may terminate in neurosis lie in the abyssal zones of the unconscious. In a broad sense, Kubie dumps the mind's garbage into the unconscious and assigns its treasures to the preconscious.

Preconscious mentation is free-flowing and inventive. Its symbols are relatively transparent; its mechanisms are efficient, versatile, yet vulnerable. Unconscious processes, on the other hand, are rigid and repetitive, and cannot be altered without resort to special techniques such as psychoanalysis, hypnosis, drug or electrical therapy. The creative activity of the preconscious is subject to attack on two fronts. It may be inhibited by the premature censorship of the conscious mind, which bears the pedantic burden of conscious purpose and which tethers the preconscious to literal reality. Or it may be sabotaged from below by inalterable, negative unconscious processes which are anchored in unreality, and which block or warp the stream of preconscious material. According to Kubie, the straightjacket of the unconscious accounts for recurring themes in an artist's work, for one-book authors, for painters and composers who produce the same work over and over again, and for the scientist whose first important contribution is his last.

Creativity research is greatly indebted to modern theories of perception which have matured and advanced in a direction William James would have approved. A person's account of how things look and feel to him, and his explanation of why he does what he does, are increasingly respected as scientifically valid and are welcomed as essential to an understanding of man's nature. The individual's "right to be believed" has been restored.

Exponents of modern perceptual theory object to regressive psychoanalytical concepts of creativity. They contend that "openness to the world" accounts for creativity and not regression to primitive thought processes, even if the latter are authorized by the ego. Ernest G. Schachtel points out that in the negative psychoanalytical formulation, creativity derives from the need to *reduce* the tension which results from unacceptable drives. The perceptual formulation, on the contrary, regards curiosity, exploratory drives, and creativity as expressions of man's affirmative need to encounter the world, and to *seek* tension and excitement. Perceptual theory maintains that the explanation of creativity lies in the way the individual as a total person perceives and relates to the world, and in his ability to transcend the closed patterns of conventional wisdom.

In Schachtel's formulation man has a choice of two modes of perception. The uncreative or *auto*centric mode is defensive, closed, and centered on the perceiver who reacts primarily to the way the object or experience affects him, rather than to what it is like. Cautious and inhibited, the autocentric viewer eventually rejects new experiences for fear they will disturb established relationships. *Allo*centric perception is spontaneous and open, and focuses on the nature of the object itself. In this form of perception, the total person encounters the familiar world creatively and for itself. Rather than assessing experience for its ability to leave his applecart undisturbed, the perceiver sets out to discover what else the world has to offer. Allocentric perception thus becomes the basis of artistic and scientific achievement and the foundation of personal growth and development.

To the child the world appears inexhaustible and open, beckoning him to savor and explore its mysteries, to taste and test, before drawing conclusions. Neither innocent nor simple, however, perception is a selective, potentially creative act in which the individual consciously and unconsciously chooses those phenomena judged relevant from the standpoint of his unique personality. Motivation is not an "intervening variable" as the more ardent behaviorists maintain, but is implicit in the act of perception. We see what we want to see and what we are taught to see. What we choose not to see or what we fail to observe is forever missing from the events we confidently call reality.

As he is introduced to the style and attitudes of his culture, the child learns what may be expressed and what must be suppressed. At this critical point in his upbringing, the child who once "turned on" each morning as he tumbled out of bed, and for whom each day was a spontaneous "happening" is in danger of losing his former openness to experience and his delight in responding to it intimately and authentically. Gradually he turns off his own eyes and ears, dons the community's astigmatic spectacles, and installs its recording equipment. Now he sees the world as others project it and listens to the recorded sounds of indifferent drummers. His ability to grow and to transcend the closed framework of the world he inherits atrophies and he learns to judge experience in terms of what it is good for and what others will think about it. He is half blind, half deaf, and only partly alive. Homogenized in the great bland cradle of his culture, he exchanges the adventure of being human for a bit of dubious security.

Creation and Aberration

The notion that insanity is essential to genius and that mental illness fires the creative flame is a myth which persists despite the lack of evidence to support it. This deeply rooted tradition is frequently expressed by those emotionally disturbed people who, convinced that neurosis is the source of their creative power, resist therapy for fear that in being cured of the disease they may be "cured" of their creativeness. Art and literature are frequently involved with neurotic processes in human nature. As James Joyce observed, the individual setting forth from his home for the encounter with experience, meets only himself on the doorstep. But neither neurosis nor more serious mental aberration can account for an individual's creative imagination or for his power to use it productively. Truck drivers and accountants may also be neurotic and may express their emotional disturbances in their work, but no one suggests that the ability to drive or to manipulate numbers is the gift of a disturbed mind.

Dostoevsky depicted his epileptic visions in his writing and Kafka wrote to assuage the terror of his sleepless nights. Darwin translated self-doubts, chronic anxiety, and psychosomatic ailments into the dogged perseverance and domestic seclusion which in turn served the heroic task of assembling the vast evidence of natural selection. Certainly neuroses, psychopathic traits, as well as physical ailments may influence the form and content of literary and artistic works. However, neither Dostoevsky's epileptic auras, Kafka's insomnia, Keats's tuberculosis, Henry James's castration anxieties, Gide's homosexuality, nor Rousseau's father nor Proust's mother explains the source of the power to give artistic expression to personal suffering. Noncreative people are also epileptic, neurotic, and insane; they too dream, hallucinate, build defense mechanisms, and have fantasies and phobias. The paranoia of a trivial mind, it has been said, is incredibly boring, whereas paranoid distortion in a brilliant literary genius such as Kafka lent itself to the terrifying portrayal of modern man, isolated, anxiety-ridden, and embarked upon a futile search for salvation. To call art a form of sublimation, escape, or catharsis, does not explain it or distinguish it from sublimation or catharsis which is not creative. A lifelong fixation in an unsolved Oedipal complex may have been a factor in the genesis of Proust's *Remembrance of Things Past*, but one must account for those who have traveled a similar route and accomplished nothing.

No one can deny that the lives of many creative artists often read like illustrations for a textbook of abnormal psychology. The list of those like Swift and Hölderlin, Van Gogh and Strindberg who succumbed to insanity, of those addicted to drugs, like Coleridge, De Quincey, and Poe, and of the countless others whose emotional houses were not in order, is long and illustrious. One might make another list, however, of outstanding creative people who were essentially normal and reasonably well adjusted. Suicide, confinement to a mental institution, and crippling alcoholism or drug addiction are adequate evidence of an ailing psyche. It is easier to confirm mental disorder than to vouch for an individual's mental health. Among those who did not display stigmata of mental instability are Chaucer, Dürer, Bach, Rubens, Victor Hugo, Thomas Jefferson, Niels Bohr, Enrico Fermi, and Freud himself. Thus far there are no adequate statistical studies to determine whether, compared to the rest of the population, creative people are distinguished either by the incidence or style of their emotional ailments. The evidence suggests that insanity and neurosis are handicaps to creation and genius, and that the creative person who is also neurotic succeeds in spite of his afflictions, not because of them. Creative potential is depleted by mental illness, and creative output is distorted and stunted by the inhibitions of neurosis. Notwithstanding the dramatic example of Van Gogh, mental institutions are not the source of masterpieces either of art or thought, and the insane genius is the exception rather than the rule.

Popular legend implies that the sublime beauty of Beethoven's music was inspired by the composer's personal anguish, and that Dylan Thomas's muse dwelled in a bottle. The truth is that when drink, drugs, or mental derangement overtake a Dylan Thomas, Hart Crane, Hugo Wolf, Mark Twain, or a Nijinsky, the artist's creative powers are more likely to fail than flourish. Alcohol and drugs tend to release the mind from the fetters of consciousness, so deeply imprinted with society's tracks and its inhibiting codes and ordinances. Their value in creative work, however, is doubtful. They impede judgment, reduce artistic discipline, and are more likely to delude than illuminate. Moreover they invite addiction and dependence. Coleridge's literary production — a catalogue of incomplete poems and fragments of masterpieces — was diminished rather than enhanced by his drug habit. Opium may have made Coleridge's life more bearable, but judging from his *Notebooks*, his imagination did not require the drug. The unearthly melody and supernatural imagery of Coleridge's poetry were the products of a uniquely inspired imagination and a mind given to fantastic reverie without the fillip of drugs; of an extraordinary memory and omnivorous reading in preparation for his craft.

A mind unhinged from part of itself by drugs or mental illness, and left to witness the free-wheeling fantasies of the unconscious, unable to control time or space, is in no condition to undertake creative invention. The creative process requires a coalescence of originality, style, and a mature sense of relevance. Over the lively circuits of the creative mind, therefore, there must preside that essential critical control which admits pertinent, even unconventional patterns, rejects the useless productions of the free-wheeling imagination and provides behavior with focus and direction. Selecting and organizing the raw material of thought requires the most subtle cerebral discretion. If the hand on the helm becomes rigid and heavy, the bold imagination of childhood is replaced by the stolid conditioned responses and stereotyped processions of thought which clog the mental highways of so many adult minds. All levels of consciousness are involved, therefore, in the creative process as the individual moves freely among them. In the words of Coleridge, "Stuff of Sleep and Dreams, and yet my Reason at the Rudder."

Creation is an "assault on fixation," or in Arthur Koestler's definition, "the defeat of habit by originality." The victim of mental illness, on the contrary, is more likely to suffer from paralyzing work blocks, destructive doubts and anxieties, and to be afflicted with repetitive, stereotyped unconscious processes. He is not free to experiment, change, and grow. No matter what its other disorders and emotional deficits, the functioning creative mind must possess the mental integrity and discipline of spirit needed to endure the "terrific hard gardening" of creative work, and to precipitate form from the "surging chaos of the unexpressed." "The true poet dreams being awake," wrote Charles Lamb, who devoted his life to the care of his gifted sister Mary, tragically afflicted with insanity. "He is not possessed by his subject, but has dominion over it."

The creative artist has the ability to translate his suffering into art, but the suffering remains. There is no support for the popular belief that through the catharsis of his work the creative person can cure himself. Torn with rage and hate, jealous and suspicious, Beethoven suffered agonizing work blocks. His music represented a triumph over his personal anguish, but the triumph was in his art, not in his life. Art, music, and dance may be useful adjuncts to the therapeutic process, but Beethoven's music did not dissolve the cairn of private torment. Neither Thomas Wolfe, that paragon of autobiographical novelists, nor Eugene O'Neill could save himself through his writing. Nijinsky could not dance himself out of insanity, and Van Gogh took his life a few days after painting *Crows in the Wheatfield* and writing to his brother that the country was healthful.

The association of mental illness with creativity is specifically a modern one and is most prevalent in the arts. Possession by divine frenzy did not prevent Greek geniuses from going about their mundane affairs cutting stone, attending to civic duties, or serving in the army. Today few people ascribe the creative powers, or even the genius of scientists, mathematicians, political or industrial leaders to an unsound mind. The disabilities of ailing political leaders such as Woodrow Wilson and Franklin Roosevelt are sensibly assumed to account for their failures, and not for their accomplishments. Einstein, it is true, fulfilled the romantic stereotype of the absentminded professor, a role in which Newton had preceded him. The Special Theory of Relativity, however, was written while Einstein was an employee of the Swiss Patent Office, long before he donned the uniform of dissent.

The artist's irresponsibility in family matters and his lack of realism in his financial affairs is often cited as evidence of his immature, childlike nature. Similarly, one can hardly describe the squabbles of scientists over priority of invention as dignified, adult behavior. Like lawyers and businessmen, scientists are by training reticent about their personal lives in their professional communications. In reporting his discoveries, the modern scientist is encouraged to restrict his personal affiliation with his work to recording his name beneath its title. Kepler's exultant prose and Osler's gracious, humane style are the vanished indulgence of a more elegant, but less efficient scientific era. "Never any knowledge was delivered in the same order it was discovered," said Francis Bacon. Once the beauty and drama, the doubts, miscalculations, and temperaments have been removed from the arid public account of scientific discovery, all that remains is the myth of science as an act of unemotional logic motivated by the lofty desire for truth. The scientist has no reason to broadcast his idiosyncracies, and the public is largely unaware of the neurotic compulsions, the fierce competitive drives, or the withdrawn antisocial attitudes which so often characterize the scientific personality.

Self-analysis is a vocational imperative — and hazard — of the literary profession. The writer is particularly sensitive to the internal mechanisms of the psyche and to the temper of his times. Endowed not only with verbal skills but with an emotional aptitude for his work, the writer exploits these insights to support his art. In the process of portraying the conflicts, tensions, and alienations of modern life, the artist uses the neurotic elements of his own nature, his loneliness, self-doubt, impotence, and anxiety. Modern literature is populated with antiheroes and psychological misfits. Its tragedy is comic and its humor black. Art in our time is profoundly concerned with neurosis because alienation and anxiety, rather than worship of God, the search for truth, or the adoration of beauty, are major themes of contemporary life. Art today appears neurotic because so much of life is neurotic.

A work of art, however, is not an absolute projection of its author's personality, and the neurotic components of an individual work must not be assumed to be identical with those of its author. *Sanctuary* has been described as a series of male impotence fantasies, but this does not mean that Faulkner was impotent, merely that he was imaginative. Moreover, some modern authors plant the psychoanalytic perceptions others may in innocence harvest. It is unwise to review their literary works and draw psychological conclusions about the lives of writers — such as Thomas Mann and James Joyce — who consciously insert Freudian insights into their fiction.

The frequent juxtaposition of neurosis and creativity in the lives of modern artists gives credence to the false, yet cherished belief that the relationship is causal. A man who intends to become a professional poet in an age when only poets read poetry elects a difficult life. The genius who sees what no one else can see, is bound to be misunderstood. External pressures aggravate internal conflicts and in the end it is not surprising if the individual becomes cranky and queer, or even mentally ill.

Studies of the correlation between vocational choice and personality offer other explanations for what appears to be a tendency toward aberration among creative artists. It has been suggested that like Darwinian natural selection, a form of social selection may attract certain personality types to specific occupations, or enable only those creative people endowed with suitable neurotic styles to prosper professionally at a given time. The artist in whom Dionysian or adolescent personality traits predominate may thrive in a sentimental, romantic era, but fail in a classical age. The renunciation of material comfort and social status imposed by a smug bourgeois society on those who waive convention in return for creative freedom, eliminates individuals who are unable or unwilling to pay the price and poses bitter conflicts for others.

A disposition to reject conventional attitudes is, for different reasons, common both to the creative and the neurotic personality. Life on the outskirts of society where the pay is poor, but "the livin' is easy," is attractive to an assortment of uncommon people — rebels, revolutionaries, pseudo artists, sexual deviants, as well as neurotic and psychotic individuals who are already estranged from the mainstream of society. Bohemia provides a haven for the nonconformist whether he is creative, neurotic, or both.

What is the significance of the large number of homosexuals in the arts, in the fashion industry, in the theater, and in the dance? Popular belief would suggest that dancing genius is linked to femininity, and that a normal male cannot excel in this inherently female art. Male folk dancers, social dancers, acrobats, Apache warriors and Russian Cossacks are apparently immune to this genetic disability. The nature of cooking genius is also strange. In France cooking is a noble art, practiced honorably by the male sex. In America, the male cook is a rugged outdoor barbecuer, whereas indoor cooking at a stove is considered a female *talent*. Indoor cooking *genius*, on the other hand, is male — and foreign. A woman cannot be a great chef, it is argued, because she is not a man. According to this perverse logic, however, the masculinity of the master chef, a man who accepts the kitchen as his domain, is suspect. The American boy who aspires to be a chef, a hairdresser, or a dancer can expect the disapproval of his family and the scorn of his friends. Therefore, the youth who decides to become a dancer, may in fact be homosexually inclined, or must possess courage, ambition, and sufficient independence to reject conventional attitudes and ignore the stigma attached to his occupation. In this way the environment chooses its man and not everyone qualified accepts the challenge.

Torn between his creative work and society's stipulation that to support a family or a marriage he must bow to the yoke of convention, the creative person may indeed succumb to emotional illness or sacrifice his gifts. Unless blessed with a patron, a private income, or a heroic family; unless Marie Curie has her Pierre, and Beatrice Webb her Sidney, genius is likely to suffer. Sometimes he sacrifices his family, like Gauguin, and departs for the South Seas and immortality; or like the tragic Willy Sidis, the mathematical prodigy, he may reject his gifts and devote his life to proving that he is not a freak, but "normal" like everyone else.

Although neurosis is not the source of creativity, the question arises whether psychotherapy may for other reasons diminish creativity. The genuinely gifted individual who seeks psychotherapy usually does so because his conflicts paralyze rather than inspire him. The outcome of psychotherapy can never be guaranteed, but following successful therapy, the patient usually becomes freer, less rigid and afraid, and once again resumes work. "The gifted artist 'spoiled by analysis' is rare." Those individuals who turn in their pens and paintbrushes, who abandon aborting novels and sterile canvases, generally do so because they have discovered that their aspirations are not supported by the necessary talent and originality. Creative efforts which serve neurotic needs and compulsions, but nothing else, are destined to be short-lived.

If, however, the goal of therapy is simply "adjustment," and if the therapist equates emotional maturity and acceptance of reality with conformity and social responsibility, a man may be constrained to exchange his unstable way of life for a steady job and the routine social responsibilities of adult life. In such circumstances the gifted woman is reminded that her primary reality lies in the kitchen, car pool, and bedroom. Freud himself refused to do what many of his followers have expected of their patients. For all his devotion to the reality principle, Freud willingly jeopardized his livelihood and his professional reputation, and endured the derision of his contemporaries in order to pursue the work he considered important. In this sense, Freud played favorites with his "realities," giving the search for truth priority over the economic and social realities of his personal life.

Creativity makes unusual demands on an individual's time, energy, and emotional loyalties. If a person cannot earn a living through his creative work, but must hold another job in order to support his family and meet his social obligations, there may be little time or energy left for anything else. The brilliant and gifted cannot be expected to win popularity contests or citizen-of-the-year awards. Often a man must choose, as Yeats said, between "perfection of the life or of the work." Like the creative life, the life of a social hero is a demanding occupation and is perhaps best left to those who are willing to devote full time to it.

It is within the context of a positive, constructive psychology which respects the individual, accepts his need to use his abilities, and which embraces both reason and emotion, that creativity is recognized as a manifestation of health, rather than the consequence of a deranged mind. In the broadest sense creativity is considered a primary process of the universe, immanent in nature and innate in human nature. Neither compensation, escape mechanism, nor the product of a demoniac bargain with sinister or supernatural powers, man's creative potential exists in its own right. The capacity to create is not grafted to man's nature as an expensive bonus, but is instead a basic human aptitude and a source of much personal satisfaction and pleasure.

11. Strange Appetites

Whatever is received is received according to the nature of the recipient.

— SAINT THOMAS AQUINAS

FOR THOUSANDS OF YEARS man has been tinkering with his mental chemistry by fasting, holding his breath, foregoing sleep, imbibing alcohol and swallowing nauseating decoctions of plants and roots. The urge to flee from reality and to transcend the limitations of consciousness and the constrictions of selfhood appears to be, in the words of Aldous Huxley, a "principal appetite of the soul." "The desire to take medicine is one feature which distinguishes man, the animal, from his fellow creatures," was Sir William Osler's more earthy observation. Secret potions once brewed in the witch doctor's cauldron are now purified or synthesized in the chemist's flask. Aspiring mystics can achieve holy simplicity or ecstatic visions not through fasting and long training, but through a pill. The era of psychopharmacology has dawned and with it the offer of the "chemical vacation," not however without the hazards of the road.

Among the useful poisons compounded by biochemists are drugs which enable us to speed up or slow down, to tune in or tune out. There are drugs which alter mood, disguise pain and which, if they cannot yet "pluck from the memory a rooted sorrow," at least suppress and blur memory. Enzymes to facilitate learning, "antibiotic memory repellers," and "protein memory consolidators" are predicted. We already have chemicals which make the cat tremble in the presence of the mouse, and which inspire the mouse with suicidal courage.

There is a structural similarity between chemicals occurring naturally in the nervous system and the molecules found in several of the hallucinogens. The curious resemblance between drug effects and certain psychoses suggested that a study of these "mind-expanding" or psychedelic drugs might offer valuable insight into the chemical basis and etiology of hallucinations and mental illness, particularly schizophrenia. It is hoped that further research on the psychochemistry of the hallucinogens will shed light on the origin of mythological symbolism and the genesis of the mystic and creative processes. If it is possible to kick the traces of ordinary perception and take a chemical shunt to the inner mind by swallowing a pill, one wonders whether it may not be feasible to induce or enhance creativity by deliberate chemical or electrical intervention in the function of the brain. Can we tune up the gifted artist or thinker, or can we amplify the weaker creative potential of those less well endowed? Since "enzyme-assisted instruction" is predicted, should it not be possible to write a chemical recipe for a creativity stimulator?

Current evidence concerning the effects of the hallucinogens is conflicting, ranging from rhapsodic promotion of the drugs as a new chemical religion and an instant cure for alcoholism and a variety of mental ailments, to their bitter condemnation as shortcuts to madness and to the degeneration of mind and morals. Depression, confusion, long-term psychosis, and chromosomal changes have been reported on the one hand, and a variety of religious, personal, and aesthetic insights on the other. For some, the drugs conjure Dante's Inferno on the screen of the mind and the suffocating, crushing tortures of Hell in the pit of flesh. Sinister transfigurations of reality and terrifying experiences of nonexistence are the fate of those the drugs do not choose to favor. Yet for many others the drugs provide visions of sheer ecstasy and may lead to new levels of self-awareness and to the release of latent abilities.

In addition to legitimate scientific disagreement, sensational publicity and the emergence of a proselytizing Drug Movement populated by eminent intellectuals and theologians, by artists and students, and by gifted drop-outs and Hippies often seeking kicks or escape, have added to the confusion. It is reasonable to ask how one drug can produce mystic enlightenment, enhanced self-understanding, or madness. The effects of potent chemicals with the power to interfere in the complex functions of the brain, not surprisingly are dependent on who takes the drugs and under what conditions, and in a broader sense, upon the culture in which they are used. Alcohol and the hemp derivatives are harmful in some societies, yet may be safely consumed in others where their use is built into the patterns of the culture.

Although the scientific literature is sprinkled with suggestions that the hallucinogenic drugs may enhance creative problem solving and stimulate artistic imagination, reliable research on the relationship between the hallucinogens and creativity is still lacking. Extended use of the drugs is ill advised and studies of long-term drug users are few. We also know more about the use of the drugs in abnormal individuals than in those without overt mental aberration. Attempts to evaluate the conflicting claims for the drugs are at this point premature. Instead, let us examine the psychedelic experience first in terms of the effect of invader drugs on the natural chemical mechanisms of the brain and second in reference to the creative process.

The Unblown Mind

The human brain is a moist, spongy organ of pinkish-gray tissue containing about ten billion cortical nerve cells. The duties of this convoluted knot of nerve cells range from keeping our blood vessels from collapsing and preserving the threads of memory, to studying itself, planning the future or regretting the past. An impermanent collection of dancing molecules and atoms, the electrically charged nerve cell, or neuron, is a living dynamo which conducts electrical impulses along its far-reaching tendrils. Nerve cells are distinguished by their long processes which provide an intricate network linking all parts of the organism to the master organ inside the skull. Extending from one part of the cell is the trunklike axon which may reach two or three feet in length. What we call a nerve is actually a bundle of nerve fibers or axons. Also projecting from the cell body are shorter dendritic processes which divide repeatedly into tiny interlacing twigs. The delicate branching dendrites enable a single cell to reach out to neighboring nerve cells, not only transmitting the impulse entrusted to it, but making the multiple connections involved in even the simplest acts. Because of this network of neuronal fibers we are able not only to use our hands, but to know where to find them, and to remember what they look like when they are out of sight.

Conduction paths in the nervous system are made up of intricately interconnected nerve cells. A stimulus traveling along a single neuron may activate 100,000 neurons in one second. The front of impulses traveling through the cerebral cortex is not like a sleek arrow speeding toward a single destination, but resembles a mighty wave advancing in a great crescendo. Within the wave, streams of traffic moving at different speeds continually converge and diverge. Around and around the circuits of the brain, impulses may pursue each other, sometimes dying out, sometimes breaking in a pathway, or reinforcing a pattern as when a habit is set or a memory established. If we imagine the complexity and grandeur of many such traffic fronts in the brain — advancing, dying out, converging, separating, and each shifting within its own lanes — it may be easier to understand why our rich, complex mental life is woven of so many different strands; why it is difficult to separate emotion from thought, learning from memory, or why love and hate may be so fatefully entangled.

When a nerve cell fires, the electrical impulse travels to the end of the nerve fiber and arrives at a microscopic gap or synapse. Neuronal processes do not touch each other. How the impulse is transmitted across the synapse is still not fully understood, but it is known that certain chemical substances such as acetylcholine and norepinephrine (noradrenalin) liberated at the ending of the nerve fiber as the result of an electrical stimulus play a role in bridging the synaptic junction. These substances are then immediately destroyed by companion enzymes which prevent the accumulation of unneeded chemicals and subsequent chaos in the traffic patterns of the nervous system. When an electrical impulse arrives at the synaptic junction it arouses its chemical partners which bridges the gap and initiates a new impulse in the dendrites or cell body of the next neuron.

The synapse, therefore, acts as a valve or a switch, regulating the flow of nerve impulses and maintaining one-way traffic. Local conditions determine whether an impulse has permission to cross the synaptic gap or whether it must wait for further impulses which will increase or decrease the strength of the message. The "climate" of the junction — electrical properties, chemical state, oxygen supply, fatigue, poisons and drugs, as well as habit — all play baffling roles in determining the patterns of nerve traffic. Here at the microscopic junctions in the nervous system where nerve cells do not quite touch, lies part of the secret of human behavior.

As nerve impulses speeding along peripheral lines of the nervous system ascend the tracts of the spinal cord, they pour into the brain where they must be sorted and organized. Millions of impulses weaving dense patterns in the fiber of the brain must make proper connections in which the demands of the inner body, of the immediate outer environment, and of human society are integrated in significant and appropriate behavior.

It is significant that certain of the hallucinogens bear a striking resemblance to chemicals involved in the orderly transmission of sensory information in the nervous system and in the harmonious function of the brain and body, particularly in response to stress. The hallucinogen mescaline is similar to adrenalin in chemical structure, and LSD (lysergic acid diethylamide) is similar, although more complex, in molecular structure to serotonin. Both adrenalin and serotonin are chemicals which are ordinarily involved in the body's reaction to stress and which are believed to participate in the transfer of signals along the circuits of the nervous system. This resemblance between the chemical compounds manufactured by the body and the psychomimetic drugs suggested that defective handling of adrenalin or serotonin might be the organic basis for schizophrenia. It was hypothesized that schizophrenics brew their own hallucinogens. The hope of unlocking the biochemical secrets of insanity has not as yet been realized, but the search continues for drugs to relieve psychic as well as physical pain.

As part of the highest integrating processes of the brain, it is the human form of consciousness or awareness which sets man apart from beast and from which issues the full glory of human achievement. Man's essential humanity — and paradoxically, inhumanity — derives from his ability to know himself as distinct from the rest of creation, to reflect upon himself, to be aware of his location in time as well as space, and to speculate upon the emotions and experience of other human beings and of animals. He is linked by a web of consciousness not only with his fellowman but with all the creatures of the earth. The subject of consciousness is immense and perplexing and our understanding of its physiology, despite our ability to tamper with it through drugs, anesthetics, and alcohol, inadequate.

Consciousness is suspended in deep sleep, in coma, and during deep anesthesia. During the course of the day consciousness waxes and wanes, fluctuating from the extremes of drowsiness and sleep to alert states in which we are excited, vigilant, or in which awareness is narrowed to permit intense concentration. The content of consciousness also varies. Hallucinations and illusions may warp its countenance. In the form of dreams which weave their luminous trails through the dark fabric of the sleeper's night, consciousness is fragmentary and often distorted.

Subtle and multiform, the entire body its domain, consciousness is created by the integration of many complex neural states. Consciousness begins and ends with the contribution of the sensory system. The continuous stream of sensory impulses which pour into the brain from all parts of the body creates the content of conscious experience. This input is at the same time the source of the energy which keeps the nervous system awake and turned on. Consciousness alters as the contribution of the various senses is diminished or reorganized. When we daydream, sight and hearing are somewhat suspended. In deep anesthesia information coming from the major sense organs, as well as touch, pain, and organic sensations are also suppressed. The driver lulled to sleep by the tedium of the superhighway; the infant by the rocking of the cradle, and the insomniac by the monotony of counting sheep illustrate the vital role our senses play, not only in providing the content of consciousness, but in keeping us awake and tuned in.

Buried in the center of the brain stem and extending upward into the midbrain is an exceptionally intricate nerve network, known as the reticular formation. This curious tangle of nerve cells is a primary target of drugs used to expand consciousness or to "blow the mind." Whereas sensory stimuli provide the fuel for consciousness, the reticular formation is its warden. To this dense set of nerve cells is entrusted the vital task of arousing and activating the higher levels of the brain, of screening and filtering impulses before they are admitted to higher offices, and of modulating the level of our attention.

Consciousness does not reside in a cluster of privileged cells or in a hidden switch. In order to create our awareness of the outside world and of our inner selves, several intricate divisions of the nervous system must cooperate with delicate and subtle precision. By way of the sensory apparatus, impulses travel to the brain from the body and the external environment. To be well tuned to reality, human awareness requires the reticular system to keep the brain awake and to sort and amplify the messages it receives. Finally, consciousness depends on the participation of those mysterious cortical areas which contain the archives of memory and the circuits of association which orient consciousness in time and space.

Disturbances in consciousness may occur when any one of these systems is injured or disengaged so that it no longer co-operates with the rest of the mechanism or when one of these divisions becomes overactive. According to this hypothesis, dreaming may be due to a decoupling of incoming sensory information from the memory and association arrangements in the higher brain. Because the sensory system is asleep, the inner patterns are allowed to "free wheel." Mental disturbances, such as delusions and some hallucinations, may result when sensory information arriving from the external environment is for some reason improperly matched with the patterns of past experience, or when the response of overstimulated reticular cells to a flood of nerve signals is distorted. The brain is itself a sensory organ. When its nerve cells are stimulated directly by chemical or electrical means, rather than by impulses delivered through customary sensory channels, sensations of pleasure, terror, hunger, or thirst may be elicited. Artificial excitation of elements in the visual projection areas of the brain may summon to the mind's surface the flotsam of latent memory traces: wheels, discs, colored balls and clouds, stars, spirals, as well as complex fragments of acquired information.

The modes and sites of action of the hallucinogenic drugs remain a matter of speculation awaiting a better understanding of the chemistry and physiology of the normal cell. Because so little of the drug is actually found in the brain and because all trace of it has vanished before the psychedelic show begins, it is postulated that these chemicals trigger metabolic processes which in turn produce the psychic fireworks. It is believed that the hallucinogens modify the response of the reticular system to sensory experience and interfere with the integrating mechanisms by which the brain sorts and channels sensory experience. In addition to retuning the reticular system, psychochemicals affect the midbrain and other ancient centers lodged between the lobes of the cerebrum. Many secrets related to the chemistry of consciousness and emotion are lodged here in the primitive visceral brain, or limbic system, and in the tiny hypothalamus which supervises the delicate chemical balance of the body and brain, and which coordinates important physiological functions by which the body expresses emotion. Above the hypothalamus, buried between the cerebral hemispheres, lies the thalamus, a large oval mass of cells which serves as a sensory way station where impulses headed for the cerebral cortex are intercepted and crudely sorted. A primitive seat of emotion, the thalamus is concerned with the phenomena of wakefulness and sleep, with the sensation of pain, and with the manufacture of a rather general product called "feeling tone." It is to this ancient structure that we owe, in part, our vague awareness of well-being and of general comfort or discomfort.

In the process of learning to write, listening to music, swallowing aspirin or LSD, the stimulus of an experience does not enter a blank nervous system. At any given moment the performance of our nerve cells is determined by the brain's immediate and very recent input, as well as by its inherited and acquired characteristics. At birth our nerve cells already possess certain biochemical endowments which throughout life affect and limit the manner in which we act and react. In addition, past experience — habits, knowledge, and attitudes — as registered in our nerve cells, influence the thoughts and fancies traveling the cerebral highways.

From personal experience, most of us are acquainted with the variability of individual reactions to alcohol, aspirin, or sedatives. Drugs may have variable effects on different people at different times, just as the side effects of these drugs may also differ. When we introduce a drug which is nonspecific in its action into mechanisms as inconstant and chemically complex as the filtering and integrating levels of the mind, it is not surprising that the results are unpredictable.

Studies of the effect of educational environment on the brain chemistry of rats and on their ability to learn illustrate the subtle complexity of the reaction between the biochemists' compounds and the brain's own chemical components. Experiments with rats raised in a stimulating, "creative" environment and deprived rats raised in a severely impoverished environment show that the disadvantaged animals suffered deteriorative changes in the chemistry and anatomy of their brains. When the rats were given chemical memory stimulants, the drugs reacted chemically with the chemicals in the brain induced by the particular environment. The extent to which a specific drug could improve a rat's learning ability depended on the chemical status of the rat's brain, which was in turn a product of its genetic endowment and its early psychological and learning experiences — a lesson derived from experiments on rodents, but not without significance for the early education of poor and deprived children. The implication is that experience alters the chemical composition of the brain. When molecules of a drug are introduced into brain cells, they react chemically with indigenous molecules already modified by learning and experience. It is impossible to foresee, therefore, what the visiting drug molecule will find awaiting it in the structure of the native molecule.

Cactus, Mushrooms, and Smutty Rye

The array of psychochemicals is vast and ancient. Chemical mood changers include depressants such as alcohol, opium, and the barbiturates; stimulants such as cocaine and the amphetamines; tranquilizers which soothe without producing drowsiness; antidepressants which elevate mood and fight apathy; and the hallucinogens, so named because they induce dramatic alterations of perception and consciousness. The hallucinogens comprise derivatives of the hemp plant (charas, hashish, ganja, bhang, marihuana) and the sinister Devil Drugs (henbane, thorn apple, and belladonna) which once provided the chemical fillip in witches' potions and ointments. At present the most fascinating and controversial hallucinogens are the psychedelic or "mind-manifesting" drugs: mescaline, psilocybin, and LSD. These three hallucinogens differ mainly in potency and in the duration of their effects. Although legally classified as hallucinogens, these drugs usually produce pseudo hallucinations, in which the individual is aware that the drug, rather than an external sensory cue, is the source of his experience.

With the exception of alcohol, the ancient hemp drugs may be the most widely used chemical mood changers. Much of the controversy surrounding marihuana derives from confusion in the terminology used to refer to the psychoactive products of the hemp plant, *Cannabis sativa*, and the common but incorrect application of the term marihuana to cannabis of various potencies. Depending upon climate and soil, method of harvest, and the part of the plant used, the potency of cannabis decreases from charas (India) and hashish (Middle East and North Africa) to ganja, bhang, and finally marihuana, the form of cannabis native to Mexico and the United States. True charas and hashish are produced from the sticky, aromatic resin exuded by the tops of the female plant just before flowering, whereas marihuana is made from the dried chopped leaves, stems, and tops of the untreated female plant. The stalk fibers of the altogether prosaic male plant are used in the manufacture of rope.

Most adverse reactions to cannabis occur in individuals who consume the crude resin (hashish) rather than in those who smoke the plant in its natural state. According to Dr. Helen Nowlis, marihuana "may have a potency relationship to the best charas like that of beer to 190 proof alcohol." Dr. Nowlis points out that as long as the effects of excessive use of charas or hashish are attributed to any use of marihuana, controversy and misunderstanding are inevitable. The paucity of well-controlled, carefully designed laboratory and field studies, and the difficulty of obtaining experimental material of known potency and structure are further sources of confusion and uncertainty.

The subjective effects of marihuana vary in different individuals and in the same individual at different times. The drug effects are extremely sensitive to the smoker's personality, to his expectations, and to the specific circumstances in which the drug is used. Sophistication in the technique of smoking and experience in recognizing and labeling the drug effects are important factors in producing the subjective response. The marihuana smoker generally smokes only enough to attain the desired "high," as the pleasant effects may be reversed if too much of the drug is used. The typical effect of marihuana is reported as a pleasant euphoria; smokers describe feeling content, happy, gay, silly, relaxed. The airy sense of exhilaration is correctly described as a "high," not a "trip." More profound changes such as illusions, delusions, and hallucinations occur with the higher doses of cannabis found in hashish and charas, or with excessive quantities of marihuana. Compared to other powerful hallucinogens on the psychedelic menu, marihuana is relatively humble fare.

Mescaline is the active alkaloid in the hairy, gray-green "button" of the peyote cactus which has been used and venerated since antiquity by the Indians of southwestern United States and Mexico. Silas Weir Mitchell, an American physician who was one of the early investigators of mescaline, swallowed several doses of an extract of the mescal buttons and entered a dark room. The eloquent account of the marvels which unreeled before his drug-enchanted eyes has since become a classic in the literature of psychedelic experience.

I saw the stars, and then . . . delicate floating films of color. . . . Then an abrupt rush of countless points of white light swept across the field of view, as if the unseen millions of the Milky Way were to flow a sparkling river before the eye. . . . [There followed a] richly finished Gothic Tower of very elaborate and definite design . . . hung with clusters of what seemed to be huge precious stones, but uncut, some being more like masses of transparent fruit. . . . All seemed to possess an interior light, and to give the faintest idea of the perfectly satisfying intensity and purity of these gorgeous colour-fruits is quite beyond my power.

William James was less fortunate. Seemingly a fine candidate for a mystical experience, the great psychologist did not become one of the happily transfigured votaries of the drug. James took one button of the sacred cactus, saw no visions, but became violently sick for twenty-four hours. A nasty hangover followed, whereupon James wrote to his brother Henry, "I will take the visions on trust."

Aldous Huxley had still another kind of adventure. For Huxley there were no jeweled dragons or living arabesques, no color-drenched geometries or fields of precious gems. Instead the drug evoked the miraculous experience of transcending the external appearance of his environment. Gazing at the "living light" of three simple flowers in a vase, Huxley saw "what Adam had seen on the morning of his creation — the miracle, moment by moment, of naked existence."

Psilocybin, which has been synthesized in the laboratory, is another powerful psychedelic drug. Psilocybin is the psychoactive ingredient in one of the "divine" mushrooms once used by the Aztecs and still used by the Indians of southern Mexico in sacred religious ceremonies. The mycologist R. Gordon Wasson ate six pairs of the acrid, rancid mushrooms after which he participated in the mushroom rites. Awe-struck, Wasson described the experience of "seeing with the eye of the soul, not through the coarse lenses of my natural eyes." Visions of choir stalls in a Renaissance cathedral "were not black with age and incense, but as though they had just come, fresh carved, from the hand of the Master. . . . With the speed of thought you are translated wherever you desire to be, and you are there, a disembodied eye, poised in space, seeing, not seen, invisible, incorporeal." Like many others who sample the hallucinogens, Wasson experienced a "fission of the spirit," in which the rational side of the mind monitors the experiences of the hallucinating part.

The hallucinogenic properties of LSD were discovered in 1943 by the Swiss chemist Albert Hofmann. Hofmann was working with lysergic acid, a derivative of rye ergot, a fungus which is itself the source of many valuable drugs. Accidentally he ingested or absorbed through his skin some of the drug and stumbled on a mild psychedelic phenomenon. This was followed by a more formidable and terrifying experience when, underestimating the potency of the chemical, Hofmann took a second, supposedly minute dose of the drug. Terrified that he was going insane, aware of his condition but powerless to stop it, Hofmann listened to himself raving and screaming. Sounds were translated into vivid color images, faces of persons appeared as grotesque, brightly colored masks, and space and time were disorganized. His throat felt dry and shriveled, his limbs sometimes cold and numb, and at times he felt he was suffocating. At one point the frightened chemist saw his body lying dead on the sofa while his " 'ego' was suspended somewhere in space." He observed clearly that his " 'alter ego' was moving around the room, moaning." The next day Hofmann recovered, having discovered in an extremely unpleasant manner one of the most potent psychochemicals in the pharmacopoeia.

Because the drug trip depends on so many variables, it is difficult to describe a typical experience. The subjective effects of LSD can be roughly summarized as follows. As the internal performance proceeds, the viewer is entertained by a kaleidoscope of changing sense impressions in which colors, sounds, smells, and other sensations are preternaturally brilliant, greatly intensified, or portentous with meaning. Sense impressions may be transposed so that a hand clasp is "heard" as a shower of sparks, and color becomes emotion or sound. The psychedelic program may include delightful or transcendent fantasies, or the world may be transfigured for the worse. A peanut-butter sandwich becomes a delicacy for the gods and a whiff of cat excrement becomes the vapor of death. Despite the heightened impact of all sensory experience, the subject also undergoes sensory deprivation. Time seems to halt or to be meaningless, pain is diminished, and the drug taker may gaze in rapture at his hand and yet be uncertain that it is his own. Saturated with color, familiar objects are rejuvenated, old boundaries dissolve, and as the drug unlocks the dark hold of the unconscious, its images float out into the light of consciousness.

At the same time control over one's sensory input weakens. Memories and perceptions follow their own course. The mechanism which relates one impression to another, useful on the solid, narrow ground of the real world, but an obstacle to transcendence into spiritual dimensions of existence, appears temporarily to be disconnected. To the psychedelic voyager cruising the inner mind, the redness of a flower, rather than the flower itself, may offer a glimpse of beatitude, the "Is-ness" of a simple chair may become a profound revelation, and meaningfulness may become more important than meaning. As repressed memories spill from the unconscious and emotional defenses crumble, the subject, now more vulnerable and sensitive, responds to these events with some of the fresh innocence of a child. Whether traversing paradise or purgatory, the rational mind reacts to the irrational self's adventures with delight or dismay, pride or guilt, ecstasy or panic. The outcome of the psychedelic trip is related to the way the subject, directed by his guide, handles his reaction to the selves he encounters on his inward journey.

The individual returning from a drug-induced exotic voyage with an assortment of preternatural monsters and unsuspected selves to a four-walled home must plan to accommodate the mind-born trophies to ordinary reality. Properly screened, healthy subjects who take these hallucinogens under the supervision of skilled therapists or guides, may have a safe and rewarding experience. The most tragic consequences occur when people who are initially unstable take the drugs unaccompanied by a trained guide who could help them handle their reactions to the bizarre experience.

Hallucinations and insights disconnected from reality are common to states of madness and mysticism. Released from the fetters of consciousness, the dreamer is briefly exposed to the primitive emotions which burrow in his unconscious, but he is protected from himself by sleep and upon awaking may choose to forget. Whether the drug experience teaches, as the Indian peyote communicants maintain, depends upon the provision of an immediate, as well as a cultural framework to incorporate the drug-induced insights into the realities of the prosaic world. It is difficult for the drug participant to control the visions the drug induces. In providing a protective focus during the temporary suspension of one's own powers, psychological "set" and setting are important. Not unexpectedly those who take the drugs carelessly for "kicks," often get kicked instead, and others who seek escape from dreary or disappointing lives find reality even less tolerable and tend to retreat still further. The drugs may produce a memorable or rewarding experience, but most people get what they are equipped at the time to experience.

The Peyote Indians who use the cactus buttons in their religious ceremonies do not use the drug promiscuously. Peyote is consumed within the context of a stable culture and in an authentic religious setting which provides guidance, standards of moderation, and a long tradition of religious and mystic experience. These Indians have a culture which enables them to transcend the fragmented elements of their visions. We are reminded that the religions which employ drugs in their sacraments seek revelation of god, not self — undoubtedly a less hazardous objective. Specious gurus who confidently lead their innocent novitiates in search of the "true self" may find themselves unprepared to handle the psychic explosion which occurs when the seeker glimpses what he has come to find and dissolves in panic and terror.

It is obvious that aspects of the drug experience are relevant to the creative process: alterations in conventional concepts of order and time, heightened awareness, and freedom from precedent. Following the psychedelic excursion there appears to be increased tolerance of ambiguity and greater sensitivity to new possibilities. The cost of enhanced imagination and a chemical bypass to the unconscious, however, is the inhibition or disruption of other faculties necessary for creative effort. Time becomes meaningless, past and present blend in the Now, and isolation and withdrawal are encouraged. Aldous Huxley himself wrote that while under the influence of the drug "the will suffers a profound change for the worse." The mescaline taker has no desire to do anything but stare entranced at the mental show, and causes which once concerned him seem "profoundly uninteresting." Whether this is a virtue or vice of the drug depends upon the nature of these former causes. Those who are defeated or bored by the everyday world may be tempted to abandon it altogether. In the drug state judgment and discrimination are impaired and the ability to focus and make decisions suffers. Although sensations are vivid they are also fragmented and the capacity to integrate and organize experience deteriorates. Coordination and synthesis are characteristic of creative endeavor and are the very qualities lacking in the dreams of the sleeper, and the visions of the mentally ill and the drug tripper.

According to Daniel X. Freedman, a search for major productions of art, letters, music, or visionary experience reveals "few clear-cut monuments" to the drugs. Huxley's greatest output preceded his mescaline experiments; "thereafter . . . he tended to write *about* drugs, not to create with them." Dr. Freedman suggests that the serious danger of the drugs lies neither in psychosis nor genetic damage, but in reinforcing a trend to dissociation and in chronic impairment of judgment and maturation. The yearning for ecstatic melting and holy simplicity tends to reduce the vast, frustrating complexity of life to a narrow reflection of oneself. Instead of unifying the diversity of experience by confronting its contradictions, the euphoric drug tripper tries to merge everything into one over-simplified, rapturous blur.

The drugs pose the greatest threat to those who are most likely to use them — adolescents and young adults — who by objective standards are the least desirable candidates for drug experiment and most likely to take drugs in circumstances which invite disaster. This group, potentially the most unstable and rebellious of any society, accounts for most of the psychological casualties. At a critical time in the creative lives of young men and women, the drugs sabotage creative discipline, warp judgment and lure them from the acquisition of essential skills and knowledge. The youth who fancies himself grooving to the oscillations of the cosmos may instead be stuck in a groove which is a rut. Arcane experience and self-experiment have a natural attraction for the young, who possess both the courage and curiosity to embark upon dangerous adventures. But to seek in Instant Revelation what otherwise must be obtained through experience is to neglect the cultivation of qualities of personality and of creative skills which ordinarily occur in a natural sequence during youth, and which, their moment lost, are only poorly acquired later.

The development of tenacity and independence, of craftsmanship and intellectual competence is youth's obligation to itself. It is in the act of seeking and integrating experience that character is forged and that the individual cultivates those creative powers needed to unite the fragments of vision and to use inner experience to illumine and enlarge reality. Even musical prodigies such as Bach and Mozart, whose Instant Genius was a genetic provision, were not ready to compose mature works of genius until they had fused the experience of living and the skills of their craft with their hereditary gifts. The young creative person must acquire that blend of logical and intuitive judgment and the synthesizing gifts needed to distinguish illusions from illumination. Without creative discipline and an urge to do something with his powers, he will remain forever nothing more than wilted potential and broken promise.

A safe chemical means of tuning into the inner vibrations of the mind may be useful, but we must be sure that the drug will not lure us into dropping out from the *real* world. The drugs stimulate imagination, encourage openness, and help one escape the bonds of conscious thought. These advantages are offset by distorted judgment, inhibition of will and ambition, by indecision, and a lack of concern with the problems of reality. The creative artist or thinker may take a jaunt through the wilderness of his unconscious, but unlike the psychotic he goes there with a purpose and knows the route back to the mainland; unlike the chemically wafted dreamer he knows what to do with his experience when he returns.

LSD is an important tool in exploring the chemistry of the brain, but unfortunately the experiments are proceeding unscientifically, conducted in the wrong place and on the wrong people. Popular experiment and proselytizing by irresponsible members of the drug cult and by exultant youth, delighted to be sitting in the catbird seat, have crippled the research of undrugged scientists on the chemical mechanisms of the mind and the psychedelic realms of experience. Comparing advances in the control of mental disease to the conquest of infectious diseases such as cholera in the nineteenth century, Isaac Asimov observed, "College students in the late nineteenth century didn't think it was exciting fun to inject themselves with cholera bacilli."

Manipulation of the mind by chemical or electrical means, including the facilitation of learning, is a prospect we may anticipate, and in some cases fear. Creativity is, however, neither a single monolithic trait, nor even a group of traits. It blooms from the mysterious interaction of unique human powers in a living, changing human being, as he responds to the variables of his environment. Of all man's faculties, his privileged form of consciousness and his subtle, enigmatic creative powers are the most likely to elude scientific analysis. The chemistry of creation must await formidably difficult basic research on relatively simpler puzzles of the mind such as memory and perception. Until then we are not likely to write a chemical recipe for the effortless stimulation of creativity.

12. The Creation of Creation

The mind is never passive; it is a perpetual activity, delicate, perceptive, responsive to stimulus. You cannot postpone its life until you have sharpened it.

— ALFRED NORTH WHITEHEAD

Prediction

Mastering the art of taking tests has become an "educational" imperative for those required to climb the ladder, not of life, but of test batteries. In recent years the flagrant abuse of aptitude, achievement, and personality tests which prejudice rather than predict has been widely reported. A reliable test which could measure creative potential and predict creative performance would enable us to identify the creative child and to adapt his education to his special needs. Although such a test would certainly be valuable, there is at present no such oracle.

Psychologists can select a set of behavior patterns which they define as creative and then construct tests to comply with this profile, but the discrepancy between test scores and creative performance in real life — the test's validity — remains discouraging. The validity of a test refers to the extent to which, on the basis of accepted criteria, the test measures what it claims to measure. Its predictive validity is the degree of correlation between test score and actual performance. The reliability of a test is its ability to yield consistent results within the test itself, under varying circumstances, and upon retesting.

Measuring the reliability and validity of a specific test is not only expensive, but often difficult and complicated. Psychologists may be aware of the limitations and predictive fallibility of the tests they construct, but those who market and promote the tests, administrators who use them, and a public easily impressed by claims of scientific validity are quick to forget the tests' deficiencies.

Tests are always more accurate in predicting failure than success because the absence of a single factor such as intelligence or artistic ability may equal probable failure, whereas even in the presence of all the measurable factors, success is still uncertain. In using a test to choose gifted children or promising job applicants, what appears to be a process of selection is actually one of rejection. If the test criteria differ from those required in actual creative performance so that the test fails to correlate — or correlates negatively — with actual performance, the test will blindly reject a high percentage of those who might succeed. Rejection and selection carry different emotional and practical weights in our social system. Selection, with its attendant expectations, has its burdens, but the individual who is denied the opportunity to demonstrate his ability, who is refused access to educational opportunity and is given a psychological vote of no-confidence, may fulfill the negative prophecy.

"Creativity tests" which focus on those emotional traits and divergent intellectual qualities ignored by narrow intelligence and aptitude tests are an important and welcome addition to the professional tester's equipment. There are, however, no available tests sufficiently reliable to use as a sole measure of predicting creativity. The notion that this most unpredictable quality can be measured and tested should cause misgivings to all who are familiar with the defects of earlier tests and with the misuse of their results. In addition, genuinely creative people are often difficult to test, as they may refuse to cooperate or may accept some of the tests, but reject those they consider stupid or absurd.

Tests which propose to identify creative talent differ from traditional objective tests in that they are scored for the number of answers as well as for the novelty and variety of response. The task of balancing subjective and objective scoring techniques, of maintaining reliability and yet providing for richness and complexity in the subject's response, is a major challenge in this type of test.

Factor-type tests, such as those developed by J. P. Guilford and his associates to test divergent thinking, use complicated statistical analyses of test scores to identify and name mental traits common to creative people. The test designer hypothesizes that certain responses to certain kinds of questions will serve as a measure of the attribute he seeks to identify. Creativity traits vary in different studies, but may include factors such as: originality, sensitivity to problems, associational fluency, sense of destiny, cognitive flexibility, and intellectual competence. If a psychologist wishes to measure originality, he may decide to do this by testing for three variables:

Uncommonness of response: word association test; listing uses for an object such as a newspaper.

Remote associations: listing consequences of a discovery which makes eating unnecessary; given two unrelated words, find a word which relates to both.

Cleverness: writing titles for short-story plots.

As a means of studying the creative person, factor analysis cannot explain how the individual employs these traits to produce actual creative productions. It is like knowing the elements in a compound but knowing neither the formulas nor catalysts necessary for synthesizing it. Factor analysis also seems unable to distinguish creativity from productive thinking and from general ability. Finally, this technique is always limited by the qualities the tester includes in his test and by the individuals comprising the study which provided the original factors. If the test does not acknowledge "aesthetic sensitivity," the tester is not likely to find it. If the subjects used in factor-analytic studies are to begin with highly selected, the results are bound to be distorted.

In another species of divergent thinking test, indebted in part to factor analysis, the subject is given test problems which are models of the creative process — or of the psychologist's theory of the process. These tests, which can be adapted to children as well as adults, attempt to take into account the personality of the subject and the conditions necessary for creative achievement. The battery of tests developed by Dr. Paul Torrance contains a series of problems of which the following are but a small sample. In the *Ask-and-Guess* test the subject is shown a picture and told to ask questions to obtain information needed to understand what is happening. The *Figure Completion* test theoretically tests the tendency toward structuring and integrating. According to Torrance premature closure of the partial drawing because of an inability to deal with the tension inherent in the incomplete figures yields an uncreative and ordinary response. *Product Improvement, Unusual Uses,* and *Just Suppose* tests are among other tests employed.

The "work sample" technique is another simpler means of testing creativity. The subject is given a task involving imagination and inventiveness and his production is judged by experts in the field. This method avoids the elaborate inventories of other creativity tests, but is limited by its lack of objectivity in scoring. It is probably an effective technique providing one is not dealing with unfledged talent, exceptional originality, or a major genius who prefers to find his own problems.

Studies of the intellectual traits and the character, emotions, and idiosyncrasies of actual creative adults are an integral part of creativity research. However, personality tests, attempting to predict future success, are of little value when applied to the general population. The misuse of personality tests has been vividly reported. Despite the popularity of these tests in the hiring and promotion protocols of many large corporations, personality tests are generally ineffective as a means of predicting a person's future performance. Self-report tests supposedly tell whether a subject is extroverted or introverted, aesthetically or scientifically inclined, or whether he has the disposition of a teacher, writer, advertising executive or salesman. Although they may do this, their success in predicting actual performance may be no better than chance. Projective tests purport to reveal the subject's "psycho-dynamic makeup" through the images he projects on vague patterns of inkblots, on incomplete drawings, or in the situations suggested to him by a series of pictures. Even when administered and scored by an expert, the validity of the well-known Rorschach test is often zero.

Armed with batteries of pencil-and-paper probes, some of which are designed primarily for the psychiatric clinic, the tester attempts to describe the "inner nature" of the job applicant. In the incompetent hands of many a tester, the personality audit yields an absurd garble of adjectives which may describe the individual as reliable, loyal, outgoing, mature, clean, and emotionally unstable. Such descriptions cannot be validated against job performance and therefore are useless. Another alternative is to decide that the job requires certain personality characteristics — not specific skills. Using tests which supposedly detect these personality attributes, the tester attempts to recruit candidates who meet the predesignated specifications. Proper validation studies are usually lacking, and if the psychologist goes to the effort and expense of checking his predictive accuracy the answer is generally negative.

The psychologist attempting to locate a creative personality, a temperament which according to hypothesis is aggressive, spontaneous, imaginative, independent, open to experience, and at home with chaos, may discover as many potential bank robbers as genuinely creative people. In general, the prediction of adult performance is most successful at the level of specific skills such as typing and mechanical aptitude. The more complex the cluster of traits, the more difficult it is to predict success. When factors of motivation and temperament are involved, the validity of the test is further impaired. Of all the attributes for which we test, creative potential is the most evasive and unpredictable. Even in the presence of so obvious a gift as musical talent, we cannot make comfortable predictions about whether the musical prodigy will fulfill his early promise.

Creativity tests are subject to the same limitations and perversions as other predictive tests. Because the professional tester is usually paid by the corporation he serves, his appraisal of his client's requirements is rarely impartial. His test criteria tend to reflect individuals already employed by the firm, or his client's description of what he thinks he needs. In conventional hiring procedures, the employer's intuitive judgment and his subjective interpretation of the very criteria he may have supplied, tend to modify the rigid definition of the job as represented by the test. Extroversion, aggressiveness, or independent judgment may have different connotations to employer and psychologist.

Creativity tests are not yet in common use in the public school system. The premature use of tests whose reliability-validity index is even less certain than that of the intelligence test would label students as creative, less creative, or noncreative on the basis of a tenuous psychological hypothesis incorporated in the test. In the statistical shuffle of children through school, we face the familiar danger that professional testers may exploit the tests to shrink children to quantitative terms, and that ignorant, harassed educators and gullible parents will misinterpret other evidence and accept the tests as a sole guide for important decisions in the child's education. Creative capacity is especially subject to motivation, maturity, and other variables such as the ability to concentrate. Unless tests are repeated frequently, unless their form is varied, and unless the test results are interpreted in terms of the child's actual performance, they may be seriously misleading. The creative faculties of different individuals develop in a highly personal fashion and on a private time schedule, determined not only by personality and opportunity, but by the nature of the specific talent. Musical and mathematical precocity appear early, but a gift for scholarship or leadership may emerge at a more ripe age.

Finally, creativity tests which test divergent thinking rather than those designed to discover specific artistic aptitudes — often obvious without a test — are still heavily weighted toward the abilities of the middle-class child. Reasonable practice in handling an Ask-and-Guess test or a Remote Associations test will improve test scores in the same way that a child's score on an intelligence test profits from previous experience with the style of the test and the mind of the test designer.

Tests for creativity and divergent thinking, first developed toward the end of the nineteenth century, were long eclipsed by the intelligence test. Moreover, they were thwarted by Terman's attractive redefinition of genius as an individual with an IQ over 140 and the subsequent rehabilitation of the genius's public image. No longer sickly, eccentric, and willful, Terman's "genius" was a normal, well-behaved, successful individual whose gifts were at the disposal of American society. Although they became outstanding adults, Terman's geniuses were in fact, non-geniuses who, if they failed to behave in the maladjusted romantic fashion so distasteful to the pragmatic American public, also failed to produce the singular, superlative contributions which are ordinarily the *raison d'être* of genius. Following Sputnik's ominous and dramatic debut, the frantic search for scientific talent and the chilling conviction that national security depended on locating hidden talent and slighted genius spurred serious interest in tests to predict creativity.

In a more general and profound sense, rapid technological progress and accelerating social change require a creative society, better prepared to plan, innovate, and adapt to new circumstances. In the past the privilege of creative enterprise was reserved for a relatively small group of potentially gifted people. We no longer can afford to waste the resources of those who either by birth or other circumstances, are denied the opportunity to develop and contribute their aptitudes, or of those whose capacities remain unused and unsuspected even by themselves. Jerome Wiesner suggests that in the absence of a useful method for predicting creative ability, we might gain a statistical increase in available talent by improving education for all and by tapping groups such as Negroes, women, and the disadvantaged.

Efforts to prevent the attrition of creative resources tread a narrow line between serving the individual's needs and exploiting him. Unfortunately, the current pursuit of creative talent cannot be attributed to expanding altruism or to a desire to support art or scholarship in the humanities. It is inspired instead by the need to supply strategic areas of science and technology with brainpower and to serve the needs of national security and of industry. Enthusiasm for identifying the creative person and the financial support necessary for research in this area are inspired more by the thought of what the gallant gifted can do for the nation than by what a generous nation might do for them.

Genius and the unfashionably gifted have often in the past been condemned to harsh lives of bleak poverty and social ostracism. But if the genius was ignored, he was at least reasonably free to do his work. No one believed that the nation's security or economy depended on his efforts. Although the outside world persecuted Galileo, hooted Darwin, and guillotined Lavoisier, public molestation took place only after their work was completed. To the independent, inner-directed creative person, poverty or the poor opinion of his neighbors may be far less damaging than the restrictions imposed by the shadowy presence of enthusiastic sponsors peering over his shoulder while he is at work. The specter of the grant administrator is an unwholesome apparition during the critical but vulnerable period in which an individual assembles his ideas and formulates his plans. It may seem ungrateful to impugn the hand that supports, rather than scorns, creative talent, but gratitude is a virtue which plays a role neither in the creative process nor in the design of the creative temperament.

Mission-oriented, as opposed to basic, scientific research, like most industrial research seeks solutions to specific problems and understandably must accept certain restrictions in pursuing its goals. If creativity recruiters intend to corral the creatively gifted and encourage them with scholarships and research grants, and if they propose to intervene in the creative person's environment organizing it to produce maximum results, what will they expect in return for their generosity? What may the recipient feel obligated to do for his benefactors?

No one wishes to underwrite trivia or folly; no one wants charity. What is anticipated, of course, is some form of worthwhile contribution to society. Since the most brilliant ideas are often first dismissed as nonsense or impractical, we must ponder whether projects regarded as "impractical" would receive support, and whether unfashionable projects would find sponsors. We must consider whether the creative person would retain the independence needed to pursue his work in circumstances where he is judged and financed by a government and a public, each bent on getting something in return for its money. It is dangerous to regard brainpower literally as a natural resource to be captured, tamed, and harnessed.

Warren Weaver reminds us that one area in which creativity is badly needed but dismally slighted is in the art of administering grants. Unless the research worker acquires skill in the art of "grantsmanship," those who control the purse strings ultimately dictate both the problems and the problem solvers. Government support is not sympathetic to research as a creative activity. Access to the federal purse is cluttered with procedural booby-traps and institutional obstacles to genuine creative venture. An agency or a scientist asked, two years in advance, to submit a detailed statement of its future research requirements, must indulge in the solemn pretense that it can predict what these will be. If political events do not sever the financial lifeline and the project actually gets what it said it needed, then no matter how circumstances have changed, it "must proceed to need what it has got." Furthermore, clumsy, massive federal agencies have no way of recognizing drive, determination, and competence if these virtues occur outside the formal structure of organized academic society.

The most serious danger of the unimaginative, short-sighted pursuit of talent is that the exceptionally or unconventionally gifted, and those whose interests do not enjoy high national priority will be excluded from the basic research on the salient features of the creative species. Although funds have been provided for studies of creativity in architects and writers, many important research programs concerned with the identification of creative talent have dealt more specifically with scientific talent — an undertaking which the government has sponsored with keen interest. Organizations such as the Air Force, the National Science Foundation, and the National Aeronautical and Space Administration (NASA) have supplied research appropriations for well-publicized creativity studies and have encouraged the development of methods for measuring and testing creativity. The Air Force and NASA have used tests developed under their auspices to help identify gifted personnel or to select job applicants.

Already afflicted with the testing virus, large corporations hoping to profit from the fallout of government-sponsored research, have added creativity tests to their burgeoning test inventories. That a test developed from studies of military engineers and intended to supply more of the same might not be appropriate for identifying advertising, sales, or management talent is not likely to occur to personnel directors who understand little about testing and less about creativity. Although creative people have certain traits in common, each creative activity has specific and discrete features. To blur the distinctions between copywriters and mathematicians, architects and editors, is as foolish as not to recognize those elements which overlap. It would be fatal mischief if tests based on a highly selected population and skewed toward the identification of specific forms of "worthwhile" creativity were to be used to judge and control schoolchildren and college students, with all the blindness of the sightless prophets of old, but none of the vision.

If the country's talent is harnessed to drawing the national juggernaut, it will betray us in the end. We can be grudging, myopic, and overly efficient in our investment in creative excellence; or we can be generous, patient, and daring. The serious purveyors of creativity would do well to take time from raking the gardens of creative talent to consider, not only what is to be found there, but what must wither on the vine and what cannot possibly grow there.

Colleagues and Catalysts

We cannot predict creativity with any degree of certainty. We cannot buy it, breed it, "turn it on" with drugs, or train people directly to be creative. Creativity is a product of genetic qualities, formative childhood experiences, and an environment which offers the opportunity to develop and demonstrate ability. It is possible to teach people more effective methods of solving problems, to foster a child's creative promise and recover some of an adult's lost capacity, but if there is a formula for raising creative people, it remains unknown.

Although creativity cannot be taught, it can be nourished. The first step in converting creative potential into performance is simply to refrain from destroying it. Creativity is trampled to death by formal and informal educational procedures which drill compliance and conformity, and which support neurotic rather than creative potential. At the other extreme, it is corrupted by exploitation and solicitude, thinly disguised as patronage, encouragement, or "science." The sad fate of the child prodigy cruelly victimized by ignorant parents and misguided promoters stands as a monument to the avarice and ineptitude of an earlier breed of creativity cultivators.

The second step in the nurture of creativity is to provide conditions conducive to its development. Some individuals thrive on encouragement, whereas others require the stimulus of opposition or competition. Some work best during times of relative tranquillity and security; others during periods of misery. To some the habit of work is so deeply ingrained that they work whether the climate of their lives is fair or foul. There are those who cannot work under pressure, and yet others require it. Faced with deadlines of death or publishers, they rise to the challenge. Evariste Galois, the French mathematician who was killed in a duel at the age of twenty-one, left a major creative testament in the work he produced in the hours before that final tragic dawn.

We can make certain general statements about the ecological conditions which encourage creativity. The argument that creativity thrives on adversity is a fiction convenient to those who wish to believe it. Reasonable, but not excessive, abundance, rather than overwhelming hardship is the more propitious atmosphere for creative work. Despite Modigliani in his garret and hungry Hemingway, and in spite of Kepler's domestic and financial distress, Schubert's poverty, and Beethoven's deafness and debts, the popular cliché that "genius will out" is self-righteous cant and grossly unfair. No one will ever count the potential geniuses and the gifted men and women lost to society because they either lacked the temperament or physical stamina to persist through hardship and opposition, or were denied the education and opportunity to prove themselves. How many of the culturally and economically disadvantaged will never discover themselves because at birth their numbing environment has already begun to blight their genetic potential? And to how many victims of slum rot is the sense of destiny, believed to characterize the creative person, a sense, instead, of inadequacy and despair?

Reasonable quiet and stretches of uninterrupted time in which to reflect upon one's work is another requirement for creative effort. For the child this means a day which is not overscheduled; for the adult it means everything from freedom from serious financial worry to some protection from trivia and distraction. American children are very early conditioned to the idea that the reward is to the fleet rather than the profound. Few of them have the courage and self-confidence to look while all others are leaping. In discussing problems of protein synthesis, Leo Szilard once told a group of scientists, "If you do stupid experiments, and finish one a year, it can take fifty years. But if you stop doing experiments for a little while and *think* how proteins can possibly be synthesized, there are only about five different ways, not fifty." Only the computer with its electronic speed can afford the waste of stupid experiments.

Human beings must think, imagine, and hypothesize. Ringing telephones, meetings, paperwork, and incessant interruptions drain the spirit and dissipate the time of all but the most fiercely motivated. Work, which according to Parkinson's Law, "expands so as to fill the time available for its completion," also encroaches on the time reserved for thought and reflection. The caustic complaint that "you can't work at Work" is a terse commentary on this irritating situation. Promotions and increased administrative duties, the rewards we bestow upon many of the most talented individuals in our society, often bring a creative life-span to a premature close. Unless an artist or public celebrity is wary and firm, the disaster of success will deliver him into the public embrace, devour his time, corrupt his values, and addle his talent.

There may also be a seasonal or diurnal variation in an individual's work pattern and in the specific demands of different disciplines. The student who is excited about a particular subject and who shows talent in that field, may be discouraged if forced by inflexible curriculum requirements to postpone his enthusiasm. Similarly, teachers cannot arrange to have all their best ideas during rigidly spaced sabbatical leaves.

It is an indication of the adaptive requirements of creative industry that exceptional energy, drive, and powers of concentration characterize genius as well as the less august creative personality. The burdens of success are becoming increasingly lethal to creative thought. Not everyone can endure the mentally and physically exhausting day demanded of many successful people, and of women with families, and still find the reserves of time and strength for serious creative work. Growing environmental pressures, the elevation of trivia, and the shrinkage of useful time suggest that selection will place a high premium on mental and physical stamina, and perhaps on youthful vigor. Wealth, we recall, afforded Darwin freedom from mundane affairs and from the compulsions of the business or academic world; a modest stipend from a city appointment permitted Anton van Leeuwenhoek to abandon the hustle of business life in Amsterdam and to retire to the peace of Delft and to his microscopes.

The ideal climate for creativity, whether at work, at home, or in the broader cultural community, is one which provides both stimulation and reasonable security, in which an open environment challenges the individual and at the same time indicates that his work is needed. The chance of innovation improves if innovation is expected. Children thrive in an atmosphere which is neither hostile nor permissive, but warm, consistent, and democratic: one which encourages free interplay of differences rather than detached acceptance. It has been suggested that necessity is actually the father of invention, whereas its mother is security. The atmosphere favorable to creative accomplishment has also been described as a state of creative tension resulting in a stimulating feedback, rather than compromise, between the forces of stability and the forces of challenge. Adequate income, prestige, specialization, freedom to choose one's projects, and the assurance that research funds will not be discontinued abruptly contribute to stability and security. Constructive criticism, competition, deadlines, and healthy disagreement are sources of stimulation and challenge.

Hybrid vigor, the increase in vitality resulting from the interbreeding of different races or species, is a biological example of such stimulation. The confluence of people of one race, culture, or academic institution with those of another is usually an occasion for innovation. The interaction of ideas and the contrast in systems of knowledge and customs, suggesting the need to reconcile these differences, may provide a stimulus to creativity similar to the challenge presented by incongruent scientific theories. "New occasions teach new duties." War and crises often release a flood of innovation. A shift in society's values, such as the emphasis on power rather than wealth during wartime, may induce people to seek new means of obtaining customary social rewards. Nationalist movements which make citizens conscious of a larger national identity, or personal crises and social upheavals which alter the self-image of an individual or a group may inspire an outpouring of linguistic, literary, and political creativity.

A rapid survey of history demonstrates that geniuses are not evenly distributed throughout civilization, but are clustered in specific periods and cultures. Among the glittering constellations of genius one thinks of the Athens of Pericles, Sophocles, and Phidias; the Florence of Michelangelo, Raphael, and Machiavelli; the Vienna of Hayden, Mozart, and Beethoven; or the Budapest of Von Neuman, Szilard, and Wigner. In seeking to explain these "outbursts" of genius or talent, Henry Steele Commager examines the remarkable efflorescence of American political leadership in the last quarter of the eighteenth century. With a population of less than three million, the United States provided a peerless galaxy of political leaders which has never since been equaled. In one generation Virginia alone produced Washington, Jefferson, Mason, Wythe, Madison, and Marshall. That statesmanship was the specialty of these frontier colonies, according to Commager, ensued from attitudes evoked by the interlocking circumstances of opportunity, geography, material rewards, prestige, education, and philosophical concepts.

Colonial society, pastoral and uninstitutionalized, offered few temptations to amass great wealth and little distraction in the form of elaborate social life. There was no formal army or navy, and there were no great universities to welcome scholars. The law and the clergy were the only professions, but the Church in this new land held little appeal. A career in public life, therefore, was almost the only challenging outlet for talented young men in an age when political heroes were in style. In contrast, a public career today demands not only financial sacrifice, but subjects the vulnerable public servant to the potshots of unstable demagogues, irresponsible Congressional committees, tireless security investigators, and sadistic journalists — not to mention epidemics of assassins' bullets.

Eighteenth-century education instilled in its young men a fervent sense of duty and of service to the commonwealth. The founders of our nation were raised on Plutarch and Cicero, on the contemporary philosophy of political liberty, and were encouraged to assume the virtues of antiquity. The new nation had been born in a dramatic act of free will. Now its leaders had the opportunity to prove that neither history nor human nature was predetermined by inexorable laws of God and nature, but that using these laws, man might by his own effort bend his fate and the fate of his nation to his will that both might grow and prosper.

The physical bounty and glory of the land itself offered freedom, possibility, and space — the latter a blessing we are only now beginning to appreciate. Its lakes and rivers, virgin forests and rich soil declared that here in this vast, untamed expanse a man could triumph over his heritage. The New World was physically, as well as politically, socially, and morally isolated from the Old World. For the first time in history "a numerous and virtuous people were vouchsafed an ideal environment and were freed from the tyrannies, the superstitions, the injustices, the vices, the miseries that had for centuries made a shambles of the history of the Old World."

Eighteenth-century America was prepared to use and reward its political talent, while the youthful Founding Fathers were well aware that the world was watching and waiting to see what they would do. Unlike young people today, who have to pound desperately against the massive, impervious walls of the social machine, often driven to social and political temper tantrums in order to make their efforts felt, Washington, Jefferson, Paine, and the other leaders of the new nation knew that their actions could make a difference and that immortality — which they confidently sought — would be their reward if successful.

Political leadership in the eighteenth century was not fortuitous. It thrived in a relatively simple, open society which was prepared to use and honor its talent. Remarkably free of frivolous and materialistic distractions, the America of Washington and Jefferson offered freedom, incentive, and inspiration, and that essential tension between challenge and security, between opportunity and need.

The ability to hold large stores of information in mind is a characteristic trait of genius and of highly original thinkers. The proliferation of information and the overlap of once discrete realms of knowledge make impossible demands on even the most brilliant and capacious mind. The days of scientific research with "love and string and sealing wax" are gone. Scientists need accelerators and electron microscopes; mathematicians who once required nothing more than pencil and paper now wait their turn at the crowded consoles of giant computers. In technically sophisticated fields it has become necessary to assemble scientific prima donnas and mathematical virtuosi in small coordinated groups to constitute a problem-solving unit whose combined power is greater then the sum of its parts. It is important, however, to distinguish between an intimate, closely knit group of researchers in related disciplines, each working on his own problem, and literal "team research" in which team members are organized in a task force whose target is a common goal.

To the question of whether a team or an individual is a more effective thinking unit there seems to be no clear-cut answer. One must consider what is meant by the team, who its members are, and the basis of comparison. The team product, for example, may be compared either to the single output of *any* of its members, or of its *best* member. Team research in science and industry is most useful in mission-oriented studies where specific goals can be outlined in advance. It also may be helpful if a few members of the team are truly creative thinkers. Otherwise, extended service on a research team may suppress initiative and stifle originality. The Manhattan Project which developed and built the world's first atomic bomb was perhaps the greatest collection of genius ever assembled to work on a single program. The coordination of so proud, egotistical, and willful an assortment of scientists would have been impossible without the administrative and diplomatic genius of Robert Oppenheimer and without the urgency of the wartime crisis.

Brainstorming is a special team technique which enjoyed considerable popularity among business and advertising executives. In a brainstorming session ideas are suggested in rapid succession, somewhat in the manner of free association. Quantity of ideas rather than quality is emphasized, and during the session criticism is deferred. Brainstorming may be useful in demonstrating some of the techniques employed in creative thinking and as a form of mental calisthenics to stimulate the uninhibited flow of ideas. Studies of this method show that, proportionately, brainstorming yields neither more nor better ideas than when individuals work separately but are free from the pressure of immediate evaluation of their ideas. In certain instances brainstorming may actually inhibit creative thinking. The galloping free-association process may seize a vague, incipient idea and quickly run it in the wrong direction, or may strangle an ephemeral strand of thought.

The mutual interaction of creative individuals assembled in relatively small groups within such organizations as the Pasteur Institute, the Lawrence Radiation Laboratory, or the Rockefeller University can be stimulating and profitable. We face a major challenge in developing practical means of accommodating the needs of the individual creative person to the necessity for sharing not only the problem but also the credit and recognition. There are many motives which attract men to difficult tasks, but to eliminate the fun and adventure from his vocation is to deprive the creative individual of essential nourishment. Involvement and pride in his work, the right to decide its nature and direction, the privilege of making his own discoveries, and the responsibility for success or failure are emotional rewards the creative person cannot long forgo. He will work for long hours and low pay, but he will not work at all if denied those deep satisfactions and that personal sense of fulfillment on which his dedication is nurtured. Inflexible organizations and academic research projects, tied not only to the financial apron strings of government agencies and philanthropic foundations but to their special interests as well, will inevitably stifle creative experiment and scholarship.

If the group is designed to avoid the squabbles and tensions which often arise when a pride of creative lions is required to work in close mental, emotional, and even physical quarters, and if the cherished individuality and autonomy of its members is respected, then the group environment may enhance and stimulate creativity. At its best the group provides access to the intellectual resources of different minds and to kindred fields of knowledge, and offers the informed criticism and pertinent suggestions of one's professional peers.

The cloistered environment of the group also offers companionship and support during times of discouragement, and buffers its members from the distractions of the outside world. Within the confines of such miniature worlds it is easier to ignore the values — money and prestige — of the larger environment, and to detach oneself from its philosophical concepts and cultural predilections. The isolation and insulation of the group's sympathetic environment protect the individual during the critical gestation of an unfledged idea when premature exposure to a hostile environment might dissuade him from his course. Not until the rudimentary idea is mature, is it required to face the assault of the larger professional community.

The tendency of a single dissenting individual to yield to the pressure of the majority is markedly reduced if he finds one other person who supports his judgment. Although the expression of divergent opinion may not alter the beliefs of the majority, it may reinforce the wavering independence of a timid, inaudible minority. Whether he finds a "partner in dissent" in a formal group of scholars and scientists, in a circle of disciples and collaborators, in a friendship, or within his family, the creative person usually requires someone with whom he can interact, or who senses his potential ability and values him for it.

Widespread acceptance of the creative person's work and recognition of its merit may be delayed. The genius must often resign himself to posthumous honor. But in the life of almost every creative person there is usually at least one man or woman who admires and believes in him and whose esteem helps to counteract the damp chill of the larger environment and to balance its opinion. This supportive role may be filled by a parent, sibling, or spouse, by a mistress or lover, friend or colleague. During his lifetime, Van Gogh's devoted brother Théo was one of the few who believed in him, providing encouragement and affection as well as financial support. Galileo had his Grand Duke of Tuscany, Goethe his literate and astute Frau von Stein, Rilke his mistress-mother, Lou Andreas-Salomé.

The partner may also be a collaborator, whose knowledge and skills are at the disposal of the innovator. In the early critical years of his work, Freud was heavily indebted to Professor Fliess for both encouragement and ideas. Later he was insulated from the hostility of the outside world by his warm family life and by his circle of students and apostles. If the nature of the work lends itself to division of labor and the temperament of the workers permits, full-fledged collaboration is possible. Marie and Pierre Curie were remarkable examples of that perfect complementation of imagination, intellect, and personality in the pursuit of a common goal.

Teachers

There are wives and mistresses, patrons and colleagues, but in the prediction and support of creativity, ultimately the teacher is the one other person who exerts a profound and central influence on the life of the creative person. It is the astute and perceptive teacher, rather than the machine or the test performance, who recognizes the single-ability student and the "late bloomer"; who looks beyond the classroom to the football field and there in the bold play and dogged courage of one of his pupils discerns a suggestion of future promise.

The distinguishing characteristic of a good teacher is neither affection for students nor efficiency in imparting knowledge. According to long, honorable tradition, the ideal teacher is one who expands and develops the student's abilities, excites his curiosity, and inspires a need for learning and achievement. Creativity thrives on the interaction of inquiring minds, the stimulation of discussion, and on the example of a teacher who serves as a model to be emulated and surpassed. "The courtesy of conversation," writes Jerome Bruner, "may be the major ingredient in the courtesy of teaching." Whether a teacher is solemn or jolly, austere or amusing, his enthusiasm and encouragement are inspiring and invaluable at all times, and especially when the student is affected with self-doubt and uncertainty.

The increase in student rebellion and in campus strikes is attributed not merely to the struggle for civil rights or to antiwar sentiment, but to disillusion with irrelevant, hypocritical education and to the students' deep and bitter sense of neglect. Whether they are in grade school or graduate school, students want teachers who are professionally competent, who want to teach, and who are concerned with them intellectually and personally. They have begun to demand not only their civil rights, but their educational rights. We may be justified in condemning violent methods of protest and leaders whose motives are purely destructive. We may grow impatient with students who demand adult prerogatives, yet hide behind the university's skirts refusing to accept the legal consequences of their acts. Fundamentally, however, the students are right. As one educator wrote, in many school systems all students tend to be disadvantaged.

Most teachers, unfortunately, are not the master instructors we have described. They are more interested in piloting a student through a prescribed course of study than in leading him to the "threshold of his mind." Teachers in the primary and secondary schools generally prefer students who are docile and easily dominated to the more independent nonconformists, even when the latter are equally competent in their studies. In a later stage of his education a gifted student or a promising young scholar may have the misfortune to be dependent on an academic superior whose creative powers are either blocked or exhausted. In his bitter frustration, the disappointed teacher may unconsciously sabotage the student's development, undermine his confidence, and contaminate his thoughts.

Our society is willing to devote funds to identify and sponsor the creative person, but myopically it neglects the care and nurture of the men and women who are his teachers and to whom his creative future is linked. We are a species destined to stumble or soar on the flexibility and strength of its brainpower. Today, more than ever, an outburst of genius, of talent, or even of competence in the art of teaching is a prime necessity.

Of all professions, teaching is perhaps the most nobly creative. It offers a peerless opportunity to lead a young mind to the discovery of itself and of new realms of intellect and spirit. Teaching should attract men and women who enjoy adventure, diversity, and challenge; who are daring, independent, and highly intelligent; and who prefer the unpredictable with its opportunity for invention and innovation to the security of the pedagogical catechism. Instead, this crucial profession is heavily populated by the ill-educated, the timid, conservative, and conformist, while the Establishment breaks the spirit of its gifted teachers and stunts the growth of those who show promise.

Teachers are too often burdened with the impossible task of pretending that children share common interests and that all children are equally able, and equally and similarly motivated. It is common, although unpopular, knowledge that, apart from the vicissitudes of environment, there are inherited differences in learning ability. We are all unequally endowed: some people are born smarter, just as some have better teeth. We must be sufficiently mature to reconcile our democratic ideals with biology's undemocratic distribution of its blessings. A democratic system should offer equal opportunity to fulfill one's potential; it cannot provide equal potential, nor should it assume, therefore, identical goals and needs for all. To permit each individual to achieve his full intellectual and emotional growth requires that we help not only the average child, but also the disadvantaged, the unpromising, and the handicapped. At the other extreme, however, we must have the courage to protect the gifted — the inconveniently as well as the agreeably gifted.

The politics and economics of mass education are opposed to the needs of the creative child and to the basic creative needs of all children. The problem of preserving the creative resources of our nation's children is complicated by the urgent task of rescuing the ghetto child whose afflictions are far more serious than the decay of his creative powers. It is not enough to integrate schools and classes. Unless we provide for the individual educational needs of both privileged and underprivileged children, they will sit in the classroom jealous and suspicious, misunderstanding one another. No more than it is expedient to teach first- and fifth-grade children together, is it possible for one teacher to teach mathematics to a class composed of children of exceptional and average endowment and of children who hate school and see no reason to be there. Equal opportunity was never served by the one-room schoolhouse.

Lower education needs not so much a change in curriculum as a change in its attitude toward the creative foundations of learning. The essential problem is to teach people to be rational, yet spontaneous; imaginative, yet disciplined. Creativity may be stimulated by the impetus of ideas which outrage or fail, as well as by those which are congenial. But discipline is not domination, and control implies guidance and direction rather than suppression and restriction. The good teacher knows how to achieve this delicate balance between freedom and control.

Parents

It is not necessary to preside over a formal schoolroom to be a teacher. At some time in our lives, we are all teachers. Older children teach the younger, husbands and wives teach each other, parents teach their children and children teach parents. Just as the good teacher of young children must be imbued with a measure of parental instinct, so the good parent possesses the attributes of a natural teacher.

In an era when children in the same family may soon find themselves on opposite sides of the generation gap, the task of raising children is beset with awesome hazards. To expect parents to rear children who abstain from drugs, stay out of jail, talk to them, and then to charge mothers and fathers with the preservation of their children's fragile creative potential is a formidable mandate. Writing detailed prescriptions for being the creative parent of a creative child has become a major industry. Yet, apart from the special training required for the child of exceptional intellectual or artistic ability, the nurture of youth's creative powers, both at home and in school, is basically simple: to recognize individuality and to provide both guidance and freedom in developing natural endowments. This, the credo of all good teachers, is nevertheless a difficult challenge even for the most capable and virtuous parents.

When asked what kind of child they are hoping for, enlightened young parents, aware of the grim psychological consequences of expecting a child of one sex and getting the other, often reply evasively, "We don't want a genius . . . all we want is a nice healthy, happy baby." By this they mean a child who, in addition to being physically sound, will grow up to be an average better-than-average child. Wishing happiness for one's child is rather cavalier on the part of parents who are uncertain of what happiness is, and who probably know few people whose lives are so uncomplicated and serene as to be called happy. These parents sense that geniuses are likely to bring "happiness" neither to themselves nor to their families. Middle-class parents may be appalled by children who practice the liberal principles they themselves were only willing to preach. Parents who advocate a creative way of life must consider whether the scruffy leader of a student protest is what they envisioned when they encouraged their sons and daughters to think for themselves.

To translate the precepts for the nurture of creativity into a way of dealing with each of one's own children is the central fascinating challenge of parenthood. The child is not a flower or a pet. He is a complex, intelligent, changing individual to whom parents react with powerful emotion. They like and dislike him, admire and envy him, fear him and fear for him. They may experience all of these emotions during the course of the day, or simultaneously in a poignant blend of ambivalence. There are parents who tend the garden with more intelligent devotion and who are more consistent and understanding in their treatment of the family pet than their own children. And with good reason. Dependent and devoted, pets are less intelligent, less wily and confusing, and more easily dominated.

It may be disconcerting to respect a child's individuality and to "treat him as a person" when he is rapidly growing into a person quite different from the model you would have chosen: one with whom you feel comfortable, whom you admire and understand. Husbands and wives love and hate but they also choose each other. Children and parents experience similar emotions but they have neither a voice in the selection process, nor are they free to divorce, run off, or give each other away. Parental rapport varies with the individual child, and a parent may indeed have a favorite child, preferred because of a resemblance or a welcome lack of it.

It is assumed that men and women who say they love each other, and parents who maintain they love their children know what they mean. But apart from the passions of new love or the overwhelming emotions of loss through death or blighted marriage, it is not always certain what is meant by love within the context of daily life. Parents who take it for granted that they love their children and who would consider it unnatural not to, might have second, more useful thoughts if asked whether they like their children, or like them equally. There are fine, virtuous people who discover too late that they have little talent for the vocation of parenthood over its full course and in all its variety of experience. A parent cannot be a specialist in certain kinds of children or certain periods of childhood. Parenthood may involve learning to understand and appreciate a child one does not automatically like, and whom one may have good cause to dislike.

The health of the relationship between a parent and a creative child depends on the parent's reaction to those who disagree with him and who intrude their differences into his life. Parents may lavish tender care on a helpless infant and may be paragons of sympathy and patience with a three-year-old to whom father and mother are still the sun and moon. Understandably, parents are hurt, tired, and confused when the child becomes more independent, is less easily bribed or overpowered, when his demands are less clearly right or wrong, and when parenthood is no longer a novelty. Born helpless and unable to survive unless its call is answered, the infant's demands represent the broad, clear needs of the human species. But as the child assumes his specific human guise, and as his individual traits and his intelligence develop, his parents must abandon their preconceived image and accept the child as he is.

A mother responds to her baby's cry for food, knowing that he will not always be so impatient and insistent. But when, unheralded by loud screams, a child asks a question at an inconvenient moment — most of the time, for some parents — his reply is too often that deadly leitmotiv of childhood, "Not now," or "Later." By then the child may have lost interest or have forgotten what he wanted to know. When one is a child, *later* is usually *never*. Physical love and care are more easily given than the gift of one's attention, of trying to understand what is really being said, and of ideas produced for the specific occasion. It is not enough to look at a child, however fondly; one must also join him in looking out at his world.

Curiosity and the urge to explore cannot be safely or simply regulated. Creative adults know they cannot schedule their good ideas. Questions may arise and the desire to experiment may occur frequently and unpredictably during the day. Aside from those moments which are plainly unsuitable, a parent has many opportunities to encourage or discourage the habit of independent observation and thought. If a child is asked repeatedly to postpone his ideas and queries, he may decide to reserve his thoughts for those who welcome them. If he is also discouraged in school, curiosity, the foundation of his intellectual life, shrinks and fails and one day is gone. Parents feel hurt and rejected when they discover that their children do not talk to them. This may be youth's revenge for "later."

To live with an adolescent is a prickly task for most parents. Adolescence is the age when a child must assert his independence if eventually he is to leave the parental nest. His fumbling attempts to find himself may proceed with something less than charm and grace, and parents are unlikely to assume a neutral, objective attitude to the domestic tremors and upheavals generated by the adolescent. Even in the best circumstances, the teen-ager may find it awkward to communicate with his parents. Certainly it is impossible if the groundwork of devotion and guidance has not been established in all those odd, inopportune moments when the child chose to open himself to his parents.

A division in approach to social and world problems is a major cause of the current tension between the generations. But long before children reach the age of social awareness, parents themselves begin to sever the lines of communication. Although willing to lecture and dictate, many parents do not like to converse with their children and have arranged their lives so that they have neither opportunity nor patience for an occupation which is now more demanding than ever before. The father whose excuse for neglecting his children is that as a devoted parent he expends all his time and effort in providing his family with material prosperity, should not be surprised when his ungrateful children become affluent dropouts from parental devotion. In the long run children admire their parents for what they did *with* them, not *for* them.

The contemporary American mother is assured that she will not harm her children if she works while they are in school. If she stays home, squandering her talents and her education, she invites the agonies of the empty-nest syndrome when her children have flown or when she is widowed. Remain a housewife, she is warned, and she risks emasculating her sons, dominating her daughters, and turning into a nag, a martyr, or an alcoholic. The woman who wants to work is persuaded that it is the quality, not the quantity, of the time she spends with her children that counts. By working she not only earns her children's respect, but her ambition and enterprise stand as a model of achievement. This theory is admirable, if not realistic.

Fundamentally, our culture educates women as if they were men, encourages them to work, but does not discover a woman's sex until she applies for a job. The married woman who works is expected to fulfill the roles of both sexes. She must do a man's job — if she can get it, on a man's terms, but for a woman's salary. Her domestic duties may be somewhat simplified, but if she has children she must continue to serve as their mother, teacher, and inspiration. Moreover, each woman individually is expected to solve the problem of meshing her multiple roles without help from outside social agencies. In a society which maintains inflexible working conditions for the woman with children and which shows neither the imagination nor the inclination to invent the jobs for which she is uniquely suited, it is not surprising if at the day's end the working mother is so weary, torn and tense that the quality of her moments with her children is a delight to no one. The quality of her work hours may also be shabby. Studies of the relationship between age and achievement show that in certain fields, particularly in science, the peak of creative ability is reached in the late twenties or early thirties. This is precisely the period in which women retire to raise families. The woman who chooses to work, therefore, may find that her work contributes less to her own fulfillment than her income does to the support of the family's "high standards of consumption."

This is not to suggest that the modern parent should hang his head in shame, or that the quality of parenthood in the latter half of the twentieth century has suddenly deteriorated. Rather, it is harder to be a parent today. The demands children make on their parents in the traditional name of love and devotion have become more difficult to fulfill as older values and social customs tumble, and as parents find their own experience less apposite to their children's problems. Young people are more perplexed, ask knottier questions, and have more doubts than earlier generations. The bolder depart the parental doorstep in search not of love or fortune, of which so many have had all they want, but of "meaningful dialogue," of which they have had very little. In the absence of dialogue, a monologue will do — as long as the young do the talking. Idealistic and bold, youth intends to be heard. But youth is also inexperienced and inept. It would be better for everyone concerned if young people, with their vision, decency, and enthusiasm had someone to talk to. Otherwise they may use their gift for protest and criticism to destroy old structures, but will be powerless and unprepared to construct new institutions to replace those which have failed. Revolution is the work of the youthful sprinter, but protest is not sufficient. Creative construction is accomplished only by the mature, independent, and competent person who will not sell out once beyond the magic threshold of thirty, and who is emotionally and intellectually equipped to persist, alone if necessary, beyond the heady days of group protest.

The Paradox

There is an ironic paradox in the contrary direction of man's emerging awareness of his own individualism, now reinforced by scientific knowledge, and his increasing failure to affirm that self in his everyday life. The conflict between the rights of the individual and the welfare of the society which controls his life, grows more difficult to reconcile as the demands of both enlarge. In some form the problem of balancing the equation between the particular and the general is inherent in most of the problems with which we struggle today. In contrast to our enlightened philosophy and psychology of the dignity of the individual, the progressive dehumanization and fragmentation of the human being remains a sad phenomenon of our times.

There will be no efflorescence of creative capacity until we rescue the individual human being from becoming the most self-absorbed statistic in mankind's history, and until we deliver him from the contraction of time and the shrinkage of space. Creative endeavor requires physical and mental space; without privacy, solitude, and time it suffocates. It is not easy to be independent in a crowd and it is impossible to pursue original thought in the scattered remnants of a day or of a lifetime. The key to the nurture of creativity lies exactly where our technico-scientific society least likes to look for it: in respect and affection for people, in the cultivation of individuality and diversity, and in the courtship of exceptional ability and brilliant inconvenience. Finally, the creative life requires an environment which is free, open, and never so logical and efficient that it cannot be unpredictable.

It has been said that perhaps the best thing we can do for the creative person is to stay out of his way. Unfortunately, this is not always feasible because so much of the social apparatus is in his way. The seemingly simple policy of not obstructing creative talent, or of leaving genius alone, requires effort, planning, and the dedication of those willing to champion unpopular causes. The nurture of creativity cannot be left to specialized school programs or to talent hunts originating in fear and cupidity. Only massive reform of our entire school system to provide high quality education for all, and fundamental revision of social attitudes toward excellence and success will suffice.

The goals we pursue today with their emphasis on the efficient production and compulsive use of material goods, the sacrifice of the individual to these ends, the emotional and physical drain of human energy, and the sabotage of leisure time are inimical to creative activity. Conversely, in an age in which work is often boring, where increased leisure looms as a psychological disaster, and where the spread of automation threatens self-esteem, the development and expansion of personal creative resources are imperative. Not only do nations need the creative resources of their citizens; each individual human being needs his own reserves if he is to please himself and if he is to contend with the abrupt and premature arrival of the future.

Creativity is a dimension of mind intimately linked to man's most prized mental faculties and most cherished human rights. The cost of its nurture, in keeping with its value and nobility, is a commitment to freedom and challenge, and to the right of each individual to fulfill the promise of his birth.

Notes

1. Man and the Mindless Inventor

PAGE

5 "laws of biological organization . . . obscure"
L. L. Whyte, "How Is It Patterned," *Saturday Review* (Oct. 1, 1966), 78–79; also in L. L. Whyte, *Internal Factors in Evolution* (New York: Braziller, 1965).

5 "in interaction with other cellular constituents"
Barry Commoner, "Is DNA Really the Master Key to Heredity?" *Saturday Review* (Oct. 1, 1966), 73.

5 "cells form . . . control molecules"
John Kendrew, "What Switches It On?" *Saturday Review* (Oct. 1, 1966), 76–77; also in John C. Kendrew, *The Thread of Life* (Cambridge: Harvard University Press, 1966).

5 "The course of nature"
Isaac Newton, *Opticks*, Query 30.

5 "whose creator is itself"
see, Edmund W. Sinnott, *Matter, Mind and Man: The Biology of Human Nature* (New York: Atheneum, 1962), 100; "Life is not undetermined, but its determinism resides in its own nature." See also Chs. 9 and 10 for discussion of nature and man as creators.

6 "sexual reproduction . . . almost universal"
G. G. Simpson, *The Meaning of Evolution* (New Haven: Yale University Press, 1949), 213–14; "Even the protozoans, which usually reproduce by simple fission of the whole body, normally undergo from time to time a form of sexual reproduction." See also, Ch. 14, for further discussion of the mechanisms of evolution.

6 "Modern theories of evolution"
Theodosius Dobzhansky, *Evolution, Genetics, and Man* (New York: Wiley, 1955), 122–23.

7 "Natural selection . . . opportunistic"

PAGE

Dobzhansky, *Evolution*, 367; see also, Simpson, *Meaning of Evolution*, 160–86.

7   " 'slipped . . . out of the green twilight' "
Loren Eiseley, *The Immense Journey* (New York: Random House, 1957), 112.

8   " 'Art . . . deliberate skill' "
Eric Gill, *Art and Prudence: An Essay* (Great Britain: The Golden Cockerel Press, 1928), 1.

9   "an average of thirty thousand"
R. Buckminster Fuller, "Vision 65 Summary Lecture," *American Scholar*, Vol. 35, No. 2 (Spring 1966), 209.

9   "130 million years"
Simpson, *Meaning of Evolution*, 12; Edwin H. Colbert, *Evolution of the Vertebrates* (New York: Science Editions, 1961), 212.

10 " 'blind spot' "
H. J. Muller, "Perspectives for the Life Sciences," *Bulletin of the Atomic Scientists* (Jan. 1964), 7.

10 "immunological defenses"
P. B. Medawar, *The Future of Man* (New York: Basic Books, 1959), 96.

11 "man proceeds with knowledge"
see, Alfred North Whitehead, *Modes of Thought* (New York: Putnam, 1958), 229: according to Whitehead, "mentality" involves the "entertainment of alternatives."

12 " 'long-sought missing link' "
Konrad Lorenz, *On Aggression* (New York: Harcourt, Brace and World, 1963), 229.

12 " 'naked reasoner' "
Clifford Geertz, "The Impact of the Concept of Culture on the Concept of Man," *Bulletin of the Atomic Scientists* (April 1966), 4.

13 "Throughout history, human nature"
Paul Goodman, *Growing Up Absurd* (New York: Random House, 1960), 6–7.

13 "man is to be defined . . . second.' "
Geertz, "Concept of Man," 7; ". . . the generic potentialities focused in specific performance."

15 "Erich Fromm and John Dewey"
Erich Fromm, *Escape From Freedom* (New York: Avon Books, 1941), 53. John Dewey, *Freedom and Culture* (New York: Putnam, 1939), 3–23. "Yet as we look at the world we see sup-

posedly free institutions in many countries not so much over-thrown as abandoned willingly, apparently with enthusiasm." p. 4. ". . . men may be brought by long habit to hug their chains." p. 8.

15 " 'educated' learning"
Jerome Bruner, "The Will to Learn," *Commentary* (Feb. 1966), 41. Also appears as Ch. 6 in J. Bruner, *Toward a Theory of Instruction* (Cambridge: Harvard University Press, 1966).

16–17 On technology and social change
see, Kenneth Keniston, "Social Change and Youth in America," *Daedalus*, Vol. 91, No. 1 (Winter 1962), 147–51.

17–19 On biological freedom and human responsibility
see, G. G. Simpson, *The Meaning of Evolution*, 309–24; also, C. Wright Mills, "On Reason and Freedom," in *Identity and Anxiety*, R. Stein, A. J. Vidich, D. M. White, eds. (Glencoe: Free Press, 1960), 110–19. "Freedom is, first of all, the chance to formulate the available choices, to argue over them — and then, the opportunity to choose. That is why freedom cannot exist without an enlarged role of human reason in human affairs." p. 117.

2. Person — Process — Product

20 "reports appeared"
George V. Dearborn, "A Study of Imagination," *American Journal of Psychology*, Vol. 9 (1898), 183–90; Laura M. Chassell, "Tests for Originality," *Journal of Educational Psychology*, Vol. 7, No. 6 (1916), 317–28; S. S. Colvin and I. F. Meyer, "Imaginative Elements in the Written Work of School Children," *Pedagogical Seminary*, Vol. 13 (1906), 84–93; R. M. Simpson, "Creative Imagination," *American Journal of Psychology*, Vol. 33 (1922), 234–43.

21 "IQ's of 120 or above"
Anne Roe, "Psychological Approaches to Creativity in Science," in *Essays on Creativity in the Sciences*, Myron A. Coler, ed. (New York: New York University Press, 1963), 166.

21 "Other studies"
Catherine M. Cox, *Early Mental Traits of Three Hundred Geniuses*, in *Genetic Studies of Genius*, L. M. Terman, ed., Vol. 2 (Stanford: Stanford University Press, 1926).

22 "Virtuosity"
Webster's New International Dictionary, 2nd ed.

22 "Talent"
Webster, 2nd ed.

PAGE

22 " 'impossible for . . . genius' "
Henri-Frederic Amiel, *Journal,* quoted in *Bartlett's Familiar Quotations,* 11th ed. (1937), 1073.

22 Theory of talent and interaction of heredity and learning see, N. C. Meier, "Factors in Artistic Aptitude: Final Summary of a Ten-year Study of Special Ability," *Psychological Monographs,* Vol. 51, No. 5 (1939), 140–58.

22 William James called genius
William James, *Psychology: The Briefer Course,* (New York: Harper Torchbooks, 1961), 195.

22 "Albert Szent-Györgyi"
Gordon R. Taylor, *The Science of Life: A Picture History of Biology* (New York: McGraw-Hill, 1963).

23 Definition of genius
Webster, 2nd ed.

24 "chaos in this field"
Quinn McNemar, "Lost: Our Intelligence? Why?" *American Psychologist,* Vol. 19, No. 12 (1964), 876.

24 " 'a novel work' "
Morris I. Stein, "Creativity and Culture," *Journal of Psychology,* Vol. 36 (1953), 311.

24 " 'disposition to make' "
Harold D. Lasswell, "The Social Setting of Creativity," in *Creativity and Its Cultivation,* H. H. Anderson, ed. (New York: Harper, 1959), 203.

24 " 'ability to see' "
Erich Fromm, "The Creative Attitude," in *Creativity and Its Cultivation,* 44.

24 " 'process extended in time' "
Donald W. MacKinnon, "The Nature and Nurture of Creative Talent," *American Psychologist,* Vol. 17 (1962), 485.

24 " 'successful step into unknown' "
Paul Torrance quoted in H. C. Espy, "The Dimension of Creativity," *Woman's Day* (Oct. 6, 1963), 47. For Torrance's research definition see, "Scientific Views of Creativity and Factors Affecting its Growth," *Daedalus,* Vol. 94, No. 3 (Summer 1965), 663–64.

24 " 'the encounter' "
Rollo May, "The Nature of Creativity," in *Creativity and Its Cultivation,* 68.

24 "different levels of creativity"
I. A. Taylor, "The Nature of the Creative Process," in *Creativity: An Examination of the Creative Process,* P. Smith, ed.

(New York: Hastings House, 1959), 51–82; see also, L. L. Thurstone, "Creative Talent," *Reports from the Psychometric Laboratory, University of Chicago*, No. 61 (1950); also in L. L. Thurstone, ed., *Applications of Psychology* (New York: Harper, 1952).

25 "genius . . . difference . . . in kind"
Nathaniel D. M. Hirsch, *Genius and Creative Intelligence* (Cambridge, Mass.: Science-Art Publishers, 1931).

25 Creativity may also be conceived in terms of specific traits of intellect and personality
see, J. P. Guilford, "Factors that Aid and Hinder Creativity," *Teachers College Record*, Vol. 65 (1962), 380–92. J. P. Guilford, *Personality* (New York: McGraw-Hill, 1959). Also, Ralph J. Hallman, "The Necessary and Sufficient Conditions of Creativity," *Journal Humanistic Psychology*, Vol. 3, No. 1 (Spring 1963), 16–29.

25 "Margaret Mead"
"Creativity in Cross-cultural Perspective," in *Creativity and Its Cultivation*, 223.

26 "Jacques Maritain"
Creative Intuition in Art and Poetry (New York: Pantheon, 1953), 49; see also, Paul Valéry, *Collected Works*, Jackson Mathews, ed., Bollingen Series XLV, Vol. 12 (New York: Pantheon Books, 1960), 36–38.

26 "problem of defining creativity"
Thomas B. Sprecher, "A Proposal for Identifying the Meaning of Creativity," in *The Third (1959) Univ. of Utah Research Conference on the Identification of Creative Scientific Talent*, C. W. Taylor, ed. (Salt Lake City: University of Utah Press, 1959); Brewster Ghiselin, "Ultimate Criteria for Two Levels of Creativity," *The Second (1957) Univ. of Utah Research Conference on the Identification of Creative Scientific Talent*, C. W. Taylor, ed. (Salt Lake City: University of Utah Press, 1958), 141–55; Lindsey R. Harmon, "The Development of a Criterion of Scientific Competence," *Creative Scientific Talent* (1958), 42–52; Anne Roe, "Psychological Approaches to Creativity in Science," in *Creativity in the Sciences*, 154–59.

27 "who evaluates the evaluators?"
Henry A. Murray, "Vicissitudes of Creativity," in *Creativity and Its Cultivation*, 99.

27 "postulated by Carl Rogers"
Carl Rogers, "Toward a Theory of Creativity," in *Our Language and Our World*, S. I. Hayakawa, ed. (New York: Harper, 1959), 179.

PAGE

28 "study of personality variables"
Ernest R. Hilgard, "Creativity and Problem-solving," in *Creativity and Its Cultivation*, 169.

28 "Ernest Hilgard and investigators"
E. R. Hilgard, R. D. Edgren, R. P. Irvine, "Errors in Transfer Following Learning with Understanding: Further studies with Katona's card-trick experiments," *Journal of Experimental Psychology*, Vol. 47 (1954), 457–64.

28–29 Discussion of personality theory
Calvin S. Hall and Gardner Lindzey, *Theories of Personality* (New York: Wiley, 1957), 1–28, 538–58.

29 "no single valid theory"
Calvin S. Hall and Gardner Lindzey, *Theories of Personality*, 554 ff.

29 "definitions of personality . . . almost fifty"
Gordon W. Allport, *Personality: A Psychological Interpretation* (New York: Holt, 1937).

30 " 'Our meddling intellect' "
Wordsworth, "The Tables Turned," *Selected Poetry* (New York: Modern Library, 1950), 83.

30 " 'criterion mess' "
Quinn McNemar, "Lost: Our Intelligence? Why?" 877.

30 "interviews of 166 physical scientists"
C. W. Taylor, B. Ghiselin, R. Ellison, "Explorations in the Measurement and Prediction of Contributions of One Sample of Scientists," USAF ASD tech. rep., No. 61–96 (April 1961).

31 " 'intelligence has . . . little relationship' "
J. L. Holland, "Creative and Academic Performance Among Talented Adolescents," *Journal of Educational Psychology*, Vol. 52 (1961), 143; For evaluation of Holland's statistics, see Quinn McNemar, "Lost: Our Intelligence? Why?" 877.

31 "as Paul Torrance cautions"
E. Paul Torrance, "Scientific Views of Creativity and Factors Affecting Its Growth," *Daedalus*, Vol. 94, No. 3 (Summer 1965), 674–75.

32 "biologist George Wald"
"Innovation in Biology," *Scientific American*, Vol. 199, No. 3 (Sept. 1958), 113.

32 "Definitions, said Samuel Butler"
"Thought and Language," *The Importance of Language*, Max Black, ed. (Englewood Cliffs, N.J.: Prentice-Hall, 1962), 13.

33 "self-actualizing creativity"

PAGE

Abraham H. Maslow, *Toward a Psychology of Being* (Princeton, N.J.: Van Nostrand, 1962), 127–37.

33 " 'creative attitude' "
Erich Fromm, "The Creative Attitude," in *Creativity and Its Cultivation,* 44–54.

34 "atomic age . . . described"
William Barrett, *Irrational Man: A Study in Existential Philosophy* (New York: Doubleday, 1958), 57.

35 "Rainer Maria Rilke"
Briefe aus Muzot, November 13, 1925 letter to Witold von Hulewicz in Rainer Maria Rilke, *Duino Elegies,* translated and edited by J. B. Leishman and Stephen Spender (New York: Norton, 1939), 128.

35 " 'creative' or 'real' existence"
Norbert Fuerst, *Phases of Rilke* (Bloomington, Indiana: Indiana University Press, 1958), 170–71.

35 " 'spiritual creativity' "
Paul Tillich, *The Courage to Be* (New Haven: Yale University Press, 1952), 46 ff.

36 " 'special talent creativity' "
Maslow, *Toward a Psychology of Being,* 129.

36 "capacity to be motivated"
Philip H. Abelson, "Relation of Group Activity to Creativity in Science," *Daedalus,* Vol. 94, No. 3 (Summer 1965), 606.

40 " 'White as a white cow's milk' "
Elinor Wylie, "Velvet Shoes," *Collected Poems of Elinor Wylie* (New York: Knopf, 1932), 40.

40 " 'pearly monotones' "
Elinor Wylie, "Wild Peaches," *Collected Poems,* 12.

40 John Ruskin
Modern Painters (New York: Dutton, 1923), 194, 195.

41 Walter Pater
The Renaissance (New York: Random House, 1901), 199.

42 "In an interview on automation"
John Diebold, *Glamour* (June 1964), 148.

44 "Thoughtful observers"
Kenneth Keniston, "Social Change and Youth in America," *Daedalus,* Vol. 91, No. 1 (Winter 1962), 166; David Riesman, "The Search for Challenge," *Abundance For What?: And Other Essays* (Garden City, New York: Doubleday, 1964), 349–67.

45 "or the serpent in Genesis"

Herbert A. Simon, "A Computer for Everyman," *American Scholar*, Vol. 35, No. 2 (Spring 1966), 261.

3. Creativity and Crisis

47 " 'turmoil and transition' "
Talcott Parsons, "Youth in the Context of American Society," *Daedalus*, Vol. 91, No. 1 (Winter 1962), 97.

49 "astronauts"
David G. Mandelbaum, "The Interplay of Conformity and Diversity," *Conflict and Creativity: Part Two of Control of the Mind*, Seymour M. Farber and Roger H. L. Wilson, eds. (New York: McGraw-Hill, 1963), 247.

51 "lover's quarrel"
Robert Frost, "The Lesson for Today," *A Witness Tree* (New York: Holt, 1942), 52.

53 "education of citizens"
Raymond Aron, "The Education of the Citizen in Industrial Society," *Daedalus*, Vol. 91, No. 2 (Spring 1962), 249–63.

53 " 'Answers to Hard Questions' "
E. B. White, *The Second Tree From the Corner* (New York: Harper, 1965), 89.

54 "deterrent no one dares use"
Aron, "The Education of the Citizen in Industrial Society," 261.

54 "another critic asks"
Barry Commoner, *Science and Survival* (New York: Viking, 1966).

55 " 'safety valves' "
Aldous Huxley, "Education on the Nonverbal Level," *Daedalus*, Vol. 91, No. 2 (Spring 1962), 292; see also, William James, "The Moral Equivalent of War," *McClure's Magazine* (August 1910), 463–68, for an earlier expression of the "safety valve" concept.

55 " 'engineering of consent' "
Robert S. Morison, "The Need for New Types of Excellence," *Daedalus*, Vol. 90, No. 4 (Fall 1961), 778.

55 " 'proliferation . . . contraction' "
Nevitt Sanford, "The Human Problems Institute and General Education," *Daedalus*, Vol. 94, No. 3 (Summer 1965), 648.

55 Willard Libby, "Man's Place in the Physical Universe," *Bulletin of the Atomic Scientists* (September 1965), 12–17; quoted, p. 16.

56 " 'vital national resource' "
Stephen R. Graubard, "Preface to the Issue 'The Contemporary University: U.S.A.,' " *Daedalus,* Vol. 93, No. 4 (Fall 1964), 1032; see also, Julius A. Stratton, "Commencement Address, Massachusetts Institute of Technology, June 12, 1964," *Daedalus* (Fall 1964), 1238–43.

56 "women . . . according to . . . reports"
G. Gurin, J. Veroff, S. Feld, *Americans View Their Mental Health: A Nationwide Survey* (New York: Basic Books, 1960), 41–43.

57 "George Kistiakowsky"
"On Federal Support of Basic Research," *Daedalus* (Summer 1965), 714–15.

58 "national computing power"
David Sarnoff, "No Life Untouched," *Saturday Review* (July 23, 1966), 22.

60 "Albert Szent-Györgyi"
"The Brain, Morals, and Politics," *Bulletin of Atomic Scientists* (May 1964), 3.

61 " 'statistical morality' "
C. H. Waddington, *The Scientific Attitude* (Harmondsworth, Middlesex: Pelican Books, 1941), 26; Robert S. Morison, "The Need for New Types of Excellence," *Daedalus* (Fall 1961), 771 ff.

61 " 'reality of action at a distance' "
Robert S. Morison, "The Need for New Types of Excellence," 774.

62 "Moral Tourism"
David Hawkins, "The Informed Vision," *Daedalus* (Summer 1965), 541.

62 "334 conventional B-29's"
Alfred Goldberg, ed., *History of U.S. Air Force 1907–1957,* Vol. 13 (Princeton, N.J.: Van Nostrand, 1957), 86, 87.

62 "Students entering medical school"
Robert S. Morison, "The Need for New Types of Excellence," 766.

62 "change as an end in itself"
see, K. Keniston, "Social Change and Youth in America," *Daedalus* (Winter 1962), 148–49.

63 "much expected of younger generation"
Kaspar D. Naegele, "Youth and Society: Some Observations," *Daedalus* (Winter 1962), 47–67. Naegele observes that in our youth culture, adults value "youngness" rather than young

people, p. 65; see also, Talcott Parsons, "Youth in the Context of American Society," 108 ff.

64 On the rapid pace of social change
see, K. Keniston, "Social Change and Youth in America," 149–153; Lynn White, Jr., "On Intellectual Gloom," *American Scholar* (Spring 1966), 223–26.

64 "Bertrand Russell"
"An Outline of Intellectual Rubbish," *Unpopular Essays* (New York: Simon and Schuster, 1950), 100.

66 "life expectancy of Neanderthal Man"
H. Vallois, "La Durée de la Vie Chez l'Homme Fossile," *L. Anthropologie*, Vol. 47 (1937), 499–532.

66 "life-span of ancient Roman or Greek"
Encyclopaedia Britannica, Vol. 13 (1968), p. 1091, chart, p. 1099.

66 life expectancy in U.S.
Historical Statistics of the U.S.: Colonial Times to 1957 (Washington, D.C.: Bureau of the Census), 24–25. *Statistical Abstract of the U.S., 1963* (Washington, D.C.: Bureau of the Census).

67 "predicted . . . learning might occupy half"
Libby, "Man's Place in the Physical Universe," 17.

67 John Finley Scott, "So You're Going to College"
(New York: Public Affairs Pamphlets), quoted in the *New York Times Magazine* (Nov. 20, 1966), 119.

68–69 student uprisings
see, Joseph Katz and Nevitt Sanford, "Causes of the Student Revolution," *Saturday Review* (Dec. 18, 1965), 64–66, 76, 77; see also, Martin Meyerson, "The Ethos of the American College Student: Beyond the Protests," *Daedalus*, Vol. 95, No. 3 (Summer 1966), 713–39.

71 "selective stimulus of the environment"
Clifford Geertz, "The Impact of the Concept of Culture on the Concept of Man," *Bulletin of Atomic Scientists* (April 1966), 6–7.

71 culture and the brain
Albert Szent-Györgyi, "The Brain, Morals and Politics," *Bulletin of Atomic Scientists* (May 1964), 2–3; George W. Beadle, "The New Biology and the Nature of Man," *Bulletin of Atomic Scientists* (March 1964), 17, and "Genes, Culture, and Man," *Columbia University Forum* (Fall 1965), 15–16.

72 "Aldous Huxley"
"Education on the Nonverbal Level," 280.

73 "Balancing population"

PAGE

Archibald T. McPherson, "Synthetic Food for Tomorrow's Billions," *Bulletin of Atomic Scientists* (Sept. 1965), 7.

74 Buckminster Fuller
"Vision 65 Summary Lecture," *American Scholar* (Spring 1966), 217.

4. Fashions in Human Nature

76 "popular magazine article"
Joan Cook, "Diagnosis: 'This child is creative,' " *Glamour* (Jan. 1963), 104.

77 "A British psychologist"
T. R. Miles, "On Defining Intelligence," *British Journal of Educational Psychology*, Vol. 27 (1957), 153–65.

77 "validity of creativity tests"
Quinn McNemar, "Lost: Our Intelligence? Why?" *American Psychologist*, Vol. 19, No. 12 (Dec. 1964), 879–80.

80 " 'over-achiever' . . . long study hours"
David E. Lavin, *The Prediction of Academic Performance* (New York: Russell Sage Foundation, 1965), 24–25; see also, John Curtis Gowan, "Some Newer Theoretical Implications for Creative Learning," in *Creativity: Its Educational Implications*, J. C. Gowan, J. Curtis, G. D. Demos, E. P. Torrance, eds. (New York: Wiley, 1967), 79–82; J. P. Guilford, "Potentiality for Creativity," in *Creativity: Its Educational Implications*, 88.

80 " 'nothing but' school"
T. H. Huxley and Julian Huxley, *Touchstone For Ethics, 1893–1943* (New York: Harper, 1947), 29.

81 "C. S. Lewis"
The Abolition of Man (New York: Collier Books, 1962), 91.

81 "Judson Herrick"
The Evolution of Human Nature (Austin: University of Texas Press, 1956), 48.

81 "Herbert Muller"
Science and Criticism: The Humanistic Tradition in Contemporary Thought (New York: Braziller, 1956), 260.

82 " 'I'm afraid you've got a bad egg,' "
Punch, Vol. CIX (1895), 222, quoted in *The Oxford Dictionary of Quotations*, 403.

83 "Morris Cohen"
Charles S. Peirce, *Chance, Love, and Logic: Philosophical Essays*, Morris R. Cohen, ed. (New York: Harcourt, Brace, 1923), xxv.

85 " 'Sentence first' "
Lewis Carroll, *Alice's Adventures in Wonderland and Through the Looking-Glass* (U.S.A.: John C. Winston, 1923), 144.

85 "Taking his cue"
Benjamin Spock, "Toilet Training," *Redbook* (Nov. 1963), 38.

86 "Alfred North Whitehead"
Dialogues of Alfred North Whitehead, Lucien Price, ed. (New York: New American Library, 1954), 277.

87 "genius . . . IQ of 140 or over"
Lewis M. Terman, *et al.*, *Mental and Physical Traits of a Thousand Gifted Children*, in *Genetic Studies of Genius*, L. M. Terman, ed., Vol. 1 (Stanford: Stanford University Press, 1926), 26.

88 "Follow-up studies"
B. S. Burks, D. W. Jensen, L. M. Terman, *The Promise of Youth: Follow-up Studies of a Thousand Gifted Children*, in *Genetic Studies of Genius*, Vol. 3, 1930; L. M. Terman and M. H. Oden, *The Gifted Child Grows Up: Twenty-five Years' Follow-up of a Superior Group*, in *Genetic Studies of Genius*, Vol. 4, 1947; L. M. Terman and M. H. Oden, *The Gifted Group at Mid-Life: Thirty-five Years' Follow-up of the Superior Child*, in *Genetic Studies of Genius*, Vol. 5, 1959.

89 " 'IQ Tests Called Harmful' "
New York Times (June 16, 1964). This article reports a conference for Education for Creativity in Science held at New York University.

90 "lie detector test"
R. A. Sternbach, L. A. Gustafson, R. L. Colier, "Don't Trust the Lie Detector," *Harvard Business Review*, Vol. 40 (Nov. 1962), 127–34; see also, letter from Richard A. Sternbach, *Science* (June 5, 1964), 1177.

90 "Our affluent society"
see, J. K. Galbraith, *The Affluent Society* (Boston: Houghton Mifflin, 1958), 159–60 on "Dependence Effect."

93 "Eric Gill"
Art (New York: Devin-Adair, 1950), 108.

5. The Birthright Lost

95 " 'to create what he is' "
Paul Tillich, *The Courage to Be* (New Haven: Yale University Press, 1952), 150: "Man creates what he is."

95 "source of the true myth"
H. and H. A. Frankfort, "Myth and Reality," in *The Intellectual Adventure of Ancient Man*, H. Frankfort, *et al.*, eds. (Chicago: University of Chicago Press, 1946), 7.

97 " 'full possession . . . powers' "
E. A. Speiser, ed., *Anchor Bible: Genesis* (Garden City: Doubleday, 1964), 26.

99 "almost no occupational specialization"
V. Gordon Childe, *Man Makes Himself* (New York: New American Library, 1951), 56.

99 Lewis Mumford
The City in History (New Haven: Yale University Press, 1952), 102.

99 "archaeological 'ages' "
Childe, *Man Makes Himself*, 41–42.

100 " 'biochemical processing plant' "
Arthur C. Clarke, *Man and Space* (New York: Time-Life, 1964), 153.

100 On division of labor in Neolithic age
Childe, *Man Makes Himself*, 74–75, 80; J. Hawkes and L. Woolley, *Prehistory and the Beginnings of Civilization*, in *History of Mankind*, Vol. 1 (New York: Harper, 1963), 265–67.

100 "Community tradition"
Childe, *Man Makes Himself*, 81.

101 "intimate village life"
according to Hawkes and Woolley, *Prehistory and Beginnings of Civilization*, p. 267; Mumford, *City in History*, p. 14, and Childe, *Man Makes Himself*, pp. 81–82, early communities were small, relatively quiet, and peaceful. According to Childe one acre might be the area of a typical village. Mumford writes that a community might contain no more than "six to three score families," p. 14. Early communities were probably peaceful because of sufficient land, Hawkes and Woolley, 265.

102 "meaningful life of a complete Neolithic human being"
Mumford, *The City in History*, 102–103, 109; Hawkes and Woolley, *Prehistory and the Beginnings of Civilization*, 266.

103 "stronghold and shrine . . . city"
Mumford, *City in History*, 36–37, 64; W. F. Albright, *The Archaeology of Palestine* (Harmondsworth, Middlesex: Penguin, 1949), 86 ff, 205.

106 "written records were at first"
Even when simplified, cuneiform script required 600–1000 distinct characters. Egyptian hieroglyphic and hieratic scripts were

PAGE

similarly clumsy. A long apprenticeship was required to master
the art of writing and inevitably the oriental scribe became
a member of a privileged class. Alphabetic script was invented
much later, in Phoenicia (1300 B.C.).

106 "creative birthright . . . usurped"
Mumford, *The City in History*, "Monopoly of Creativity," 99–
100. I am especially indebted to Lewis Mumford for the concepts in this section. See also, Edith Hamilton, *The Greek Way*
(New York: Norton, 1964), 18; Thorkild Jacobsen, "Mesopotamia," in Frankfort, *et al.*, *The Intellectual Adventure of
Ancient Man*, 182–83, 198.

106 "servant of the gods"
Henri Frankfort, *The Birth of Civilization in the Near East*
(Bloomington: Indiana University Press, 1954), 59.

107 " '*Verily, savage-man*' "
James B. Pritchard, ed. *Ancient Near Eastern Texts Relating to
the Old Testament* (Princeton, N.J.: Princeton Univ. Press,
1955), 68.

107 "It has been suggested . . . civilized man"
Henri Frankfort, *Kingship and the Gods: A Study of Ancient
Near Eastern Religion as the Integration of Society and Nature*
(Chicago: University of Chicago Press, 1948).

108 " 'divinely imposed responsibility' "
William A. Irwin, "The Hebrews," in *The Intellectual Adventure
of Ancient Man*, 350; E. A. Speiser, ed., *Anchor Bible: Genesis*,
199.

109 king as integrated, free-standing individual
Henri Frankfort, *Kingship and the Gods*; also, Mumford, *The
City in History*, 110.

110 "One in seven"
Richard E. Wycherley, *How the Greeks Built Cities*, 2nd ed.
(London: MacMillan, 1962), 13–14.

110 "two thousand plays . . . . five to six thousand musical"
William Scott Ferguson, *Greek Imperialism* (Boston: Houghton
Mifflin, 1913), 59–60.

110 "forty-thousand full-fledged citizens"
R. E. Wycherley, *How the Greeks Built Cities*, 14.

111 "Many factors . . . genius"
see, Moses Hadas, *Humanism: The Greek Ideal and Its Survival*
(New York: Harper, 1960), 15–20; Edith Hamilton, *The Greek
Way*, 22–34; L. Mumford, *City in History*, 119–71.

112 "The heroic tradition"

see, C. M. Bowra, *The Greek Experience* (London: Weidenfeld
and Nicolson, 1957).

113 "mother goddess"
E. O. James, *The Ancient Gods: The History and Diffusion of
Religion in the Ancient Near East and the Eastern Mediter-
ranean* (New York: Putnam, 1960), 77 ff. Mother goddess cults
were found in Mesopotamia, Egypt, Western Asia, and the
Iberian Peninsula.

113 " 'waters which wander' "
Thorkild Jacobsen, "Mesopotamia," in *Intellectual Adventure
of Ancient Man,* Frankfort *et al.,* 146, 146–48.

113–114 Gods immanent in nature and Hebrew transcendent deity
For an interesting discussion of this see, H. and H. A. Frankfort,
The Intellectual Adventure of Ancient Man, 363–88.

116 " 'divine madness' "
Plato, "Ion," *Dialogues of Plato,* B. Jowett, trans. (New York:
Random House, 1937), Vol. 1, 289–91.

116 "blasphemous . . . God alone"
Roland H. Bainton, "Man, God, and the Church in the Age of
the Renaissance," in *The Renaissance: Six Essays,* W. K. Ferguson, *et al.,* eds. (New York: Harper and Row, 1962), 80–81.

117 "churchmen denounced"
e.g., St. Bernard; see, Herbert J. Muller, *Freedom in the Western World* (New York: Harper and Row, 1963), 50–51.

117 " *'Creatura non potest creare'* "
St. Augustine, *De Trinitate,* III, 9.

117 " *'creatio ex nihilo'* "
Thomas Aquinas, *Summa Theologiae,* I, 45, 8.

117 "St. Augustine . . . maintained"
Confessions, XII, 7.

117 "others who disagree"
W. A. Irwin, "The Hebrews," in *The Intellectual Adventure of
Ancient Man,* 259.

117 " 'Outrageous as a Sea' "
Milton, *Paradise Lost* (Modern Library), Book VII, 253.

117 "The Middle Ages"
Herbert J. Muller, *Freedom in the Western World,* 48–50, 107;
J. H. Randall, *The Making of the Modern Mind* (Boston: Hough-
ton Mifflin, 1940), 58, 89.

118 " 'free and proud shaper' "
Pico della Mirandola, *Oration on the Dignity of Man,* A. R.
Caponigri, trans. (Chicago: Henry Regnery, 1956), 4.

PAGE

118 "Dürer describes"
Erwin Panofsky, *The Life and Art of Albrecht Dürer*, one vol.
ed. (Princeton, N.J.: Princeton University Press, 1955), 279–80.

118 "sixteenth-century English critic"
Richard Puttenham, *The Arte of English Poesie* (London,
1589); quoted in Panofsky, "Artist, Scientist, Genius: Notes on
the 'Renaissance-Dämmerung,' " in *The Renaissance: Six Essays*,
172.

118 "Leonardo avoided . . . 'create' "
Panofsky, *Albrecht Dürer*, 281. Also, Panofsky, "Artist Scientist,
Genius," in *The Renaissance: Six Essays*, 173–74.

119 " 'The rise of man' "
Panofsky, "Artist, Scientist, Genius," in *The Renaissance: Six
Essays*, 172.

119 "two kinds of madness"
Plato, "Phaedrus" *Dialogues of Plato*, Vol. 1, 268–69.

121 "Italian Quattrocento"
Panofsky, "Artist, Scientist, Genius," in *The Renaissance: Six
Essays*, 174.

122 " 'master architects' "
Schiller, quoted in E. Kretschmer, *The Psychology of Men of
Genius* (London: Kegan Paul, 1931), 136.

122 " 'Many small' "
Chaucer, *The Persones Tale*, Section 21.

124 " 'rule of the cord' "
William Cecil Dampier, *A Shorter History of Science* (New
York: Meridian Books, 1957), 11, 19.

124 "suggested that Pythagoras"
Herbert Westren Turnbull, "The Great Mathematicians," in
The World of Mathematics, James R. Newman, ed., Vol. 1
(New York: Simon and Schuster, 1956), 83–84.

124 "believed that Galileo"
I. Bernard Cohen, "Galileo," editors of *Scientific American*, in
Lives in Science (New York: Simon and Schuster, 1957), 16.

124–125 story of Newton and Halley
I. B. Cohen, "Newton," in *Lives in Science*, 27–28. John May-
nard Keynes, "Newton: The Man," in *The World of Mathematics*, Vol. 1, 278–79; see also, E. N. Da C. Anrade, "Isaac Newton," in *The World of Mathematics*, Vol. 1, 264–66, for a slightly
different account.

125 "Faraday postulated his theories"
Helmholtz, Faraday Lecture of 1881, quoted in J. Kendall,
Michael Faraday (London: Faber, 1955), 138.

PAGE

126 " 'what science does' "
J. H. Randall, *The Making of the Modern Mind*, 459–60, 478.

126 "J. Bronowski"
Science and Human Values (New York: Harper and Row, 1959), 91–94.

127–128 For an account of Kepler's physics and metaphysics
see, Arthur Koestler, *The Act of Creation* (New York: Macmillan, 1964), 124–30.

128 "aesthetic emotions"
Henri Poincaré, "Mathematical Creation," in *The Creative Process: A Symposium*, Brewster Ghiselin, ed. (New York: New American Library, 1955), 33–42, esp. pp. 40–41; also in Newman, ed., *The World of Mathematics*, 2041–50.

129 "Norbert Wiener"
The Human Use of Human Beings: Cybernetics and Society (New York: Doubleday, 1954), 188 ff., 193.

129 " 'Der Herrgott' "
Albert Einstein quoted in Wiener, *The Human Use of Human Beings*, 188.

129 "L. L. Whyte"
The Unconscious Before Freud (New York: Basic Books, 1960), 73.

129 "hidden unity"
J. Bronowski, *Science and Human Values*, 31–32. "And if science were a copy of fact, then every theory would be either right or wrong, and would be so forever." See also, J. Bronowski, "The Creative Process," *Scientific American*, Vol. 199, No. 3 (July 1958), 59–65.

129 "the science of weather"
Oliver Lodge, "Johann Kepler," in *The World of Mathematics*, Vol. 1, 234.

129 "Clerk Maxwell"
in J. G. Crowther, *Men of Science* (New York: Norton, 1936), 320.

131 "major effect of twentieth-century . . . physics"
see, Randall, *The Making of the Modern Mind*, 459–60, 472–78.

131 "Scientific imagination"
Mario Bunge, *Intuition and Science* (Englewood Cliffs, N.J.: Prentice Hall, 1962), 92–99.

132 For an account of Einstein's discovery
see, Max Wertheimer, *Productive Thinking* (New York: Harper, 1959), 213–33.

132   " 'common sense' "
      M. Bunge, *Intuition and Science*, 87–89.

133   "to *un*learn"
      M. Bunge, *Intuition and Science*, 75–76; H. Lasswell, "The
      Social Setting of Creativity," in *Creativity and Its Cultivation*,
      213–14.

135   "Einstein called, 'the deep shudder' "
      quoted in Arthur Koestler, *The Act of Creation* (New York:
      Macmillan, 1964), p. 258; from Carl Seelig, *Albert Einstein*
      (Zürich: Europa Verlag, 1954), 45.

6. Psychology Goes Scientific

137   "ideal primary school pupil"
      John L. Holland, "Some Limitations of Teacher Ratings as
      Predictors of Creativity," *Journal of Educational Psychology*,
      Vol. 50, No. 5 (1959), 219–23; Anne Roe, "Psychological Ap-
      proaches to Creativity in Science," in *Essays on Creativity in
      the Sciences*, Coler, ed., 170; Jerome Kagan, "Personality and
      the Learning Process," *Daedalus* (Summer 1965), 556–58.

137   " 'late bloomers' "
      For "late bloomers" and "morning glories" see, David C. Mc-
      Clelland, *et al., Talent and Society: New Perspectives in the
      Identification of Talent* (New York: Van Nostrand, 1958), 9.

137   "Winston Churchill"
      Arnold J. Toynbee, "Churchill — Progress of a 'Slow Grower,' "
      New York Times Magazine (November 1, 1964), 40–42, 46, 48.

137   " 'peak-and-valley' "
      Cliff W. Wing, Jr., "Student Selection, the Educational Environ-
      ment, and the Cultivation of Talent," *Daedalus* (Summer 1965),
      633.

138   "Freud . . . forced the public"
      L. L. Whyte, *The Unconscious Before Freud* (New York: Basic
      Books, 1960), 10.

138   Historical forces affecting psychology in the nineteenth century
      see, Gardner Murphy, *Historical Introduction to Modern Psy-
      chology* (New York: Harcourt, Brace and World, 1949) ; A. A.
      Roback, *History of American Psychology* (New York: Library
      Publishers, 1952) ; E. G. Boring, *A History of Experimental
      Psychology* (New York: Appleton-Century-Crofts, 1950).

139   "fatal uncertainty"
      Lawrence Cremin, *The Transformation of the School: Progres-*

PAGE

sivism in American Education, 1876–1957 (New York: Knopf, 1961), 265–70; James D. Koerner, *The Miseducation of American Teachers* (Boston: Houghton Mifflin, 1963), 26.

139 "George Stoddard"
"Creativity in Education," in *Creativity and Its Cultivation*, 181.

140 " 'What is mind' "
Thomas Hewitt Key. Quoted by F. J. Furnivall, *Bartlett's Familiar Quotations*, 360.

140 " 'great ravelled knot' "
Charles Sherrington, *Man On His Nature* (Garden City: Doubleday, 1955), 183.

141 "Democritus"
Bertrand Russell, *A History of Western Philosophy* (New York: Simon and Schuster, 1945), 66 ff.

141 "Plato and his successors"
Russell, *A History of Western Philosophy*, 134 ff.

142 "True knowledge"
B. A. G. Fuller, *A History of Philosophy* (New York: Holt, 1945), 128–29, 147–49.

142 For the nature of reality in Plato and Aristotle
see also, Ross Stagner and T. F. Karwoski, *Psychology* (New York: McGraw-Hill, 1952), 3–6.

143 " 'an act of sight' "
Descartes, "Meditation II," in *Meditations and Selections from the Principles of Philosophy by René Descartes*, L. Lévy-Bruhl, ed. (La Salle, Illinois: Open Court, 1948), 38.

144 "unanswerable metaphysical questions"
A. C. Crombie, "Early Concepts of the Senses and the Mind," *Scientific American*, Vol. 210, No. 24 (May 1964), 111.

145 Psychology as study of soul or mind
Floyd L. Ruch, *Psychology and Life*, 6th ed. (Glenview, Ill.: Scott, Foresman, 1963), 10.

145 "general problem of 'mind' "
Gardner Murphy, *General Psychology* (New York: Harper, 1933), 2.

146 "Auguste Comte"
Positive Philosophy, quoted in Herbert J. Muller, *Freedom in the Modern World* (New York: Harper and Row, 1966), 204.

146 "William James"
Psychology: The Briefer Course, Gordon Allport, ed. (New York: Harper, 1961), 335.

146 "Wundt trained so many"
Robert I. Watson, *The Great Psychologists* (Philadelphia: Lippincott, 1963), 258.

147 "Psychology as a natural science"
William James, *Psychology: The Briefer Course*, 334.

147 "whose author James admired"
Ernest Jones, *The Life and Work of Sigmund Freud*, Vol. 2 (New York: Basic Books, 1955), 57.

147 "exact science of physics"
E. Hilgard, *Theories of Learning*, 2nd ed. (New York: Appleton-Century-Crofts, 1956), 479.

148 "James preferred"
James, *Psychology*, Allport, ed., xv, 328–29; Gay Wilson Allen, *William James* (New York: Viking, 1967), 496–98.

149 " 'intra-organic stimuli' "
Gardner Murphy, *Historical Introduction to Modern Psychology*, 265.

150 "study of *behavior*"
Murphy, *Historical Introduction to Modern Psychology*, 259–260; Hilgard, *Introduction to Psychology*, 3rd ed. (New York: Harcourt, 1962), 17; A. A. Roback, *History of American Psychology*, 225–26.

150 "merely ignored it"
see, Ralph Barton Perry, *Realms of Value* (Cambridge: Harvard University Press, 1954), 17, 20.

150 "psychology . . . losing its mind"
F. L. Ruch, *Psychology and Life*, 10.

151 "studies of rats and pigeons"
"People, after all, are not rats (with a few exceptions), and they are not pigeons (with similar exceptions)." J. P. Guilford, "Factors that Aid and Hinder Creativity," in *Creativity: Its Educational Implications*, Cowan, *et al.*, 122.

152 "whole determines the parts"
Robert S. Woodworth and Mary R. Sheehan, *Contemporary Schools of Psychology*, 3rd ed. (New York: The Ronald Press, 1964), 218–19.

153 Wertheimer, Köhler, and modern physics
Roback, *History of American Psychology*, 308; Murphy, *Historical Introduction to Modern Psychology*, 284, 287, 297–98.

154 "in real life food is not"
Murphy, *Historical Introduction to Modern Psychology*, 432.

154 Learning theory
see, Ernest R. Hilgard, *Theories of Learning*, and O. Hobart

Mowrer, *Learning Theory and Behavior* (New York: Wiley, 1960).

155 "Jacques Hadamard"
The Psychology of Invention in the Mathematical Field (Princeton: Princeton University Press, 1949).

155 "Einstein once told"
M. Wertheimer, *Productive Thinking*, 228.

156 " 'latent learning' . . . 'incidental learning' "
Hilgard, *Theories of Learning*, 196, 214.

157 latent learning in schools
Martin Mayer, *The Schools* (Garden City, N.Y.: Doubleday, 1963), 87.

158 Hilgard on Skinner
Hilgard, *Theories of Learning*, 106.

158 B. F. Skinner
see, *The Behavior of Organisms: An Experimental Analysis* (New York: Appleton-Century-Crofts, 1938), 442. "I can say that the only differences I expect to see revealed between the behavior of rat and man (aside from enormous differences of complexity) lie in the field of verbal behavior."

159 "Bertrand Russell once observed"
Bertrand Russell, *An Outline of Philosophy* (London: Allen and Unwin, 1956), 33.

159 "taught with confidence"
Hilgard, *Theories of Learning*, 457.

159 "thinking, or something like it"
D. O. Hebb, *Organization of Behavior* (New York: Wiley, 1961), xvi. "Something like *thinking*, that is, intervenes."

162 "Learning processes . . . a combination"
Hilgard, *Theories of Learning*, 475; Hilgard, *Introduction to Psychology*, 3rd ed., 280.

162 "According to Watson"
J. B. Watson, *Behaviorism,* revised ed. (Chicago: University of Chicago Press, 1930), 247.

162 Guthrie and Hull
E. R. Guthrie, *The Psychology of Learning* (New York: Harper, 1935), 25. C. L. Hull, *A Behavior System* (New Haven: Yale University Press, 1952), 56; see also Hilgard, *Theories of Learning*, 152.

163 "manipulating variables"
B. F. Skinner, *Science and Human Behavior* (New York: Macmillan, 1953), 252 ff.

163 "Watson had boasted"

J. B. Watson, *Behaviorism*, revised ed. (Chicago: University of Chicago Press, 1930), 104.

7. *Adventures in Education Land*

165–166 school attendance statistics
U.S. Bureau of the Census, *Statistical Abstract of the United States: 1968*, 89th ed. (Washington, D.C., 1968), 105; I. L. Kandel, *American Education in the Twentieth Century* (Cambridge: Harvard University Press, 1957), 29.

166 "science of education suffered"
see, James D. Koerner, *The Miseducation of American Teachers* (Boston: Houghton Mifflin, 1963), 25–34.

167 "scorned the 'zoopsychologists' "
I. P. Pavlov, "Physiology and Psychology in the Study of the Higher Nervous Activity of Animals," *Essays in Psychology and Psychiatry* (New York: Citadel Press, 1962), 84.

167 "forbade . . . psychological terms"
Pavlov, "Physiology and Psychology in the Study of the Higher Nervous Activity of Animals," 71.

167 classical and operant conditioning
Stagner and Karwoski, *Psychology*, 281–82, 308; D. O. Hebb, *Organization of Behavior*, 174–76.

170 " 'specificity doctrine' " E. L. Thorndike, *Educational Psychology II. (The Psychology of Learning)* (New York: Teachers College, 1913), 213–17.

170 "specific stimulus-response connections"
Thorndike, *Educational Psychology II*, 55, "learning is connecting."

171 "Law of Effect"
Thorndike, *Educational Psychology II*, 4, and *Educational Psychology I. (The Original Nature of Man)* (New York: Teachers College, 1913), 172.

172 "affect all nerve cell connections"
Thorndike, *Educational Psychology, I*, 221 ff., and *Educational Psychology II*, 417; also, Hilgard, *Theories of Learning*, 20, 44, 45.

172 "Jerome Bruner observes"
Jerome Bruner, *Toward a Theory of Instruction* (Cambridge: Harvard University Press, 1966), 127–28.

173 "Since 1950"
D. E. Berlyne, "Curiosity and Exploration," *Science*, Vol. 153 (July 1, 1966), 25–33.

PAGE

173 " 'will to learn' "
Jerome Bruner, "The Will to Learn," *Commentary* (Feb. 1966), 41–46; also in *Toward a Theory of Instruction*, Ch. 6, 113–28.

173 "Identical Elements"
E. L. Thorndike, *Educational Psychology II* (1913), 417.

174 "transfer of learning"
Hilgard, *Theories of Learning*, 24.

174 " 'faculty training' "
Kandel, *American Education in the Twentieth Century*, 91.

175 "Intelligence in Thorndikian terms"
Hilgard, *Theories of Learning*, 25.

175 "did not deny ideas or insight"
Hilgard, *Theories of Learning*, 4–5, 45.

175 "Köhler's celebrated study"
Wolfgang Köhler: *The Mentality of Apes* (New York: Vintage Books, 1959), 158, 174–75.

176 For story of Archimedes
see, J. R. Newman, ed., *The World of Mathematics*, Vol. 1, 185–186.

177 "overlearning"
Hilgard, *Theories of Learning*, 472 ff.

177 "mechanized habits persist"
see, N. R. F. Maier, N. M. Glaser, J. B. Klee, "Studies of Abnormal Behavior in the Rat: III," *Journal Experimental Psychology*, Vol. 26, No. 6 (1940), 521–46. "Frustration causes a position habit to become fixated," 541.

178 " 'Unfinished Revolution' "
Paul Goodman, *Growing Up Absurd* (New York: Random House, 1960), 216–17, 225; and *Compulsory Mis-education and the Community of Scholars* (New York: Random House, 1964), 40.

179 "Dewey's criticisms relevant"
Oscar Handlin, *John Dewey's Challenge to Education* (New York: Harper, 1959), 39, 45–49.

180 "Paul Torrance"
"Scientific Views of Creativity and Factors Affecting its Growth," *Daedalus*, Vol. 94, No. 3 (Summer 1965), 677, 677–79.

181 "expectation of success or failure"
Jerome Kagan, "Personality and the Learning Process," *Daedalus* (Summer 1965), 555–56.

182 content and method in Dewey
see, D. Hawkins, "The Informed Vision," *Daedalus* (Summer 1965), 546.

PAGE

183 " 'zeal' "
E. L. Thorndike, *Educational Psychology II* (1913), 22.

184 On "impulse-release" as a central doctrine of education
Jules Henry, "American Schoolrooms: Learning the Nightmare,"
Columbia University Forum (Spring 1963), 29–30. Also appears
in Jules Henry, *Culture Against Man* (New York: Random
House, 1963), 319–20.

185 "disintegration of . . . progressive education"
see, Sidney Hook, "Some Educational Attitudes and Poses,"
Harvard Educational Review, Vol. 36, No. 4 (Fall 1966), 496–
504.

185 "the young hero . . . observed"
J. D. Salinger, *The Catcher in the Rye* (New York: New American Library, 1951), 166.

187 "World War II"
James B. Conant, *The Child, the Parent, and the State* (Cam-
bridge: Harvard University Press, 1957), 17; Frank G. Jennings,
"The Revolution in Education: It Didn't Start with Sputnik,"
Saturday Review (Sept. 16, 1967), 77–79, 95–97.

188 "never possessed a clear statement"
Anthony G. Oettinger, "The Myths of Educational Technology,"
Saturday Review (May 18, 1968), 76–77, 91.

188 " 'science of nonthought' "
Jacques Barzun, *The House of Intellect* (New York: Harper,
1959), 137.

188 "modern mathematics curricula"
Morris Kline, "A Case History," *Harvard Educational Review*,
Vol. 36, No. 4 (Fall 1966), 509.

189 "concede, as Thorndike did"
statement made by E. L. Thorndike at the International Congress
of Psychology, New Haven, Sept. 1929. Quoted in Hilgard,
Theories of Learning, 25.

190 quotes from Creative Playthings catalogues
"Help Them Grow Every Day" (1964), 3; "The Power of Play"
(1967), 4; "Help Them Grow Every Day" (1964), 2; "Creative
Playthings, Inc. 68/69" (1968), 36, 37; "The Power of Play"
(1967), 4; "Play and Learning in the Home" (1964), 8; "Help
Them Grow Every Day" (1964), 13; "Play and Learning in the
Home" (1964), 2.

8. Machines

193 " 'necessary technical excellence' "
A. N. Whitehead, *The Aims of Education and Other Essays* (New York: Macmillan, 1959), 144.

194 " 'teach-test' "
Sidney L. Pressey, "Re-Program Programing?" *Psychology in the Schools* (July 1967); reprinted by Van Valkenburgh, Nooger and Neville, Inc., p. 5.

195 "Skinner's response-reinforcement technique"
B. F. Skinner, "The Science of Learning and the Art of Teaching," in *Teaching Machines and Programmed Learning: A Sourcebook*, A. A. Lumsdaine and Robert Glaser, eds. (Washington, D.C.: National Education Association, 1960), 99–100; also appears in *Harvard Educational Review*, Vol. 24, No. 2 (Spring 1954), 86–97.

196 Socratic method and empirical science
Bertrand Russell, *A History of Western Philosophy* (New York: Simon and Schuster, 1945), 92–93.

198 "only behavior is real"
Skinner, "The Science of Learning and the Art of Teaching," in *Teaching Machines and Programmed Learning*, 111.

199 "not the hardware but the software"
Patrick Suppes in the *Christian Science Monitor* (Aug. 10, 1967) writes: "This absence of a tough-minded intellectual tradition of study of how we can best individualize instruction is, in my own judgment, the most serious handicap we have to overcome in using computers as instructional devices."

199 "eliminate . . . the entire school system"
James D. Finn, "Technology and the Instructional Process," in *Teaching Machines and Programmed Learning*, 390.

200 inadequacy of middle-class nursery school
see, Maya Pines, "Slum Children Make Up for Lost Time," *New York Times Magazine* (Oct. 15, 1967), 66; see also, Susan S. Stodolsky and Gerald Lesser, "Learning Patterns in the Disadvantaged," *Harvard Educational Review*, Vol. 37, No. 4 (Fall 1967), 546–93.

200 "Bereiter-Engelmann method"
Carl Bereiter and Siegfried Engelmann, *Teaching Disadvantaged Children in the Preschool* (Englewood Cliffs, N.J.: Prentice-Hall, 1966); see review of Bereiter and Engelmann by Ilse Mat-

tick, *Harvard Educational Review*, Vol. 37, No. 2 (Spring 1967), 319–25.

201 "slum environment offers"
Bereiter and Engelmann, *Teaching Disadvantaged Children in the Preschool*, 62–63.

201 " 'think when the teacher says' "
Bereiter and Engelmann, *Teaching Disadvantaged Children in the Preschool*, 214.

201 "relating personal experience"
Bereiter and Engelmann, *Teaching Disadvantaged Children in the Preschool*, 80.

201 " 'appropriate schoolroom behavior' "
Bereiter and Engelmann, *Teaching Disadvantaged Children in the Preschool*, 78.

202 "a mistake to conclude"
Frank Riessman, *The Culturally Disadvantaged Child* (New York: Harper and Row, 1962), 77–78.

203 On misuse of the machine in the classroom
see, Jonathan Kozol, *Death at An Early Age* (Boston: Houghton Mifflin, 1967), 169.

203 " 'teacher-proof' "
Robert J. Schaefer, *The School as a Center of Inquiry* (New York: Harper and Row, 1967), 38.

204 "little organized research"
Patrick Suppes, *Christian Science Monitor* (Aug. 10, 1967), and "The Uses of Computers in Education," *Scientific American*, Vol. 215, No. 3 (Sept. 1966), 219–20.

204 " 'It was programmed . . . but I'm not' "
Time (May 19, 1967), 98.

204 "David Hawkins observed"
David Hawkins, "The Informed Vision," *Daedalus*, Vol. 94, No. 3 (Summer 1965), 551.

205 "exaggerated stress on detail"
S. L. Pressey, "Some Perspectives and Major Problems Regarding 'Teaching Machines,' " *Teaching Machines and Programmed Learning*, 498–99.

206 " 'premonition of things unknown' "
C. G. Jung, *Memories, Dreams, Reflections* (New York: Pantheon, 1963), 356.

207 "Gardner Quarton mentions"
Gardner Quarton, "Deliberate Efforts to Control Human Behavior and Modify Personality," *Daedalus*, Vol. 96, No. 3 (Summer 1967), 840.

PAGE

208 "too soon to tell"
Ben B. Seligman, *Most Notorious Victory: Man in an Age of Automation* (Glencoe: Free Press, 1966), 112; W. J. Carr, "A Functional Analysis of Self-Instructional Devices," *Teaching Machines and Programmed Learning*, 541–42. In addition to evaluation studies of the effectiveness of machine teaching as compared to standard methods of instruction, Dr. Carr believes that the "major portion of research effort should be devoted to an experimental analysis of the parameters which influence the effectiveness of the self-instructional devices." These variables are: characteristics of the device, of the program, and of the learner.

208 "it has been suggested"
review of Arthur Koestler's *Act of Creation* in the *Times Literary Supplement* (July 2, 1964), 562.

209 "Skinner concluded"
see, Robert S. Woodworth and Mary R. Sheehan, *Contemporary Schools of Psychology* (New York: Ronald Press, 1964), 168–169. The authors observe that Skinner ignores perceptual factors in the learning process. Many words and phrases are learned simply by listening, rather than by direct prompting.

210 " 'trial and success' "
J. H. Martin, "A Report on the Freeport Public Schools Experiment on Early Reading Using the Edison Responsive Environment Instrument" (Englewood Cliffs, N.J.: Responsive Environments Corp., n.d.), 3.

210 "*what* tested principles?"
see, S. L. Pressey, "Teaching Machine (and Learning Theory) Crisis," in *Educational Technology: Readings in Programmed Instruction*, John P. DeCecco, ed. (New York: Holt, Rinehart and Winston, 1964), 455. "The archvillain, leading so many astray, is declared to be learning theory!" Pressey pleads for a closer look at concepts of programming.

211 " 'Come forth and bring' "
Wordsworth, "The Tables Turned," *Selected Poetry* (New York: Modern Library, 1950), 83.

212 "One wonders what . . . children will become"
see, Stanley Foster Reed, "Automation, Education, and Creativity," in *Automation, Education, and Human Values*, William W. Brickman and Stanley Lehrer, eds. (New York: School and Society Books, 1966), 323–24; W. Brickman, "The Scholar-Educator and Automation," in *Automation, Education, and Human Values*, 176–79.

213 "*properly used . . . fully understood*"

Chris A. De Young and Richard Wynn, *American Education,* 5th ed. (New York: McGraw Hill, 1964), 400.

214 "the vast waste"
G. Howard Goold, *et al.,* "The Education Industries," *Harvard Educational Review,* Vol. 37, No. 1 (Winter 1967), 117.

214 "have not been adequately tested"
A. A. Lumsdaine and Robert Glaser, "Concluding Remarks," *Teaching Machines and Programmed Learning,* 565–66; B. Seligman, *Most Notorious Victory,* 112–13; Douglas Porter, "A Critical Review of a Portion of the Literature on Teaching Devices," *Teaching Machines and Programmed Learning,* 122–29.

215 " 'product of high intellectual quality' "
Edward L. Katzenbach, "The Education Industries," *Harvard Educational Review* (Winter 1967), 123.

215 " 'I know of no market' "
E. L. Katzenbach, "The Education Industries," 119.

215 "Less than one half of one percent"
Wilbur J. Cohen, "Education and Learning," *Annals of the American Academy of Political and Social Science* (Sept. 1967), 97.

216 "commitment to specific programs and devices"
Lumsdaine and Glaser, "Concluding Remarks," *Teaching Machines and Programmed Learning,* 565.

216 "Who will have the courage"
Gerald Holton, "The Education Industries," 115. Holton writes, "Who will ask the big and dangerous questions?" On industry's vested interests, see also, Roy C. Buck, "Education, Technological Change, and the New Society," *Automation, Education, and Human Values,* 195–212, esp. 199.

216 " 'to help teach people how to know' "
"A Publisher and More," McGraw-Hill advertisement.

216 " 'unreasonable to expect' "
G. Howard Goold, "The Education Industries," 117.

217 "Many educators fear"
Paul Goodman, "The Education Industries," 107–10; Donald W. Oliver, "The Education Industries," 110–13; C. A. De Young and R. Wynn, *American Education,* 496.

217 "individualizing the *presentation*"
Patrick Suppes, "Computers Aid Instruction," *RCA Education News* (Aug. 8, 1967), 4.

9. In Old Vienna

222 "statistical composite"
L. M. Terman, *et al.*, *Mental and Physical Traits of a Thousand Gifted Children* in *Genetic Studies of Genius*, L. M. Terman, ed., Vol. 1 (Stanford: Stanford University Press, 1926).

222 "myth of the sick artist"
see, Mason Griff, "The Commercial Artist: A Study of Changing and Consistent Identities," *Identity and Anxiety: Survival of the Person in Mass Society*, M. R. Stein, A. J. Vidich, D. M. White, eds. (Glencoe, Ill.: Free Press, 1960), 220–22.

222 " 'gray and ashen' "
Goethe, *Faust*, Pt. I, *Studirzimmer*.

222 romanticism
see, J. H. Randall, *Making of the Modern Mind* (Boston: Houghton Mifflin, 1940), 389–425.

223 "Max Nordau proclaimed"
Max Nordau, *Degeneration* (New York: Appleton, 1895).

223 "Cesare Lombroso declared"
Cesare Lombroso, *The Man of Genius* (London: Walter Scott, 1891).

223 " 'world calls genius' "
Poe, quoted in Lorine Pruette, "A Psychoanalytical Study of Edgar Allan Poe," Hendrik M. Ruitenbeek, ed., *The Literary Imagination* (Chicago: Quadrangle Books, 1965), 410.

223 "Herbert Muller"
Herbert J. Muller, *Freedom in the Modern World* (New York: Harper and Row, 1966), 21, see also, pp. 21–25.

225 "Lionel Trilling observes"
Lionel Trilling, "Art and Neurosis," *Art and Psychoanalysis*, William Phillips, ed. (Cleveland: World Publishing, 1963), 502–520.

225 "disease as an instrument of knowledge"
see, Thomas Mann, "Freud and the Future," in *Art and Psychoanalysis*, 372–73. Mann writes, "he [Nietzsche] seems to instruct us that there is no deeper knowledge without experience of disease, and that all heightened healthiness must be achieved by the route of illness." p. 372.

226 " 'great wits' "
Dryden, "Absalom and Achitophel," Pt. 1.

226 For description of Freud's professional quarters

PAGE

see, Ernest Jones, *The Life and Work of Sigmund Freud,* Vol. 2 (New York: Basic Books, 1955), 379–82.

226 Freud's mode of life
see, E. Jones, *The Life and Work of Sigmund Freud,* Vol. 2, 382 ff.

227 " 'free, friendly . . .' "
E. Jones, *The Life and Work of Sigmund Freud,* Vol. 2, 388.

227 " 'romantic mechanist' "
Floyd W. Matson, *The Broken Image* (Garden City: Doubleday, 1966), 180.

227 " 'last pre-Freudian rationalist' "
L. L. Whyte, *The Unconscious Before Freud* (New York: Basic Books, 1960), 179.

227 "fatalistic system"
Crane Brinton, *The Shaping of the Modern Mind* (New York: New American Library, 1953), 227–30; see also, E. Jones, *The Life and Work of Sigmund Freud,* Vol. 1 (New York: Basic Books, 1953), p. 377. "Freud's psychology was undoubtedly deterministic: whether the epithets 'materialistic' or 'mechanistic,' often used as terms of abuse, should be applied to it is a question that could be answered only by philosophers."

227 "slighted man's unique biological assets"
Herbert J. Muller, *Freedom in the Modern World,* 208–209.

227 "disparity . . . of Freud's personal life"
see, Ernest Jones on "the two opposite sides of Freud's nature," *The Life and Work of Sigmund Freud,* Vol. 1, 384; also, F. Matson, *The Broken Image,* 182.

227 "quantifiable science of the mind"
E. Jones, *The Life and Work of Sigmund Freud,* "Project for a Scientific Psychology," Vol. 1, 379–93.

227 "Neurosis, according to Freud"
Freud, "Three Contributions to the Theory of Sex," *The Basic Writings of Sigmund Freud,* A. A. Brill, ed. (New York: Random House, 1938), 573, 625; Clara Thompson, *Psychoanalysis: Evolution and Development* (New York: Hermitage House, 1950), 42.

228 On ambivalence of Freud's position
see, E. Jones, *The Life and Work of Sigmund Freud,* Vol. 1, 34, 138, and Vol. 2, 433; Herbert J. Muller, *Freedom in the Modern World,* 210; L. L. Whyte, *The Unconscious Before Freud,* 78 ff.; F. Matson, *The Broken Image,* 204.

228 "Freud was not encouraged"
Freud, *New Introductory Lectures on Psychoanalysis* (New

York: Carleton House, 1933), 142. "Unfortunately the testimony of history and our own experience . . . confirm the judgment that the belief in the 'goodness' of man's nature is one of those unfortunate illusions."

228 "Freud did not discover"
L. L. Whyte, *The Unconscious Before Freud, passim.*

230 "tragedy and pessimism"
Freud, "Analysis Terminable and Interminable," in *Complete Psychological Works of Sigmund Freud,* James Strachey, ed., Vol. 23 (London: Hogarth Press, 1964), 216–53; *New Introductory Lectures on Psychoanalysis,* 112; *Civilization and Its Discontents,* James Strachey, trans. (New York: Norton, 1961), *passim;* see also, L. L. Whyte, *The Next Development in Man* (New York: New American Library, 1950), 190.

231 "behavior in primitive cultures"
Patrick Mullahy, *Oedipus Myth and Complex* (New York: Hermitage House, 1953), 238–40; Clara Thompson, *Psychoanalysis: Evolution and Development,* 135. "It is disappointing to find that Freud took little interest in the study of comparative cultures which was coming more into the center of attention in the 1920's. . . . there is no evidence that his thinking was in any way modified by the findings of modern anthropology"; see also, Abram Kardiner and Edward Preble, *They Studied Man* (Cleveland: World Publishing, 1961), 224–39.

231 "underestimated the influence"
see Erich Fromm, *Escape From Freedom* (New York: Holt, Rinehart & Winston, 1961), 10–11. Fromm writes, "The relation of the individual to society in Freud's theory is essentially a static one: the individual remains virtually the same and becomes changed only in so far as society exercises greater pressure on his natural drives (and thus enforces more sublimation) or allows more satisfaction (and thus sacrifices culture)." Karen Horney, *New Ways in Psychoanalysis* (New York: Norton, 1939), *passim;* Ira Progoff, *The Death and Rebirth of Psychology* (New York: Dell, 1956), 5–6; also, Freud, *New Introductory Lectures on Psychoanalysis,* 203–204. Freud regarded society's role as primarily suppressive. "The function of education, therefore, is to inhibit, forbid and suppress . . ."

231 "Anthropological studies"
see, Ralph Linton's study of the Marquesan culture in Abram Kardiner, *The Individual and His Society* (New York: Columbia University Press, 1939), 137–250, esp. 246–49; A. Kardiner, *The Individual and His Society,* 481. The Oedipus complex is absent in the Trobriand culture; see also, Malinowski's studies

PAGE

of primitive societies of eastern New Guinea. B. Malinowski, *The Argonauts of the Western Pacific* (New York, Dutton, 1922).

231 "Freudian mental topography"
Freud, "The Anatomy of the Mental Personality," *New Introductory Lectures on Psychoanalysis*, 82–112.

231 "mind-body dualism"
see, discussion of Freud in L. L. Whyte, *The Next Development in Man*, 188–96.

232 " 'uneven and careless' "
Freud, *New Introductory Lectures*, 88.

232 "primitive id . . . sublimated"
Sublimation is a process of diverting the aim and object of sexual instinct to related but socially acceptable goals. Thus the surgeon employs his "sadism" in a socially useful manner; see, Freud, *A General Introduction to Psychoanalysis*, Joan Rivière, trans. (Garden City: Garden City Publishing Co., 1943), 302; *Three Contributions to the Theory of Sex*, 625; *New Introductory Lectures*, 133; *Civilization and Its Discontents*, esp. 70 ff.

232 "Ambiguity and confusion"
Freud's recommendations on therapy require tolerance and detachment. The therapist is not supposed to take a moral stand (Freud, *A General Introduction to Psychoanalysis*, 377). Yet, psychoanalysis is also described as "re-education" (p. 392), a condition difficult to meet without a viewpoint and a system of values.

232 "Scylla . . . and the Charybdis"
New Introductory Lectures, 204.

233 "little admiration for it"
Freud, *New Introductory Lectures*, 103–104, 142 ff.; F. Matson, *The Broken Image*, 183, 187.

233 " 'Where id was' "
Freud, *New Introductory Lectures*, 204.

233 " 'would not fail to concede' "
Freud, *New Introductory Lectures*, 234.

233 "The price of civilization"
Freud, *Civilization and Its Discontents*, 69–75, 81.

233 impasse created by the death instinct
E. Jones, *The Life and Work of Sigmund Freud*, Vol. 3 (New York: Basic Books, 1957), 272–73.

234 " 'prefer to think in torment' "
E. Jones, *The Life and Work of Sigmund Freud*, Vol. 3, 245.

PAGE

234 "Freud failed to comprehend"
David Riesman, "The Themes of Work and Play in the Structure
of Freud's Thought," *Individualism Reconsidered* (Glencoe, Illinois: Free Press, 1954), 310–33; also, H. J. Muller, *Freedom
in the Modern World*, 208–209; Clara Thompson, *Psychoanalysis: Evolution and Development*, 13, 131–52; L. L. Whyte, *The
Next Development in Man*, 194–95; I. Progoff, *The Death and
Rebirth of Psychology*, 16–45, 255.

235 " 'unrestrained sexual licence' "
Freud, *A General Introduction to Psychoanalysis*, 377.

236 "cruelty may be learned"
Clara Thompson, *Psychoanalysis: Evolution and Development*,
53–58.

236 suicide and the death instinct
Elizabeth Kilpatrick, "A Psychoanalytic Understanding of Suicide," Harold Kelman, ed., *Advances in Psychoanalysis: Contributions to Karen Horney's Holistic Approach* (New York:
Norton, 1964), 202; Clara Thompson, *Psychoanalysis: Evolution
and Development*, 51–52.

236 "toward greater variety"
C. Judson Herrick, *The Evolution of Human Nature* (Austin:
University of Texas, 1956), 50.

237 L. L. Whyte
The Next Development in Man, 189 ff.

238 " 'unitary man' "
L. L. Whyte, *The Next Development in Man*, 196.

239 "tantamount to sacrilege"
Freud, *Collected Papers*, Vol. 3 (London: Hogarth, 1924), 527,
and *Collected Papers*, Vol. 1, 338. Freud criticized Adler for
attempting to explain the character and behavior of human
beings as a whole instead of limiting himself to the individual's
neurotic and psychotic ailments.

239 " 'style of life' "
Alfred Adler, *Social Interest: A Challenge to Mankind* (London: Faber and Faber, 1938), 37 ff.; see also, Adler, *The Practice and Theory of Individual Psychology* (New York: Harcourt,
Brace, 1924), *passim*.

239 "Jungian unconscious"
C. G. Jung, *The Psychology of the Unconscious* (New York:
Dodd, Mead, 1927).

240 "refused to accept sex"
see, C. G. Jung, *The Psychology of the Unconscious*, 145, and
The Theory of Psychoanalysis, Nervous and Mental Disease
Monograph Series, No. 19, pp. 23, 35, 40.

PAGE

240 "self acts as a symbolic goal"
Progoff, *The Death and Rebirth of Psychology*, 177–87.

240 "suppress . . . positive attributes"
C. G. Jung, *Two Essays on Analytical Psychology* (New York: Dodd, Mead, 1928), 178.

240 "Rank . . . Jung's equal in breadth"
Progoff, *The Death and Rebirth of Psychology*, 191.

240 "Rank's 'will' psychology"
Otto Rank, *Will Therapy and Truth and Reality* (New York: Knopf, 1945); see also, Ruth L. Monroe, *Schools of Psychoanalytic Thought* (New York: Holt, Rinehart and Winston, 1955).

240 "close kin to the Jungian self"
Progoff, *Death and Rebirth of Psychology*, 206; Thompson, *Psychoanalysis: Evolution and Development*, 178.

241 "artist and creative person"
see, Rank, *Will Therapy and Truth and Reality*, 95–96, 212, 265; Rank, *Art and Artist: Creative Urge and Personality Development* (New York: Knopf, 1932); Rank, *Beyond Psychology* (Camden: Haddon Craftsmen, 1941).

241 " 'artisan of technical skill' "
Rank, *Beyond Psychology*, 101.

243 " 'He only deserves freedom' "
Goethe, *Faust* II, Act. 5, *Grosser Vorhof des Palasts*.

10. The Birthright Restored

244 "health, harmony, and growth"
Abraham H. Maslow, *Toward a Psychology of Being* (Princeton, N.J.: Van Nostrand, 1962), 3; see also, Ira Progoff, *The Death and Rebirth of Psychology* (New York: Dell, 1956), 254–66. Although "harmony" was Freud's goal, he postulated a basic dualism which the humanistic psychologies try to avoid. "Growth" in Freudian terms implies constructing defenses and overcoming the normal neurosis of childhood which occurs because each individual is destined to repeat the experience of ancient man. Maslow, Allport, and Fromm, among others, speak of the existential concept of "becoming" or of fulfilling one's potential, in contrast to the analytical development of capacities required in adapting to society.

244 " 'third force' "
Maslow, *Toward a Psychology of Being*, 9.

244 "psychosynthesis"

PAGE

Floyd Matson, *The Broken Image* (Garden City: Doubleday, 1966), 208, 318.

244 "'partly known and partly knower'"
William James, *Psychology: The Briefer Course*, Gordon Allport, ed. (New York: Harper, 1961), 43.

244 "mind imposes logic"
see, Jean Piaget, "The Mental Development of the Child" and "The Thought of the Young Child," *Six Psychological Studies* (New York: Random House, 1967), 3–73, 77–86.

245 "Parts of the ego and superego"
Freud, *New Introductory Lectures on Psychoanalysis* (New York: Carleton House, 1933), 98, 102.

246 "the preconscious"
Freud, "The Psychology of the Dream-Processes," *The Interpretation of Dreams* in *The Basic Writings of Sigmund Freud*, A. A. Brill, ed. (New York: Random House, 1938), 544.

246 "'fringe of consciousness'"
William James, *Psychology: The Briefer Course*, 33 ff.

246 "dimensions . . . of unconscious vary"
Lawrence Kubie, *Neurotic Distortion of the Creative Process* (New York: Noonday Press, 1961). Kubie distinguishes between the preconscious system which is responsible for creative activity, and the unconscious system which accounts for repression, rigidity, and neurosis.

247 "steps in the creative process"
Graham Wallas, *The Art of Thought* (New York: Harcourt, Brace, 1926), 80 ff.

247 "'imaginative muddled suspense'"
A. N. Whitehead, quoted in Brewster Ghiselin, *The Creative Process: A Symposium* (New York: New American Library, 1955), 14.

247 "'deep well of unconscious cerebration'"
Henry James, *The American* (Scribner, 1935), vii.

247 "Contrary to Freudian theory"
see, Freud, *New Introductory Lectures on Psychoanalysis*, 142.

247 "neutral or antecedent"
Maslow, *Toward a Psychology of Being*, 3.

248 "'carry the feelings'"
J. Donald Adams, "Speaking of Books," *New York Times Book Review* (April 30, 1961).

250 "William Barrett emphasizes"
William Barrett, *Irrational Man* (Garden City: Doubleday, 1958), 239.

251 " 'courage of despair' "
W. H. Auden, *Age of Anxiety* (New York: Random House, 1946) ; also, Paul Tillich, *The Courage to Be* (New Haven: Yale University Press, 1952), 139–54.

252 " 'heart has its reasons' "
Pascal, *Pensées* iv., 277.

252 " 'the truth of poetry' "
Edith Hamilton, *The Greek Way* (New York: Norton, 1964), 31.

253 "ecstasy and elation"
Rollo May, "The Nature of Creativity," *Creativity and Its Cultivation*, H. H. Anderson, ed. (New York: Harper, 1959), 61–65.

253 " 'peak-experience' "
Maslow, "Creativity in Self-Actualizing People," *Creativity and Its Cultivation*, 89–91.

253 "Maslow observes"
Maslow, "Creativity in Self-Actualizing People," *Creativity and Its Cultivation*, 88.

254 Leonardo not a neurotic
Freud, *Leonardo da Vinci: A Study in Psychosexuality* (New York: Random House, 1947), 110.

254 "practical concept of illness"
Freud, *Leonardo da Vinci*, 110–11; Freud, *A General Introduction to Psychoanalysis* (Garden City: Garden City Publishing Co., 1943), 398.

254 "neuroses . . . originate in a *'conflict'* "
Freud, *A General Introduction to Psychoanalysis*, 305, 307; Freud, "Three Contributions to the Theory of Sex," *The Basic Writings of Sigmund Freud*, in Brill, ed. (New York: Random House, 1938), 625. According to Freud, "the neurosis is the negative of the perversion."

254 " 'prosthetic god . . . ' "
Freud, *Civilization and Its Discontents* (New York: Norton, 1962), 38–39.

254 "love of beauty"
Freud, *Civilization and Its Discontents*, 29–30.

254 " 'Before the problem . . . creative artist' "
Freud, "Dostoevsky and Parricide," *Complete Psychological Works of Sigmund Freud*, James Strachey, ed., Vol. 21 (London: Hogarth Press, 1961), 177.

254 "creativity results from the sublimation"
Freud, *General Introduction to Psychoanalysis*, 327–28, and *Leonardo da Vinci*, 30–31; see also, Ernst Kris, "The Contribu-

tion and Limitations of Psychoanalysis," *Art and Psychoanalysis*, William Phillips, ed. (Cleveland: World, 1963), 271–91, esp. 283–84.

255 " 'flexibility of repression' "
Freud, *General Introduction to Psychoanalysis*, 327

255 "retreat from duty and reality"
Freud, *A General Introduction to Psychoanalysis*, 327 ff.; David Riesman, *Individualism Reconsidered* (Glencoe, Ill.: Free Press, 1954), 315–16, 329–30.

255 " 'chewing and sucking' "
A. A. Brill, "Poetry as an Oral Outlet," *Psychoanalytic Review*, Vol. 18, No. 4 (Oct. 1931), 358.

255 " 'mild narcosis' of art"
Freud, *Civilization and Its Discontents*, 28.

255 Characteristics of the creative personality
see, D. W. MacKinnon, "The Nature and Nurture of Creative Talent," *American Psychologist*, Vol. 17 (1962), 485–95; D. W. MacKinnon, "What Makes a Person Creative," *Saturday Review* (Feb. 10, 1962), 15–17, 69; Frank Barron, "The Psychology of Imagination," *Scientific American*, Vol. 199, No. 3 (Sept. 1958), 163–66; Raymond B. Cattell, "The Personality and Motivation of the Researcher from Measurements of Contemporaries and from Biography," in *Scientific Creativity: Its Recognition and Development*, C. W. Taylor and F. Barron, eds. (New York: Wiley, 1963), 121–24.

256 " 'negative capability' "
Keats, *The Complete Works of John Keats*, H. Buxton Forman, ed., Letter XXVI to George and Thomas Keats, Dec. 28, 1817, Vol. IV (Glasgow: Gowars and Gray, 1901), 50.

256 " 'regression in the service of the ego' "
see, Ernst Kris, "On Preconscious Mental Processes," *Psychoanalytic Quarterly*, Vol. 19 (1950), 551–52.

257 "Lawrence Kubie draws"
Lawrence S. Kubie, *Neurotic Distortion of the Creative Process*, 34–35, 137, 139.

257 "According to Kubie"
Neurotic Distortion of the Creative Process, 140.

258 " 'right to be believed' "
Gordon W. Allport, *Personality and Social Encounter: Selected Essays* (Boston: Beacon Press, 1960), 97; see also, Maslow, "Toward a Humanistic Psychology," in *Our Language and Our World*, S. I. Hayakawa, ed. (New York: Harper, 1959), 195.

PAGE

258 "Ernest G. Schachtel"
Metamorphosis (New York: Basic Books, 1959), 83, 184–88, 238–45.

259 "individual setting forth"
James Joyce, *Ulysses* (New York: Modern Library, 1946), 210.

260 "neither neurosis nor . . . mental aberration"
Kris, "The Contribution and Limitations of Psychoanalysis," 278–79.

260 "paranoia of a trivial mind"
William Phillips, ed., *Art and Psychoanalysis* (Cleveland: World, 1963), xviii.

261 "might make another list"
see, Hilgard, "Creativity and Problem-solving," *Creativity and its Cultivation*, 174.

261 "no adequate statistical studies"
Phillips, *Art and Psychoanalysis*, xviii; William Barrett, "Writers and Madness," in *Art and Psychoanalysis*, 402.

261 "Creative potential is depleted"
Kubie, *Neurotic Distortion of the Creative Process*, 6; Maslow, "Emotional Blocks to Creativity," *The Humanist*, Vol. 18, No. 6 (1958), 325–37; Arthur C. Jacobsen, "Literary Genius and Manic Depressive Insanity with Special Reference to the Alleged Case of Dean Swift," *The Literary Imagination*, Hendrik M. Ruitenbeek, ed. (Chicago: Quadrangle, 1965), 443.

261 "insane genius the exception"
see, Ardyth A. Hebeisen, "The Performance of a Group of Schizophrenic Patients on a Test of Creative Thinking," in *Creativity: Third Minnesota Conference on Gifted Children*, E. P. Torrance, ed. (Minneapolis: Center for Continuation Study, University of Minnesota, 1960), 125–29; W. R. Brain, "Some Reflections on Genius," *Eugenics Review*, Vol. 40, No. 1 (April 1948), 20.

262 On Coleridge's poetry and drug addiction
see, John Livingston Lowes, *The Road to Xanadu: A Study in the Ways of the Imagination* (New York: Vintage Books, 1959), 377–88; Loren Eiseley, "Darwin, Coleridge, and the Theory of Unconscious Creation," *Daedalus*, Vol. 94, No. 3 (Summer 1965), 591–95.

262 " 'Stuff of Sleep' "
Coleridge, *Notebook* XVI, 6–13, Dec. 1803, Kathleen Coburn, ed., Vol. I (1794–1804), Bollingen Series L (New York: Pantheon, 1957), series 1718, entry 16.105.

262 " 'assault on fixation' "

Ghiselin, "The Creative Process and Its Relation to the Identification of Creative Talent," *Scientific Creativity*, 362.

262 " 'defeat of habit' "
Arthur Koestler, *The Act of Creation* (New York: Macmillan, 1964), 96.

262 " 'terrific hard gardening' "
Katherine Mansfield, from her *Journal* (New York: Knopf, 1927), quoted in *The Creative Process*, B. Ghiselin, ed. (New York: New American Library, 1955), 29.

263 " 'surging chaos' "
Lowes, *The Road to Xanadu*, 12.

263 " 'The true poet' "
Charles Lamb, "Sanity of True Genius," *Complete Works and Letters of Charles Lamb* (Modern Library, 1935), 167.

263 "catharsis of his work"
Kubie, *Neurotic Distortion of the Creative Process*, 3; see also, Richard and Editha Sterba, *Beethoven and His Nephew* (New York: Pantheon, 1954).

263 "triumph was in his art"
William Barrett, "Writers and Madness," in *Art and Psychoanalysis*, 410–11.

264 "Scientist has no reason to broadcast"
James D. Watson's *The Double Helix* (New York: Atheneum, 1968) is a striking exception.

264 "Self-analysis . . . vocational imperative"
see, Lionel Trilling, "Art and Neurosis," in *Art and Psychoanalysis*, 510–11.

265 *"Sanctuary* . . . described"
L. Kubie, "The Literature of Horror," *Saturday Review of Literature*, Vol. XI (1934), 218, 224–26; see also, Stanley Edgar Hyman, "Maud Bodkin and Psychological Criticism," in *Art and Psychoanalysis*, 490.

265 "Thomas Mann and James Joyce"
S. E. Hyman, "Maud Bodkin and Psychological Criticism," in *Art and Psychoanalysis*, 499; Thomas Mann, "Freud and the Future," *Art and Psychoanalysis*, 386–87.

265 "Studies of . . . vocational choice and personality"
Kubie, "Some Unsolved Problems of the Scientific Career," *American Scientist*, Vol. 41, No. 4 (Oct. 1953), 596–613 and Vol. 42, No. 1 (Jan. 1954), 104–12; E. Kris, "The Contribution and Limitations of Psychoanalysis," in *Art and Psychoanalysis*, 278–79, 287–88.

265 "a form of social selection"

Otto Rank, "Life and Creation," in *Art and Psychoanalysis*, 312–13; Phillips, *Art and Psychoanalysis*, xx.

266 On homosexuality and the artist
see, Lawrence J. Hatterer, *The Artist in Society: Problems and Treatment of the Creative Personality* (New York: Grove, 1966), 138–71.

267 "The outcome of psychotherapy"
Hilgard, "Creativity and Problem-solving," *Creativity and Its Cultivation*, 175; Kubie, *Neurotic Distortion of the Creative Process*, 4–6; Barron, "The Psychology of Imagination," *Scientific American*, Vol. 199, No. 3 (Sept. 1958), 160–63.

267 " 'spoiled by analysis' "
E. Kris, *Psychoanalytic Explorations in Art* (New York: International Universities Press, 1952), 29.

267 "search for truth"
see, Ernest Jones, *The Life and Work of Sigmund Freud*, Vol. 2 (1955), 433. Jones writes that Freud's passion to discover the truth was the deepest and strongest motive in his nature.

268 " 'perfection of the life' "
Yeats, "The Choice," *Collected Poems* (New York: Macmillan, 1949), 284.

11. Strange Appetites

269 " 'principal appetite' "
Aldous Huxley, *The Doors of Perception and Heaven and Hell* (New York: Harper and Row, 1963), 67.

269 " 'The desire to take medicine' "
William Osler, *Aequanimitas and Other Addresses* (Philadelphia: Blakiston's, 1904), 181.

270 "deliberate chemical intervention"
Walter R. Hess, "Causality, Consciousness, and Cerebral Organization," *Science* (Dec. 8, 1967), 1281–82; George A. Miller, "Some Psychological Perspectives on the Year 2000," *Daedalus*, Vol. 96, No. 3 (Summer 1967), 895–96; E. Callaway, G. Stone, L. E. Hollister, H. Isbell, "Psychologic Effects of Drugs," Panel Discussion, *Conflict and Creativity: Control of the Mind, Part II*, S. M. Farber and R. H. L. Wilson, eds. (New York: McGraw-Hill, 1963), 171–81.

270 " 'enzyme-assisted instruction' "
David Krech, "The Chemistry of Learning," *Saturday Review* (Jan. 20, 1968), 48.

PAGE

271 "dependent on who takes the drugs"
Leo E. Hollister, "Evaluation of Drugs in Psychiatric Patients,"
in *Conflict and Creativity*, 128–29.

271 "reliable research . . . lacking"
Helen H. Nowlis, *Drugs on the College Campus*, Drug Education Project of National Association of Student Personnel Administrators (NASPA) under Contract FDA 67–3 (Dec. 1967),
93–94; Sidney Cohen, *The Beyond Within* (New York: Atheneum, 1964), 81; R. E. L. Masters and J. Houston, *The Varieties of Psychedelic Experience* (New York: Dell, 1967), 61–62.

273–274 On chemistry of the hallucinogens
see, S. Cohen, *The Beyond Within*, 246–56; F. Barron, M. E.
Jarvik, S. Bunnell, Jr., "The Hallucinogenic Drugs," *Scientific
American*, Vol. 210, No. 4 (April 1964), 31–33; Richard H.
Blum, ed., *Utopiates: The Use and Users of LSD-25* (New York:
Atherton Press, 1964), 118–23.

274 "schizophrenics brew . . . hallucinogens"
Isaac Asimov, *The Human Brain* (New York: New American
Library, 1965), 218–19, 334–38; Barron, Jarvik, Bunnell, Jr.,
"The Hallucinogenic Drugs," 32–33; Robert S. De Ropp, *Drugs
and the Mind* (New York: Grove, 1961), 167–201.

276 "excitation . . . visual projection areas"
W. R. Hess, "Causality, Consciousness, and Cerebral Organization," 1282.

276 "postulated that drugs trigger"
H. Nowlis, *Drugs on the College Campus*, 8–10, 91–92; Masters
and Houston, *The Varieties of Psychedelic Experience*, 56; Peter
Laurie, *Drugs* (Baltimore: Penguin Books, 1967), 97–99; E.
Fingl and D. M. Woodbury in *The Pharmacological Basis of
Therapeutics*, L. S. Goodman and A. Gilman, eds., 3rd ed. (New
York: Macmillan, 1965), 1. The authors caution that until more
is learned about the biochemistry and physiology of the normal
cell, only superficial explanation of the mechanism of drug
action is possible.

278 Educational environment and brain chemistry
David Krech, "The Chemistry of Learning," *Saturday Review*
(Jan. 20, 1968), 48–50, 68.

279 "pseudo hallucinations"
Barron, *et al.*, "The Hallucinogenic Drugs," 29; H. Nowlis,
Drugs on the College Campus, 90, 92. Dr. Nowlis writes, "True
hallucinations are relatively rare . . . although the individual
has a visual experience with no appropriate sensory cues, he is
usually well aware of the fact that it is subjective and is a
result of the drug." p. 92.

PAGE

279 "marihuana 'may have a potency relationship' "
Nowlis, *Drugs on the College Campus*, 83.

280 "Sophistication in the technique"
J. H. Jaffee, "Drug Addiction and Drug Abuse," *The Pharma-cological Basis of Therapeutics*, 300; H. D. Kleber, "Student Use of Hallucinogens," *Journal of American College Health Association*, Vol. 14 (1965), 115; J. O. Cole and M. Katz, "The Psychotomimetic Drugs: An Overview," *Journal of American Medical Association*, Vol. 187 (1964), 758.

280 "Silas Weir Mitchell"
"The Effects of Anhelonium Lewinii," *British Medical Journal*, Vol. 2 (Dec. 1896), 1626; see also, H. Ellis, "Mescal: A New Artificial Paradise," *The Contemporary Review* (Jan. 1898); also in *Annual Report of the Smithsonian Institution* (1898), 537–48.

281 " 'take the visions on trust' "
William James quoted in G. W. Allen, *William James* (New York: Viking, 1967), 383. *The Letters of William James*, Henry James, Jr., ed. (Boston: Atlantic Monthly Press, 1920), William James to Henry James, June 11, 1896.

281 " 'living light' "
A. Huxley, *The Doors of Perception and Heaven and Hell*, 18.

281 " 'what Adam had seen' "
A. Huxley, *The Doors of Perception and Heaven and Hell*, 17.

281 "Wasson described"
R. Gordon Wasson, "The Hallucinogenic Mushrooms of Mexico: An Adventure in Ethnomycological Exploration," *Transactions of the New York Academy of Sciences*, Vol. 21 (1959), 331; also, Wasson "Seeking the Magic Mushrooms," *Life* (May 13, 1957).

282 For description of Hofmann's experience
see, W. A. Stoll, "LSD-25, A Hallucinatory Agent of the Ergot Group," *Swiss Archives of Neurology*, Vol. 60 (1947), 279; also in Masters and Houston, *The Varieties of Psychedelic Experience*, 49–50; S. Cohen, *The Beyond Within*, 26–30.

284 "Whether the drug . . . teaches"
Daniel X. Freedman, "The Use and Abuse of Psychedelic Drugs," *Bulletin of the Atomic Scientists* (April 1968), 7.

284 "equipped . . . to experience"
S. Cohen, *The Beyond Within*, 240.

284 "We are reminded"
D. X. Freedman, "The Use and Abuse of Psychedelic Drugs," 13.

285 " 'the will suffers' "
A. Huxley, *The Doors of Perception and Heaven and Hell*, 25.

285 " 'few clear-cut monuments' "
D. X. Freedman, "The Use and Abuse of Psychedelic Drugs,"
14; see also, S. Cohen, *The Beyond Within*, 81.

285 " 'thereafter . . . [Huxley] tended to write' "
D. X. Freedman, "The Use and Abuse of Psychedelic Drugs," 14.

286 "threat . . . adolescents and young adults"
D. X. Freedman, "The Use and Abuse of Psychedelic Drugs,"
12; see also, R. E. Nixon, "Psychological Normality in Adolescence," *Adolescence*, Vol. 1 (1966), 211–23; Cole and Katz,
Psychotomimetic Drugs: An Overview, 758–61.

287 " 'College students . . . nineteenth century' "
Isaac Asimov, "That Odd Chemical Complex, The Human
Mind," *New York Times Magazine* (July 3, 1966), 18.

12. The Creation of Creation

289 validity and reliability
Richard H. Lindeman, *Educational Measurement* (Glenview,
Ill.: Scott, Foresman, 1967), 35–37, 41, 43–44.

289 "discrepancy . . . discouraging"
D. W. MacKinnon, "The Nature and Nurture of Creative Talent," *American Psychologist*, Vol. 17 (1962), 485.

290 "success is still uncertain"
J. W. Getzels and P. W. Jackson, *Creativity and Intelligence:
Explorations with Gifted Children* (New York: Wiley, 1962),
16–17.

290 "actually . . . rejection"
S. Rains Wallace, "Prediction and Individual Behavior," *Con-
flict and Creativity: Control of the Mind, Part II*, Farber and
Wilson, eds. (New York: McGraw-Hill, 1963), 44.

290 "often difficult to test"
Donald W. MacKinnon, "Prediction of Creativity and Success,"
in *Conflict and Creativity*, 66.

291 "a major challenge"
J. W. Getzels and P. W. Jackson, *Creativity and Intelligence:
Explorations with Gifted Students*, 198–99.

291 Creativity tests
see, Anne Anastasi, *Psychological Testing*, 3rd ed. (New York:
Macmillan, 1968), 373–81; list of published tests, 644.

291 "Factor-type tests"

PAGE

J. P. Guilford, *Psychometric Methods*, Ch. 16, "Factor Analysis" (New York: McGraw-Hill, 1954), 470–538; S. R. Wallace, "Prediction and Individual Behavior," in *Conflict and Creativity*, 49–50.

291 Description of factor-type tests
see, J. P. Guilford, R. C. Wilson, P. R. Christensen, D. J. Lewis, *A Factor-Analytic Study of Creative Thinking: I. Hypothesis and Description of the Tests* (Los Angeles: University of Southern California, 1951) ; also, E. Hilgard, "Creativity and Problem-solving," *Creativity and Its Cultivation*, 171–74.

291 "factor analysis cannot explain"
Frank S. Freeman, *Theory and Practice of Psychological Testing*, 3rd ed. (New York: Holt, Rinehart and Winston, 1962), 181.

292 Torrance's test batteries
E. P. Torrance, "Scientific Views of Creativity and Factors Affecting its Growth," *Daedalus*, Vol. 94, No. 3 (Summer 1965), 668–72, and "Explorations in Creative Thinking in the Early School Years: A Progress Report" in *Scientific Creativity*, C. W. Taylor and F. Barron, eds. (New York: Wiley, 1963), 174–76.

292 " 'work sample' technique"
Ruth Strang, "Developing Creative Powers of Gifted Children," P. Witty, J. B. Conant and R. Strang, in *Creativity of Gifted and Talented Children* (New York: Teachers College, Columbia University, 1959), 23.

292 "little value when applied"
S. R. Wallace, "Prediction of Creativity and Success," in *Conflict and Creativity*, 64.

292 "personality tests . . . future performance"
S. R. Wallace, "Prediction and Individual Behavior," in *Conflict and Creativity*, 46; A. Anastasi, *Psychological Testing*, 2nd ed. (New York: Macmillan, 1961), 519–23.

293 validity of Rorschach
Robert M. Allen, *Personality Assessment Procedures: Psychometric, Projective, and Other Approaches* (New York: Harper, 1958), 164–67, 181–83; Bruno Klopfer and Helen H. Davidson, *The Rorschach Technique: An Introductory Manual* (New York: Harcourt, Brace and World, 1962), 24–25; A. Anastasi, *Psychological Testing*, 2nd ed. (1961), 572. Anastasi writes that studies of Rorschach validity are not encouraging; S. R. Wallace, "Prediction and Individual Behavior," in *Conflict and Creativity*, 47.

293 "Proper validation studies"
S. R. Wallace, "Prediction and Individual Behavior," in *Conflict*

PAGE

    and Creativity, 51; see also, Martin L. Gross, *The Brain Watchers* (New York: Random House, 1962), 78.

295 "waste the resources"
    see, John W. Gardner, *Excellence* (New York: Harper and Row, 1961), 33–38.

296 "Jerome Wiesner suggests"
    "Education for Creativity in the Sciences," *Daedalus* (Summer 1965), 533.

296 "current pursuit of creative talent"
    see, K. Kreuter and G. Kreuter, "The Useful Genius: Intelligence, Creativity, and American Values," *Saturday Review* (Oct. 17, 1964), 64–67; also, Loren C. Eiseley, "No Secret Formula for Making Scientists," *New York Times Magazine* (Oct. 18, 1964), 66, 68, 74, 76. "We are making things easier now, but, with the professional touch, there can emerge also a cold and glittering sterility, a too-early selectivity that leaves a quiet and uncertain child hesitating at the door." p. 76; Frank Barron, *Creativity and Psychological Health: Origins of Personal Vitality and Creative Freedom* (Princeton, N.J.: Van Nostrand, 1963), 7–10.

296 On creative person as national asset
    see, Mark Harris, "Government as Patron of the Arts," *New York Times Magazine* (Sept. 13, 1964), 35, 139–40.

297 "Warren Weaver reminds us"
    "The Encouragement of Science," *Scientific American* (Sept. 1958), 171–72; quote on 172.

298 "more specifically with scientific talent"
    see, Kreuter and Kreuter, "The Useful Genius: Intelligence, Creativity, and Scientific Values," 66.

300 For an account of Galois
    see, Jacques Hadamard, *The Psychology of Invention in the Mathematical Field* (Princeton: Princeton University Press, 1949), 119–20.

300 "Reasonable, but not excessive"
    Donald C. Pelz, "Creative Tensions in the Research and Development Climate," *Science,* Vol. 157 (July 14, 1967), 160–65; Harold D. Lasswell, "The Social Setting of Creativity," in *Creativity and Its Cultivation,* 215; see also, John W. Gardner, *Self-Renewal: The Individual and the Innovative Society* (New York: Harper and Row, 1963), 19.

300 " 'genius will out' "
    see, Albert Szent-Györgyi, "Secret of the Creative Impulse," *New York Times Magazine* (July 30, 1961), 14, 34, 36. "The belief seems to be that genius will reveal itself of its own accord.

PACE

This is completely wrong. Most genius entails a great sensitivity and nothing is easier than to discourage it." p. 14. See also, D. C. McClelland, "Issues in the Identification of Talent," in *Talent and Society: New Perspectives in the Identification of Talent*, D. C. McClelland, A. L. Baldwin, U. Bronfenbrenner, F. Strodtbeck, eds. (Princeton, N.J.: Van Nostrand, 1958), 15–19; R. Strang, *Helping Your Gifted Child* (New York: E. P. Dutton, 1960), 219.

301 " 'If you do stupid' "
Leo Szilard, quoted in John R. Platt, "Strong Inference," *Science*, Vol. 146 (Oct. 16, 1964), 348.

301 "administrative duties"
Anne Roe, "Changes in Scientific Activities with Age," *Science*, Vol. 150 (Oct. 15, 1965), 313–18. A high administrative position is likely to put an end to all research. Very few scientists who have taken administrative posts return to research, p. 316.

301 "seasonal or diurnal variation"
Philip H. Abelson, "Relation of Group Activity to Creativity in Science," *Daedalus* (Summer 1965), 613.

301 "inflexible curriculum requirements"
Cliff W. Wing, Jr., "Student Selection, The Educational Environment, and the Cultivation of Talent," *Daedalus* (Summer 1965), 636; J. Douglas Brown, "The Development of Creative Teacher-Scholars," *Daedalus* (Summer 1965), 625–29.

302 "chance of innovation"
H. D. Lasswell, "The Social Setting of Creativity," in *Creativity and its Cultivation*, 212–13.

302 "Children thrive"
Ruth Strang, "Developing Creative Powers of Gifted Children, in *Creativity of Gifted and Talented Children*, 24.

302 "its mother is security"
D. C. Pelz, "Creative Tensions in the Research and Development Climate," 160.

302 "creative tension"
T. S. Kuhn, "The Essential Tension: Tradition and Innovation in Scientific Research," in *Scientific Creativity*, 341–54.

302 "Hybrid vigor"
Lasswell, "The Social Setting of Creativity," in *Creativity and Its Cultivation*, 213.

303 " 'New occasions teach new duties' "
Robert Lowell, "The Present Crisis," quoted by Henry Steele Commager, "Leadership in Eighteenth-Century America and Today," *Daedalus*, Vol. 90, No. 4 (Fall 1961), 655.

PAGE

303 "Nationalist movements"
Lasswell, "The Social Setting of Creativity," in *Creativity and Its Cultivation*, 214.

303 "geniuses . . . clustered"
Wolfgang Kroeber, *Configurations of Cultural Growth* (Berkeley: University of California Press, 1947).

303 "Henry Steele Commager examines"
"Leadership in Eighteenth-Century America and Today," *Daedalus*, 652–73.

304 " 'numerous and virtuous' "
Commager, "Leadership in Eighteenth-Century America and Today," 665.

305 "to use and honor"
Nevitt Sanford, *Self and Society: Social Change and Individual Development* (New York: Atherton Press, 1967), 212. Sanford writes that rather than selecting potentially creative people, it is more important to nurture potential in everybody and to foster an environment favorable to creative work.

305 "no clear-cut answer"
Hilgard, "Creativity and Problem-solving," in *Creativity and Its Cultivation*, 170.

305 "outlined in advance"
P. H. Abelson, "Relation of Group Activity to Creativity in Science," *Daedalus* (Summer 1965), 609.

306 "Brainstorming"
A. F. Osborn, *Applied Imagination: Principles and Procedures of Creative Thinking* (New York: Scribner, 1957).

306 "Studies of this method"
D. W. Taylor, P. C. Berry, C. H. Block, "Does Group Participation when Using Brainstorming Facilitate or Inhibit Creativity?" *Admin. Science Quarterly*, Vol. 3 (1958), 23–47; S. J. Parnes and A. Meadow, "Development of Individual Creative Talent," in *Scientific Creativity*, 317–18.

306 "mutual interaction"
Caryl P. Haskins, "The Changing Environments of Science," *Daedalus* (Summer 1965), 698–99.

307 "designed to avoid"
P. H. Abelson, "Relation of Group Activity to Creativity in Science," *Daedalus* (Summer 1965), 610–11.

307 "companionship and support"
H. D. Lasswell, "The Social Setting of Creativity," in *Creativity and Its Cultivation*, 217.

307 "single dissenting individual"

PAGE

Richard S. Crutchfield, "Independent Thought in a Conformist World," in *Conflict and Creativity*, 216, 228.

308 " 'partner in dissent' "
R. S. Crutchfield, "Independent Thought in a Conformist World," in *Conflict and Creativity*, 228.

308 "mistress-mother"
Norbert Fuerst, *Phases of Rilke* (Bloomington: Indiana University Press, 1958), 18.

309 " 'courtesy of conversation' "
J. S. Bruner, "Culture, Politics, and Pedagogy," *Saturday Review* (May 18, 1968), 90.

309 "student rebellion . . . attributed"
J. Katz and N. Sanford, "Causes of the Student Revolution," *Saturday Review* (Dec. 18, 1965), 65–66; Martin Meyerson, "The Ethos of the American College Student: Beyond the Protests," *Daedalus*, Vol. 95, No. 3 (Summer 1966), 731.

309 "all students . . . disadvantaged"
Peter Schraag, "Why Our Schools Have Failed," *Commentary*, Vol. 45 (March 1968), 34.

310 "Teachers . . . prefer students"
J. W. Getzels and P. W. Jackson, *Creativity and Intelligence* (New York: Wiley, 1962), 30–31; E. P. Torrance, "Explorations in Creative Thinking in the Early School Years: A Progress Report," in *Scientific Creativity*, 183; see also, p. 338 of Notes, "ideal primary school pupil."

310 "unconsciously sabotage"
Kubie, "Unsolved Problems of Scientific Education," *Daedalus* (Summer 1965), 577–78.

312 "balance . . . freedom and control"
see, A. N. Whitehead, *The Aims of Education and Other Essays* (New York: Macmillan, 1959), 45–65.

312 "difficult challenge"
see, Clark E. Moustakas, *Creativity and Conformity* (Princeton, N.J.: Van Nostrand, 1967), 45–63.

314 "whether they like their children"
see, David Hawkins, "Childhood and the Education of Intellectuals," *Harvard Educational Review*, Vol. 36, No. 4 (Fall 1966), 478. "Much of our present zeal for reform in education is consistent with the interpretation that we don't really like children and want to get them over being children as early as possible."

315 "division in approach"
Kenneth Keniston, *The Young Radicals: Notes on Committed Youth* (Cambridge: Harvard University Press, 1968).

PAGE

317 "Studies of . . . age and achievement"
Alice S. Rossi, "Women in Science: Why So Few?" *Science,*
Vol. 148 (May 28, 1965), 1199; H. Lehman, *Age and Achievement* (Princeton, N.J.: Princeton University Press, 1953).

317 " 'high standards of consumption' "
Margaret Mead, "The Life Cycle and Its Variations: The Division of Roles," *Daedalus,* Vol. 96, No. 3 (Summer 1967), 871.

Suggestions for Further Reading

Allport, Gordon W. *Personality and Social Encounter: Selected Essays.* Boston: Beacon Press, 1960.

Anderson, Harold H., ed. *Creativity and Its Cultivation.* New York: Harper and Row, 1959.
Broad, interdisciplinary in scope. Highly readable contributions provide a good introduction to the subject.

——, ed. *Creativity in Childhood and Adolescence: A Variety of Approaches.* Palo Alto, California: Science and Behavior Books, 1965.

Barnett, Homer G. *Innovation: The Basis of Cultural Change.* New York: McGraw-Hill, 1953.
An interesting book on the development of novelty in different cultures.

Barron, Frank. *Creativity and Psychological Health: Origins of Personal Vitality and Creative Freedom.* Princeton, New Jersey: D. Van Nostrand Co., 1963.
Summary of ten years of research. This excellent book explores such topics as prediction, originality, psychotherapy, religious beliefs, the role of conflict, and personal creativity.

Blum, Richard H., ed. *Utopiates: The Use and Users of LSD-25.* New York: Atherton Press, 1964.
A major study. Highly recommended.

Bronowski, J. *Science and Human Values.* New York: Harper and Row, Harper Torchbooks, 1959.
An inspiring essay on the nature of the creative mind and the fundamental meaning of science to contemporary human life.

Bruner, Jerome S. *The Process of Education.* New York: Random House, Vintage Books, 1960.
An influential work.

Cohen, Sidney. *The Beyond Within: The LSD Story.* New York: Atheneum, 1964.
Discussion of good and bad trips, "good" uses and "bad" uses by an authority.

Coler, Myron A., ed. *Essays on Creativity in the Sciences.* Creative Science Seminar Division of General Education of New York University. New York: New York University Press, 1963.

A valuable collection of essays.

Cremin, Lawrence. *The Transformation of the School: Progressivism in American Education, 1876–1957.* New York: Alfred A. Knopf, 1961.

DeCecco, John P. *Educational Technology: Readings in Programmed Instruction.* New York: Holt, Rinehart and Winston, 1964.

de Ropp, Robert S. *Drugs and the Mind.* New York: Grove Press, Evergreen Black Cat, 1961.
A fascinating and reliable book written by a biochemist.

Dewey, John. *Experience and Education.* New York: Macmillan, 1938.

———. *The School and Society.* Chicago: University of Chicago Press, 1943.

Erikson, Erik H. "The Problem of Ego Identity." *Journal of the American Psychoanalytic Association* 4 (1956): 58–121.
An important psychoanalytic study of youth's search for identity.

Farber, Seymour M., and Wilson, Roger H. L., eds. *Conflict and Creativity: Control of the Mind, Part Two.* New York: McGraw-Hill, 1963. Essays and discussions on the forces in man and society which encourage creativity or conformity. See papers on mood and drug action.

Freud, Sigmund. *Leonardo da Vinci: A Study in Psychosexuality.* Translated by A. A. Brill. New York: Random House, Vintage Books, 1947.

Fry, Edward B. *Teaching Machines and Programmed Instruction.* New York: McGraw-Hill, 1963.
Provides examples of typical programs and a good bibliography.

Gardner, John W. *Excellence: Can We Be Equal and Excellent Too?* New York: Harper and Row, 1961.

———. *Self-Renewal: The Individual and the Innovative Society.* New York: Harper and Row, 1963.
Two small, excellent books. Constructive, optimistic, and readable.

Gerard, R. W. "The Biological Basis of Imagination." *The Scientific Monthly* 52 (1946): 477–79.
Fascinating speculation on the neural mechanisms of imagination and original thought.

Getzels, Jacob W., and Jackson, Philip W. *Creativity and Intelligence: Explorations with Gifted Students.* New York: John Wiley and Sons, 1962.
Studies of highly intelligent and highly creative children. Contains a good summary of the use of IQ in defining creativity and an excellent review of the major psychoanalytic theories of creativity.

Ghiselin, Brewster., ed. *The Creative Process: A Symposium.* New York: New American Library, Mentor, 1955.
Genius at work. Selections from the personal accounts of the creative process of thirty-eight artists and writers with an illuminating essay on the creative process by the editor.

Goodman, Paul. *Compulsory Miseducation and The Community of Scholars.* New York: Random House, Vintage Books, 1964.
A vivid and biting critique of the schools. See Chapter 6, "Programmed," on automation and its spirit in the classroom.

Gowan, John Curtis; Demos, George D.; Torrance, E. Paul, eds. *Creativity: Its Educational Implications.* New York: John Wiley and Sons, 1967.
A special merit of this collection of papers is its provision of an extensive bibliography, as well as separate annotated bibliographies.

Graubard, Stephen R., ed. "Creativity and Learning." *Daedalus* 94, Summer 1965.
Major focus is on science and scholarship. Stimulating potpourri.

Gruenberger, Fred. "A Measure for Crackpots." *Science* 145 (1964): 1413–15.
A checklist to help distinguish between authentic scientific research and the work of the charlatan or boob.

Guilford, J. P. "Creativity." *American Psychologist* 5 (1950): 444–54.
The need for a better measure of originality than the intelligence test.

———. *Personality.* New York: McGraw-Hill, 1959.

Hadamard, Jacques. *The Psychology of Invention in the Mathematical Field.* Princeton, New Jersey: Princeton University Press, 1949.

Heist, Paul, ed. *The Creative College Student.* San Francisco: Jossey-Bass, 1968.

Highet, Gilbert. *The Art of Teaching.* New York: Alfred A. Knopf, 1950.
Teaching as an art, not a science.

Holt, John. *How Children Fail.* New York: Pitman Publishing Corp., 1964.
A disturbing book.

———. *How Children Learn.* New York: Pitman Publishing Corp., 1967.

Huxley, Aldous. *The Doors of Perception and Heaven and Hell.* New York: Harper and Row, Harper Colophon, 1963.
Huxley's personal experiments with mescalin. A psychedelic classic.

———. "Young Archimedes." In *Fantasia Mathematica,* edited by Clifton Fadiman. New York: Simon and Schuster, 1958.
The profoundly moving story of an Italian peasant boy born with mathematical genius.

James, William. *The Varieties of Religious Experience.* New York: Modern Library, 1942.

Jung, C. G. *Modern Man in Search of a Soul.* New York: Harcourt, Brace and Co., 1933.

———. *Psychology of the Unconscious.* New York: Dodd, Mead and Co., 1925.

——. *Two Essays on Analytical Psychology.* New York: Dodd, Mead and Co., 1928.

Kandel, I. L. *American Education in the Twentieth Century.* Cambridge, Mass.: Harvard University Press, 1957.
An authoritative work.

Koestler, Arthur. *The Act of Creation.* New York: Macmillan, 1964.
A vast, sprawling book on the psychological processes underlying creative activity in art, science, and humor. Contains a brilliant and devastating section on aspects of modern learning theory.

Kris, Ernst. *Psychoanalytic Explorations in Art.* New York: International Universities Press, 1952.

Krutch, Joseph Wood. *Human Nature and the Human Condition.* New York: Random House, 1959.
See, Chapter 5, "The Average and the Norm," on the failure to distinguish between what is normal (ideal) and what is average (usual; statistically probable).

Kubie, Lawrence S. *Neurotic Distortion of the Creative Process.* New York: Noonday Press, 1961.
The role of neurosis in blocking creative preconscious processes. Implications for education.

——. "Some Unsolved Problems of the Scientific Career." *American Scientist* 41 (October 1953): 596–613; and 42 (January 1954): 104–12.

Kuhn, Thomas S. "The Essential Tension: Tradition and Innovation in Scientific Research." In *Scientific Creativity: Its Recognition and Development.* Edited by Calvin W. Taylor and Frank Barron, pp. 341–54. New York: John Wiley and Sons, 1963.
An admirable essay by a physicist and historian of science.

Lowes, John Livingston. *The Road to Xanadu: A Study in the Ways of the Imagination.* New York: Vintage Books, 1959.
A well-known study of Coleridge.

Lumsdaine, A. A. and Glaser, Robert, eds. *Teaching Machines and Programmed Learning: A Sourcebook.* Washington, D.C.: National Education Association, 1960.

McClelland, David C.; Baldwin, Alfred L.; Bronfenbrenner, Urie; Strodtbeck, Fred L., eds. *Talent and Society: New Perspectives in the Identification of Talent.* Princeton, New Jersey: D. Van Nostrand, 1958.

MacKinnon, Donald W., ed. *The Creative Person.* Institute of Personality Assessment and Research, University of California, Berkeley. Berkeley: University of California, 1961.
Conference proceedings.

——. "The Nature and Nurture of Creative Talent." *American Psychologist* 17 (1962): 485–95.

Maritain, Jacques. *Creative Intuition in Art and Poetry.* New York: Pantheon, 1953.

Discussion of the philosophy of art and the role of intellect in art and poetry.

Maslow, Abraham H. *Toward a Psychology of Being*. Princeton, New Jersey: D. Van Nostrand Co., 1962.
A psychology of growth and self-actualization by a leading exponent of the humanistic trend in psychology.

Mayer, Martin. *The Schools*. Garden City, New York: Doubleday and Co., Anchor Books, 1963.
An excellent introduction to life in the schools. See the chapters on progressivism and learning.

Montagu, Ashley. *The Humanization of Man*. New York: Grove Press, Evergreen Black Cat Book, 1962.
Includes a valuable discussion of the nature of human nature and the means by which human beings acquire it.

Moustakas, Clark E., ed. *The Self: Explorations in Personal Growth*. New York: Harper, 1956.
Essays by the humanistic psychologists. A useful introduction to their work.

Murphy, Gardner. *Historical Introduction to Modern Psychology*. New York: Harcourt, Brace and World, 1949.
———. *Human Potentialities*. New York: Basic Books, 1958.
A stimulating and illuminating book.

Neumann, Erich. *The Origins and History of Consciousness*. Bollingen Series, No. 42. New York: Pantheon Books, 1954.
A distinguished book containing many bold and original insights.

Nowlis, Helen H. *Drugs on the College Campus*. A Guide for College Administrators. Drug Education Projects of the National Association of Student Personnel Administrators under Contract FDA 67–3, Food and Drug Administration, 1967.
Useful and compact. Includes annotated bibliography.

Parnes, S. J., and Harding, H. F., eds. *A Source Book for Creative Thinking*. New York: Charles Scribner's Sons, 1962.
A valuable anthology oriented toward industry.

Phillips, William, ed. *Art and Psychoanalysis*. Cleveland: World Publishing Co., Meridian Books, 1963.
A collection of outstanding studies in the application of psychoanalytic theory to the creative process, particularly in literature.

Poincaré, Henri. "Mathematical Creation." In *The Foundations of Science* by Henri Poincaré. Translated by George Bruce Halsted. New York: Science Press, 1946.
A classic.

Polanyi, Michael. *Personal Knowledge: Toward a Post-Critical Philosophy*. Chicago: University of Chicago Press, 1958.
A monumental study of the limitations of science as an objective study and the role of subjective values and personal commitment in scientific knowledge.

Polya, George. *How to Solve It.* Princeton, New Jersey: Princeton University Press, 1945.
A brilliant and delightful book exploring the techniques of discovery and problem solving.

Progoff, Ira. *The Death and Rebirth of Psychology.* An Integrative Evaluation of Freud, Adler, Jung, and Rank and the impact of their culminating insights on modern man. New York: Dell Publishing Co., Delta Book, 1964.

Rank, Otto. *Art and Artist: Creative Urge and Personality Development.* Translated by Charles Francis Atkinson. New York: Alfred A. Knopf, 1932.

———. *Will Therapy and Truth and Reality.* In one volume. Translated by Jessie Taft. New York: Alfred A. Knopf, 1945.

Rilke, Rainer Maria. *Letters to a Young Poet.* Translated by M. D. Herter Norton. New York: W. W. Norton and Co., 1934.

Roback, A. A. *History of American Psychology.* New York: Library Publishers, 1952.

Roe, Anne. *The Making of a Scientist.* New York: Dodd, Mead and Co., 1952.

Rossman, J. *The Psychology of the Inventor.* Washington, D.C.: Inventors Publishing Co., 1931.

Ruitenbeek, Hendrik M., ed. *The Literary Imagination: Psychoanalysis and the Genius of the Writer.* Chicago: Quadrangle Books, 1965.
A useful collection of studies of nineteenth-century literary geniuses.

Russell, Bertrand. *The Basic Writings of Bertrand Russell, 1903–1959.* Edited by Robert E. Egner and Lester E. Denonn. See the following essays: "How I Write," pp. 63–65; "Education," pp. 401–12; "The Aims of Education," pp. 413–29; "Emotion and Discipline," 430–34; "The Functions of a Teacher," pp. 435–42.

Sanford, Nevitt. *Self and Society: Social Change and Individual Development.* New York: Atherton Press, 1966.
Especially Chapter 13, "Creativity and Conformity."

Schachtel, Ernest G. *Metamorphosis: On the Development of Affect, Perception, Attention, and Memory.* New York: Basic Books, 1959.

Scientific American. "Innovation in Science." 199, September 1958.
A valuable issue.

Smith, P., ed. *Creativity: An Examination of the Creative Process.* New York: Hastings House, 1959.

Stein, M. I., and Henze, Shirley J. *Creativity and the Individual: Summaries of Selected Literature in Psychology and Psychiatry.* Glencoe, Illinois: The Free Press, 1960.
An invaluable bibliography reviewing important empirical and theoretical studies of creativity.

Strang, Ruth. *Helping Your Gifted Child.* New York: E. P. Dutton, 1960.

Taylor, Calvin W., ed. *Creativity: Progress and Potential*. New York: McGraw-Hill, 1964.
Results of University of Utah research conferences on creativity (1955, 1957, 1959, 1961). Oriented toward scientific creativity. Prediction of creative potential, the influence of educational environment, and establishing criteria of creativity are the main themes.

—— ed. *Widening Horizons in Creativity*. Proceedings of the 1962 Utah Conference. New York: John Wiley and Sons, 1964.
This volume includes studies of creativity in special fields.

——, and Barron, Frank, eds. *Scientific Creativity: Its Recognition and Development*. New York: John Wiley and Sons, 1963.
A useful book consisting of selected papers from the first three University of Utah conferences on "The Identification of Creative Scientific Talent." The last chapter provides a helpful summary of the research, followed by an extensive bibliography.

Torrance, E. Paul. *Guiding Creative Talent*. Englewood Cliffs, New Jersey: Prentice-Hall, 1962.
An excellent book on the identification, instruction, and guidance of gifted children by an authority on the subject.

——. *Rewarding Creative Behavior: Experiments in Classroom Creativity*. Englewood Cliffs, New Jersey: Prentice-Hall, 1965.

Trilling, Lionel. "Art and Neurosis." In *Art and Psychoanalysis*, edited by William Phillips, pp. 502–20. Cleveland: World Publishing Co., Meridian Books, 1963.
A cogent essay on the myth of the sick artist.

——. "Of this Time, of that Place." *Partisan Review*, January–February 1943.
A subtle, haunting story of brilliance and madness in the classroom.

Wertheimer, Max. *Productive Thinking*. Enlarged edition. Edited by Michael Wertheimer. New York: Harper and Bros., 1959.
A classic study of thought processes by a pioneer Gestalt psychologist.

Whitehead, Alfred North. *The Aims of Education and Other Essays*. New York: Macmillan, 1959.
An eloquent protest against dead knowledge and inert students.

Whyte, L. L. *The Unconscious Before Freud*. New York: Basic Books, 1960.
An important contribution to the history of ideas.

Index

ACETYLCHOLINE, 273
Adam and Eve, 96–97
adaptation to the environment, 14, 17–19
Adler, Alfred, 238–239, 240, 242
adrenalin, 274
advertising, exploitation by, 90
Aeschylus, 110
affluence, problems of, 90–94, 134, 249
aggression, 14, 54–55, 235–236
"Aha" experience, the, 161
Alexander the Great, 23
alienation, 63
analysis vs. synthesis, 81
Andreas-Salomé, Lou, 308
anthropology, 13, 154
apes, psychological studies of, 152, 175–176
Apollo, 233, 249, 252–253
aptitude, natural. *See*, talent
Aquinas, Thomas, 78, 84, 117, 269
Archimedes, 161, 176
Aristarchus, 132
Aristotle, 23, 28, 78, 116, 120; and mind-body problem, 142–143
Aron, Raymond, 53
art: defined, 8, 26, 51; children's, 22, 37–40; evaluation of, 52, 127; vs. science, 121, 122–123, 125–126; response to, 126–127; in the schools, 165; modern, 251–252; Freud on, 255; and neurosis, 264–266
artist(s): attitude to creativity studies, 78; in modern society, 93; Plato's conception of the, 116; as mad, 222–226; manqué, 241; irresponsibility of, 263–264; and neurosis, 264–268; and drugs, 285–287
Asimov, Isaac, 287
atomic bomb. *See*, bomb, thermonuclear
atomism, 81, 141, 153
Augustine, Saint, 14, 117, 205
auto-instructional device. *See*, programmed instruction; teaching machine

BACH, JOHANN SEBASTIAN, 261
Bacon, Francis, 78–79, 121, 264
Barrett, William, 250
Barzun, Jacques, 188
Beethoven, Ludwig van, 23, 261, 263, 300, 303
behavior: genetically programmed, 8; actual, vs. innate capacities, 13; modification of, 13–14; education and, 14; patterns of, 14–15, 153; creative, 28, 134; conscious and unconscious determinants, 29; fundamental questions of, 29–30; theories of, 84, 88–89; effect